Database Theory and Practice

INTERNATIONAL COMPUTER SCIENCE SERIES

Consulting editors **A D McGettrick** University of Strathclyde
J van Leeuwen University of Utrecht

OTHER TITLES IN THE SERIES

Programming in Ada (2nd Edn) *J G P Barnes*

Software Engineering (2nd Edn) *I Sommerville*

The UNIX System *S R Bourne*

Computer Science Applied to Business Systems *M J R Shave and K N Bhaskar*

Office Automation: Concepts, Technologies and Issues *R A Hirschheim*

UNIX for Super-Users *E Foxley*

Introduction to Expert Systems *P Jackson*

Modula-2: Discipline & Design *A H J Sale*

The UNIX System V Environment *S R Bourne*

System Simulation: Programming Styles and Languages *W Kreutzer*

The Craft of Software Engineering *A Macro and J Buxton*

PROLOG Programming for Artificial Intelligence *I Bratko*

Text Processing and Typesetting with UNIX *D W Barron and M J Rees*

Performance Measurement of Computer Systems *P McKerrow*

Syntax Analysis and Software Tools *K J Gough*

Concurrent Programming *N Gehani and A D McGettrick* (Eds)

Practical Compiling with Pascal-S *M J Rees and D J Robson*

Functional Programming *A Field and P Harrison*

Ada from the Beginning *J Skansholm*

Database Theory and Practice

Lars Frank

Privatbanken, Denmark

Translated by
Ole Helmersen
Copenhagen School of Economics and
Business Administration

ADDISON-WESLEY
PUBLISHING
COMPANY

Wokingham, England · Reading, Massachusetts · Menlo Park, California
New York · Don Mills, Ontario · Amsterdam · Bonn
Sydney · Singapore · Tokyo · Madrid · San Juan

First published in Danish as *Databaser*

Cover graphic by Laurence M Gartel.
Cover designed by John Gibbs and printed by
The Riverside Printing Co. (Reading) Ltd.
Typeset by Times Graphics, Singapore.
Printed and bound in Great Britain by Mackays of Chatham PLC, Chatham, Kent.

First printed 1988. Reprinted 1988

British Library Cataloguing in Publication Data

Frank, Lars
Database: theory and practice. —
(International computer science series).
1. Data base management 2. File organization
(Computer science)
I. Title II. Series
005.74 QA76.9.D3

ISBN 0–201–18041–3

Library of Congress Cataloging in Publication Data

Frank, Lars.
Database.

(International computer science series)
Translation of: Databaser.
Bibliography: p.
Includes index.
1. Data base management. I. Title. II. Series.
QA76.9.D3F713 1988 005.74 87–35077
ISBN 0–201–18041–3 (pbk.)

Preface

The past few years have witnessed rapid progress as regards both database theory and database software products. This book aims to present an up-to-date description of the most important subjects within the database field. Special emphasis is placed on subjects that are relevant to administrative data processing; that is, how a database is built-up in practice and what are the most important considerations when selecting a database software product. Database recovery is discussed in particular detail since the built-in security of software products is not always sufficient.

Third-generation database languages are represented by the CODASYL proposal for a standardization of database languages. This language comprises so many facilities that most other third-generation languages can be regarded as subsets of it.

Fourth-generation languages are represented by SQL. SQL has had a great influence, both theoretically and practically, on developments within fourth-generation programming languages, and has become a standard for relational database languages.

Synopsis

This book is primarily designed for Computer Science courses in higher education and for refresher courses for data processing staff. The only requirement needed to read the book is a basic knowledge of data processing.

The book can be read at two different levels: (1) following the text without paying too much attention to the advanced mathematics, which is only used in the appendices and a few examples, thereby acquiring a general knowledge of the subject; or (2) studying the text alongside the advanced mathematics in depth. Whatever the route chosen, the reader will find many examples throughout the book illustrating the contents.

- Chapter 1 deals with the design of the logical database; that is, the design of the logical files of the database and the connection between them. Special emphasis is placed on designing the database so that it is flexible to the extensions that new, unforeseen tasks will require. The chapter also describes the most important methods used to describe a logical database.

- Chapters 2 and 3 describe the design of the physical database; that is, the methods for implementing the files of the logical database and the search paths between the records of these files.
- Chapters 4 to 8 outline the facilities that are often supplied with a database management system (DBMS); that is, software that manages the access to the database.
- Chapters 9 and 10 describe the special circumstances involved with the use of database machines and distributed databases. Chapter 10 also takes a brief look at the most important tasks to be performed by the database administrator.
- Chapter 11 deals with an example of a database language that can be used via a third-generation programming language, such as COBOL, PL/1, ALGOL, BASIC, FORTRAN or Pascal. As an example, the CODASYL standard has been chosen, since a lot of DBMSs follow this standard and because this system is so comprehensive that it contains practically all types of database instructions used from a third-generation programming language.
- Chapters 12 and 13 give examples of fourth-generation programming languages; that is, programming languages that are especially oriented towards databases and in which the individual instructions are so strong that they operate on sets of records, instead of one record at a time.
- Finally, the appendices contain a more technical description of the subjects covered in the body of the book.

Acknowledgements

I would like to thank my colleagues in Privatbanken's Data Processing Section for their inspiring cooperation which has been invaluable in preparing the examples and exercises in the book. I would also like to thank Uffe Møller of Aalborg University for his valuable criticism in connection with the new equation for the estimation of search lengths in files. This equation makes it possible to estimate the search length for several different file organizations, a task that previously could only be done by means of simulation.

I am grateful to Privatbanken's Foundation for supporting me in preparing this book.

Lars Frank

Copenhagen 1987

Contents

Part One
DATABASE STRUCTURES

Chapter 1
The Logical Database

1.1 Introduction

A **database** can be defined as a set of master files, organized and administered in a flexible way, so that the files of the database can be easily adapted to new, unforeseen tasks. A large number of different methods are available to ensure such a flexibility of a database, and these are described in the first three chapters. It used to be common practice to create new files simultaneously with the introduction of a new data processing system. However, new database techniques have made it possible to integrate a firm's data processing systems, so that the various subsystems can use the same files. This principle is illustrated in the following example.

EXAMPLE 1.1

The system flowchart shown in Figure 1.1 illustrates how a bank might have built up isolated data processing systems for each of its separate products – that is, without integrated databases. In this system, the customer's name and address are stored in separate account records and deposit records. Consequently, if the bank decides to develop a new product system, it is not possible to take advantage of the fact that the names and addresses of the bank's customers are already held. In the system flowchart of Figure 1.2, the data processing systems have been integrated, using the same data held in the customer file of the database.

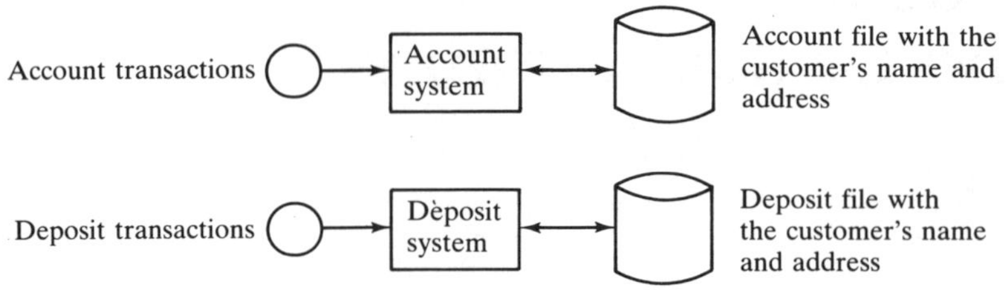

Figure 1.1 Bank system without integration. Customer details are duplicated.

Following the American National Standards Institute's proposals (ANSI/SPARC, 1975), it has become the norm to recognize three forms of database description, which are as follows:

(1) The **conceptual schema** (or **conceptual view**) is a machine- and software-independent description of the total database. The conceptual schema will often be referred to in the rest of the book as the logical database.

(2) The **internal schema** (or **internal view**) is a description of the physical database. It is close to the machine level and describes such things as file organization and access paths.

(3) The **external schema** (or **user view**) is a user-oriented description of part of the database. It corresponds to the way in which a program needs to 'view' the database. Since there are many different purposes to which the data in a database may be put, there will be many different external schemas corresponding to the different programs interpreting the database in particular ways.

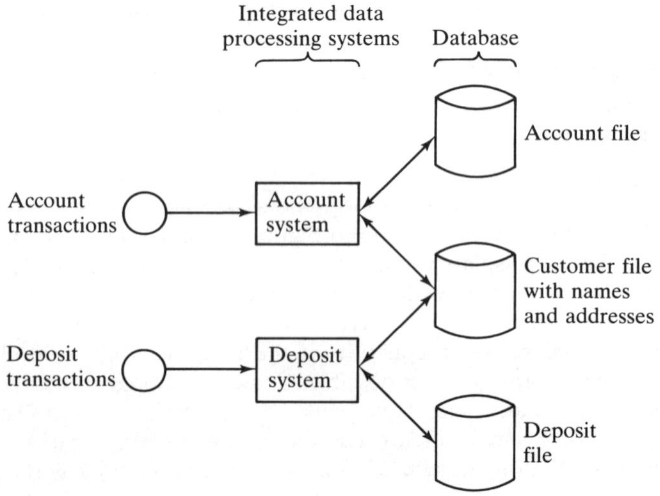

Figure 1.2 An integrated banking system. Duplication is minimized.

A program that reads data held in a database will refer only to the external schema. The database management system (DBMS) translates the database statements of the program accessing the database so that data in the physical database can be read. To do this it must make use of the conceptual schema and the internal schema.

The three levels of the ANSI/SPARC model (see also Tsichritzis and Klug, 1978) have gradually become generally accepted, although many older DBMSs operate only with two levels: the internal schema is often integrated into the conceptual schema (see Section 5.2 on Data independence).

1.2 Elements of the conceptual schema

The description of the conceptual schema includes:

- a description of the kinds of logical files and record types comprising the database;
- a description of the fields included in a record type;
- a description of the relationships (i.e., connections) between the different record types of the database (see Section 1.2.2 on Relationships);
- A description of any limitations in the values that can be taken by individual fields as well as constraints upon the relationships between records (see Sections 6.6 and 6.7 on Consistency control and Validity control).

A conceptual schema may be thought of as a model of the enterprise using it. The selection of files and relationships between data records to be included in the conceptual schema is based on the requirements or preferences of the users of the database. However, it is possible to construct many different conceptual databases on the basis of a given set of user requirements. Given several alternatives, the schema that is 'closest to reality' should be chosen; that is, record types in the conceptual database should describe physical items or concepts as they exist in the real world. If the conceptual database describes the external world in this way, it is more likely that the database can be easily adapted to future requirements. A further advantage of constructing the database to 'look like' reality is that redundancy in the data can be reduced because data can be stored where it naturally belongs.

1.2.1 Entities

An **entity** or **entity occurrence** is an item or a concept in the real world about which we want to record data. The data associated with an entity are called its **attributes**, and these are normally recorded as field values in a record.

An **entity type** is a classification of all the entities describing the same type of item or concept from the real world. Thus, entity types correspond to the record types of the database. The description of an entity type in the conceptual database normally includes the following:

- a unique name for each entity type;
- a field containing a unique identifier for each individual entity – such a field is called a **primary** or **identification key**;
- a description of the attributes or fields of the entity type;
- an indication of the number of occurrences of an entity type the database will be required to hold – this is known as the **cardinal number** of the entity type.

The attributes belonging to an entity may be:

- **mandatory** or **optional** depending on whether a field should or should not always have a value; for example, not everyone has a telephone, so that the telephone number attribute of the entity 'person' may have no value;
- **single valued** or **multivalued**; for example, a person or a firm may have several different telephone numbers, so we may say that their telephone number attribute is multivalued. A multivalued attribute could be stored in a **repeating field.**
- **aggregate** or **simple,** corresponding to whether the attribute is formed from a combination of other attributes or not; for example a telephone number consisting of an area code, a number and an extension number could be considered an aggegrate attribute. An aggegrate attribute thus corresponds to a **combined field** or a **group field** in a record.

The concepts entity, entity type and attribute are used in connection with things or concepts taken from the external world, or in connection with conceptual schemas to which a DBMS does not have access. If the conceptual schema is implemented in such a way that the description is accessible to a DBMS (that is, if there is a direct relationship between the structure of the conceptual data base and that of the physical database), the words **record, record type** and **field value** may be used.

EXAMPLE 1.2

Sometimes it may be difficult to define an entity type precisely, as the different users within an enterprise may have different views of what an entity type is. As an example of this, consider the concept of 'customers' in a bank. A customer can be an individual person or a family in which both spouses share the same rights and obligations. A customer could also be an association, whose membership fees are paid into an account, or a large business firm, which may be divided into subsidiary companies. Although all these customer types may be seen as belonging to distinct entity types (they are different *kinds of* customer), it may still be practical to regard them as belonging to the same entity type: *customer*. The bank, however, also has to record information about guarantors and other persons who are not necessarily customers of the bank. Hence, the entity type has to be extended to include everyone and everything having its name and address held in connection with one of the bank's services. However, the bank's employees are also 'customers' of the bank, since they at least have a wage account. But with respect to the employees, the bank will need to record attributes that are irrelevant in connection with all the other customers, such as salary, length of service, days of leave taken or sickness, etc. To satisfy the different user requirements for data it may be necessary to have fields in the database that are not relevant to all the entities of the entity type. The external schema, making use of the DBMS, allows separate users, at a later stage, to read the records of the file in such a way that they see only those fields that are of interest to them.

1.2.2 Relationships

Within database theory a distinction is usually drawn between the term **relationship,** which is used to describe a connection between entities, and the term **relation,** which is used to designate a logical table describing a set of similar entities. However, these two terms are related in the sense that a connection between entities can be described by means of a table with rows corresponding to entities and columns corresponding to attributes (see Section 1.3.3).

A relationship is by definition directional, which means that we distinguish between whether the related entity B is searched for from entity A or vice versa. In practice, we shall often need to implement both search directions. When we invoke a relationship we therefore often also imply its inverse relationship.

A **relation occurrence** is defined as an individual entity's connections with other entities as regards a specific relationship. The **branching factor** of a relationship is defined as the number of relationship branches that branch off from a particular entity. Sometimes this is also referred to as the relationship's cardinal number for the entity. The **maximum branching factor** of a relationship is defined as the maximum number of relationship branches that can branch off from an entity in a relationship occurrence. If this number can be arbitrarily large, this is symbolized by the letter n or m. The **minimum branching factor** of a relationship is defined as the minimum number of relationship branches that can branch off from an entity in a relationship occurrence.

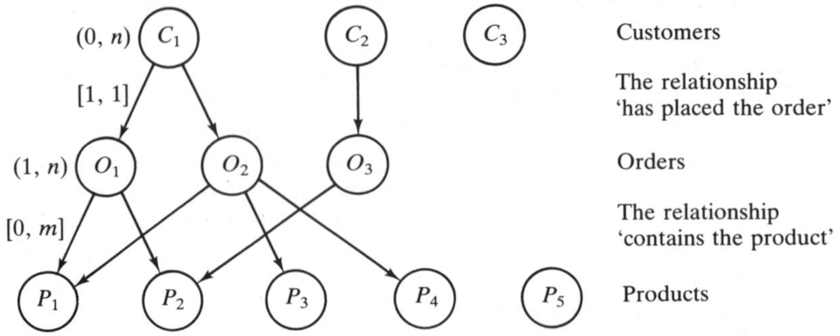

Figure 1.3 Relationships between customers, *C*, orders, *O*, and products, *P*. Branching factors for the downward search direction are shown in round brackets; thus, (0, *n*). Branching factors for an upward search are shown in square brackets, [1, 1]. The minimum branching factor is shown first in each case.

EXAMPLE 1.3

In Figure 1.3, the circles indicate orders, customers and products. The arrows symbolize two different relationships. One of these combines a customer with the orders he has placed, while the other combines an order with the products specified in it.

Each relationship in the figure is associated with two pairs of numbers, which indicate the minimum and maximum branching factor for the two search directions of the relationship. The minimum branching factor for the search direction from customers towards orders is zero, as a customer need not always have placed an order, and the maximum branching factor is *n*, because a customer may have placed an arbitrary number of orders.

The minimum and maximum branching factor for the search direction from orders towards customers is 1, since an order is always placed by one and only one customer. The minimum branching factor for the search direction from orders towards products is 1, because an order, by definition, always includes at least one item; the maximum branching factor is *n*, as an order may include an arbitrary number of products. The minimum branching factor for the search direction from products towards orders is zero, because a product need not always be included in any orders, and the maximum branching factor is *m*, since a product may be included in an arbitrary number of orders. The maximum branching factors for the two search directions of the relationship are labelled *n* and *m*, respectively, to indicate that their size is arbitrary, but probably different.

The relationships just outlined could be used, for example, for invoicing, since a program could be written to follow the path of the relationships. For each customer record we could select the order records related to it, and for each order record we could select the related product records.

However, many other relationships could be used. For example, we may have a relationship that divides the customers according to the discounts they receive, or which groups them by the sales district in which they operate. A relationship may connect a customer with the products on which he receives special discounts, or it may divide products into raw materials, components and finished products, and – by using components as an intermediary link – connect the raw materials with the finished products corresponding to the sequence in which they are used in the production process.

Attributes can be attached to a relationship in the same way as attributes can be attached to an entity. As an example of this, consider the relationship that holds between customers and orders in Example 1.3. This relationship may have a delivery address associated with it, showing where the products specified in the order are to be delivered. There will always be data attached to the relationship between orders and products as we need to know the quantity of a particular product included in a particular order.

If a relationship is to be described in the conceptual schema, the following points should be noted:

- the relationship must have a unique name;
- if attributes are attached to the relationship, these must be described;
- if the maximum and minimum branching factor of the relationship are stored in the database description, the DBMS can use this information later to validate the database;
- the relationship type should be specified (see later).

In the sections that follow, we shall describe the most common relationship types occurring within administrative data processing. The main reason for distinguishing between these different types is that they are implemented in different ways in the physical database. (This topic is dealt with in detail in Chapter 2.)

The one-to-many relationship

In this relationship type (also known as the **1 to *n*** or **1 : *n* relationship**), entities are connected in such a way that the maximum branching factor is 1 in one direction and *n* in the other.

Entities from which the maximum branching factor of the relationship is *n* are called 'owners', while entities from which the maximum branching factor is 1 are called 'members'. An example of this relationship type is shown in Figure 1.4.

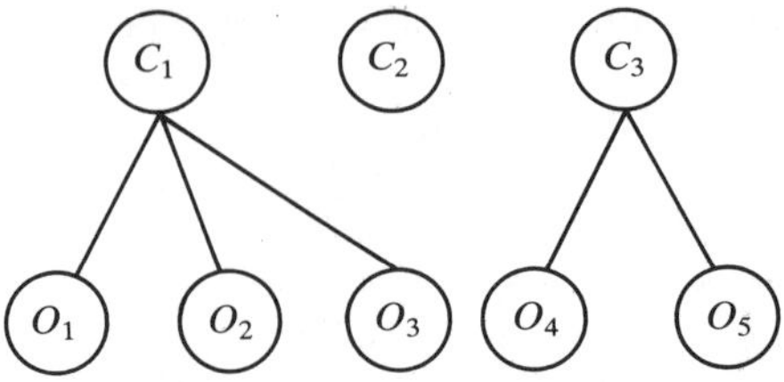

Figure 1.4 The 1 : *n* relationship. A customer may place an arbitrary number of orders (or none at all), while an order can only belong to a single customer.

The many-to-many relationship

In this relationship type (also known as the ***n* to *m*** or ***n* : *m* relationship**), entities are connected in such a way that the maximum branching factor is *n* in one search direction of the relationship and *m* in the other. An example of this relationship type is shown in Figure 1.5.

The one-to-one relationship

In this relationship type (also known as the **1 to 1** or **1 : 1 relationship**), entities are connected in such a way that the maximum branching factor is 1 in both search directions. An example of this relationship type is shown in Figure 1.6, which illustrates the relationship 'head of' between a department and an employee. We assume here that there can be only one head of a department.

The sequential relationship

By means of a sequential relationship we can organize a set of entities in a fixed order, as shown in Figure 1.7. An application of this relationship is provided by a set of customers that is organized according to the customers' total purchases during a certain time period. Similarly, it may sometimes be practical to organize a set of products according to their rate of turnover.

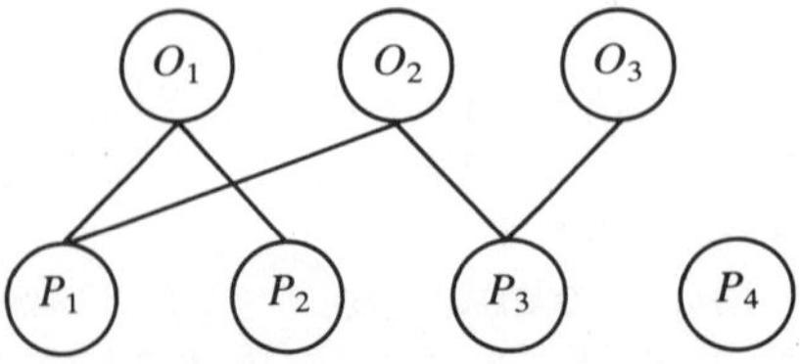

Figure 1.5 The $n : m$ relationship. An order may contain orders for several products (but must order at least one product), while a product may be ordered in several different orders (or in none at all).

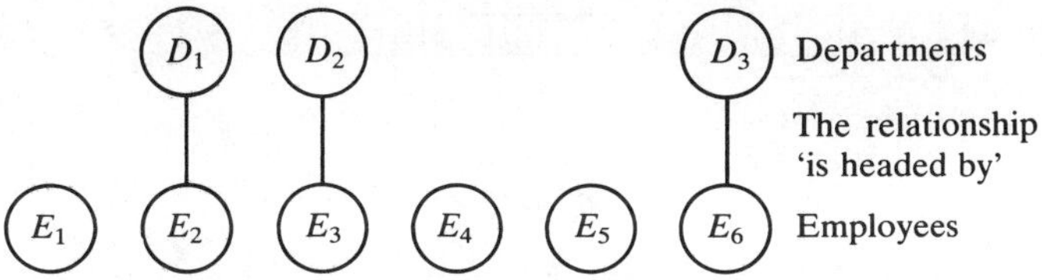

Figure 1.6 The 1 : 1 relationship. Employee E_2 is head of department D_1, E_3 head of D_2 and E_6 head of D_3.

The equivalence relationship

The equivalence relationship makes it possible to group a set of entities into separate subsets. By using search criteria corresponding to these subsets, we can retrieve all the entities in a particular group. The equivalence relationship is **symmetrical,** which means that it is identical to its inverse relationship. For example, it may be practical to group a set of customers according to the firm's sales districts. At the design stage the equivalence relationship is often described as a $1:n$ relationship between, for example, the entity types 'sales districts' and 'customers'. But if we already know, at the design stage, that we are not going to create a sales district file, it will be sufficient to describe the customer entity type and the equivalence relationship that divides the customers into districts, as shown in Figure 1.8. The branching factor of an equivalence relationship is the same as the number of entities that are equivalent to each other.

Trees

A **tree** is a relationship with the following characteristics:

- In one search direction, the maximum branching factor is 1. This search direction includes a final entity called a **root**. If there is more than one root, the relationship is called a **forest**. Figure 1.9 illustrates a forest consisting of two trees.
- In the other search direction, the maximum branching factor is n. This search direction also has an end, and the final entities are called **leaves**.

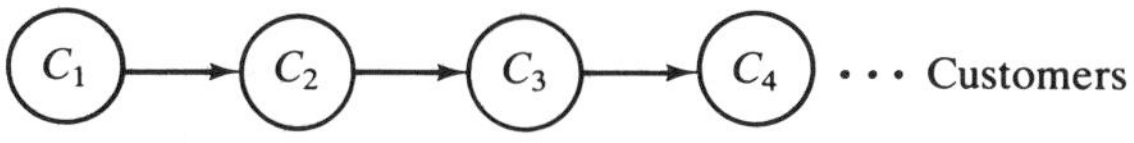

Figure 1.7 The sequential relationship. Customer C_1 has purchased more than customer C_2, who has purchased more than C_3, etc.

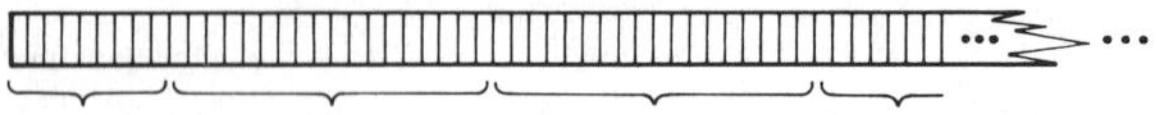

Figure 1.8 The equivalence relationship. All the customers in customer group 1 are equivalent to each other. The same applies to each of the customer groups.

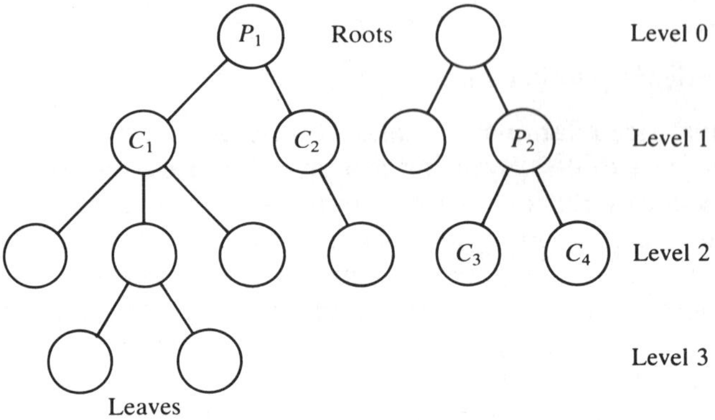

Figure 1.9 A forest consisting of two trees. P_1 at level 0 is the parent of C_1 and C_2, while P_2 at level 1 is the parent of C_3 and C_4 at level 4.

In the search direction from the root towards the leaves, an entity's successors are called its **children** (c), while an entity's predecessor is called its **parent** (p).

A tree is always represented with the root at the top. The **nodes** of the tree are represented in levels, so that the root is at level zero and the children of the root are at level 1, etc. The **height** of a tree is the number of the highest level at which there are leaves. A **subtree** is a node with its related children, grandchildren, etc.

In Section 2.4, which discusses index organization, a special type of tree, called a **search tree**, will be described.

EXAMPLE 1.4

A tree relationship may be illustrated with reference to the three entity types finished products, components and raw materials. The nodes in Figure 1.10 are finished products F, components C and raw materials R. The numbers against the branches indicate the numbers of the product entering into the production process. For example, product F_1 is produced from 2 C_1 and 3 C_2. Assume that these numbers 2 and 3 are

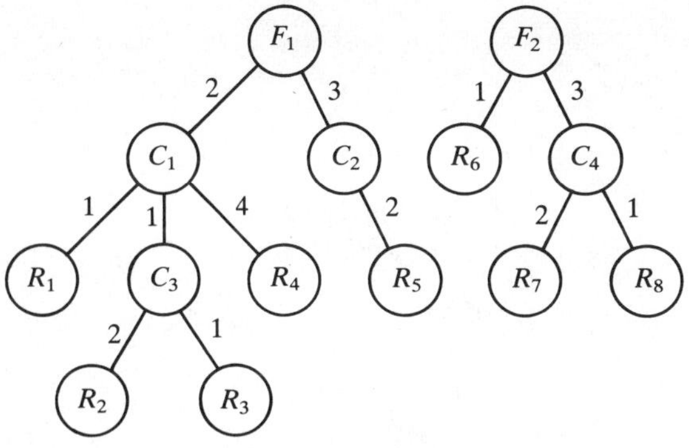

Figure 1.10 Tree showing relationships between finished products, *F*, components, *C*, and raw materials, *R*. The numbers between the nodes show the quantities used.

attributes of C_1 and C_2 respectively. If the relationship just described is implemented it can be used to answer queries of the following type:

(1) What raw materials and what quantity of each must be purchased in order to produce 1 F_2?

(2) How many F_2 can we produce, given that we have to produce five F_1 and given that we have 50 R_1, R_2, . . . and R_8 in stock?

(3) What finished products does the raw material R_3 form part of?

In fact, this example, as set out, makes it easy to answer these queries by inspection. However, the situation is quite different if the finished products are different types of aeroplanes and the raw materials are screws, aluminium sheets, transistors, etc. In this case, the chain from raw materials to finished product may comprise several thousand components and consequently the calculations become very time consuming.

The network relationship

An **oriented network** can be defined as a tree that branches both upwards and downwards. The maximum branching factor in the two search directions of the relationship is *n* and *m*, respectively.

EXAMPLE 1.5

Figure 1.11 illustrates the production structure for Example 1.4, only this time C_3 and C_4 are taken together as it is assumed that they represent the same component. The figure has now become an oriented network because C_3 now has two different parents.

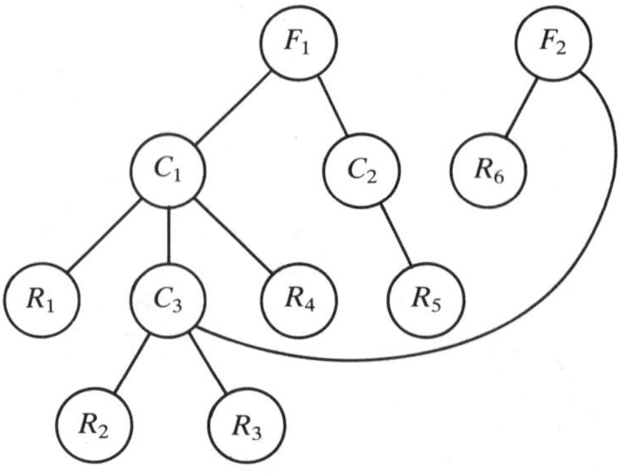

Figure 1.11 The production structure of Figure 1.10 where components C_3 and C_4 are identical. The tree is transformed into a network.

A **general network** is a symmetrical relationship in which each node may be related to an arbitrary number of the other nodes in the network. An example of a general network would be the cooperative relationships between a group of people or the transmission lines in a data transmission system. It is assumed that the transmission lines are so arranged that data can be transmitted in either direction between two connected computers. Otherwise the relationship would not be symmetrical.

Relationships of order *n*

In this section, we have looked at examples of relationships that are defined on one single set, in addition to relationships that connect entities in two different sets. Relationships of order n connect entities in n different sets.

EXAMPLE 1.6

Assume that a firm employs more than one motor-car dealer who sells cars from more than one car manufacturer, which also produces more than one type of vehicle (e.g., private car, bus, truck, etc.) If we are to describe the connection between the entities (motor-car dealer, car manufacturer, and vehicle type), we may have to use a relationship of the 3rd order. This example is illustrated in Figure 1.12, where the maximum and minimum branching factor for searches starting from these entities are indicated against the entity, and will be analysed further in Section 1.4.

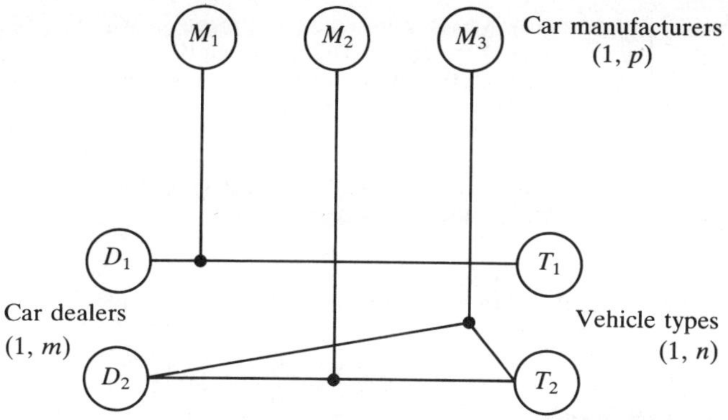

Figure 1.12 Relationships of third order. The figures in brackets show minimum and maximum branching factors. Dealer D_1 stocks only type T_1 from manufacturer M_1, while D_2 stocks only T_2 from M_2 and M_3.

1.3 Data models

A **data model** is a method used to describe the entity types and relationships of the conceptual database. Table 1.1 contains a survey of the data models to be described in this section and shows what database types the method is appropriate for. While the description of the individual database types is postponed to Section 4.2, it can be seen from Table 1.1 that the E–R diagram is so general that it can appropriately describe all database types, while the Bachman diagram and the relational model are more specialized.

In practice, the E–R diagram is often used for top-down analysis of new systems, while the relational model is good for bottom-up analysis of existing files.

Table 1.1 Survey of data models.

Database type	***Data model***		
	E–R diagram	*Bachman diagram*	*Relational model*
Relational	✓		✓
Hierarchical	✓	✓	
Network	✓	✓	
Inverted list	✓		

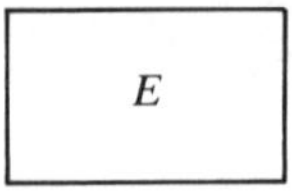

An entity type is represented as a rectangle with the name of the entity. This can often be thought of as a file containing all the entities of the particular type.

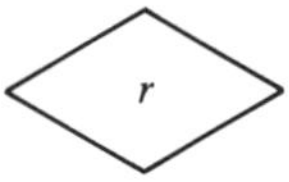

A relationship is represented as a rhomboid with the name of the relationship.

Figure 1.13 The basic symbols of an E–R model.

1.3.1 The E–R diagram

E–R diagram is an abbreviation of **entity–relationship diagram.** The account of the method given here follows Chen (1976) and Frank (1971).

An E–R diagram is made up of the symbols shown in Figure 1.13. A relationship connecting one entity type to another can be symbolized as shown in Figure 1.14. The symbols n and m in the figure show that it is an $n : m$ relationship. A $1 : n$ relationship or a $1 : 1$ relationship can be indicated in a similar way.

Figure 1.15 illustrates how we can describe relationships of order n. As an example, we use the 'dealer relationship' mentioned in Example 1.6. The symbols m, n and p mean, respectively, that a motor-car dealer may sell an arbitrary number of vehicle types, and that each car type may be manufactured by an arbitrary number of car manufacturers who may supply cars to an arbitrary number of motor-car dealers.

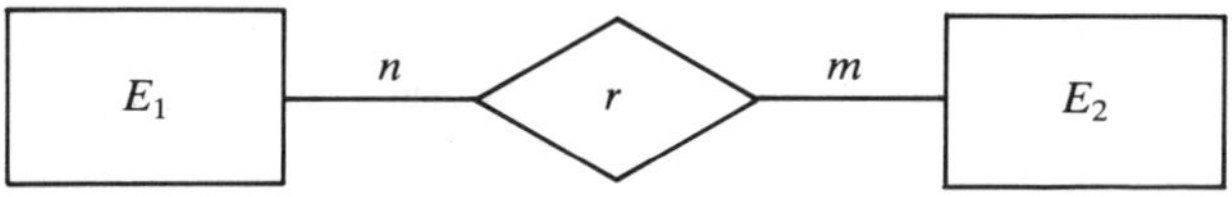

Figure 1.14 E–R representation of a relationship.

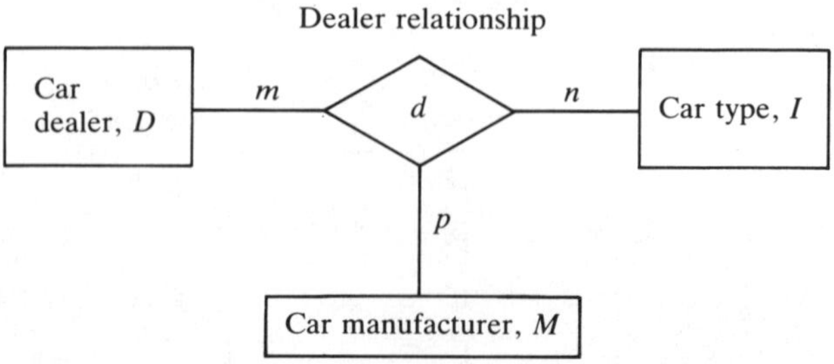

Figure 1.15 E–R diagram of a relationship of third order.

Table 1.2 Alternative symbols used to represent E–R diagrams.

Relationship type	***Descriptive method 1***	***Descriptive method 2***	***Descriptive method 3***
1 : *n* relationship	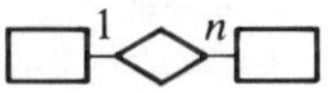		
n : *m* relationship	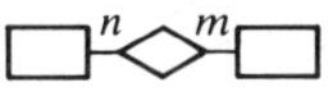		
Hierarchical relationship (tree)	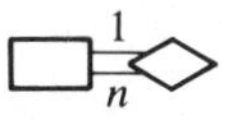		
Network relationship	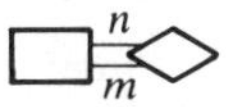		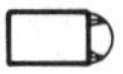
Relationship of 3rd order	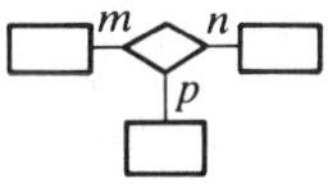	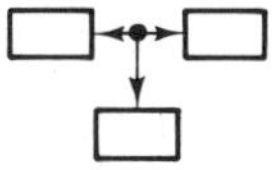	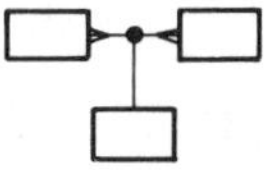
1 : 1 relationship			
Sequential or equivalence relationship	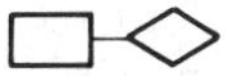		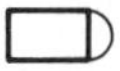

A tree or network relationship can be depicted by connecting the rectangle and the rhomboid by two lines with the symbols '1, *n*' and '*n*, *m*', respectively.

Sometimes alternative symbols are used to represent the E–R diagram and these are shown in Table 1.2.

EXAMPLE 1.7

Figure 1.16 shows an E–R diagram covering that section of a firm's database concerned with the invoicing system, the inventory management system and the back order system. During the invoicing process, the relationship r_1 is used to fetch data on customers, while the relationship r_5 is used to get the prices, names, etc. of the products. Assume that the back order forms request products that are out of stock. When the invoicing program is run, the back order file E_3 is increased by a new record each time that a product cannot be supplied. The relationships r_2 and r_4 are used when the firm has received new supplies,

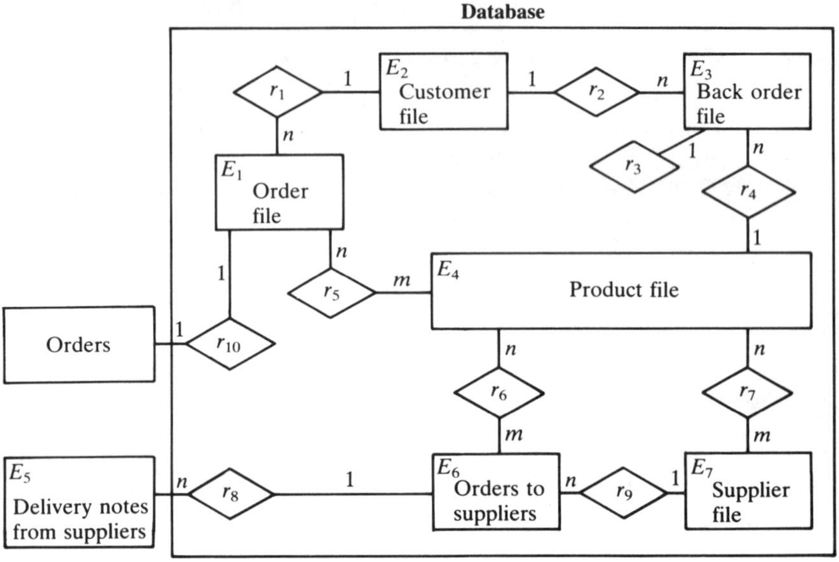

Figure 1.16 E–R diagram of an invoicing and inventory management system.

so that some of the back orders can be invoiced. The invoicing program updates the fields 'present volume of stocks' in the product file. If 'present volume of stocks' ≤ 'minimum volume of stocks', and if new supplies have not already been re-ordered, the invoicing program can find the name and address of a supplier by means of relationship r_7, after which a new order to the supplier can be printed. A copy of the order can be created in E_6, so that the system can automatically give an alarm message if the supplier does not meet his delivery date.

When supplies are received from the supplier, the relationship r_8 can be used to locate the corresponding order in E_6. By means of **combined relationship**†, E_6, r_6, E_4, r_4 and E_3, it is possible to locate the back orders that are ready to be invoiced. r_3 is a sequential relationship managing the order in which back orders for a given product are to be executed.

If a supplier suspends payments, the combined relationship r_9, E_6, r_4, E_3, r_2 and E_2 can be used to retrieve the names and addresses of customers who will be affected by the delay in delivery.

There are a number of symbols that can be used to improve the E–R diagram to provide a more detailed description of reality. For

†The expression 'combined relationship' can be seen as shorthand for the JOIN statement of relational algebra (see Chapters 12 and 13). JOIN operations make it possible to expand an entity by adding to it attributes from other entities to which it is related. The resulting entity can have further attributes added to it by successive applications of the JOIN statement.

example, the minimum and maximum branching factors can be indicated against the relationships of the diagram. The identification keys of the entities, foreign keys and other keys can also be shown.

A **foreign key** in an entity is a field having the characteristic that it serves as identification key for another entity. Thus, making the foreign keys in an entity explicit illustrates that the entity is related to another entity via the contents of this key.

It would also be an advantage to indicate a repeating field in the E–R diagram, as this would serve as an independent entity.

If a large number of entities share keys and/or relationships, they can be boxed in a 'shared entity box', in which the shared relationships and keys are referred to. This illustrative technique is particularly important in the case of very large databases, which tend to become unwieldy unless entities are grouped together in some way. In databases containing several hundred entities it is more practical to divide the E–R diagram into levels, so that the top level shows only the relationships between high-level entities, such as the shared entity boxes. In this way, more detailed E–R diagrams can be produced for each of the shared entity boxes and the entities related to it.

EXAMPLE 1.8

The database in a large bank normally consists of several hundred entities and relationships. The E–R diagram shown in Figure 1.17 describes the bank's main entities and the connections between them. At the top level, the bank's database can be illustrated with a few mutually related products that are also related to the customers, account managers, staff etc.

The detailed E–R diagram shown in Figure 1.18 specifically considers that section of the database concerned with customers and their relationships to accounts and transactions in foreign currency. In this figure, keys are represented by arrows which point to the entities. This symbol is used because the keys are likely to be implemented later, as 'entrances' to the files. A repeating field is represented by a double arrow. Repeating fields may be needed because, for example, it is necessary to record several exchange rates for each currency, since the contract date and settlement date for foreign exchange transactions need not be the same.

Many different transactions are associated with foreign currency. These are grouped together in the figure to give a good visual overview. The record formats of the individual foreign currency transactions vary considerably, although they all share a number of keys and relationships. This is shown by referring the shared keys and relationships to the group entity 'foreign currency transactions'.

It should be noted in passing that the E–R diagram of Figure 1.18 is a highly simplified description of the bank's database. In practice, yet another level in the database description will be needed.

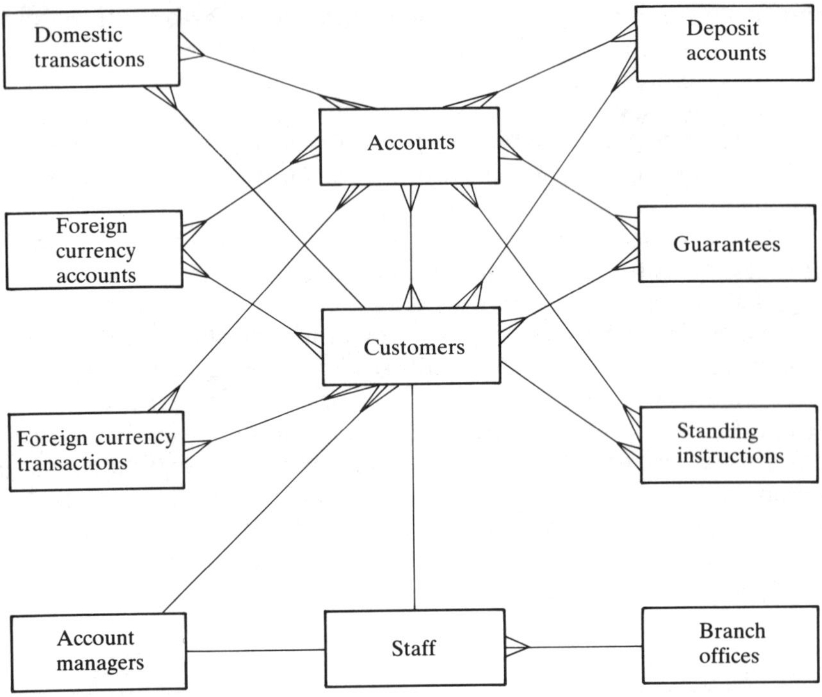

Figure 1.17 High-level description of a bank's main activities.

1.3.2 The Bachman diagram

A **Bachman diagram** (Bachman, 1969), also called a **datastructure diagram**, can only be used to illustrate $1:n$ relationships. However, many relationship types can be transformed to $1:n$ relationships. Example 1.9 illustrates how $n:m$ relationships can be transformed into a subentity and two $1:n$ relationships. The symbols used in Bachman diagrams are shown in Figure 1.19. In Bachman diagrams, $1 : n$ relationships are called **sets**. Sets and entities may be given names.

EXAMPLE 1.9

The Bachman diagram shown in Figure 1.20 illustrates the connection between orders, customers and products discussed in Example 1.3. To implement the $n:m$ relationship between orders and products it is necessary to insert an entity type suborder, which contains an order for one single product. In this example, the relationships are not named because there is no more than one relationship between each entity type.

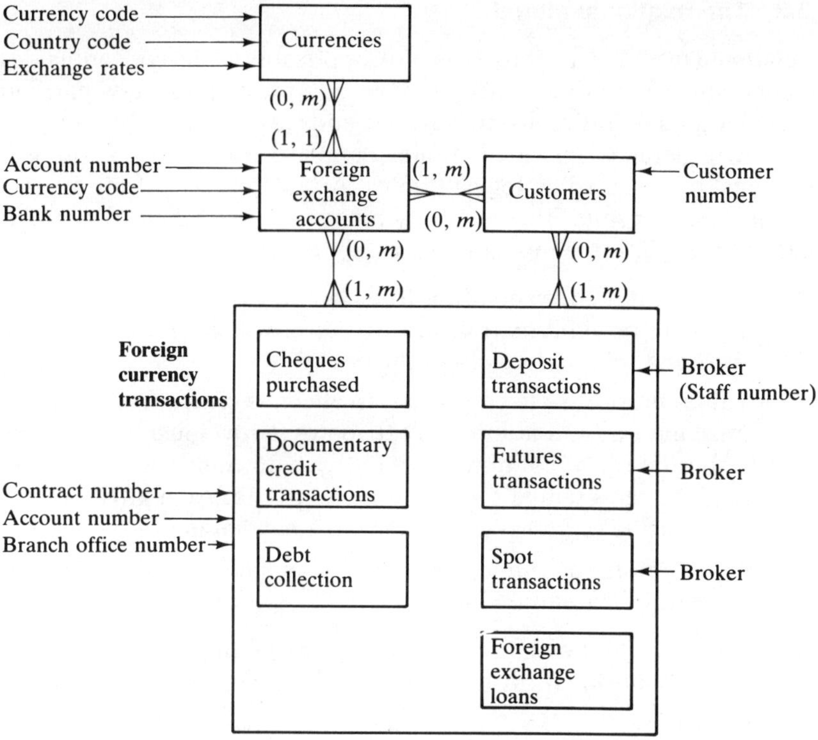

Figure 1.18 Details of the foreign currency area of a bank's business.

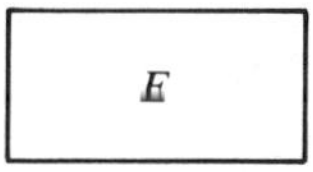

An entity is presented as a rectangle with the name of the entity.

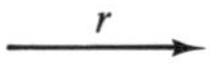

An arrow must always combine two entities. The arrow always symbolizes a 1 : n relationship.

Figure 1.19 The basic symbols of a Bachman diagram.

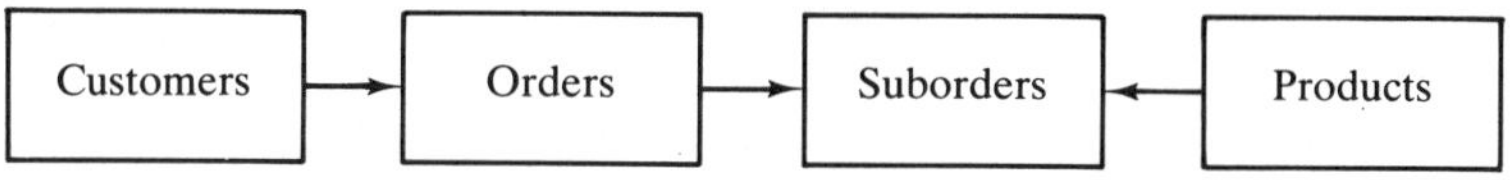

Figure 1.20 Bachman diagram of an $n : m$ relationship between customers and products.

1.3.3 The relational model

A **relational model** of a database is only applicable to the conceptual level of database description, since it does not presuppose any particular internal implementation for the entities and relationships that it sets up.

In general terms, a relational database consists of nothing but 'relations' represented as logical tables. A table can stand for an entity type or a relationship. These will often have data attached to them. The tables of the relational model must satisfy the following requirements:

- Each entity, corresponding to a row in the table, must have an attribute or combination of attributes, which serves as an identifier and refers uniquely to the entity.
- Tables must be of fixed format. In effect, this means that an entity must have a fixed number of attributes (a row must be made up of a specific set of columns). An entity with multivalued attributes must be represented by a separate entity for each attribute value and thus be given several rows in the new table.
- A table must be homogeneous; that is, all the rows in the table must be of the same kind.

Figure 1.21 shows a relational model of the customer–product system already outlined in the examples. It makes use of the following tables:

- A CUSTOMER table consisting of a unique CUSTOMER NUMBER (the identifier attribute for this table), a NAME and an ADDRESS.

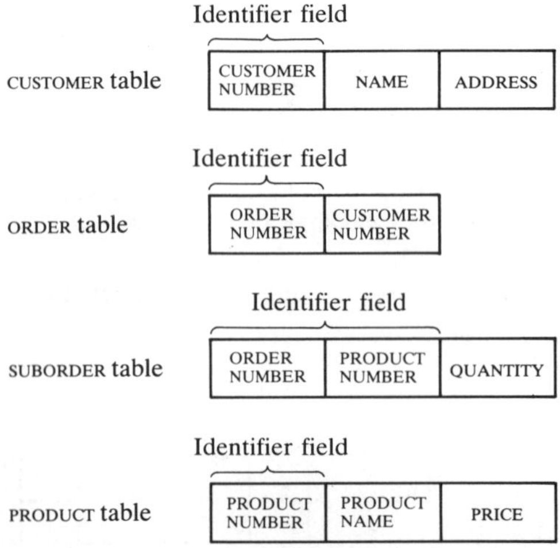

Figure 1.21 Relational model of a customer–product database. The model requires tables for customers, products, orders and suborders.

- An ORDER table consisting of an ORDER NUMBER (identifier) and a CUSTOMER NUMBER.
- A SUBORDER table with ORDER NUMBER together with PRODUCT NUMBER as identifier and a further attribute for the QUANTITY of the product ordered.
- A PRODUCT table consisting of PRODUCT NUMBER (identifier), PRODUCT NAME and PRICE.

As can be seen from the figure, a table can describe an entity (e.g., a product or a customer) or a relationship (e.g., a suborder).

The relational model is very simple because it is built up only of files or tables. However, it does not give a very good visual overview of the database because the model describes relationships in the same way as entities. In the case of very large, complex databases, it is important to have a comprehensive overview of the database, and it therefore may be useful to supplement a relational model with an E–R diagram.

The relational model was originally developed by Codd (1970), whose article prompted comprehensive theoretical research within database theory as well as practical cooperation between researchers and software producers. Practical experience with the relational model has led to some adjustments (Codd, 1979) of its original definition, of which the following are the most important:

- In practice, users do not always need an identifier field in a record, as this field may only be used for purposes of searching. In such cases, the identifier field can be replaced by another unique key, such as the file name followed by the record's relative address.
- A 'null value' may be allotted to a field to indicate that the value of the field is unknown or non-existent. An example of this is the telephone number field in a staff record where an employee's telephone number is unknown. However, the identifier field or a part thereof cannot be allowed to have a null value.
- An identifier field or a part thereof may not be updated. The record, and therefore also the identifier field, can only be created or deleted.

1.3.4 User view diagrams

As mentioned earlier, an external schema or a user view is a description of that part of the conceptual database used by a program. Likewise, a **user view diagram** is a data model of that part of the conceptual database used by a program.

The data models already outlined can be used, amongst other things, for top-down design of the conceptual database, whereas the user view diagrams discussed here can be used for bottom-up construction of

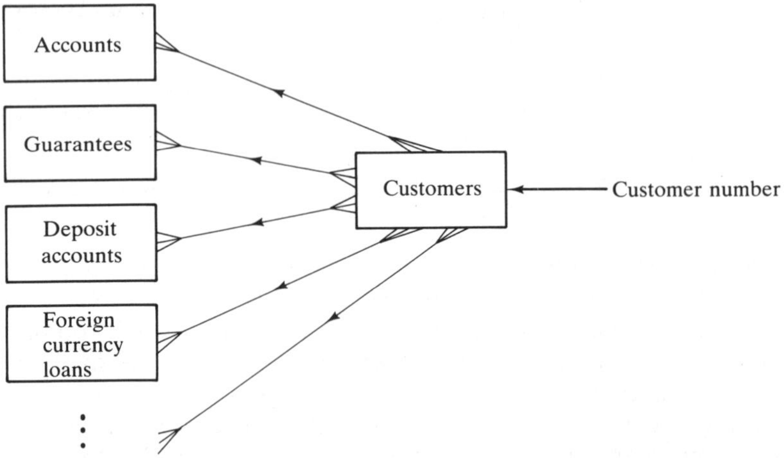

Figure 1.22 User view diagram of an on-line query system accessed by means of a customer number.

the conceptual schema. In the process of a bottom-up construction, the various users' demands, represented on user view diagrams, are used to correct the first draft of a data model. Then, as the user view diagrams are incorporated, the data model of the conceptual database can be made more complete.

EXAMPLE 1.10

Figures 1.22 and 1.23 are two user view diagrams used for the construction of the bank database introduced in Example 1.8. Figure 1.22 describes that part of the database concerned with the on-line display of a customer's total obligations on the basis of a customer number. Figure 1.23 outlines that part of the database that deals with the payment of dividends on a particular type of security, depositing the money in the account related to the security and notifying the customer of the deposit. The arrows in the figures indicate the search paths between files and the access needed to the files by the programs. Information of this kind can prove very valuable when constructing the physical database for the following reason: if a number is written against the arrows, indicating how frequently the program uses the illustrated search direction, numbers can be summed and transferred to the conceptual data model. When the physical database is constructed, it is then possible to use the numbers to decide which search directions or access routes are to be optimized at the expense of the less frequently used ones.

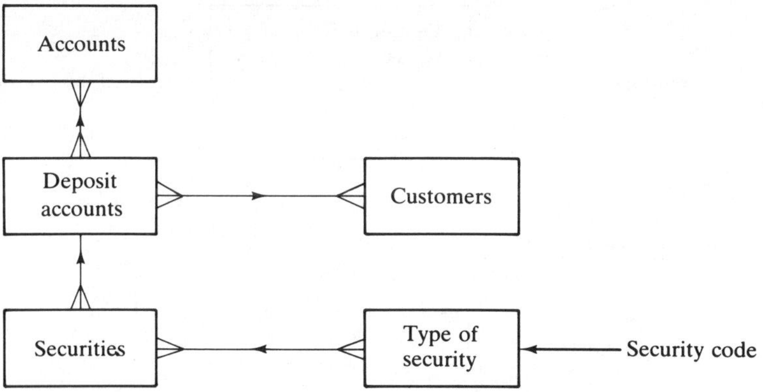

Figure 1.23 User view diagram of a dividend payment system.

1.4 Design of the conceptual schema

There are several methods of designing the conceptual schema. The method described in this section is heavily influenced by relational database theory, as the emphasis is placed on designing the conceptual schema of a relational database. However, this method can also be used to design schemas for other database types, since it is relatively simple to alter the relational model to fit their conceptual schema.

The three most important stages in the design of the conceptual schema, illustrated in Figure 1.24, are as follows:

(1) Input for the first stage is the users' requirements or preferences for the application uses and thus indirectly those of the database itself. The gathering of user requirements is usually performed as a separate activity, although it is often advantageous to perform it at the same time as the analysis to determine what entities and relationships are relevant for the various users' views of reality. When the user views have been collected, they have to be incorporated into an appropriate data model to provide a shared conceptual schema, which must be sufficiently general for users to understand and accept. In this first conceptual schema, therefore, it is not essential to consider any constraints the DBMS may later impose. However, as the entities and relationships of the conceptual database are decided upon on the basis of the users' views, particular attention must be paid to the problems arising as a result of the use of homonyms and synonyms: different concepts may be referred to by the users by means of the same entity name and vice versa, several names may be used by different parts of the firm for what is essentially the same entity (see Example 1.2, for instance, which analyses what the entity 'customer' may mean).

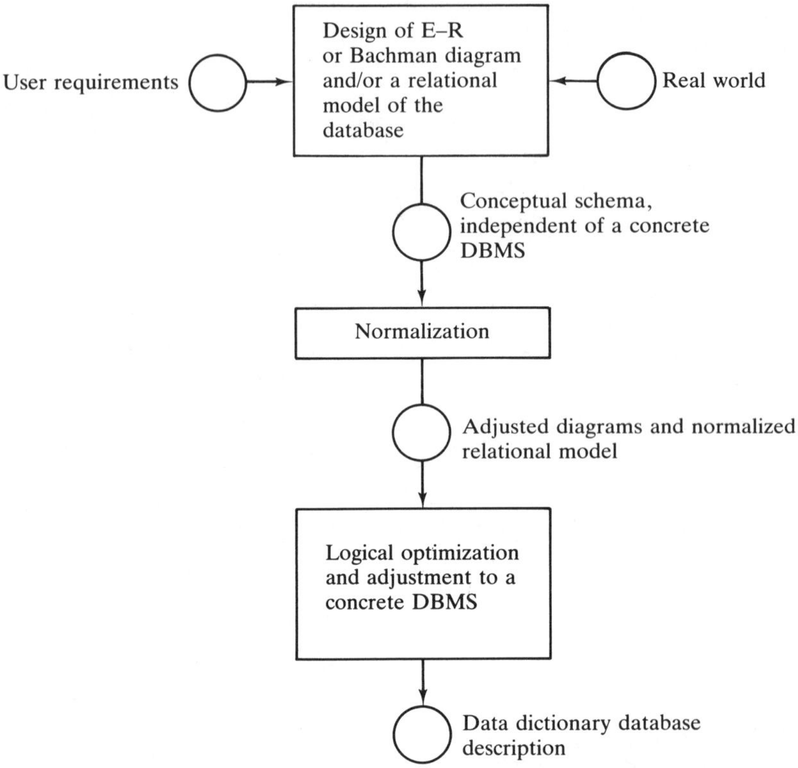

Figure 1.24 Design of the conceptual schema. *Phase 1* : choice of a model; *Phase 2* : normalization; *Phase 3* : optimization.

Another problem that must be addressed is that the users may make conflicting demands on the entities. For example, the accounts department of a firm often needs data relating to the last day of an accounting period, while another department may need the most up-to-date data.

Normally, the entity types and relationships of a database are stable, so that new demands on the database can often be satisfied merely by inserting new fields into existing entity types. If the database is a model of the external world, then the addition of new systems will only require the creation of new entities and relationships, which can be easily linked in with the existing database. If, however, the database is not a model of the external world, there is a risk that new systems will not be able to be integrated into the existing database.

(2) The second stage of the design of the conceptual schema consists of the **normalization** of the provisional model. In this context, normalization means that redundant data is systematically deleted from the logical database, so that data is only inserted where it naturally belongs. By the process of normalization, it is also possible to check whether the original logical database is adequate, or whether new logical files need to be created to bring the logical database more in line with concepts and physical objects of the external world. The normalization rules will be outlined in the following sections.

(3) During the third stage, any redundant data necessary to optimize the searches of application programs is inserted. It is often practical to retain the data in its original location in the normalized database, from which it can then be copied to where it is required. If this leads to inconsistencies occurring in the database, it is usually possible to regenerate the redundant data by repeating the copying of it.

During this stage, the description of the logical database is also adapted to a concrete DBMS. (If the DBMS is relational no such adaptation is necessary, but in the case of hierarchical and network databases this adaptation often consists of deleting the identification fields of the relationship files either partly or completely, and replacing them by physical pointers that directly link up a record with the records it is related to.) The result of this stage is a data dictionary database description (see Section 4.3); that is, a conceptual schema that can be used by the DBMS. The construction of a database is an iterative process, as new knowledge may necessitate the system designer backtracking to an earlier stage to redesign the database description. For example, a designer will only optimize by means of redundancy if, during the construction of the physical database, it emerges that the users' response time demands cannot be met without taking this step.

1.4.1 Normal forms

One of the central ideas of relational database theory is to formulate constraints on the structures of tables in the database to obtain a logical database that is 'like the external world'. Applying different sets of constraints results in differently structured tables. In database terminology these are said to be in various normal forms.

The terminology of relational database theory uses several terms of its own which should be introduced here. They apply equally to the abstract objects of relational algebra and to the real components of a

SALESMAN NUMBER	SALES CODE	CITY	PRODUCT NUMBER (PN)	AMOUNT (A)	PN	A	PN	A	PN	A	PN	A
S_1	10	Aarhus										
S_2	30	Copenhagen	P_1	200	P_3	100						
S_4	20	Odense	P_5	200	P_8	100						
S_5	30	Copenhagen	P_1	50	P_3	500	P_4	800	P_5	500	P_8	100

Figure 1.25 The SALESMAN file before normalization. Note the repeating PN and A fields.

relational database. Thus, the term **relation**† designates a file with a fixed record structure; a **tuple** is the same as a record in such a file; **domain** designates a field's value area; and a field is called an **attribute**. Instead of relation, tuple and attribute the terms **table**, **row** and **column** are often used. The reason for this will become clear in Example 1.11.

First normal form

For a file to be a representation of a relation, it is necessary that:

- only one type of record appears in the file (tuples are of the same kind); and
- each tuple must contain a unique identifier.

If the relation is to be of **first normal form**, we must ensure, in addition, that tuples have only atomic values in their attributes. In other words, repeating fields are excluded under first normal form.

EXAMPLE 1.11

Figure 1.25 shows the details of a SALESMAN file. Each salesman record includes a salesman NUMBER, a SALES CODE and the salesman's home town (CITY). In addition, there is a repeating group for the individual product numbers the salesman has sold, and another for the QUANTITY he has sold. The file has variable record length because not all the salesman sell all types of products.

† A relation is defined mathematically as follows: Assume that $A_1, A_2, \ldots, A_n$ are sets whose individual elements are $p_1\ q_1, p_2\ q_2, \ldots\ p_n\ q_n$. A relation R on the set $A_1, A_2, \ldots, A_n$ can be defined as a subset of the Cartesian product $A_1 \times A_2 \times \ldots \times A_n$. In other words, a relation can be defined as a set of elements in which each individual element consists of n subelements $(p_1, p_2, \ldots, p_n)$, so that the first subelement must belong to the set A_1, the second to A_2, etc. If these elements are thought of as records with the field values $p_1, p_2, \ldots, p_n$, it can be seen that it is easy to think of the relation as a file.

SALESMAN NUMBER	SALES CODE	CITY	PRODUCT NUMBER	AMOUNT
S_1	10	Aarhus		
S_2	30	Copenhagen	P_1	200
S_2	30	Copenhagen	P_3	100
S_4	20	Odense	P_5	200
S_4	20	Odense	P_8	100
S_5	30	Copenhagen	P_1	50
S_5	30	Copenhagen	P_3	500
S_5	30	Copenhagen	P_4	800
S_5	30	Copenhagen	P_5	500
S_5	30	Copenhagen	P_8	100

Figure 1.26 The SALESMAN file in first normal form. The repeating fields are represented by means of new rows in the table.

In Figure 1.26, the SALESMAN file has been altered so that it satisfies first normal form. The fixed record build-up has been achieved by repeating all the salesman data for each individual Product Number the salesman sells.

(This example is used throughout the rest of the book. A similar example, including exercises and solutions, is described in Date (1986).)

Second and third normal forms

To define second and third normal forms, it is first necessary to introduce the notion of functional dependency. Assume that *X* and *Y* are fields in the same record. Field *Y* is said to be **functionally dependent** on field *X* if, and only if, it is the case that for all pairs of records in the file, that if they have the same value in field *X*, they also have the same value in field *Y*. Field *Y* is said to be **fully functionally dependent** on field *X* if *Y* is functionally dependent on *X*, and not functionally dependent on any subset of *X's* possible subfields. A field on which another field is fully functionally dependent is called the **determinant** for that field. Furthermore, field *Y* is said to be **transitively functionally dependent** on *X* if there is some other field *Z* such that *X* determines the value of *Z* and *Z* determines the value of *Y*.

We can now define second and third normal forms. A file is in **second normal form** if it is in first normal form, and if all non-identifier fields are fully functionally dependent on the record's identifier field. In popular terms, we can say that a file is in second normal form if the ordinary record fields contain data that is attached to the entire record's identifier field.

SALESMAN NUMBER	SALES CODE	CITY
S_1	10	Aarhus
S_2	30	Copenhagen
S_4	20	Odense
S_5	30	Copenhagen

(a)

SALESMAN NUMBER	PRODUCT NUMBER	AMOUNT
S_2	P_1	200
S_2	P_3	100
S_4	P_5	200
S_4	P_8	100
S_5	P_1	50
S_5	P_3	500
S_5	P_4	800
S_5	P_5	500
S_5	P_8	100

(b)

Figure 1.27 The SALESMAN file represented as two files satisfying third normal form provided that SALES CODE and CITY are independent.

A file is in **third normal form** if it is in second normal form, and if, in addition, the record's non-identifier fields are not transitively dependent on the record's identifier field. In popular terms, this means that the ordinary record fields must contain data that is attached to the identifier field, to the entire identifier field and to nothing but the identifier field. If this last condition – 'and to nothing but the identifier field' – is omitted, then the record type is only in second normal form. If a file does not satisfy second and third normal forms respectively, it should be divided up (see Codd, 1970).

EXAMPLE 1.12

In the salesman table in first normal form in Example 1.11, the identification key field is composed of the field SALESMAN NUMBER and PRODUCT NUMBER. This table is not in second normal form because the column CITY contains information not connected to the entire identification key field. In this situation, the file must be divided up, so that the ordinary record fields can be collected around the identification key fields they are connected to. This is illustrated in Figure 1.27 in which SALESMAN NUMBER is identification key column in the first table (a), and (SALESMAN NUMBER, PRODUCT NUMBER) is identification key column in the second table (b).

The SALESMAN file is in third normal form if both SALES CODE and CITY are connected to SALESMAN NUMBER. However, the record description could also be understood to mean that SALES CODE contains data connected to the contents of CITY. In this case, SALES CODE 30 would represent information about the city Copenhagen.

If SALES CODE is connected to CITY, the file is not in third normal form, since SALES CODE may not be connected to anything but the

SALESMAN NUMBER	CITY
S_1	Aarhus
S_2	Copenhagen
S_4	Odense
S_5	Copenhagen

(a)

CITY	SALES CODE
Copenhagen	30
Odense	20
Aarhus	10

(b)

Figure 1.28 Tables showing a dependency between SALES CODE and CITY. These two tables should replace (a) in Figure 1.27 to ensure that third normal form is satisfied.

identification key field SALESMAN NUMBER. In such a situation, the file must be again divided up so that the ordinary record fields are collected around the identification key fields to which they are connected. This is illustrated in Figure 1.28 in which SALESMAN NUMBER is identification key field in the first table (a) and CITY is identification key field in the second table (b).

Figure 1.28 can also be used to illustrate the problems that may occur if the relationships of the database are not normalized to third normal form.

- If a city changes its Sales Codes, it is only necessary to alter the city's sales code field in the normalized file with city data (Figure 1.28 (b)). If the database is implemented as illustrated in Figure 1.27, then the sales codes have to be updated in all the salesman's records connected to the city that changes its sales codes. Normally, such an alteration requires the existence of an additional secondary index in the salesman file, so that all salesmen in a given city can be located.
- When one of the salesman's records in Figure 1.27 (a) is deleted, there is a risk that this might be the last salesman for a given city. If this the case, all data recorded for that city will be lost – data that will be needed next time a salesman record for that city is created. If the database is implemented as illustrated in Figure 1.28, this problem can be avoided.

Boyce/Codd normal form

Boyce/Codd normal form makes use of the concept of a determinant. The definition already given may be difficult to understand, so for practical purposes we can say that a field is the determinant for other fields in the record if all the fields make up a description of a type of object or concept from the external world in such a way that the determinant can be used as identification key field for the new type of object or concept. Using this concept of a determinant, we can now define a relation in **Boyce/Codd normal form** as one in which any determinant attribute can be used as the tuple's identification key field.

If a relation does not satisfy this normal form it is usually because the table describes a concept or object that incorporates other concepts or objects. The table should therefore be divided into two or more relations, each describing its own proper concept or object.

It can be easily proved that a relation satisfying the Boyce/Codd normal form also satisfies third normal form. Third normal form, however, contains an unfortunate constraint, which the Boyce/Codd normal form does not. A relation in the Boyce/Codd normal form may well contain several different unique identification key fields, which the mathematical derivation of third normal form does not allow. So, for most purposes the Boyce/Codd normal form is more practical than third normal form.

EXAMPLE 1.13

In practice, relations containing several different identification key fields are relatively common. As an example, consider a salesman's record. In addition to the SALESMAN NUMBER, we must also store a national register number (also a unique identification key), since this is needed in connection with reports to the Inland Revenue.

Fourth normal form

Fourth normal form invokes the concept of **multivalued dependencies** between attributes. A multivalued dependency holds between two attributes in a table if the second attribute can assume different values for a given value in the first attribute. If a relation contains two multivalued dependencies, these may be dependent on, or independent of each other, respectively. A relationship of order n will usually include many multivalued dependencies. If these are independent of each other, the relationship of order n can be reduced to $1:n$ relationships and $n:m$ relationships, as illustrated in Example 1.14.

EXAMPLE 1.14

Assume that a database contains a file for motor-car dealers, a file for car manufacturers and a file for vehicle types. An $n:m$ relationship exists between the motor-car dealers and the car manufacturers, as a motor-car dealer may sell cars from more than one manufacturer, and a manufacturer may have his cars sold by more than one motor-car dealer. Likewise, there is an $n{:}m$ relationship between the motor-car dealers and the vehicle types, as a motor-car dealer may sell several types of vehicle, and a vehicle type may be sold by several motor-car dealers. These two $n{:}m$ relationships can be implemented as shown in Figure 1.29. In the

MOTOR-CAR DEALER	CAR MANUFACTURER
Hansen	Ford
Hansen	GM
Jensen	Ford
Jensen	GM

(a)

MOTOR-CAR DEALER	VEHICLE TYPE
Hansen	car
Hansen	bus
Jensen	car
Jensen	truck

(b)

Figure 1.29 Two $n:m$ relationships implemented as two tables. (a) shows that both Hansen and Jensen each sell Ford and GM products. (b) shows that Hansen sells cars and buses while Jensen sells cars and trucks.

table of Figure 1.29(a), there is a multivalued dependency between MOTOR-CAR DEALER and CAR MANUFACTURER, because motor-car dealer Hansen sells cars from both Ford and GM. Similarly, in the table of Figure 1.29(b), there is a multivalued dependency between MOTOR-CAR DEALER and VEHICLE TYPE. These two $n:m$ relationships can also be implemented as illustrated in Figure 1.30. In this case, the two multivalued dependencies are implemented in the same table. The two multivalued dependencies are independent of each other if the contents of the first row means that Hansen acts as a dealer for the car manufacturer Ford, and that Hansen sells (private) cars. If the multi-valued dependencies are independent, it is therefore possible Hansen does not sell Ford's cars, only their buses. If they are dependent, Hansen sells private cars made by Ford. This is made explicit in the case where

MOTOR CAR DEALER	CAR MANUFACTURER	VEHICLE TYPE
Hansen	Ford	car
Hansen	Ford	bus
Hansen	GM	car
Hansen	GM	bus
Jensen	Ford	car
Jensen	Ford	truck
Jensen	GM	car
Jensen	GM	truck

Figure 1.30 The two $n:m$ relationships implemented as a single table with three columns. This table contains exactly the same information as Figure 1.29, providing that the multivalued dependencies are independent. If they are dependent upon one another, the table asserts that Hansen sells GM buses, whereas in Figure 1.29 it is only asserted that Hansen sells buses and that he sells some GM products.

MOTOR-CAR DEALER	CAR MANUFACTURER	VEHICLE TYPE
Hansen	Ford	car
Hansen	Ford	bus
Hansen	GM	car
Jensen	Ford	car
Jensen	GM	truck

Figure 1.31 A single table with dependent multivalued dependencies. Here it is explicit that Hansen does not sell GM buses.

the two multivalued dependencies are dependent upon each other, as shown in Figure 1.31. Motor-car dealer Jensen sells for both Ford and GM, but Jensen only sells Ford's (private) cars, although GM could also supply such cars.

Where the two multivalued dependencies are dependent upon each other, as shown in Figure 1.31, the file cannot be split up into two files as in Figure 1.29, since to do so implies that Jensen also sells private cars from GM.

Informally, we can say that a file satisfies fourth normal form if it satisfies third normal form and, if the file contains several multivalued dependencies, these are dependent upon each other. If a file does not satisfy fourth normal form because it contains two independent multivalued dependencies, then the file can be normalized by splitting it up into two different files, each of which contains one of the multivalued dependencies. If the multivalued dependencies are dependent upon each other, we cannot normally split up the table, as shown in Example 1.14.

One of the main problems connected with breaking fourth normal form is that doubt may arise as to how updating or maintenance is to be performed.

EXAMPLE 1.15

Figure 1.32 (a)–(d) illustrates four different maintenance strategies for a file that does not satisfy fourth normal form. These maintenance strategies are further complicated if data is attached to one or both of the multivalued dependencies

Fifth normal form

Fifth normal form is also concerned with relations containing multivalued dependencies. The fifth normalization rule sometimes makes it possible to reduce a relation containing two multivalued dependencies

(a)

MOTOR-CAR DEALER	CAR MANUFACTURER	VEHICLE TYPE
Hansen	Ford	
Hansen	GM	
Hansen		car
Hansen		bus

The multivalued fields are kept separate, so that a record contains either a car manufacturer or a car type. This filing method is very similar to splitting up the file.

(b)

MOTOR-CAR DEALER	CAR MANUFACTURER	VEHICLE TYPE
Hansen	Ford	car
Hansen	GM	bus

The multivalued fields are mixed at random, but in such a way that the number of records is minimized.

(c)

MOTOR-CAR DEALER	CAR MANUFACTURER	VEHICLE TYPE
Hansen	Ford	car
Hansen		bus
Hansen	GM	

Random filing.

(d)

MOTOR-CAR DEALER	CAR MANUFACTURER	VEHICLE TYPE
Hansen	Ford	car
Hansen	Ford	bus
Hansen	GM	car
Hansen	GM	bus

All possibilities of combination must be filed. This maintenance strategy leads to redundancy.

Figure 1.32 Maintenance strategies for a file not satisfying fourth normal form. (a) separation of multivalued fields; (b) random mixing; (c) random filing; (d) all combinations.

that are dependent upon each other. The prerequisites for making a reduction possible can be illustrated with the help of Example 1.16, in which car dealers sell car types from different car manufacturers.

EXAMPLE 1.16

In Figure 1.33, the two multivalued dependencies are dependent upon each other because Jensen sells private cars and GM produces private cars but Jensen does not sell GM cars. However, the following rule can be deduced:

MOTOR-CAR DEALER	CAR MANUFACTURER	VEHICLE TYPE
Hansen	Ford	car
Hansen	Ford	truck
Hansen	GM	car
Hansen	GM	truck
Jensen	Ford	car

Figure 1.33 Dependent multivalued dependencies.

- If a motor-car dealer sells a particular vehicle type, and if the dealer represents a car manufacturer, then the dealer sells this particular vehicle type from the car manufacturer.

If two multivalued dependencies in a relation satisfy symmetric constraints of this type, the relation can be reduced as shown in Figure 1.34. All the tables shown in this figure satisfy fifth normal form, whereas the table of Figure 1.33 only satisfies fourth normal form.

The principal purpose of normalization theory is to produce a database that models the real world. In this way, it is more likely that the database can be easily adaptable to unforeseen requirements. From this point of view, fifth normal form can be dispensed with, since by normalizing the two dependent multivalued dependencies the immediate information that the multivalued dependencies are dependent upon

MOTOR-CAR DEALER	CAR MANUFACTURER
Hansen	Ford
Hansen	GM
Jensen	Ford

(a)

MOTOR-CAR DEALER	VEHICLE TYPE
Hansen	car
Hansen	truck
Jensen	car

(b)

CAR MANUFACTURER	VEHICLE TYPE
Ford	car
Ford	truck
GM	car
GM	truck

(c)

Figure 1.34 Figure 1.33 reduced to three files in fifth normal form.

each other is concealed. In terms of filing technique, however, problems may arise if the fifth normal form is not observed, as it may be necessary to introduce redundancy to be able to store the data where it logically belongs.

EXAMPLE 1.17

Assume that two multivalued dependencies are dependent upon each other, as shown in the Figures 1.33 and 1.34. Furthermore, assume that data is connected to one of the multivalued dependencies – because Hansen, for example, receives a fixed commission for selling for Ford. If we wish to file this piece of information in the file with two multivalued dependencies, it is natural to store the information redundantly in all the instances where a connection between Hansen and Ford is filed. We could also create a separate file for this information, but in so doing the connection between Hansen and Ford would become redundant.

Other normal forms

The normal forms dealt with so far are all concerned with deleting redundant data by splitting up the file into smaller ones. Within the database theory, there are also normal forms that can be used to delete redundant information distributed on several different files. This problem is illustrated in Example 1.18.

EXAMPLE 1.18

The employees of a bank can also be regarded as customers of that bank, since they have, at least, a wage account. The field 'name and address' can therefore be inserted in both the customer file and the employee file in a natural way. However, if names and addresses are stored in both files, redundant data will be inserted without being detected by the normalization rules that have been outlined.

EXERCISES

1.1 Describe how the equivalence relationship can be replaced by a $1:n$ relationship.

1.2 The graph in Figure 1.35 shows a network relationship outlining the production structure for two products, P_1 and P_2. P_1 is produced from one P_3 and two P_4s, and P_2 is produced from four P_3s and one P_5. Most DBMSs cannot implement network relationships directly, as the network relationship has to be implemented as $1:n$ relationships. Show, by using a graph, how this network relationship can be implemented as two $1:n$ relationships.

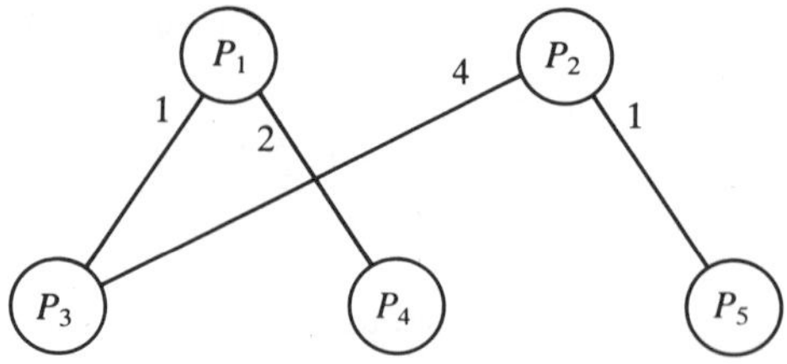

Figure 1.35 Network relationship showing production structure for two products.

1.3 In Section 1.3.1, an E–R diagram for a wholesale firm was shown.

(a) Transform the E–R diagram so that it only comprises files that at least satisfy third normal form.

(b) Assume that the government introduces a new differentiated VAT system. What changes does this imply for the logical database if the database is to be kept in third normal form?

1.4 Produce an E–R diagram and a relational model of a database that can be used for project management in a large data processing department. The database has to be used to solve the following tasks:

- Printing of activities in the 'critical path' (see the following description of network planning).
- Printing of project surveys indicating the status of each individual project in relation to the time schedule.
- Printing of surveys of activities, which, for each activity, shows who is responsible and who is taking part. These surveys must show what proportion of total working time each employee is spending on the activity.
- Working plans for all employees. Note that an employee may be working on more than one activity at a time. The working plans must also contain data on planned holidays and course participation.
- If an employee falls ill it has to be possible to have a print out of the number of days an employee can be absent before it delays the completion of projects the employee is working on. It also has to be possible to have the names of other employees who are qualified to replace the absentee.

Figure 1.36 illustrates how the 'critical path' of a project can be calculated by means of network planning. The figure is a system flowchart, in which the arrows illustrate activities and the ellipses illustrate events. The figures against the activities indicate the duration of the activities. The ellipses in the figure consist of three fields: the field to the left contains

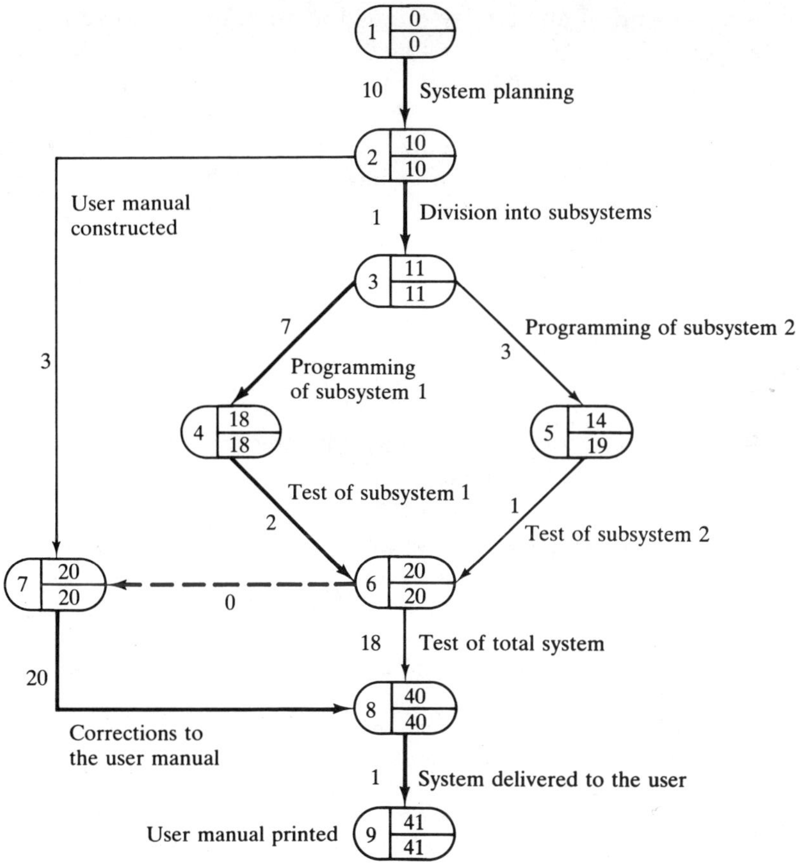

Figure 1.36 Critical path for a project. The critical path is indicated by the thick lines and arrows.

the number of the event; the top field contains the earliest time at which the event can take place; and the bottom field contains the latest time at which the event can take place if the project is not to be delayed. Note that the earliest and latest times can be calculated if only the duration of the individual activities is known. If the first event is given the starting time 0, the successive starting times of the subsequent events can be calculated. The latest time for the last event is defined as having the same value as the earliest time for the event. Thus, we can calculate backwards from the finishing time and calculate the latest times for the other events. The difference between the earliest and the latest time for the event is called the **slack** of the event. The event must fall within this period, otherwise the entire project is delayed. The difference between the latest time for an event at the beginning of an activity and the earliest time of an event at the end of an activity minus the duration of the activity is called the **float** of the activity. The float of an activity is equal to the time the activity can be delayed before it has an impact on the finishing time of the entire project. The path through a network consisting of activities without float, which combines events without slack, is called the **critical path**. This is the most time-consuming path through the network and any delay along this path has an immediate effect upon the calculated finished time of the project.

EXERCISES

1.5 A local authority wants to build up a data processing system to help its libraries in the following tasks:

- Recording books lent.
- Reservation of books. It must be possible for a borrower to reserve a book in his local library, so that it is delivered as soon as it is available in any of the local authority's libraries.
- Printing overdue notices. The overdue notices must include the name of the borrower, the title of the book and the name of the author.
- Printing manual index card files, so that books can be searched for manually. The search argument may be the title of the book, the subject or the name of the author. Note that there may be more than one author of a single book, and that the book may deal with more than one subject.
- It must be possible to combine the search arguments on-line.

(a) Design an E–R diagram that describes how the library can build up the conceptual schema.

(b) What relationship types does the E–R diagram contain?

(c) Show, by means of combined relationships, that it is possible to produce the required output.

(d) Describe the conceptual schema by means of a Bachman diagram.

(e) Transform the conceptual schema so that the files of the database satisfy at least third normal form, and describe the database by means of the relational model. To limit the extent of this exercise, you should only include the most necessary record fields. Design the conceptual schema in such a way that it does not record redundant data.

1.6 Example 1.7 showed how searches of application programs can be outlined by means of combined relationships. However, it is also possible, in these combined relationships, to indicate where we want to update. For example, the searches and updatings necessary for the invoicing of back orders are:

Back orders, FP, product file (updating of stock)
Back orders (deletion), FC, customer file.

Outline, by means of combined relationships, the searches and updatings required for the following tasks:

(a) Invoicing of orders and creation of records for any unfilled orders and printing of orders to suppliers.

(b) Updatings of the database on the basis of the delivery notes from the suppliers.

1.7 The E–R diagram shown in Figure 1.37 illustrates the conceptual schema in a project-oriented production firm. Describe the conceptual schema by means of the relational model so that all files satisfy fifth normal form.

1.8 Assume that a file satisfies Boyce/Codd normal form and that the file does not contain several mutually independent or dependent multivalued fields.

(a) Does the file also satisfy fourth and fifth normal form?

(b) Is it possible to avoid redundant data in such a file?

1.9 The E–R diagram shown in Figure 1.38 illustrates the most important entities and relationships in a bank database. As it is essential for the bank to quickly survey which products a customer has, the bank has built up a shared relationship file between the relationships for customers and products. The relationship file has a fixed record format and contains the fields shown in Figure 1.39. The data relating to account relationships is

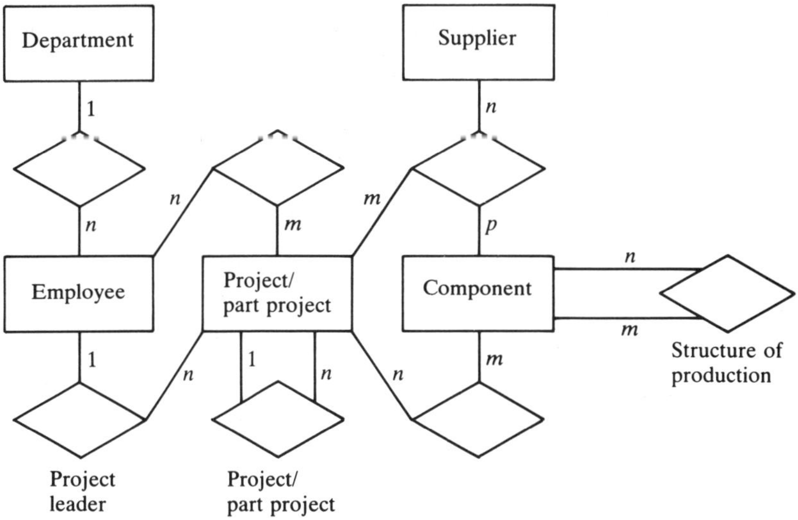

Figure 1.37 E-R diagram for a project-orientated production enterprise.

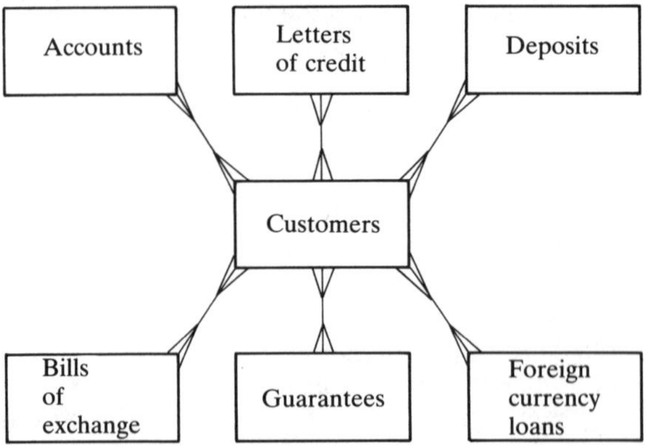

Figure 1.38 Entities and relationships in a bank database.

only stored in relationships pointing to account records. A similar rule applies to data relating to deposit relationships, etc. Thus, there are many fields with null values in each individual relationship record. This does not matter, however, if the DBMS has data compression.

Which normal form does this relationship file satisfy?

1.10 It appears from Section 1.3.3 that the original demands on a relational database have been changed.

(a) Give examples of entities that do not need a unique identification field in a record.

(b) Why do you think an identification field may not be updated?

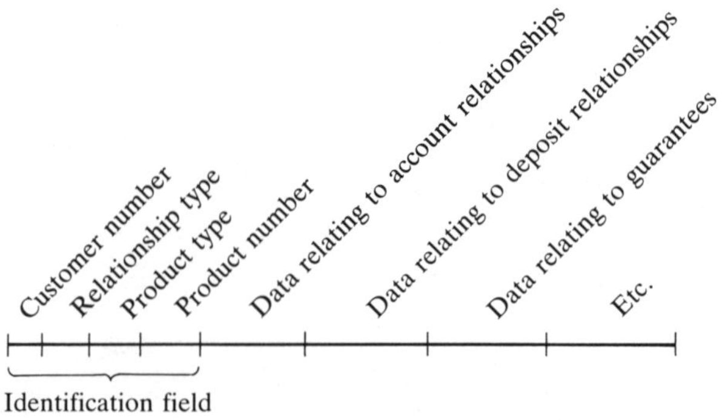

Figure 1.39 Fields in the relationship file linking customers to products in the bank database.

1.11 An $n : m$ relationship between two master files can be implemented by the creation of a relationship file whose identification field is made up of the two master files' identification fields.

(a) Which normal forms does the relationship file satisfy if redundancy is introduced by storing data from one of the master files in the relationship file?

(b) Which normal forms does one of the master files satisfy if redundancy is introduced by storing data from the relationship file in it?

1.12 (a) Can a domain contain two identical elements?

(b) Can a relation contain two identical records?

(c) Give examples of transitive relationships; that is, relationships that meet the following conditions: If X is related to Y and Y is related to Z, then X is also related to Z.

(d) What is a null value and how can it be implemented?

1.13 The files in a database, shown in Figure 1.40, satisfy first normal form, and the unique identification field is underlined. Which normal form does each individual file satisfy? Specify any assumptions that you make in arriving at a solution.

1.14 Figure 1.41 shows the most important types of input and output for an insurance company, which can be summarized as follows:

- Insurance proposals and policies include the following fields: number of the policy, annual premium and type of policy.
- Notices of claims and outgoing payments include: number of the policy, amount of loss and data relating to the claim.
- Ingoing payments and giro paying-in forms include: number of the policy, premium and date of payment.
- The insurance agents receive index cards on clients living in their district. Each card includes an overview of the policies that a client has taken out with the insurance company.
- The letters asking for payment include: number of the policy, overdue premium and date of payment.
- The insurance agents receive commission on new policies and on increases of premiums. The specification of commission contains: the name of the agent, the agent's address, commission period and, for each new policy sold in the period in question, a policy number and a commission sum. The commission sum is calculated as a percentage of the increase of the annual premium and is paid out the first time the client pays the premium of the new or increased policy. The percentage is dependent on the type of policy.
- It has to be possible to output annual statistics of the total sum of premiums per district. The system must allow for the possibility of a client changing districts.

Department record

DEPARTMENT NUMBER	DEPARTMENT NAME	HEAD OF DEPARTMENT NUMBER	DEPUTY HEAD OF DEPARTMENT NUMBER

Employee record

DEPARTMENT NUMBER	DEPARTMENT NAME	EMPLOYEE NUMBER	EMPLOYEE NAME	PROJECT NUMBER

Project record

PROJECT NUMBER	PROJECT LEADER NUMBER	PROJECT NAME

Work ticket

DATE	EMPLOYEE NUMBER	EMPLOYEE NAME	WORKING HOURS	PROJECT NUMBER

Training record

COURSE NUMBER	EMPLOYEE NUMBER	COURSE NAME	START DATE	FINISH DATE

Course-type record

COURSE NUMBER	COURSE NAME	TEACHER NUMBER	COURSE LENGTH	DEMANDS FOR COURSE PREMISES

Course-evaluation record

COURSE NUMBER	TEACHER NUMBER	EMPLOYEE NUMBER	DATE	COURSE EVALUATION

Course record

COURSE NUMBER	TEACHER NUMBER	COURSE ROOM NUMBER	START DATE	NUMBER OF PARTICIPANTS

Premises record

ROOM NUMBER	ROOM FACILITIES

Figure 1.40 Files in an employee database. Unique identification fields are underlined.

- It has to be possible to output annual statistics of the total sum of premiums per agent. Note that an agent may change districts and that there may be more than one agent in a district.

(a) Use an E–R diagram to describe how the insurance company can build up the conceptual schema so that the required output can be

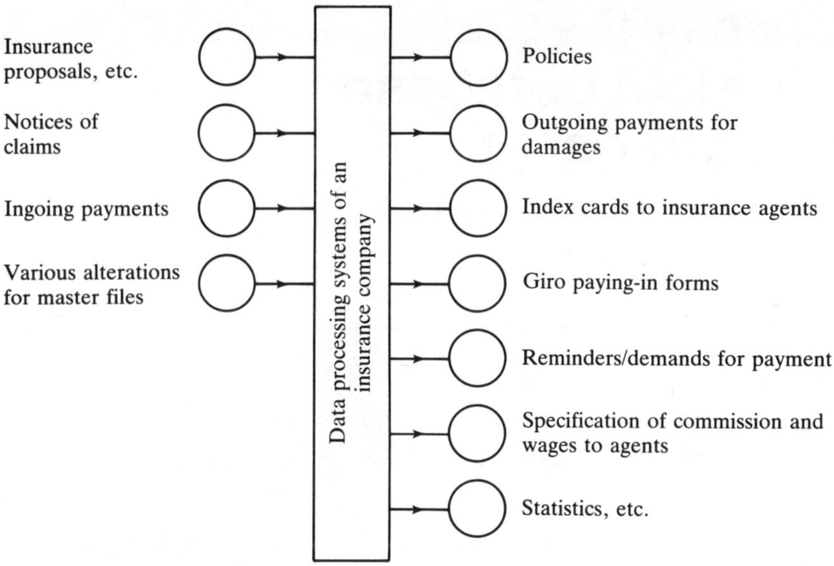

Figure 1.41 Input and output for an insurance company.

produced. The conceptual schema must also show that a policy may be re-insured with other insurance companies.

(b) What relationship types does the E–R diagram comprise?

(c) Show, by means of combined relationships, that it is possible to produce the required output.

(d) Describe the conceptual schema by means of a Bachman diagram.

(e) Transform the conceptual schema so that the files of the database satisfy at least third normal form, and describe the database by means of the relational model. To limit the extent of the exercise, you should only include the most necessary record fields. Design the conceptual schema so that it does not store redundant data.

Chapter 2
Physical Database Structures – I

2.1 Introduction

This chapter demonstrates how the conceptual database can be transformed into a physical database; that is, it shows how the entities of the conceptual database are implemented as physical files and the relationships as access paths, which enable searches for related records. These access paths can, of course, also be used for various user applications.

The organization of a file depends on where the individual records are to be stored physically and by the **access paths** of the file. Since files may have several different organizations, corresponding to the number of access paths possible for that file, a distinction is made between **primary** and **secondary organization**. Primary organization is based upon the physical storage of the individual records, whereas secondary organization is not. Thus, a file may have one primary organization and any number of secondary organizations, corresponding to the access paths that have been set up for it.

When searching for data it is much faster to search by a primary access path than by a secondary one; therefore, the determination of the primary organization of the files is an important phase in the building up of a physical database. However, as the use of the database may change in the course of time, this phase should be reviewed at regular intervals. If the database is described as an internal schema, it is possible to optimize the physical database without having to make alterations to the application programs already using the database.

From the foregoing discussion, it appears that it is possible to implement a relationship between two files as an access path from one file to the other. Alternative, a technique known as **record clustering** can be used, which physically accumulates and stores records that are related to each other.

EXAMPLE 2.1

> A $1:n$ relationship between parents and their children can be implemented by physically storing the records of the children beside those of the parents. Thus, a search for related records is very fast, as they are probably stored in the same block.

First normal form requires that there is no more than one record type in the same file. Record clustering does not conflict with first normal form because relational database theory only deals with logical files or tables. From a purely physical point of view, it may be practical to mix records from different tables, but the users and the application programs that operate at the logical level should not be aware of this. Thus, it should be possible to cluster records of different type without it being necessary to make alterations in the existing application programs. Record clustering can be seen as a case of primary organization because it makes demands on the physical placing of each individual record. The other main types of file organization, which are described in this and the following chapter, are as follows:

- Sequential organization, in which the individual records are dealt with according to a fixed sequence.
- Random organization, in which a record can be traced by transforming the identifier number of the record to a block address.
- Index organization, in which records can be searched for via an index that contains references to the records of the file.
- Various forms of list organization, in which related records are chained together by pointer fields.

In this description of the different forms of organizations, mention will also be made of the most important variants and their characteristics. We will also show how each form of organization deals with the various structures of relationship described in Chapter 1.

Table 2.1 gives an outline of the most important characteristics of the main types of file organization. It should be noted that only random organization and index organization make it possible to access a record directly by using a key value. Furthermore, it also appears from the table

Table 2.1 Types of file organization.

Characteristics	*Organization* Sequential	Random	Index	List
Is it possible to gain direct access to the records?	No	Yes	Yes	No
Is sequential treatment possible?	Yes	No	Yes	Yes
Can the 1 : *n* relationship be implemented?	Yes	Yes	Yes	Yes
Can the *n* : *m* relationship be implemented?	Yes, if it is transformed to two 1 : *n* relationships	Only partly, because random is a primary organization	Yes, if it is transformed to two 1 : *n* relationships	Yes
Can the equivalence relationship be implemented?	Yes	Yes, if the group code is used as key	Yes	Yes
Can the ordering relationship be implemented?	Yes	No	Yes	Yes
Can the tree structure be implemented?	Yes	Only partly	Yes	Yes
Can the network relationship be implemented?	No	Only partly	Yes, if it is transformed to two 1 : *n* relationships	Yes
Can relationships of order *n* be implemented?	Yes	Only partly	Yes	Yes

that there are at least three different organizations that can be used to implement each type of relationship. It should also be noted that index organization is very flexible, as it satisfies all the desired criteria of the outline. However, index organization rarely provides an optimum solution.

2.2 Sequential organization

A file is organized sequentially when the individual records can be read in a fixed sequence. **Physical sequential organization** determines the physical order in which the individual records are stored. In the case of **logical sequential organization** the records of the file are able to be read in a fixed sequence, which may not correspond to the physical storing sequence.

In the early days of databases, when disk storage was relatively expensive, magnetic tape files with a physical sequential organization were often used. Nowadays, it is normal to use disk storage; but physical sequential organization is still important because in the case of large batch runs, sequential organization will often lead to a reduced use of resources (see Section 3.3 on Sequential organization versus direct organization and list organization). Although most firms now use real-time systems, there are still many tasks that it is practical to run as a batch job. Thus, the implementation of the various relationships by sequential organization is still of importance.

2.2.1 The sequential relationship

Sequential organization implements the sequential relationship by making it possible to read the records of the file in the order determined by the sequential relationship. In the case of physical sequential organization, the individual records are stored physically in the required sequence. If new records are to be inserted into, or if records are to be deleted from, a file with physical sequential organization, it is often necessary to produce a new version of the file, so that the new records are inserted in their proper places and the deleted records are removed. In case of logical sequential organization, the sequential relationship can be implemented by linking the individual records in the required order (see Appendix A Lists). These two implementation methods are often combined in practice, since blocks with records satisfying physical sequential organization within each block can be linked together (e.g., by means of pointers). If new records are to be stored in a file that has physical sequential organization this mixed technique can be used, since a pointer to an overflow block can be stored if there is no space for inserting new records in the block. This method thus makes it possible to avoid having to create a new file each time the file is to be extended.

2.2.2 The 1 : *n* relationship

Sequential organization can implement the 1 : *n* relationship as described in connection with the relational model: the member records must contain a field where the owner record's identifier number is stored. When the searches corresponding to the relationship are to be performed,

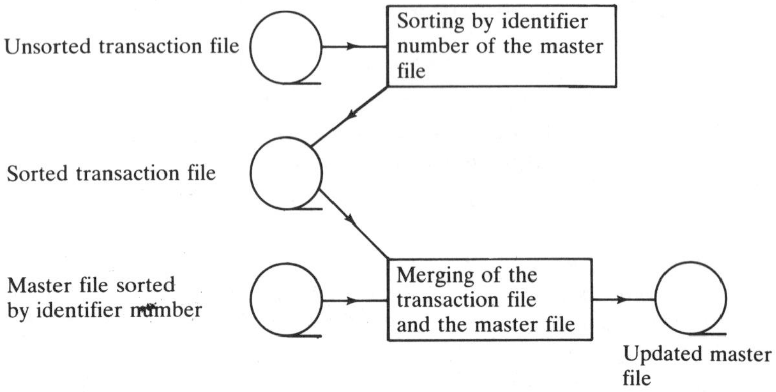

Figure 2.1 The 1 : *n* relationship with sequentially organized files. Both the transaction and master files are sorted by identifier number and then merged.

both files can be sorted by the owner's identifier number and subsequently merged.

EXAMPLE 2.2

A transaction file containing material for bringing the database up to date may contain one or more transactions for updating the data of each individual master record. Thus, there exists a 1 : *n* relationship between the transaction file and the master file. The system diagram in Figure 2.1 shows how the searches can be performed if the relationship is represented as described. This method, however, is only practical if there is a relatively large number of transactions. If there are *n* records in the master file and only one single transaction to be performed, then, on average, $(n + 1)/2$ records must be read from the master file to be able to search the master record relevant to the transaction. If the master file has physical sequential organization, and if it is stored on a medium giving direct access to the separate records, the search time can be reduced by using special search techniques, such as binary search or Fibonacci search. Space does not allow for a full discussion of searching techniques here and for further information the reader is referred to a specialist text such as Knuth (1973).

2.2.3 The *n* : *m* relationship

As mentioned earlier, in connection with Bachman diagrams (Section 1.3.2), the *n* : *m* relationship can be implemented by creating a new subfile and two 1 : *n* relationships, which link the subfile to the original files (see Example 1.8). When the searches corresponding to the relationships are to be performed, they can be done by sorting and merging the files, as explained in Section 2.2.2.

EXAMPLE 2.3

Example 1.2 dealt with customers' orders and products. It was shown that a $1 : n$ relationship exists between customers and orders, and an $n : m$ relationship between orders and products. Figure 2.2 outlines an invoicing system, in which the searches corresponding to these relationships are performed by sorting and merging. The fields of the individual files are as follows:

The order record:

ONR – order number
CNR – number of the customer who placed the order
QTY – quantity of a product specified in the order
PNR – identity number of a product specified in the order

Each order will often contain several (QTY, PNR)s.

The product record:

PNR – the product's identity number
DESCR– a description of the product
PRICE – price per unit of the product

The customer record:

CNR – the customer's identity number
ADDS – the name and address of the customer
DEBIT – the amount the customer owes the firm: the contents of this field can be increased by an invoicing program and reduced by a crediting program.

The invoice record:

ONR – order number
CNR – customer number
ADDS – the customer's name and address
SUM – invoice sum
VAT – value-added tax on the invoice sum

In addition, for each product line, there are the following fields:

QTY – quantity
PNR – product number
DESCR– the text describing the product
PRICE – the price per unit of the product

2.2.4 The equivalence relationship

As discussed in Section 1.2.2, the equivalence relationship consists of a grouping of the records of a file into separated groups. Relationships of this type are often represented by the addition of a field carrying a group code. Records belonging to the same group must have the same value in the field carrying the group code.

Searches corresponding to the equivalence relationship can be implemented either by physical or logical organization of the file's records in accordance with the group code field. Example 2.4 shows how

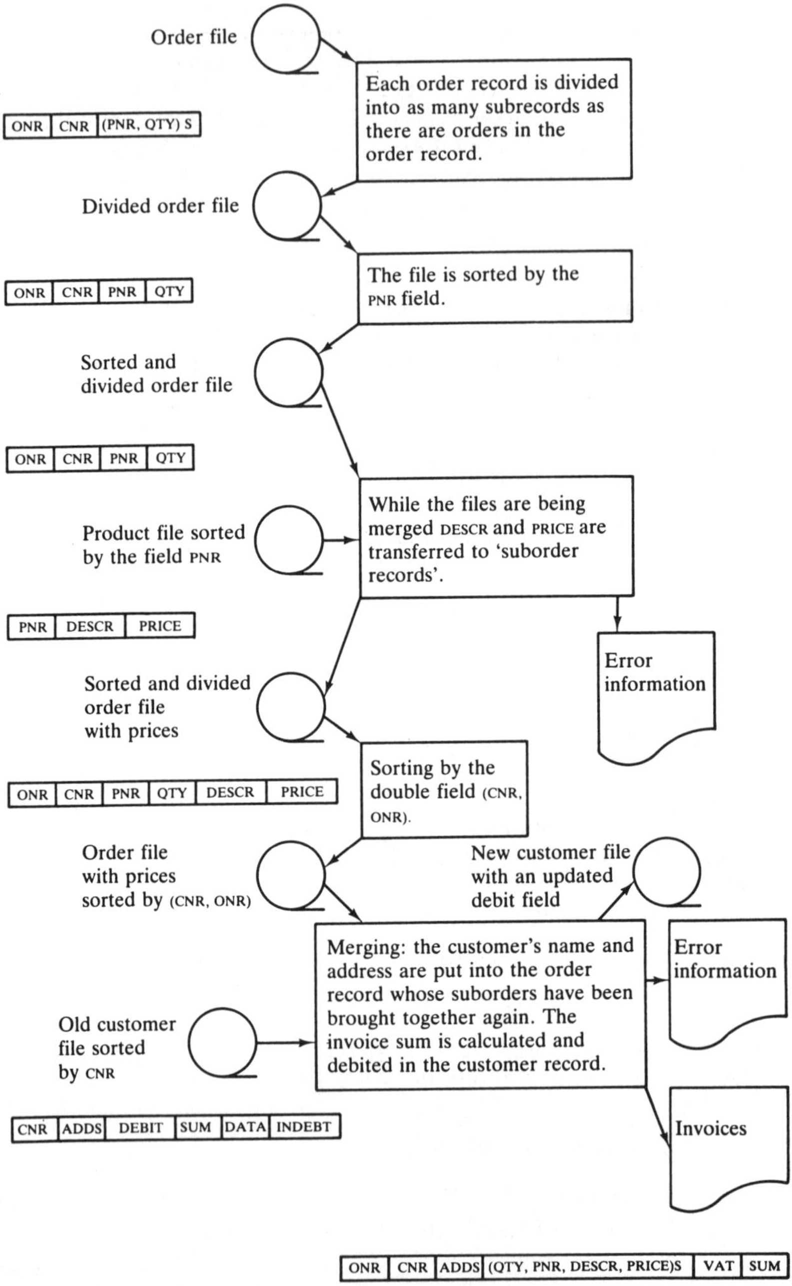

Figure 2.2 The $n : m$ relationship with sequentially organized files. The figure shows an invoicing system making use of order, product and customer files. The invoice is made up of fields from all three files and additionally contains locally generated fields (VAT, SUM).

	District 1	District 2	...	District n	Total per customer group
Customer group 1					
Customer group 2					
⋮					
Customer group n					
Total sales per district					

Total sales per customer group per district

Total sales of the firm

Figure 2.3 The equivalence relationship with sequentially organized files. The table is obtained by sorting by customer number and sales district.

information retrieval can be performed in a sequential file in which two different equivalence relationships are represented.

EXAMPLE 2.4

Sales statistics used to analyse and control a firm's sales are often organized by means of various criteria to make it easier for the firm to analyse the effects of different strategies.

The firm's customer records contain, amongst others, the following fields:

CUSTGR code for the customer group which the customer belongs to

DISTRICT code for the sales district which the customer belongs to

If the customer file is sorted by the double field (CUSTGR, DISTRICT), the n first rows of the table of the firm's sales, shown in Figure 2.3, can be obtained. The last row can be filled in after the file has been sorted by the DISTRICT field.

The method used here is only necessary if the table is too large for the main storage of the computer. If there is space for the whole table in the main storage of the computer, the table can be produced by a single pass through the file, and in that case it will not be necessary to sort it.

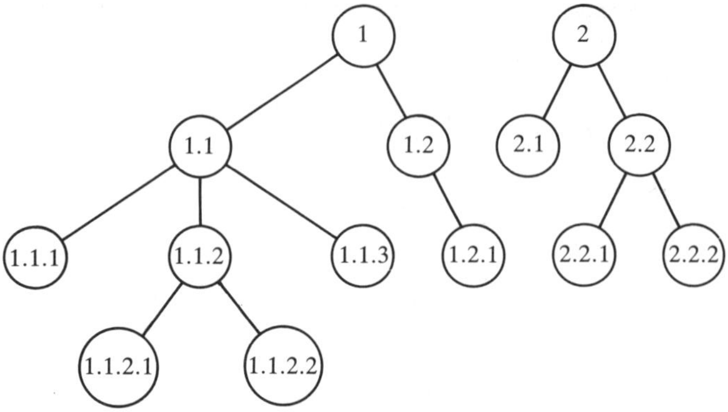

Figure 2.4 Tree structure with nodes labelled in Dewey decimal notation.

2.2.5 Tree structures

Trees can be represented by introducing an identifier number that reflects the record's location. For example, the nodes can be numbered in accordance with the **Dewey decimal notation** which represents the *n*th child of the *X*th node as $(X.n)$.

EXAMPLE 2.5

Figure 2.4 illustrates a tree structure whose nodes are numbered in accordance with the Dewey decimal notation. The books in a library are often organized according to this principle, the individual digits representing codes for subject areas and sub-subject areas. The chapters and subdivisions in this book are also organized in this way.

If the file in Figure 2.4 is sorted in ascending order by the hierarchically built-up identifier number, then it is possible to search downwards through the relationship by means of one single reading of the file. If the file is sorted in descending order, then it is possible to similarly search upwards in one single reading.

2.2.6 Relationships of order *n*

In a normalized database, relationships of the order n can be implemented by creating an independent relationship file. In such cases, there will be n different $1:n$ relationships between this relationship file and the n master files, as shown in Figure 2.5. Here, the searches between the different files can be performed by sorting and merging as described in connection with the $1:n$ and $n:m$ relationships.

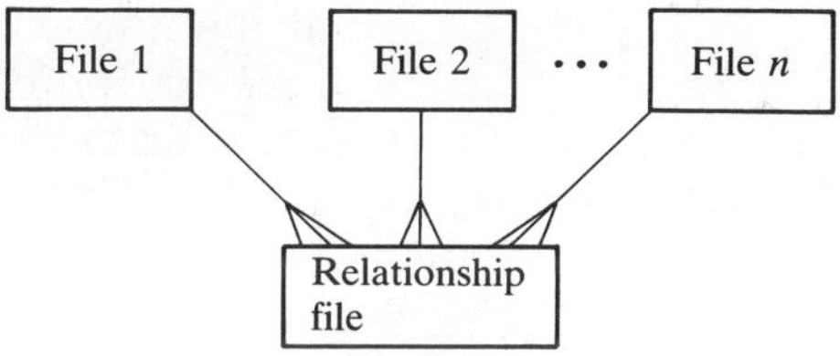

Figure 2.5 Relationships of order n. There is a $1:n$ relationship between each file and the relationship file.

2.2.7 Networks

Section 2.2.3 shows how the network relationship can be transformed to $1:n$ relationships. When this transformation has been completed, related records can be retrieved in the usual way by sorting and merging. However, it is rarely a good idea to implement network searches in this way because this technique only involves a search of the neighbouring nodes.

2.3 Random organization

Random organization is a kind of direct organization. **Direct organization** exists where files are organized in such a way that records can be retrieved if the value of their **key field** is known. It follows then that a key field is a field that makes it possible to search *directly* for all records with a particular value in the key field. A **unique key** is a key field whose value identifies the records uniquely. A **non-unique key** is a key field where more than one record may have the same key value. To search for a record directly, it is necessary to know its address. It is a question, therefore, of finding a function f, which for a given key value, gives the corresponding address where the desired records are stored:

$$address = f(key)$$

In practice, the address will often, but not necessarily, be a block address, but to avoid confusion the terms **bucket** and **bucket address** will be used. A bucket can be a cylinder, a track, a block or part of a block.

The function f can consist of a table through which the key can be transformed to an address. If the function f includes a table, the file organization is called **index organization** (this organization will be analysed in a later section). If the function f is a mathematical function, the organization is called **random organization**. The term random is used because it deals with functions that make a uniform distribution of the key values over the file's bucket addresses.

The mathematical function f is called a **randomizing** or **hashing function**. If the randomizing function transfers more records to one particular bucket address than the bucket can hold, it will create **collision** or **overflow** in the bucket. There are many different **Collision Resolution Methods (CRM)**. Most of these methods store the new record in an **overflow bucket**. The address into which a key is transformed is called the **home address** of the record. Different keys are said to give **synonyms** if they transform to the same home address.

2.3.1 Selection of the randomizing function

The most commonly used randomizing function is to choose as the address the key's remainder after integer division by n:

$$address = key \text{ modulo } n$$

where n is the number of buckets in the file. It is possible to prove that if n is selected in such a way that it does not include low prime factors, it will be more likely that the home addresses will be evenly distributed on the n buckets.

Sometimes more complicated randomizing functions are used, in which the above modulo formula may be combined with the selection of bit strings from the record key. Some of these bit strings may be added, multiplied, divided or squared prior to taking part in the further address calculation. The choice of randomizing functions is further discussed in Appendix E.

2.3.2 Overflow in files with random organization

The most important methods used to solve the problem of overflow are:

- **Linear open overflow:** a check is made to determine whether there is available space for the record in the following bucket. If this is not the case, the next bucket is checked, and so forth. There must be available overflow buckets at the end of the file, otherwise **spiral overflow** can be used – if there is no space for the record in the last bucket, a check is made to see whether there is available space in the first bucket, after which the linear open overflow method is resumed.

- **Chained overflow**: the bucket on the record's home address is used as the list head for a list of overflow buckets. In case of **coalesced chaining**, overflow records are not stored in a separate overflow storage but in the primary file itself. If overflow occurs in a bucket, another bucket with available space is searched for, and overflow records from the first bucket are subsequently stored in this second bucket. If overflow also occurs in the second bucket, the

Table 2.2 Grouping of the overflow methods.

	Chained overflow	*No chained overflow*
Separate overflow storage	Separate chaining	Dynamic overflow
No separate overflow storage	Coalesced chaining	Linear open overflow and non-linear open overflow (rehashing)

process is repeated so that there will be a coalesced overflow list for the two buckets with overflow, as well as the new bucket with available space. With chained overflow, we could also use a separate overflow file.

- **Separate overflow file**: overflow records are stored in a separate overflow file. The database management system ADABAS, for example, uses an index organized file to store overflow records. However, it is more common to use **separate chaining**. Separate chaining chains overflow buckets together with overflow records belonging to the same home address. To save space, an overflow bucket that is smaller than the buckets of the primary file is often used. With **dynamic overflow**, the home address may be the root of a *B*-tree (see the section on B-trees).
- **Non-linear open overflow**: with non-linear open overflow, as in linear open overflow, another bucket from the primary field is used to store overflow records. The address of this other bucket may be found, for example, by means of **rehashing**; that is, by choosing a new randomizing function for records that have overflowed. This process is repeated until a bucket with available space is found.

In Table 2.2 the various overflow methods are grouped according to whether chained overflow is used or not, and according to whether a separate overflow storage is used.

It is often advantageous to combine a **two-pass load** of the file with any of these overflow techniques. This means that first all the records not causing overflow are placed at their proper addresses, while the overflow records are stored as a sequential file. This file is then used as input for a program that loads the remaining records.

If linear open overflow is used, a two-pass load ensures that fewer records flow over. If chained overflow is used, and if overflow records are sorted by their home address before they are loaded, overflow records with the same home address are likely to be stored in the same overflow bucket. This requires that overflow records are stored using a joint available space list. If an available space list is used for each individual

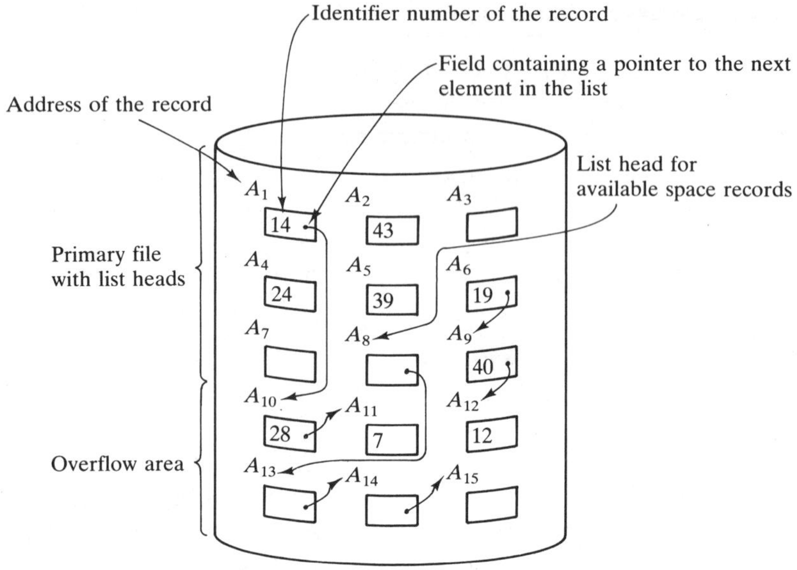

Figure 2.6 Randomly organized file with chained overflow in an overflow file.

home address, records with the same home address can still be stored in the same overflow bucket, but this technique requires more storage space, since the individual overflow buckets are likely to be only partly filled out.

Some overflow techniques are demonstrated in the following examples. The randomizing function used in these examples is:

$$address = (key \text{ modulo } 7) + 1$$

as it is assumed that the block with the address 0 is used to store file parameters, such as the number used for the modulo calculation. This function only has the values $\{1, 2, \ldots, 7\}$. These are, of course, considerably lower than the values that would be used in practice.

EXAMPLE 2.6

In Figures 2.6 and 2.7, it is assumed that one record is stored per block. The figures show a randomly organized file in which the overflow problem has been overcome by means of chained overflow in a separate overflow file. As 7 is the highest value of the randomizing or hashing function, address 8, which for convenience and to avoid ambiguities is written as A_8, is the first record in the overflow file and is used as the list head to point to the first of the free records in the overflow file that are chained together by means of pointers.

In Figure 2.6, records with identifiers 19, 14, 39, 40, 43, 28, 24, 7 and 12 have been loaded in roughly the order given. 19 hashes to 6 and is

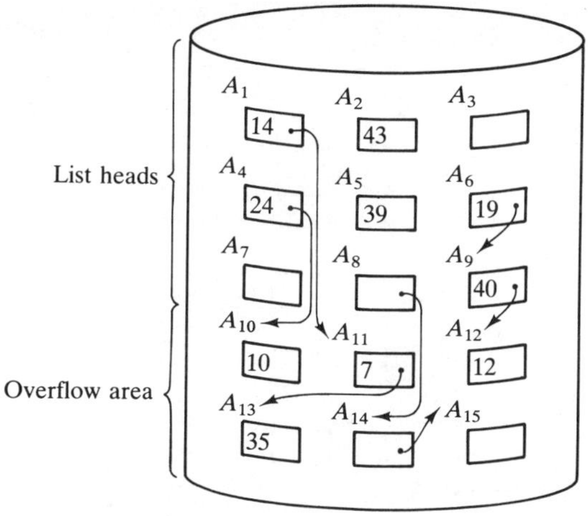

Figure 2.7 The same file after an update.

thus stored at A_6. 14 goes to A_1 and 39 to A_5. 40 also hashes to 6, but as A_6 is already occupied by 19, the list head for available overflow space at A_8 is consulted. This record contains a pointer to A_9, the first free address, so 40 is placed there and chained to 19. The first free overflow block is now A_{10}, and the pointer in A_8 is reset to point to it. 43 goes to A_2 in a straightforward manner, while 28, hashing to 1, must go in the overflow file at A_{10} chained to 14 at A_1. 24 goes in the main file at A_4, while 7, again hashing to 1, must be placed in the lowest free address in the overflow file. The list head at A_8 is by now pointing to A_{11} so 7 is placed there chained to 28 in A_{10}. Finally, 12, which like 19 and 40 hashes to 6, is placed at A_{12} and chained to 40, while the list head at A_8 is left pointing to A_{13}.

Figure 2.7 illustrates the file after an updating, which has deleted record 28 and added records 10 and 35. When record 28 has been deleted, the list head at A_8 will point to A_{10} as the first free overflow address, so 10 will be placed there chained with 24, which has the same hash value. 35 will be placed at A_{13}, and the list head reset to point to A_{14}.

EXAMPLE 2.7

Figure 2.8 illustrates a random organized file with linear open overflow, in which the records with the following keys have been created:

16, 14, 19, 28, 24, 7, 40, 39, 12, 43

Loading the records in a single pass, record 16 goes to A_3, 14 to A_1 and 19 to A_6. 28 hashes to 1 but A_1 is already occupied by 14, so 28 must be placed in the first free address, which is currently A_2. 24 goes naturally to A_4, while 7 hashes to 1, and with A_2, A_3 and A_4 occupied must be placed at A_5. 40 hashes to 6 and A_6 contains 19. A_1 to A_6 are now all occupied so

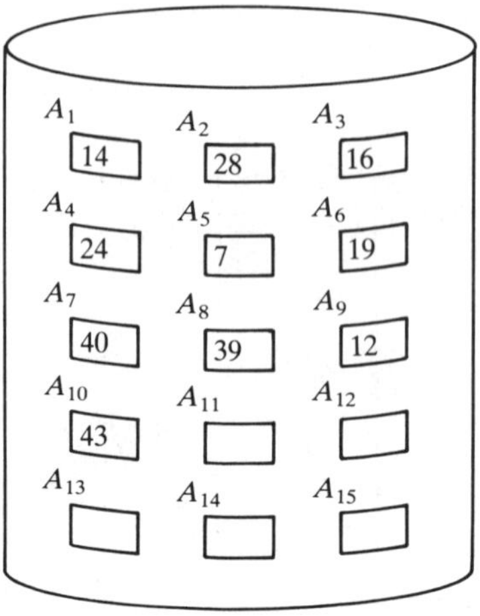

Figure 2.8 Randomly organized file with linear open overflow: loaded in a single pass.

40 is placed at A_7. All addresses that the hash function can generate are now filled, so 39, 12 and 43 are forced to go into A_8, A_9 and A_{10}.

In Figure 2.9, the same records have been created, this time with a two-pass loading of the file. Records 14, 43, 16, 24, 39 and 19 load at the addresses given by the hash function on the first pass, leaving 28, 7, 40 and 12 as a sequential file to be loaded in a second pass. A_7 is the highest address left unoccupied after the first pass, so they are placed at addresses A_7 to A_{10}.

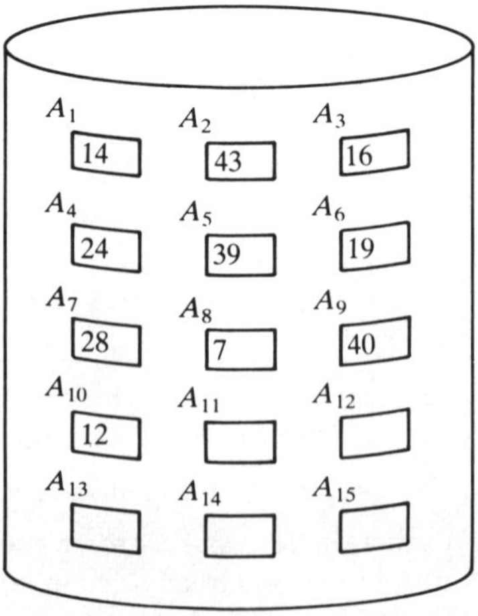

Figure 2.9 Randomly organized file with linear open overflow: loaded in two passes.

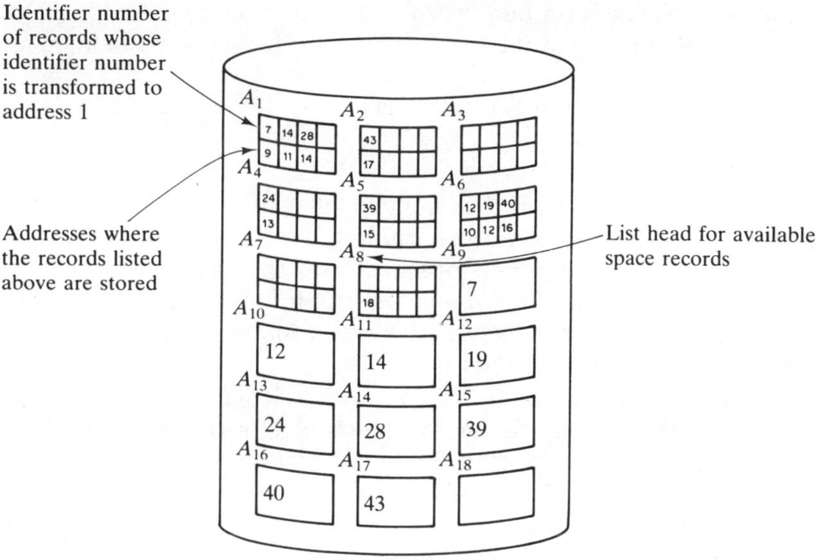

Figure 2.10 File with sequential primary and random secondary organization. Inverted list heads on the home addresses give the addresses of the records in the primary file, which is organized sequentially.

Examples 2.6 and 2.7 are examples of *primary* random organization. The following example demonstrates how random organization can be applied as a secondary organization.

EXAMPLE 2.8

Figure 2.10 shows a file in which an inverted list head, which links up all records with the same home address, is stored on the record's home address. As the highest value of the randomizing function is 7, the block on address 8 (A_8) is used as list head for available space records. Blocks 1–7 show the secondary organization of the file. In the Figure, the file's primary organization is sequential, sorted by the record's identifier number.

2.3.3 Search length in files with random organization

The **search length** for an access method is the number of blocks that need to be read into main storage to get access to the desired record(s). If the search length for an access method is known, the disk storage work time and minimum response time can be estimated by using the formulae given in Appendix B. The average search length in randomly organized files depends on the actual form of random organization used, as well as on the **blocking factor** (or number of records that can be stored in a block) and the **loading factor** of the file. As the loading factor f is defined as

$$f = \frac{\text{number of records}}{\text{number of blocks} \times \text{blocking factor}} = \frac{m}{n \times b}$$

it is not necessary to know the number of records in the file, only the blocking factor and the average number of records per block (i.e., m/n). For many forms of random organization, the search length can be calculated by means of the Poisson Distribution (see Appendix E), or by simulation. In practice, however, it is easier to look up the search length in a table or to read it off a graph.

In Figures 2.11 to 2.13, the search length is illustrated as a function of the loading factor for different blocking factors b. If the graphs do not show the blocking factor required the search length can be calculated by interpolation. Alternatively, the more extensive tables and graphs in Bratbergsengen *et al.* (1983), Knuth (1973), Sørensen (1984), and Teorey and Fry (1982) can be used.

In practice, the search lengths can also be used if the blocking factor of the overflow storage is more than 1, as the different records in an overflow block normally have different home addresses, unless a two-pass load has been applied.

EXAMPLE 2.9

A file with 100 000 records has random organization with linear open overflow (see Figure 2.11). An IBM 3380 disk with a block length of 4820 bytes is used. The file has variable record length, but on average 15 records can be stored per block, (i.e., $b = 15$). If 8334 blocks are used for the file, the loading factor is 0.8. As the blocking factor is 15, the search length cannot be read off the previous figure directly. It appears from Figure 2.11, however, that blocking factors 5 and 20 give search lengths of about 1.29 and 1.04, respectively. By interpolation it can be calculated that a blocking factor of 15 gives a search length of about 1.12.

If we have random organization with separate overflow, the file is divided into a **primary file** and an **overflow file**, used to store overflow records.

EXAMPLE 2.10

Figure 2.12 illustrates the search length for files with random organization with chained overflow in a separate overflow file. The blocking factor of the primary file is b and the blocking factor of the overflow file is 1. Note that the loading factor of a file may be higher than 1 if a separate overflow storage is used.

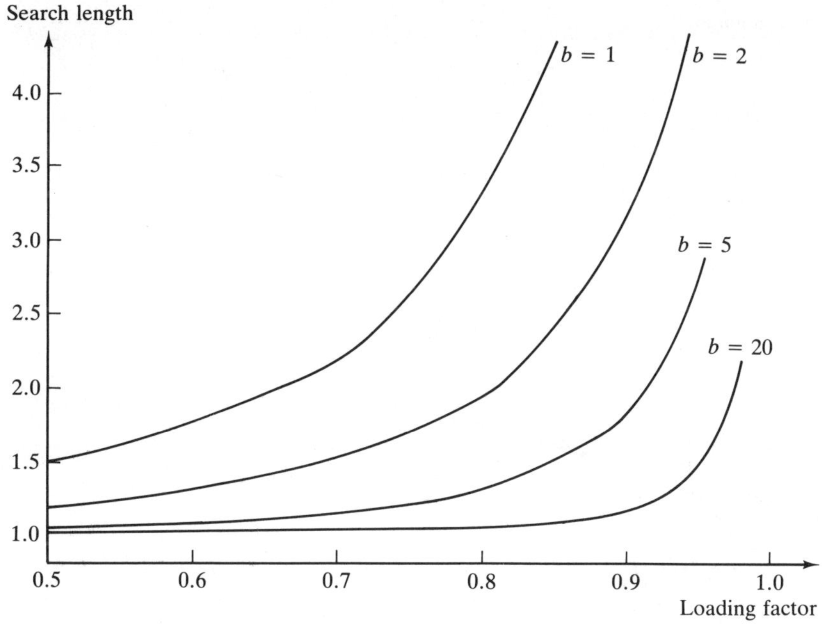

Figure 2.11 Search lengths for randomly organized files with linear open overflow for blocking factors (b) of 1, 2, 5 and 20. A blocking factor of 1 is assumed for the overflow storage.

As in the previous example, a blocking factor of 15 and a loading factor of 0.8 are used. Figure 2.12 shows that blocking factors of 5 and 20 give search lengths of about 1.20 and 1.08, respectively. By interpolation, the search length for the blocking factor 15 is calculated to be about 1.12.

The loading factor is called in Example 2.10 the **nominal loading factor** and it is calculated as the ratio of the number of records in the file to the number of records that can be stored in the primary file.

2.3.4 Estimation of storage space in files with random organization

We saw in the previous section that the access time depends very much on the loading factor and the blocking factor. As users often require certain minimum response times to be kept, it is often expedient to select a suitable search length first and then determine the blocking and loading factors so that the desired search length is achieved.

If the file has linear open overflow, the storage space required for

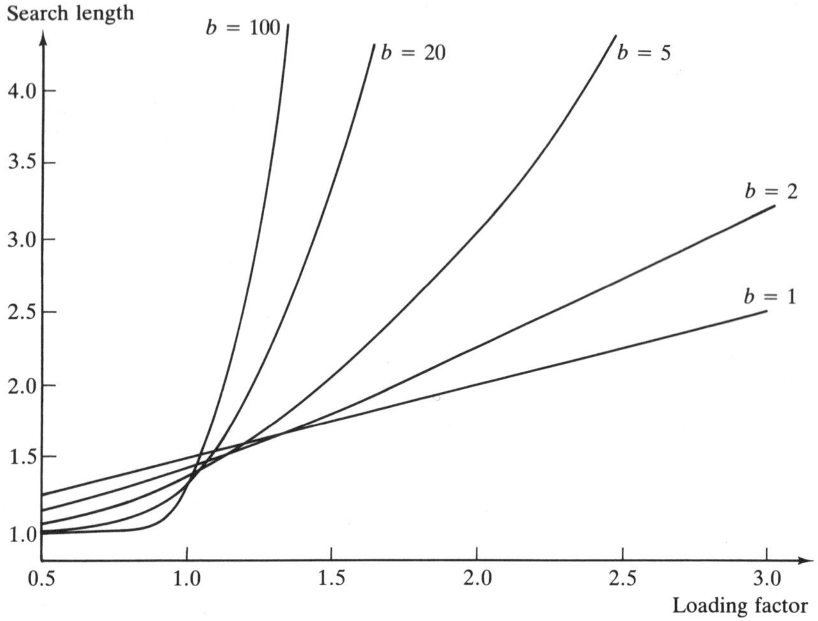

Figure 2.12 Search lengths for randomly organized files with chained overflow in a separate overflow file for blocking factors (*b*) of 1, 2, 5, 20 and 100.

the file can be calculated, as the number of records that the file must contain will normally be known. If random organization with a separate overflow file is used, the size of the overflow file can be estimated by means of the graph in Figure 2.13, which illustrates the percentage share of overflow records for different loading factors and blocking factors. If a blocking factor not corresponding to any of the graphs in the illustration is used, the percentage of overflow records can be estimated by interpolation.

EXAMPLE 2.11

EXAMPLE 2.10 considered a randomly organized file with chained overflow in a separate overflow file. The file contained 100 000 records, the blocking factor was 15 and the loading factor 0.8. From Figure 2.13, it can be seen that blocking factors of 5 and 20 give overflow percentages of about 11 and 2, respectively. By interpolation the overflow percentage can be estimated to be about 5 for a blocking factor of 15. As the file holds 100 000 records, it follows that the overflow file must provide space for about 100 000 × 5% = 5000 records. At least 5000/15 = 334 blocks of 4820 bytes each must be reserved for the overflow file. As the primary file must have a loading factor of 0.8, this file must provide space for 100 000/0.8 = 125 000 records. Therefore, about 125 000/

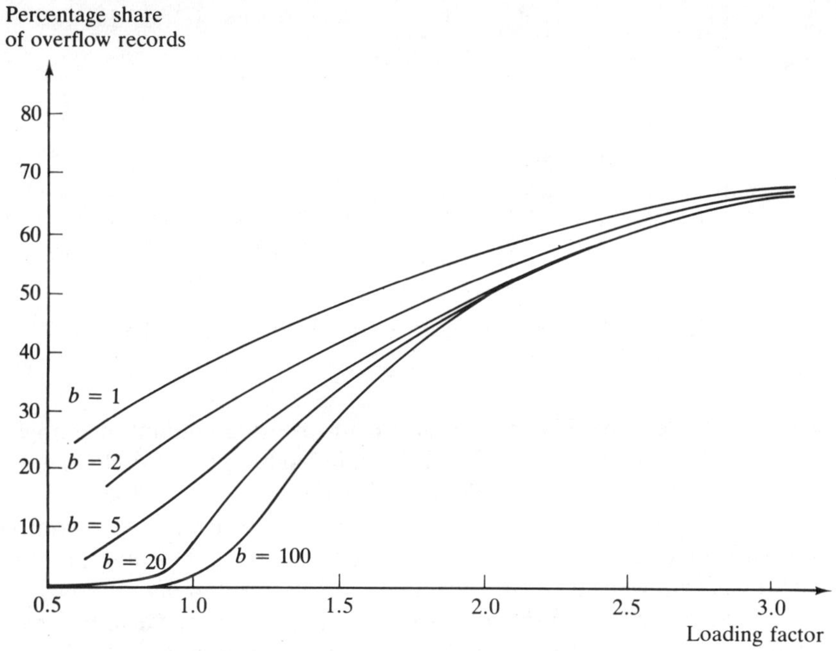

Figure 2.13 Percentage of overflow records in a randomly organized file with chained overflow in a separate overflow file for blocking factors (b) of 1, 2, 5, 20 and 100.

15 = 8334 blocks of 4820 bytes each must be reserved for the primary file. The total storage space required then is about 8334 + 334 = 8668 blocks of 4820 bytes each.

2.3.5 Dynamic hashing

The previously discussed 'classical' types of random organization all suffer from the drawback that the search length is increased to an unacceptable level if new records are created over and above what the file is designed for. On the other hand, the loading factor of the file becomes very low if a large number of records are deleted compared with the size of the file when it was designed. These problems can be solved by re-organizing the file – by giving it a new hashing function that compensates for the altered size of the file. One disadvantage of such a re-organization is that it is very time consuming. Another disadvantage is that the size of files with fluctuations in the number of records will need regular monitoring.

Since the beginning of the 1970s many forms of hashing have been presented in which the file size can be changed dynamically, so that the

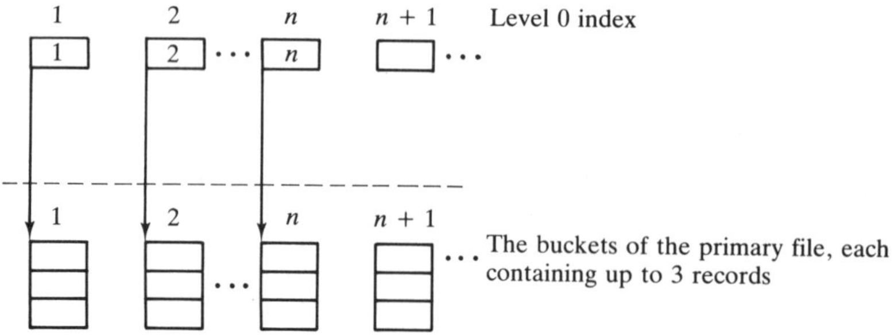

Figure 2.14 Randomly organized file with dynamic hashing.

search length and the loading factor are almost independent of changes in the number of records in the file. **Dynamic hashing** is the collective term used for these new forms of file organization.

It is more complicated to implement dynamic hashing in comparison with the classical forms of random organization. However, dynamic hashing is very well suited for implementation in a database management system. Kjellberg and Zahle (1984) give a survey of the various forms of dynamic hashing, classified according to whether an index or table is or is not used. Examples of those containing an index or table are Expandable Hashing (Knott, 1971), Dynamic Hashing (Larson, 1978), Virtual Hashing (Litwin, 1978) and Extendable Hashing (Fagin *et al.*, 1979). These techniques try to keep the index or table so small that it can be held in main memory, so that a record can be retrieved by one search operation in the secondary storage areas. The index may, for example, be a randomly organized table in which each table element contains a pointer to the bucket containing the records whose keys are transformed to the same home address in the index table. However, overflow may occur in the bucket if it has to accommodate more records than it can actually hold. If this overflow problem is solved by using the methods described in the preceding sections the search length becomes dependent upon the number of records in the file. Such a problem can be solved by the technique of **bucket split**. This means that the records of the overflow buckets are distributed into two buckets while simultaneously the index element becomes the root of a binary tree, whose leaves point to one or other of the buckets into which the records of the overflow bucket are distributed. If overflow later occurs in one of these new buckets, the splitting process can be repeated.

Figure 2.14 illustrates a randomly organized file before a bucket split. Notice that there is a unique correspondence between the index elements and the n buckets of the primary file initially. Both the index table and the primary file have available space on the addresses $n + 1$, $n + 2$, $n + 3$, etc., as this available space is to be used later for the

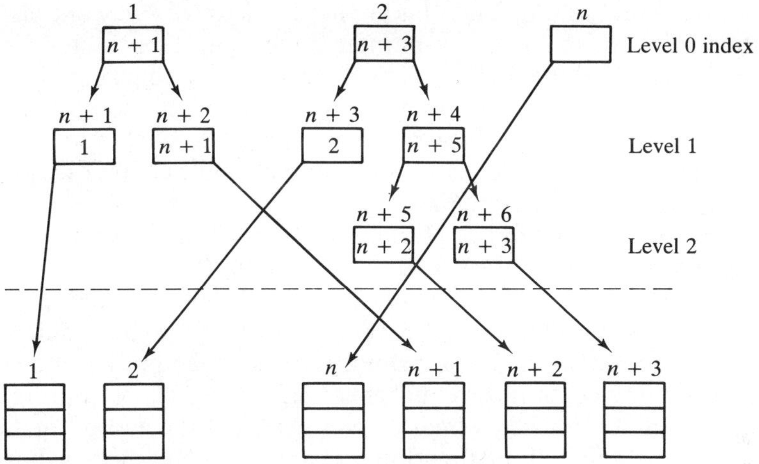

Figure 2.15 The file shown in Figure 2.14 after three bucket splits have taken place. The numbers in the index boxes indicate the highest bucket address to which the index elements point. At the leaf level, index elements point to only a single bucket.

building up of the binary trees of the index and storing the split buckets of the primary file. The primary file accommodates three records in a bucket and the index elements must be able to contain a reference and a code, which indicates whether the index element points to another index element or to a bucket in the primary file.

Figure 2.15 illustrates the file after three bucket splits. First, bucket 1 is split and its contents distributed between bucket 1 and bucket $n + 1$. At the same time, the index element 1 becomes the root in a binary tree whose leaves are stored on the addresses $n + 1$ and $n + 2$. As the two leaves are stored next to each other, the index element can accommodate both pointers, as the pointer to the second leaf is arrived at by adding 1 to the address of the first leaf.

Next, overflow occurs in bucket 2 and its contents are distributed between bucket 2 and bucket $n + 2$. At the same time, the index element 2 becomes a binary tree whose leaves are stored on the addresses $n + 3$ and $n + 4$.

Finally, overflow occurs in bucket $n + 2$ and its contents are distributed between bucket $n + 2$ and $n + 3$. At the same time, the index node in $n + 4$ is allocated two leaves, each pointing to a bucket.

To create or search for records by means of the index, a hashing function has to be used for each level in the index. The first hashing function, which belongs to level 0, is used to select the correct value from the first n index elements. The second hashing function can only take on two values, and it is used to choose between the daughters of the root element.

The subsequent hashing functions are used in a similar way until a leaf is reached from which there is a pointer directly to the primary file. If x bucket splits occur, the primary file will occupy $n + x$ buckets and the index will contain $n + 2x$ pointers, of which x pointers point directly to other index elements. It is possible to give the file a much more compact structure than has been described here, and examples of this are given in the references cited earlier.

Examples of Dynamic Hashing without an index or table include Spiral Storage (Martin, 1979), Linear Hashing (Litwin, 1980), Linear Hashing with Partial Expansion (Larson, 1980), Unified Dynamic Hashing (Mullin, 1984) and Cascade Hashing (Kjellberg and Zahle, 1984). In Linear Hashing, the primary file is expanded when a bucket split occurs. The contents of a bucket are distributed between the original bucket and a new bucket, which is then placed at the end of the file. At the same time, the hashing function is changed, so that the new bucket is added to the function value. However, the hashing function is only changed as far as the split bucket and the new bucket are concerned, so that the updates caused by a file expansion can be executed quickly. With Linear Hashing, bucket splits are executed sequentially, no matter whether overflow has or has not occurred, so that it is also necessary to be able to deal with the overflow situation. Litwin (1980) describes how overflow buckets can be chained together in separate overflow storage, but there are other articles describing Linear Hashing with other overflow methods (Larson, 1985). After a bucket split, it is likely that overflow records can be stored at their own home address.

A bucket split can be started automatically each time the loading factor of the file exceeds a predetermined value, s. Figure 2.16 (a) shows a new file with n buckets. Figure 2.16 (b) shows the file after four bucket splits, where p is a pointer that points towards the next bucket to be split. When all the buckets of the file have been split, the file level is said to be increased by 1. At this point, the pointer p has to be reset to zero, so that the bucket split process can be repeated.

If the level of the file is L, then the following hashing function can be used in the case of Linear Hashing. The first time the file is used the file level must be zero:

$$h(\text{key}) = \begin{cases} (key \bmod n \times 2^{L}) & \text{if } p \leqslant (key \bmod n \times 2^{L}) \\ (key \bmod n \times 2^{L+1}) & \text{if } p > (key \bmod n \times 2^{L}) \end{cases}$$

In Litwin's original description of Linear Hashing, buckets in the interval from p to $n \times 2^{L}$ have a relatively high average loading factor, while the remaining buckets have a relatively low average loading factor. This problem can be resolved in several different ways.

One solution is to use Linear Hashing with Partial Expansion, which executes bucket splits with several buckets simultaneously, so that

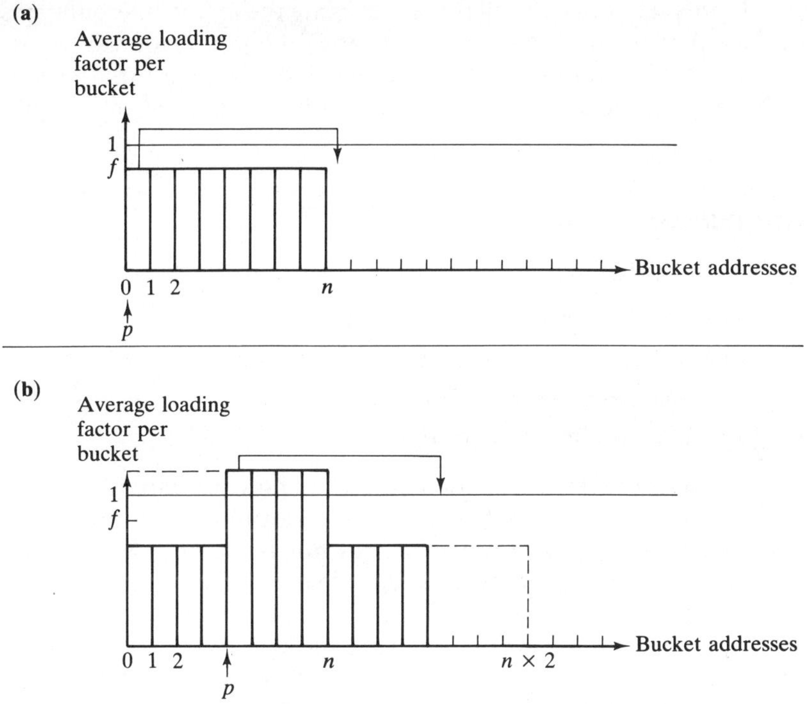

Figure 2.16 Linear hashing. (a) shows a file before any **bucket** splits have occurred. (b) shows a file after four bucket splits have been executed.

the new bucket contains relatively few records from each of the old, split buckets. Using this technique, the old buckets must be split several times before the size of the file is doubled and the file level is increased by one.

Another solution is to use Unified Dynamic Hashing, which solves the problem by using a 'biased' hashing function that distributes the records of the file on buckets at a declining frequency in accordance with the predetermined split sequence. Naturally, these two techniques can be combined so that the variation in the loading factors of the various buckets is further reduced.

2.4 Index organization

An **index** may be regarded as a table of contents containing key values and references to the corresponding records. A file is using indexed organization if it has at least one index that enables searches for records to be carried out directly.

In this section, we shall first investigate the many different types of index and then proceed to describe how the different relationships can be implemented by means of indexes. Finally, methods of estimating search lengths and storage requirements in index organized files will be discussed.

2.4.1 Different types of index

Indexes can be distinguished according to:

- whether they are primary or secondary,
- whether they are based on a unique or non-unique key,
- the organization form of the index,
- whether they are static or dynamic.

A **primary index**† makes demands as to how the individual records in the master file are stored so that a file can only have one primary organization. As a **secondary index** does not make any demands as to where the records of the file are stored, a file may have any number of secondary indexes.

An index built on the basis of a unique key contains a unique reference to the record with the unique key. A secondary index built on the basis of a non-unique key normally contains an inverted list of the records with a given non-unique key value. (This organization will be dealt with more thoroughly in Section 3.2.2 on Inverted list organization.)

An index may have many different organizations. The most common organization is a tree structure corresponding to a hierarchical table of contents. The hierarchical organization of chapters and sections in this book is an example of this. However, an index may also use random organization (see the example given in the subsection on Indexes with random organization).

A **dynamic index** is an index that does not need to be re-organized as a consequence of adding or deleting records in the master file. The opposite of a dynamic index is a **static index**, which is created permanently and is adjusted due to extension or reduction by various types of overflow list.

† A primary index is often defined as an index built on a unique identifier number. Likewise, a secondary index is one that is built on a non-unique key. These definitions are inconsistent with those used in this book because we make a sharp distinction between primary and secondary indexes, and between unique and non-unique keys and the indexes belonging to these different categories.

Hierarchical static indexes

It is assumed here that a file has physical sequential organization on the disk storage medium, so that it is sorted by the key field forming the basis of a primary index. The file may now be seen as divided into a number of smaller subfiles, or buckets (normally, a bucket is the same as a block, but it could be a track or a cylinder). The lowest level in the primary index can now be built up as a table which, for each bucket, contains the bucket's address and the highest key value of the records in the bucket. Searching for a record in the file now becomes a question of finding the row in the index table that has a key value greater than or equal to the key value of the search argument, and for which the preceding row in the index table has a key value that is less than the key value of the search argument.

EXAMPLE 2.12

Figure 2.17 illustrates the lowest level in an index and the corresponding file whose records are sorted in ascending order by the key field of the index. To search for the record with the key value JA, the index entrance KH must be used, because JA ≤ KH and JA > DG. From this entrance, there will be a pointer to a bucket on address 49, where the record with the key value JA is stored.

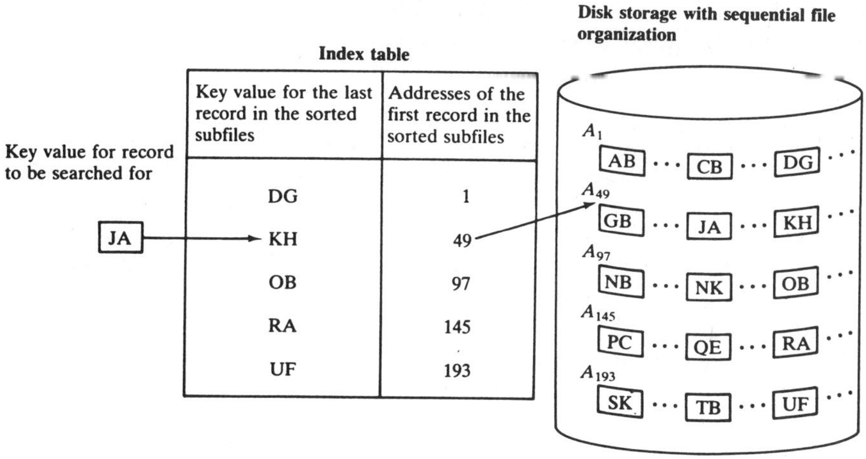

Figure 2.17 Access to a sequential file via an index table.

(a)

Cylinder index (48)

Highest key value in the cylinder	Address of corresponding track index
FS	47
QS	96
⋮	⋮

Track index 1 (47)

Highest key value in the track	Address of corresponding block index
CA	1
DF	13
FK	25
FS	37

(b)

Track index 2 (96)

Highest key value in the track	Address of corresponding block index
IC	49
KG	61
NA	84
QS	85

Figure 2.18 Cylinder and track index tables for the file illustrated in Figure 2.19.

A static, hierarchical primary index is normally built so that the top level of the index points to buckets that are whole storage disks. This first level index is called a **disk storage index**. From this index, there may be pointers to the second level of the index. This index level may point to buckets that are cylinders, and this is then called a **cylinder index**. From this index, there may again be pointers to the third level. This index level may point to buckets that are tracks, and this is called a **track index**. Finally, there may be pointers from the track index to the fourth level of the index. This level may refer to buckets that are blocks, and therefore is called a **block index**. If the file is stored in one single disk, the disk storage index can be dispensed with; similarly, if the file can be stored in one single cylinder, the cylinder index can be dispensed with, etc.

EXAMPLE 2.13

Figure 2.18 illustrates a file with cylinder, track and block indexes. In the file itself, only the key value of the last record in each block is held.

If we are to search for the record with the key value JA, we are

(c)

1

Highest key value in the block	Address of corresponding block
AB	2
AC	3
AD	4
AE	5
BA	6
BB	7
BC	8
BD	9
BE	10
BF	11
CA	12

13

CC	14
CD	15
CE	16
CF	17
CG	18
DA	19
DB	20
DC	21
DD	22
DE	23
DF	24

25

EA	26
EB	27
EC	28
ED	29
EE	30
EF	31
FG	32
FH	33
FI	34
FJ	35
FK	36

37

FL	38
FM	39
FN	40
FO	41
FP	42
FQ	43
FR	44
FS	45

49

Highest key value in the block	Address of corresponding block
CC	50
CD	51
CE	52
HA	53
HB	54
HC	55
HD	56
HE	57
IA	58
IB	59
IC	60

61

JB	62
JC	63
JD	64
JE	65
KA	66
KB	67
KC	68
KD	69
KE	70
KF	71
KG	72

84

KI	74
LA	75
LB	76
LC	77
LD	78
MA	79
MB	80
MC	81
MD	82
ME	83
NA	84

85

PA	86
PB	87
PC	88
PD	89
PE	90
PF	91
QB	92
QR	93
QS	94

Figure 2.18 (cont.)

> referred, at the QS-entrance' of the cylinder index, to the track index on address 96. In this track index we are referred via the KG-entrance to the block index on address 61, and in this track index we are referred, via the JB-entrance, to the block address 62. If the record with the key JA is located in the file, it must be stored in the block on address 62, or in an overflow area attached to this block. This arrangement of records and indexes is illustrated in Figure 2.19.

A file has **indexed sequential organization** if it has an index and if the records of the file can be read directly in the same order as when sorted by the index key. If a primary index is created as described earlier, the records of the file can be read in sequence either by means of the index or by means of the physical sorting order. When new records are to be inserted in files with static indexes, it is normal to link an overflow area to each cylinder, so that it is possible to read overflow records without having to move the read/write head. This overflow area is called a **first level overflow**. If there is no more space available for records in first level overflow, **second level overflow** is used instead. Second level overflow is an overflow area that is shared by all fully occupied cylinders.

When this method is applied to construct a primary index, the block index and the blocks it serves as an index for are normally stored in the same track. This usually means that no extra read/write head movement is required when the block pointed to in the index is to be read. Similarly, the track index is stored in the cylinder whose tracks the index points to so that again no extra read/write head movement is required.

The advantage of having the individual records stored sequentially in a block cannot be utilized in the building up of a secondary index. Here, the lowest level of the index must point to the individual records and not to blocks. The method described for building up primary indexes can, however, be applied to secondary indexes in an indirect way. If it is assumed that the primary index is built on the identifier field, the secondary index can be built up by extracting the identifier number and the value of the secondary key field from all the records of the file. It is then possible to build up a primary index whose entrance is the secondary key of the extraction file just described. When the primary index is completed, all records with a given value in the secondary key can be searched for by using the secondary key value as the entrance to the extraction file. This search results in the identifier numbers of the records with the required value in the secondary key field. By using the primary index of the file and the identifier numbers as search argument, it is possible to search for the required records directly.

The extraction file, which becomes the secondary index, may also be built up by extracting the record's physical address and the corresponding value of the secondary key field. If this method is used to build

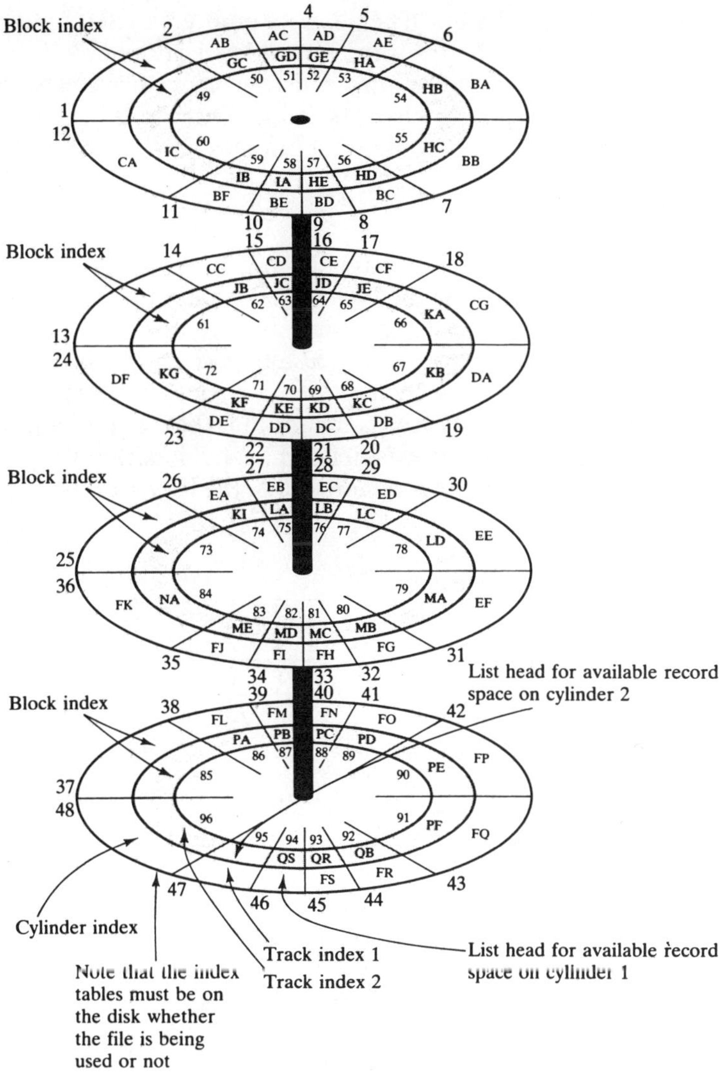

Figure 2.19 A file with cylinder, block and track indexes. The file is on two cylinders; cylinder 1 consisting of blocks 1–48 and cylinder 2 comprising blocks 49–96. The cylinder index is to be found on block 48. The cylinders each have four tracks, and the track indexes are on block 48 for cylinder 1 and on block 96 for cylinder 2; that is the track indexes are to be found at the ends of the cylinders. Each track index points to a block index stored at the beginning of each track; thus, the block index for the first track of the first cylinder is to be found on block 1, the block index for track 2 of cylinder 1 on block 13, etc. The first record in the file is thus stored on block 2. Each cylinder maintains its own list head for available record space. The list head for cylinder 1 is on block 46; that for cylinder 2 on block 95.

up the secondary index, there will be physical pointers to the corresponding records in the master file from the lowest level of the index.

A primary index is sometimes called a **block index** because the lowest level of the index points to blocks. A secondary index is sometimes called a **total index** because it contains a pointer to all records in the file.

Hierarchical dynamic indexes

In a dynamic index no overflow chains to first level overflow or second level overflow are used because the index itself is built to allow for the insertion or deletion of records. A dynamic index is normally built as a **search tree**, which is defined recursively as a tree in which the children of the root are ordered and where the children are root elements for search trees. Insertion or deletion of records means that the tree either grows or is reduced. The **height** of the tree is defined as the maximum number of branches there are between the root and one of the leaves of the tree. The

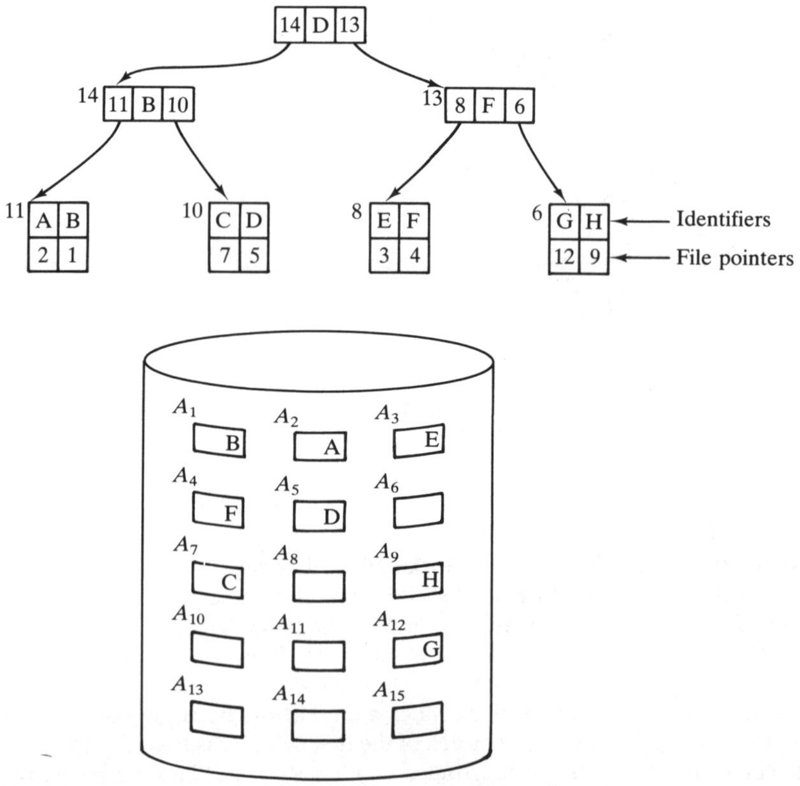

Figure 2.20 File with a dynamic index in the form of a binary tree. Each leaf holds pointers to two records.

node branching factor is defined as the number of children related to the parent record. The **branching factor of a tree** is defined as the maximum branching factor of the nodes of the tree.

EXAMPLE 2.14

Figure 2.20 illustrates a file with a dynamic index, which is built up as a tree with the branching factor 2 (this is also called a **binary tree**). The nodes of the index tree are blocks, which are also stored in the disk storage. The number to the left of each block indicates the address of the block in the disk storage. Those blocks that store the records of the file are called **data blocks**, whereas the other blocks are called **index blocks**. The nodes or blocks of the index have two different formats. The leaves are built up to hold two record identifiers and the corresponding pointers to the physical records. The other nodes are built up of three fields, of which the middle one is a record identifier.

The first field contains a pointer that must be followed if the identifier searched for is less than or equal to the record identifier in the next field. If the identifier of the records searched for is greater than the identifier of the middle field, the pointer in the last field is followed. Thus, to find E, we first follow pointer 13 to the node 8, F, 6 and then follow pointer 8 to the leaf that indicates that E is stored at 3.

When new records are to be inserted into the file, we must first find the leaf that is to contain the pointer to the new record. If there is available space for the identifier of the new record and the pointer, these are inserted into the leaf block. If there is no such space, the contents of the leaf block are distributed over two new leaf blocks, and the old leaf block is converted into a node with pointers to the two new leaf blocks.

Figure 2.21 illustrates the index after the creation of records I, J and K. Note that this has increased the height of the tree from 2 to 4.

It can be seen from Example 2.14 that the height of the different subtrees in an index may vary considerably. If an index tree is very unbalanced, the average search length increases, and at the same time the search length varies considerably, depending on the index level where the record pointer is stored. An index ought therefore to be built up as a **balanced tree**; that is, a tree in which the difference in height from the root to the leaves is no more than 1.

The index in Example 2.14 is a secondary index, since its lowest level contains pointers to individual records. The technique used in the example may, however, also be used to build up primary indexes. If the index is a primary index, then the individual records of the data blocks must be stored in sorting order, so that the leaves of the index point to an entire block with records whose identifiers are all greater than or less than the identifiers of the other data blocks. If the root of an index tree is stored in main storage, the height of the index tree is equal to the

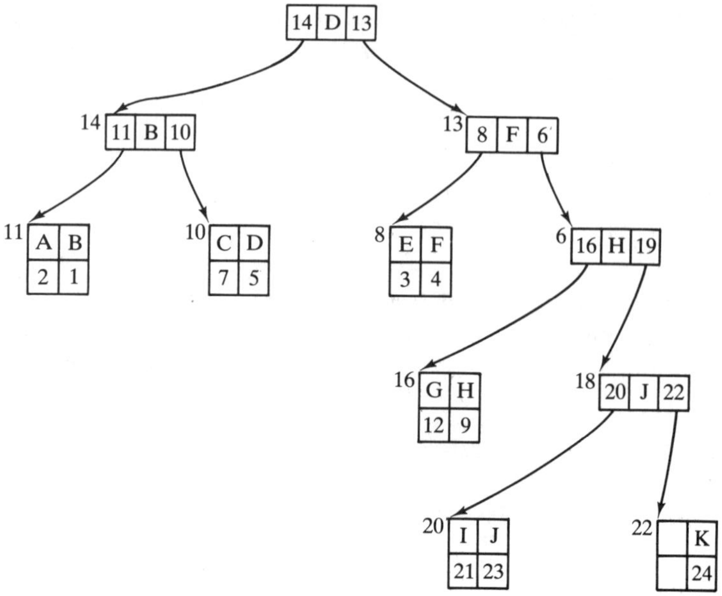

Figure 2.21 Index to the file shown in Figure 2.20 after the creation of two new records.

maximum number of block accesses that must be executed to input a leaf containing the pointers to the individual records.

Appendix F demonstrates various equations for the calculation of the height of different types of index tree. The following equations for calculating the height apply to index trees whose nodes all have the branching factor b, and whose leaves are all at the same level – that is, balanced trees:

$$\text{Height in a primary index} = \left\lceil \frac{\log n}{\log b} \right\rceil - 1$$

$$\text{Height in a secondary index} = \left\lceil \frac{\log m}{\log b} \right\rceil - 1$$

where m is the number of different key values in the secondary index, n is the number of blocks in the data file and b is the branching factor of the index, which is equivalent to the blocking factor of the index. The symbol ⌈ ⌉ means that the result should be rounded up to the next integer number.

It appears from these equations that the higher the branching factor of the tree, the lower the height of the tree. In practice, therefore, relatively large index blocks are used, so that the branching factor becomes high. However, the index blocks should not be so large as to prohibit the storage of at least the top index level permanently in main storage.

EXAMPLE 2.15

A customer file contains 500 000 records of 800 bytes each. A block size of 4820 bytes is used in the CUSTOMER file itself, while in the index a block size of 2004 bytes is used. We want to build up a primary index over the field CUSTOMER NUMBER of 10 bytes and a secondary index over the field NAME of 40 bytes. If a physical address occupies 4 bytes, the record length in the CUSTOMER NUMBER index will be 14 bytes and the blocking factor 143. If the loading factor of the customer file is 5/6, the customer file will occupy 100 000 blocks. If all the nodes of the index have the same branching factor and if all the leaves of the index are at the same level, then the height of the CUSTOMER NUMBER index can be estimated as:

$$\left\lceil \frac{\log(100\,000)}{\log(143)} \right\rceil - 1 = \left\lceil \frac{5}{2.1553} \right\rceil - 1 = 2$$

The record length in the NAME index is 44 and the blocking factor will be 45. The height of the NAME index can be estimated as:

$$\left\lceil \frac{\log(500\,000)}{\log(45)} \right\rceil - 1 = \left\lceil \frac{5.6990}{1.6532} \right\rceil - 1 = 3$$

The equations given here suggest that the search length in a dynamic index increases at slower rate as the number of newly inserted records in the file increases. This is an improvement on the static index whose search length increases linearly with the number of newly inserted records, because the overflow problem is overcome by means of overflow lists. The advantage of a dynamic index is lost, however, if the tree becomes very unbalanced. This problem cannot be solved by balancing the tree after each individual record creation, as this would mean that one single record creation may require a total re-organization of the entire index. To sum up: we want to be able to maintain an index without allowing it to grow very unbalanced, and at the same time we want to ensure that the creation of new records does not require a total re-organization of the index. The various forms of *B*-trees, described in the following subsections, satisfy those requirements.

B-trees

A *B*-tree of order *d* has the following characteristics:

- All the leaves of the tree are at the same level, so that the search length is the same for all records.

- The root of the tree contains from 1 to $2d$ key values or record identifiers, which means that the root may contain from 2 to $2d + 1$ child pointers.
- The other nodes of the tree contain from d to $2d$ key values, which means that a node may contain from $d + 1$ to $2d + 1$ child pointers.
- The leaves of the tree contain from d to $2d$ key values and the corresponding pointers to the records of the file.
- For each key value of a node, the *B*-tree contains a direct pointer to the corresponding record in the data file. If the identifier of the record searched for is less than the first key value of a node, then the first child pointer is followed. After this the search is repeated in the new node. If the key of the record searched for is less than the second – and greater than the first key value of the node – then the second child pointer of the node is followed, etc. If the key of the record searched for is greater than the $2d$th key, then the last child pointer of the node is followed.

During the updating of a *B*-tree, the following rules must be observed, so that the original characteristics of the *B*-tree are retained.

The following rules concern the the creation of new records:

- If there is available space in the leaf belonging to the new key value, the new key value and the corresponding record pointer are inserted.
- If overflow occurs in a leaf (i.e., if the leaf already contains $2d + 1$ key values), the middle key value is inserted into the node immediately above, the d lowest keys into a new leaf created to the left and the d highest keys in a leaf to the right. If this results in overflow in the node immediately above, this node is divided in the same manner. This process can be repeated until overflow occurs in the root of the tree, which thus increases its height by 1.

The following rules govern the deletion of records:

- If the key occurs in a leaf, it can be deleted immediately. If this results in fewer than d keys in the leaf, an attempt must be made to share the key values of the leaf with a neighbouring leaf which must contain more than d key values, as no leaf may contain fewer than d key values. If two neighbouring blocks together contain fewer than $2d$ keys, they must be merged, and at the same time a key value must be removed from the node immediately above.
- If a key value of a node is to be deleted, the nearest higher key value must be brought up into the node. This key value can be found in the leaf furthest to the left in the subtree branching off to the right of the deleted key value. The procedure for deleting a key

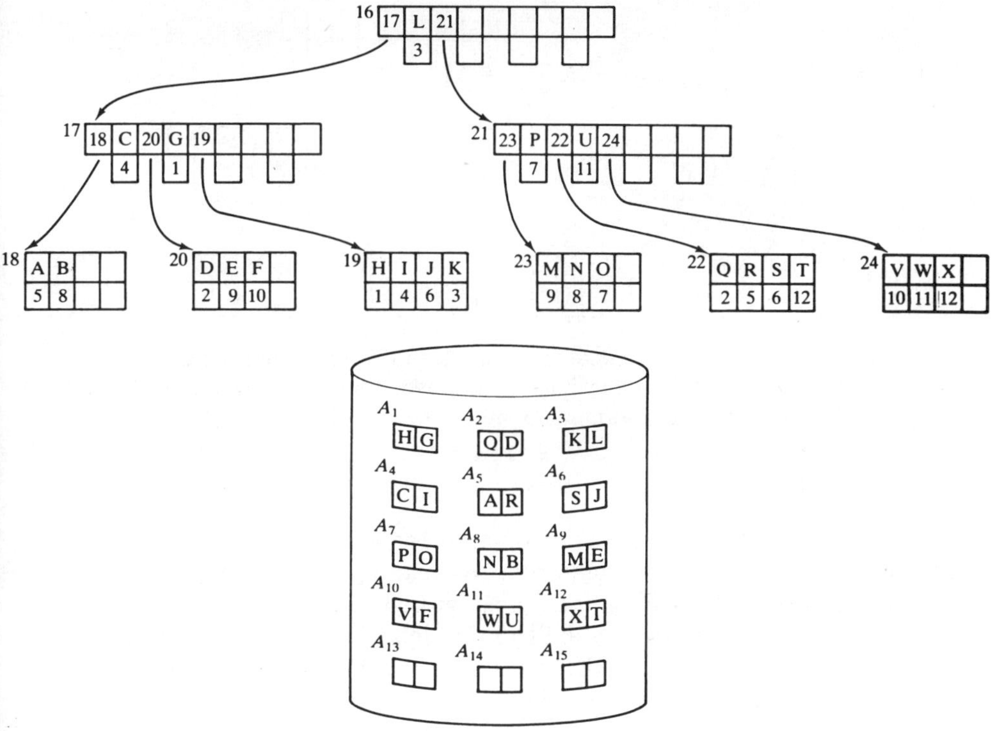

Figure 2.22 *B*-tree index and the corresponding indexed file.

value in a leaf is described above. The alternating deletion of a leaf key and a node key stops at the deletion of a key value in the root element, a process that may reduce the height of the tree by 1.

EXAMPLE 2.16

Figure 2.22 illustrates a file whose index is a *B*-tree of order 2. Its nodes are built up of fields which contain, in turn, a child pointer and a key value. The pointer to the block that stores the record corresponding to the key is located below a key value field. The leaves of the tree only contain key values and pointers to the corresponding records.

Figure 2.23 shows the *B*-tree after records Y and Z have been created and record G has been deleted.

A *B*-tree is a secondary index if the leaves contain pointers to the individual records of the file, so that these can be located arbitrarily in disk storage. If only the highest key values of the records stored in a block are inserted into leaves of the tree, the *B*-tree can be used as a dynamic primary index.

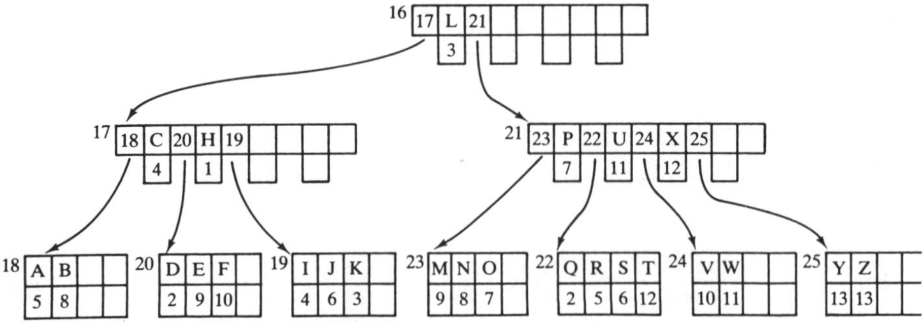

Figure 2.23 *B*-tree after update in which Y and Z are created and G is deleted. Y and Z go in a new leaf at 25 while H has moved up the tree by one level, and the leaf at 19 now contains pointers to only three records.

In addition to direct searches, the tree can also be used to read the records of the file in sorted order. By reading the tree in 'in-order'†, the records of the file can be read in ascending order by the key value.

In what follows we shall go through some important variations of the *B*-tree. Appendix F also gives a mathematical treatment of various aspects of different kinds of *B*-tree.

B^+-trees A B^+-tree is a *B*-tree in which all key values are located in the leaves. Thus, key values located in a node must also be inserted into the subtree to the left of the key value (a B^+-tree can of course also be built up by consistently inserting a key value of a node into the subtree located to the right of the key value). As all the file pointers in a B^+-tree are stored in the leaves, fast sequential treatment can be implemented by chaining the leaves together in the required sorting order. (Some writers refer to a B^+-tree as a *B**-tree but we reserve the term *B**-tree for a different kind of structure.)

EXAMPLE 2.17

Figure 2.24 illustrates a B^+-tree of first order. This tree is a primary index because the leaves only contain the highest key value in a block.

Figure 2.25 shows the B^+-tree after the creation of record AQ and the deletion of records SQ and TP.

† The reading of a *B*-tree in 'in-order' is defined recursively: we first follow the first child pointer of the root and read that subtree in 'in-order'. Next, the first key value of the root is dealt with. The second child pointer is then followed and this subtree is read in 'in-order', etc. Finally, the last child pointer of the root is followed and this subtree is read in 'in-order'.

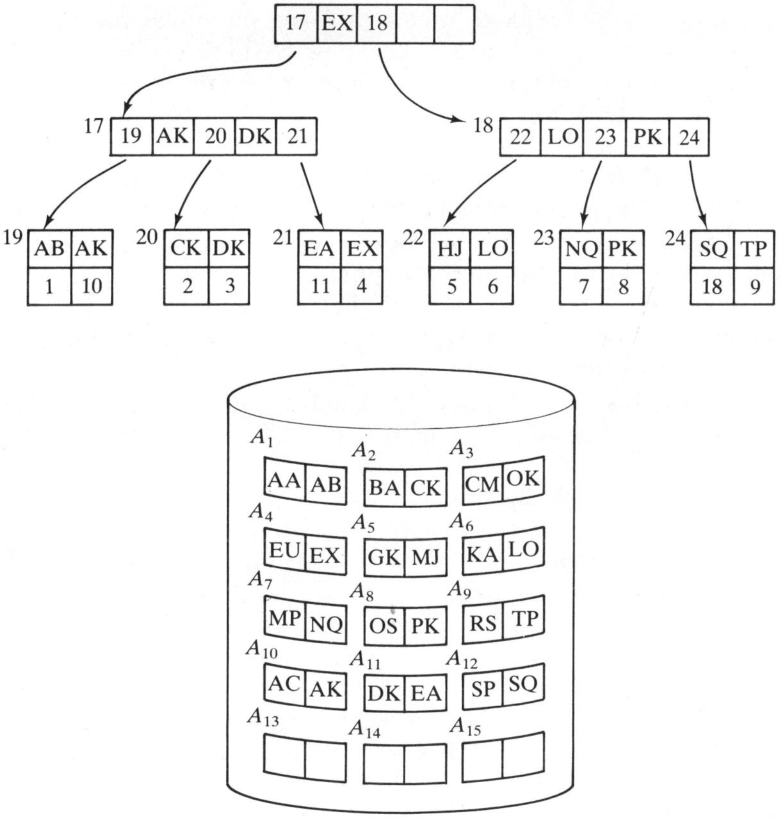

Figure 2.24 B^+-tree of first order and the corresponding indexed file.

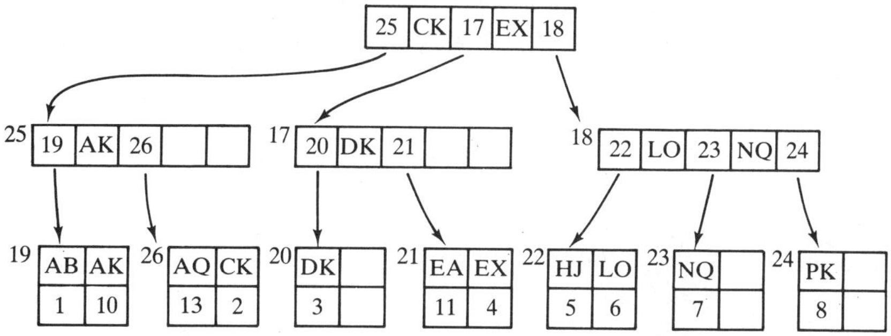

Figure 2.25 B^+-tree after update in which AQ is created and SQ and TP are deleted. A pointer to CK has been moved to the root of the tree and a new leaf 26 created. The deletion of SQ and TP results in PK being moved to leaf 24.

Prefix B^+-trees A prefix B^+-tree is a B-tree in which the index only stores enough of a key value to make it possible to determine which of the node pointers to follow. This saves storage space for the index and it also makes it faster to compare key values.

B-trees* A B*-tree is a B-tree or a B^+-tree in which the individual blocks must be at least two-thirds full. This can be achieved if, in an overflow situation, the contents of the overflow block are distributed on both of its neighbouring blocks before a block split is performed. If it is necessary to perform a block split, the contents of the overflow block and its occupied neighbouring block must by distributed on the new block, which thereby becomes two-thirds full.

B*-trees contain less free space and so searches are faster than for ordinary B-trees because their average branching factor is greater.

VSAM VSAM is a widely used software product, developed by IBM. Its index is the most well-known implementation of the concepts behind B^+-trees. However, only the dynamic expansion, and not the contraction, is implemented by VSAM. This is justified by the fact that the contraction of the index is the most time consuming of the two operations, and usually also the least necessary.

VSAM software can administer both primary and secondary indexes. In VSAM terminology, a secondary index is called an **alternate index**. The leaves in a VSAM index are chained together and called a **sequence set**. This makes fast sequential treatment in sorted order possible.

The blocks in a VSAM file are called **control intervals**. Blocks that can be pointed to from a leaf in a primary index are called **control areas**. If the cylinders of the disk storage are used as control areas and an index leaf stored in the same cylinder as the corresponding control area, then the read/write head must not be moved after the leaf block has been read. If overflow occurs and an index leaf has to be split, the records from the corresponding control area are divided between the original control area and a new one.

Indexes with random organization

An index can be defined as an independent file containing redundant data which is used to gain access to a master file. It is redundant in the sense that it can be re-created on the basis of the data which the master file contains.

The preceding sections have described indexes organized as a hierarchical tree. An index may, however, also have random organization. A randomly organized index is also called a '**scatter table**'. In Section 2.3.2, we saw an example of a file with a randomly organized static index in which an inverted list head, linking up all records with the same home address, was stored at the home address. A randomly organized index can also be built up dynamically, since the home address can be used as the root element in a B-tree. If there is no space to store the index in main storage, then the random index requires a shorter search length than a similar hierarchical index. In practice, random indexes are only used as secondary organization, because random organization as primary organization is faster than using a random index.

2.4.2 Implementation of relationships by direct organization

In what follows **direct organization** is used as a blanket term for index organization and random organization. The implementation of relationships by means of these two organizations is dealt with together because, from a logical point of view, the same techniques are used for each of them. Index organization, however, is described more fully as this method is the most common in practice. It may be necessary to use both primary and secondary organization in the implementation of relationships because many different relationships may be attached to a file. For every file we must decide which search direction we want to optimize and then use a primary organization to implement that search direction.

The one-to-many relationship

As an example of this relationship, we have previously used the connection between customers and orders. If the customer number is stored in the order records representing the orders placed by that customer, the customer number can be used to search for the corresponding customer record.

The search direction from orders to customers can be implemented if the customer file has direct organization and uses the customer number as key.

The search direction from customers to orders can also be implemented by random organization of the order file using the customer number as a non-unique key. In this case, the home address of the customer number may also contain orders placed by other customers. This is no serious problem, however, since 'false drops' (records that are selected during a search process, but which should not be represented in the final result) can be detected by testing on the customer field of the order record.

The many-to-many relationship

We represented this relationship earlier by means of the connection between orders and products, as an order may request many products and the same product may be requested in many different orders. If we

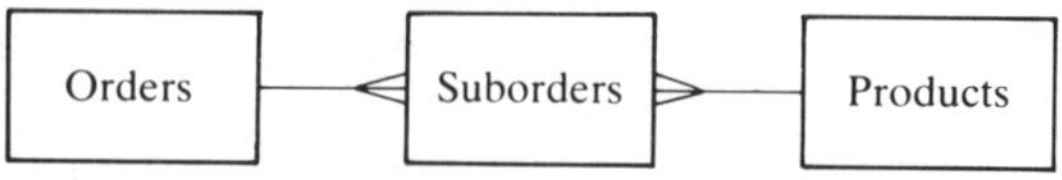

Figure 2.26 An $n : m$ relationship between orders and products represented as $1 : n$ relationships between suborders and orders, and suborders and products.

use direct organization, this relationship can be implemented by dividing it into two $1 : n$ relationships. This is illustrated in the E–R diagram shown in Figure 2.26.

The suborder file contains a record for each product mentioned in the order. Therefore, the double field (order number, product number) serves as unique identifier for records in the suborder file. As there are two different $1 : n$ relationships, the suborder file must have both product number and order number as keys. Furthermore, as the suborder file can only have one primary organization, we have to decide whether we want to optimize the search direction from orders to products or conversely from products to orders.

If we are going to search for the related product records from a given order record, the search is performed by using the order entrance to the suborder file. This makes it possible to search for all the suborders containing the original order number. The suborders all include a product number, which is used for the subsequent direct access to the product file. The reverse search direction from products to orders can be performed in a similar way, only this time the order number entrance in the suborder file must be used.

The one-to-one relationship

The one-to-one relationship is a special case of the one-to-many relationship. Consequently, it can be implemented by using the same methods utilized for the $1 : n$ relationship. However, there are a number of possibilities to choose between if we are going to implement a $1 : 1$ relationship.

EXAMPLE 2.18

Between a department file and an employee file the relationship 'head of department' is a $1 : 1$ relationship, as it is assumed that there is one and only one head of a department. In the E–R diagram shown in Figure 2.27, the branching factors of the relationship have been inserted, because these are of importance in the selection of an implementation method.

The $1 : 1$ relationship can be implemented by storing an employee number in the field 'head of department' in the department record. This employee number can be used for a direct search from a department record to the employee record of the head of the depart-

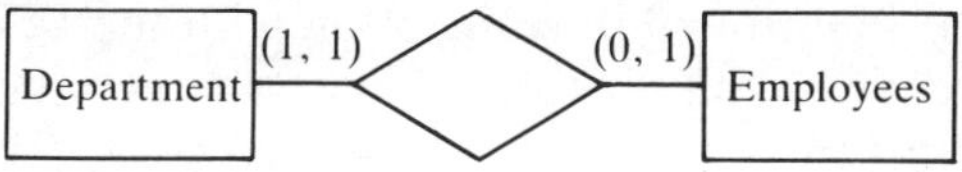

Figure 2.27 The 1 : 1 relationship 'head of department' shown as a relationship between the two entities department and employees.

ment. The search direction from an employee record to a department record where the person in question is head of the department can be implemented by constructing an index over the field 'head of department' in the department record. The disadvantage connected with this method of implementation is that a search has to be performed before it is possible, on the basis of an employee record, to find out whether a given person is or is not head of a department.

We could also implement the 1 : 1 relationship by inserting the field 'head of department' in the employee record, and storing the department number in this field, and also build up an index over the field so that from the department file we can search for the employee records related to heads of departments. A disadvantage of this solution is that the field 'head of department' is only relevant in relatively few employee records.

A third method of implementing the 1 : 1 relationship is to store the employee number of the head of department in the department record, and the department number and occupation in the employee record. This is a very simple solution, but it has the disadvantage that it contains redundancy and that inconsistency between the two files may occur (see Section 6.6 on Consistency control).

The sequential relationship

It is possible to construct randomizing functions that make it possible to read records in sorted order. However, it is difficult to construct good randomizing functions possessing this characteristic, and therefore they are seldom used. It is an advantage to use an 'address table' in connection with these randomizing functions, so that the organization becomes a form of index organization. By using hierarchical indexes, however, it is very simple to implement the ordering relationship (see Section 2.4.1).

The equivalence relationship

The equivalence relationship divides the records of the file into groups that are separated from each other. It is easy to implement a search for all records in a group by index organization in which the key is a field that uniquely identifies the separate groups. Thus, the equivalence relationship can be implemented by index organization over a non-unique key. The equivalence relationship can also be implemented by random organization, but as mentioned in connection with the 1 : *n* relationship, 'false drops' (i.e., records with the same home address but different group codes) must be removed.

Trees

Trees can be implemented by storing the identifier of the parent record in every node. If we are going to search towards the root of the tree this identifier can be used to search for the parent record directly. The search direction towards the leaves of the tree can be implemented by direct organization in which the field containing the parent record serves as key. By means of such an entrance, we can search for all records with a specific value in the field containing the parent record - that is, all the children of the parent record.

As random organization is a primary organization, only one of the search directions can be implemented by random organization.

The network relationship

As an example of an oriented network we have previously used the production structure, which illustrates how finished goods can be produced from components and raw materials. If we create a file for the nodes of the network and a file for the branches of the network, then the network can be implemented by two 1 : *n* relationships between these two files as shown in Figure 2.28.

To serve as identifier for a branch in the network, we can use the double field (parent product number, child product number), which contains the identifier of the nodes connected by the branch. The branching file must have two different direct organizations corresponding to the two 1 : *n* relationships: 'forms part of' and 'consists of'.

If we are going to search downwards through the structure, we have to use the entrance having the parent product number as key. To

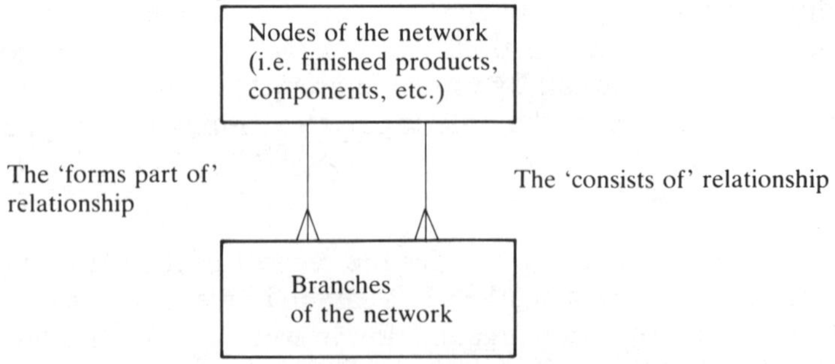

Figure 2.28 A network relationship represented as two 1 : *n* relationships between the nodes and branches of the network.

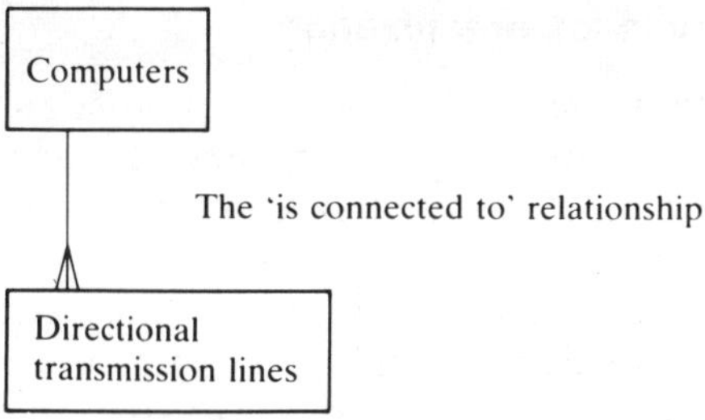

Figure 2.29 A general network represented as a single 1 : *n* relationship. Here, the relationships have implied direction; i.e., a record is required for '*B* is connected to *A*' as well as for '*A* is connected to *B*'.

search upwards through the structure we have to use the entrance having the child product number as key.

As an example of a general network, we used in Chapter 1 a data transmission net in which each computer in the network can be directly connected to several other computers. It is possible to implement a general network in the form of an oriented network, but this requires 'upward' as well as 'downward' searches if the related records are to be searched for.

An alternative is to create two branch records for each connection between two nodes. The two branch records must correspond to the two search directions; that is, a branch record can be identified with the double field (from node number, toward node number). If the branch file has direct organization, using the 'from node number' as key, this entrance can be used to search for all the branches that branch off from a particular node. By means of these branch records, we can search for the related nodes directly, as shown in Figure 2.29.

Relationships of order *n*

In Section 1.2.2 on Relationships of order *n*, the connection between car dealers, car manufacturers and car types was given as an example of a relationship of third order. If we also wish to record the profit that the dealer gets by selling a particular car type from a particular manufacturer, this connection can be implemented by the creation of a relationship file containing the fields CAR DEALER, CAR TYPE, CAR MANUFACTURER and PROFIT. The various search directions can be implemented by allowing the relationship file three different entrances corresponding to the keys CAR DEALER, CAR TYPE and CAR MANUFACTURER. The opposite search directions can be implemented by having direct organization with a unique key in the files CAR DEALER, CAR TYPES, CAR MANUFACTURERS, respectively. This method of implementation is equivalent to seeing relationships of order *n* as *n* different 1 : *n* relationships (see Figure 2.7).

2.4.3 Clustering by index organization

Clustering means that records related to one another are stored adjacently. By using clustering, an owner record and its member records, for example, can be stored in the same block so that it becomes very fast to search for related records.

Clustering is particularly applicable to the various forms of list organization because these are secondary organizations that do not make any demands on the physical location of the individual records. However, clustering can also be implemented by means of index organization. Hierarchical relationships, such as trees and 1 : n relationships, can be implemented by storing records in **preorder**, so that child or member records are stored immediately after their parent or owner record.

The preorder sequence for the elements of a tree is defined recursively. First comes the root and then the subtrees of the root in preorder. The subtrees of the root are treated successively from left to right. Figure 2.30 illustrates a tree structure whose nodes are numbered in preorder. This figure illustrates relationships between customers, orders and suborders.

Storing in preorder can be achieved by using a hierarchical primary index, whose key is the double field (owner key, member key). To be able to build up this key in all record types, the member records have to be expanded to contain a field holding the key value of the owner records. Likewise, the owner record has to be expanded by the member key field, which must contain a value less than the lowest member key actually occurring. The result of this expansion is that the owner is stored immediately before the members related to it. If the file is created with a suitable loading factor and re-organized at regular intervals, newly created member records can probably also be stored physically close to their owner.

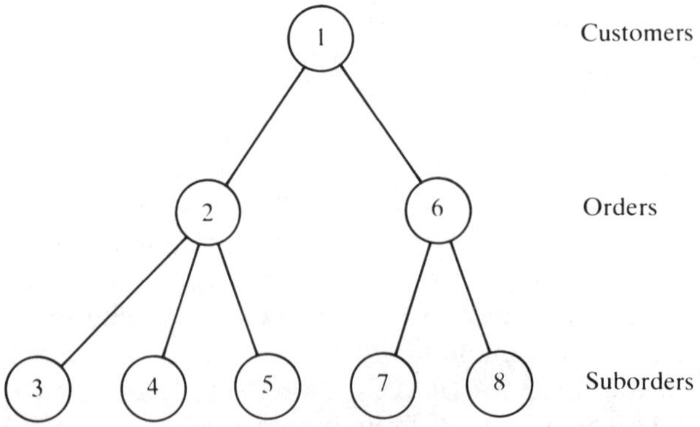

Figure 2.30 Tree with its nodes numbered in preorder.

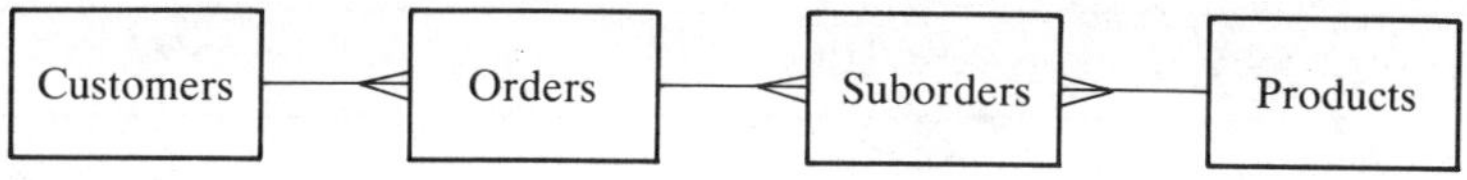

Figure 2.31 E–R diagram showing relationships between customers, orders, suborders and products.

EXAMPLE 2.19

The E–R diagram shown in Figure 2.31 illustrates the relationships between customers, orders, suborders and products that we are already familiar with. The hierarchy between customers and products can be stored in preorder by letting the two record types share the same key field (CUSTOMER NUMBER, ORDER NUMBER), in which the ORDER NUMBER has the value zero in all customer records. When searching for a customer and the related orders, the customer record is searched for first by the primary index, and then the orders are searched for by sequential reading.

If the search direction from orders to suborders is used more than the search direction from products to suborders, it may also be worthwhile to store the suborders together with the orders, which are again stored together with the customers.

The hierarchy between customers, orders and suborders can be stored in preorder by letting all three record types share the same key field (CUSTOMER NUMBER, ORDER NUMBER and PRODUCT NUMBER), in which the PRODUCT NUMBER has the value zero in all customer records and order records, while the ORDER NUMBER has the value zero in all customer records. If the search direction from products to suborders is used more than the search direction from orders to suborders, it may be worthwhile to store the suborders together with the products. This can be implemented by storing the hierarchy between products and suborders in preorder by letting the two record types share the same key field (PRODUCT NUMBER, ORDER NUMBER), in which the ORDER NUMBER has the value zero in all product records.

Example 2.19 demonstrates that clustering can be performed in many different ways. Which clustering method to choose is discussed further in Section 3.2.4. If clustering is performed by means of index organization, as described here, there will be several different record types in the same physical file. This physical storing ought to be administered by a database management system, to avoid the application programmes becoming dependent upon the physical implementation of the relationships. This is of particular importance with respect to the fourth-generation language described in Chapters 12 and 13.

EXERCISES

2.1 A firm has a master file that is updated by a batch program.

(a) Assume that the master file has random organization. What factors will have an influence on whether it will pay to sort the transactions before the master file is updated?

(b) Assume that the master file has index sequential organization. What factors have an influence on whether it will pay to sort the transactions before the master file is updated?

2.2 A firm has a product file comprising 50 000 records. The government has just introduced a new VAT system that operates with three different VAT rates for necessities, everyday commodities and luxury articles, respectively. The data processing department of the firm presents the two proposals, shown in Figure 2.32, for making the necessary changes in the product file to meet the new VAT rules.

(a) What normal forms are satisfied by the files in the two proposals?

(b) What factors should have an influence on the choice of proposal?

(c) How much storage space is occupied by the two proposals on IBM 3380 disk storage if a block size of 4820 bytes is used?

(d) Which of the two proposals will be the most flexible towards unforeseen changes in VAT rules?

(e) Which proposal will give the fastest run time for a batch invoicing program?

(f) Which proposal will give the shortest response time for real-time invoicing?

2.3 In files with direct organization, the overflow problem can be avoided by using the physical address of a record as record identification number. As

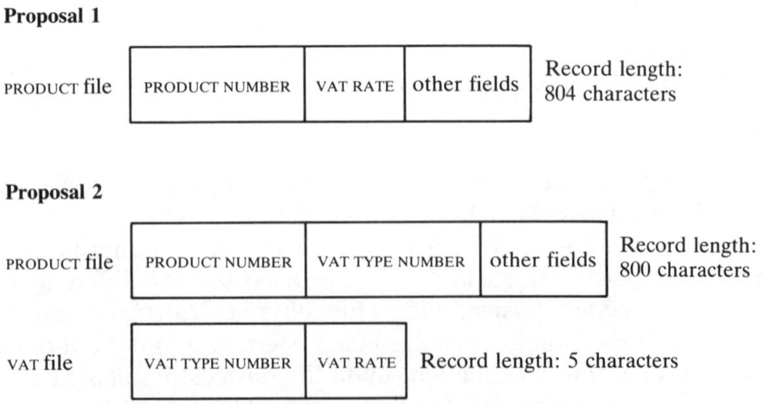

Figure 2.32 Two proposals for implementing variable VAT rates.

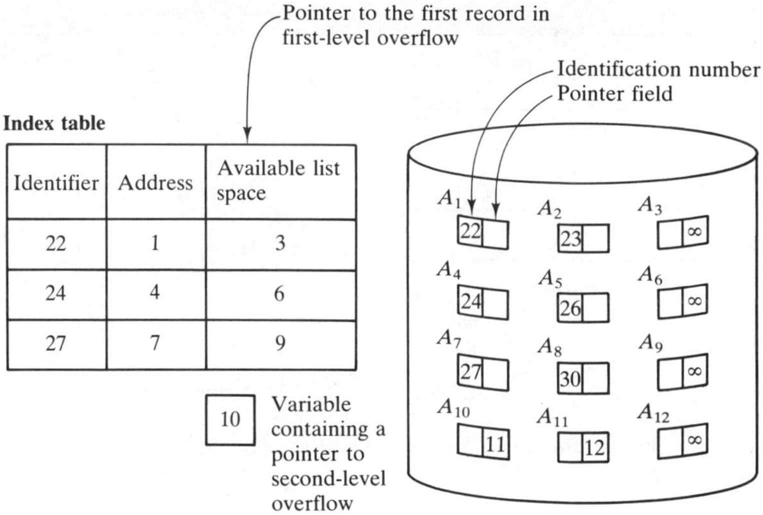

Identifier	Address	Available list space
22	1	3
24	4	6
27	7	9

Figure 2.33 File with index sequential organization. First level overflow is organized within each cylinder. Second level overflow uses an available list space.

a firm can often choose its record identification numbers freely, there are no logical obstacles to using direct organization. However, this method is not used very much in practice. Why is this so?

2.4 Figure 2.33 illustrates a new file that has index sequential organization. Each row in the figure corresponds, for example, to a cylinder on the disk storage. Within each cylinder, there is a list of available space records called **first-level overflow**. If there are no more records in the available space list belonging to a cylinder, **second-level overflow** has to be used, which is a shared list of available space records. The time required to read the file sequentially increases substantially if there are many records in second-level overflow, so that the index sequential files have to be reorganized at regular intervals. In Figure 2.33, each record contains an identification number and a pointer field, which is only used if the next record is not stored immediately after the record read. In Figure 2.34 the records 28 and 29 have been inserted into the file. Carry out the changes an updating program has to execute for the following transactions:

(a) Create RECORD 22

(b) Create RECORD 21

2.5 A bank wants to create an accounting system that makes it possible to update customer accounts on a real-time basis as entries are received. The bank has 2 million accounts of an average 3000 bytes. The new accounting system is required to update 100 accounts/second during peak hours. It has been decided to use random organization with a separate

Index table

Identifier	Address	Available list space
22	1	3
26	5	4
27.	7	∞

[11] Variable containing a pointer to second-level overflow

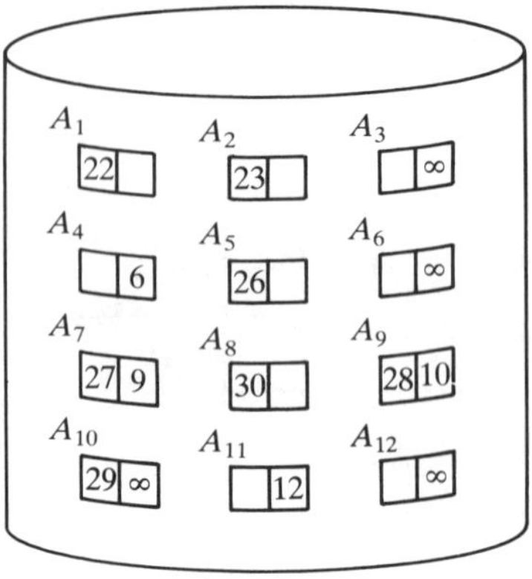

Figure 2.34 The file shown in Figure 2.33 after records 28 and 29 have been inserted.

overflow storage in which overflow records are chained together individually.

(a) The same block format and record format are required in both the master file and the overflow file, so that a shared READ statement can be used in case of sequential reading. Where would you recommend storing the address of the first overflow record of a block, and where would you recommend storing the other pointers in an overflow list? A shared available space list for empty overflow records is used. How would you propose implementing this list?

(b) What block size, blocking factor and loading factor would you recommend if the average search length can be a maximum 1.2 accesses for searching a record? How large will the master file and the overflow file be, in bytes?

(c) In connection with re-organization, the records are to be sorted by the home address. Estimate the time it takes to re-organize assuming that 1,000,000 bytes are used for the internal sorting in main storage.

(d) Once a month, 100 000 accounts are to be updated when wages, pensions, etc. are paid in. This updating is executed by a batch program that runs overnight, so that the customers can withdraw the money when the bank opens in the morning. Estimate the time required for the updating assuming that it is a direct updating.

(e) The bank adds interest to its accounts periodically by updating the accounts file sequentially. In connection with this updating, it is possible to include the batch entries, introduced in part (d). What are the advantages and disadvantages of including the batch entries in the 'interest-added run'?

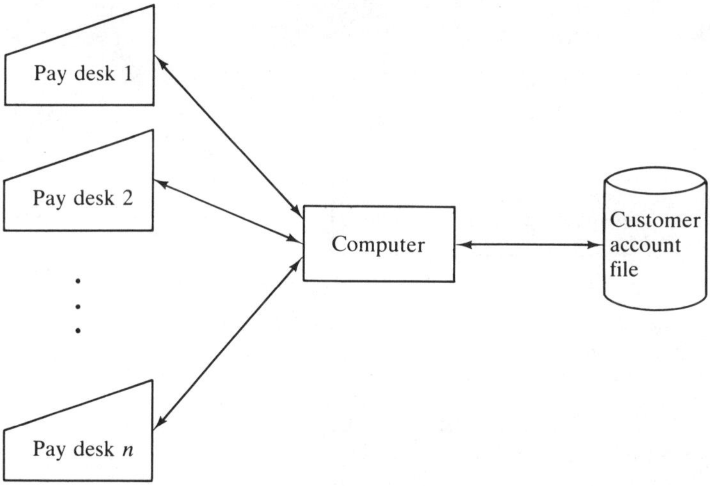

Figure 2.35 A system for credit card purchases in a department store.

2.6 A department store wants to create a real-time system that, amongst other things, can be used to debit customers who use its credit cards. This is shown in Figure 2.35. When a customer wants to use his card, the shop assistant can use a terminal to directly debit the account by the amount of the purchase. If the credit card is stolen, or if there have been irregularities concerning the customer's payments, such data can be returned to the shop assistant who can then refuse to hand over the articles to the customer. The computer has simultaneous units and a relatively large main storage. In addition to 50 terminals, the following external units are connected to the computer:

- two disk units
- one magnetic tape unit
- one line printer

The customer file contains 40 000 accounts of 200 characters each.

(a) How many terminals, in theory, can be plugged into the computer if it is to run the transaction during peak hours, when up to two debit transactions per minute may be sent to the computer from each terminal?

(b) Once a month, giro paying-in forms are to be printed and sent to those customers who have spent more than they have paid into their account. On average, these paying-in forms are printed for 90% of the 40 000 customers. Giro paying-in transactions are later delivered by the Post Office and then used as input in a program that credits the customers' accounts with the amounts paid in. Outline by means of system flowcharts how you would advise the department store to build up the program that prints the giro

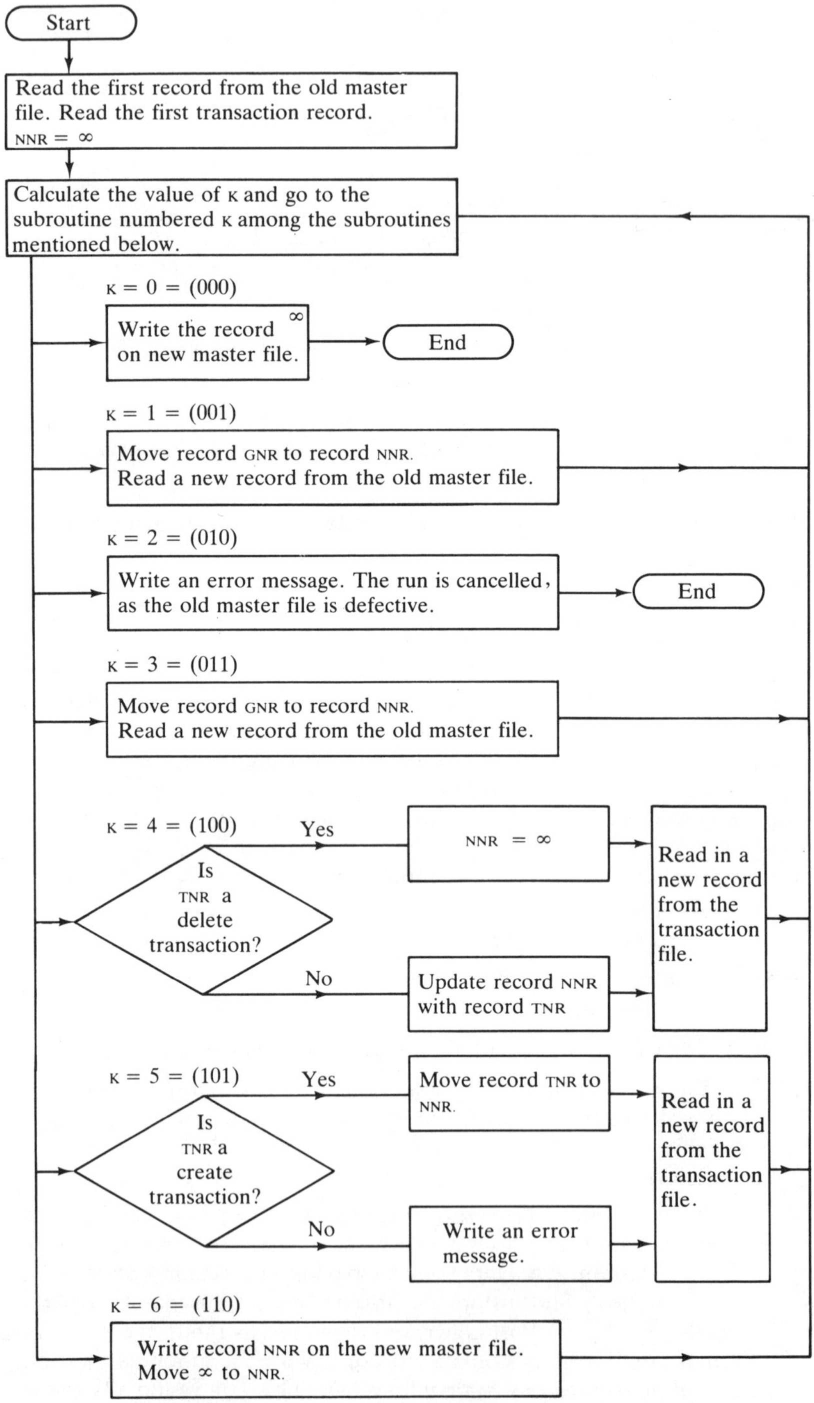

Figure 2.36 Files in an insurance company's database.

paying-in forms and credits the customers' accounts. Indicate whether the customer file is to have random or index sequential organization.

2.7 A general updating program for a sequential master file, stored on magnetic tapes, can be built up as shown in the flowchart program of Figure 2.36. The program can create, delete and change records in the master file, and an arbitrary number of transactions can be accepted for a master record in the same run. It is assumed that both the transaction file and the master file are concluded by an end-of-file record, whose identification number is greater than that of the other records. The identification number of the record is indicated by the symbol ∞ in the flowchart.

The description of the variables is as follows:

- GNR is the field with the identification number in the old master file;
- NNR is the field with the identification number in the new master file;
- TNR is the field with the identification number in the transaction file;
- K is an auxiliary variable, whose value is determined by whether GNR, TNR or NNR contains the lowest identification number.

The values for K are given in Figure 2.37. The situation in which K = 0 only occurs at the end of the program, where GNR = TNR = NNR = ∞.

(a) What happens if, by some mistake, the transaction file has not been sorted before the program runs?

(b) Is it possible, in the same run, to delete, recreate and make changes in the same master record?

(c) Assume that the master file is an account file in a bank. What subroutine should be used to print warning letters to customers who have overdrawn their account?

(d) What modifications have to be made in the flowchart if the magnetic tape master files are changed into a file with index

K	GNR	TNR	NNR	Value of K in binary
0	lowest	lowest	lowest	000
1	lowest	lowest	large	001
2	lowest	large	lowest	010
3	lowest	large	large	011
4	large	lowest	lowest	100
5	large	lowest	large	101
6	large	large	lowest	110

Figure 2.37 Values of K for various values of GNR, TNR and NNR.

sequential organization in which the individual records are updated by writing back the changed records? Note that for this solution it is not necessary to write master records for which there have been no transactions. Furthermore, note that files with index sequential organization use different statements for updating and creating new records. Reattempt part (c) on the basis of these modified assumptions.

2.8 A file contains 100 000 records of 600 bytes each. The file is stored on IBM 3380 disk storage and a block size of 1588 bytes is used. There has to be space available for the creation of new records in each block.

(a) Calculate the size of the file, the loading factor and the blocking factor.

(b) Select a more appropriate block size from the table of possible block sizes given in Appendix G. Take into account that the file is used heavily by on-line users.

(c) Assume that although the average record length is 600 bytes, 20% of the records in the file have a length of 1000 bytes, and the rest a length of 500 bytes. Calculate the average size of the file and the loading factor assuming that the block size is 1588 bytes and that the record types are distributed with the probabilities given above. In addition, calculate the maximum and minimum file size and loading factor.

2.9 A randomly organized file contains 100 000 records of 500 bytes each. The file has a blocking factor of 10. A randomizing function, which spreads the records evenly among the file's blocks, is used, so that there is an average of seven records per block.

(a) Calculate the average access time for an on-line program if linear open overflow is used.

(b) Calculate the average access time if separate chaining is used and the individual overflow records are chained together. What block size would you propose for the overflow area? Calculate the average data area required for overflow records.

2.10 Calculate the sorting time for a file of 600 000 records of 400 bytes each if a sorting area of 22 Kbytes is available. Assume that IBM 3380 disk storages are used. Which block size will be most appropriate for the sorting program?

2.11 If records in a randomly organized file are deleted with linear open overflow, we cannot know how far we have to search for a possible overflow record, as the search will have to be continued after we have read empty records. Suggest alternative solutions to this problem.

2.12 Example 2.7 gave illustrations of a file after a one-step re-organization and a two-step re-organization. Change the figure to show that record 28 has been deleted and that records 27 and 41 have been created.

2.13 How does the binary tree in the dynamic index in Example 2.14 grow if new records, with ascending key values, are created?

2.14 In Example 2.16 there is an illustration of a *B*-tree, which is a secondary index.

(a) Illustrate the creation of records 01 and 02, which are to be inserted into the *B*-tree after the key value 0.

(b) Illustrate the deletion of records U, E and F.

2.15 In Example 2.17 there is an illustration of a B^+-tree, which is a primary index.

(a) Illustrate the creation of record EZ.

(b) Illustrate the deletion of records NQ and PK.

2.16 (a) Find an equation that can be used to calculate the number of index levels for a B^+-tree built over a non-unique key.

(b) Find an equation that can be used to calculate the number of index levels for a B^+-tree built over a repeating field.

2.17 Assume that a $1:n$ relationship has been implemented exclusively by random organization; that is, the first file has random organization with a unique key and the second file has random organization with a non-unique key. How does the search algorithm have to differ depending upon whether the key is unique or non-unique?

2.18 A bank wants to implement an $n:m$ relationship between deposit records and account records. When payments from a security arrive, it has to be possible to divide the payment amongst different accounts corresponding to interest, instalment payments, fees, payments relating to shares, mortgage deeds, bonds, etc. The relationship must also be used when consistency control is executed, so that accounts that may later receive payments from securities in deposit are not deleted. In which types of database management system is it possible to implement clustering in the database, and how would you propose to utilize the clustering facility in the implementation of account–deposit relationships?

2.19 Assume that a database management system comprises an index sequential access method that makes it possible to read records in ascending order by both primary and secondary keys. There is no in-built possibility of reading records in descending order.

(a) Describe how it is still possible, in such a system, to read files in descending order both by a primary and by a secondary key.

(b) Assume that the key the index is built over can be composed of several different keys. Describe how the file can be read in ascending order by the first part of the key and in descending order by the second part of the key. As an example of this consider a file of statements of account in which an index has been built over the key (account number, date of statement). For a given account number we must be able to read the statements of account in descending chronological order because any customer enquiries are likely to be about the latest statement(s).

2.20 How many real-time updates can be stored on a magnetic tape log file with technical data as described in Appendix G? The database file, which is real-time updated, uses a fixed record length of 100 bytes. A disk storage address occupies four bytes. (A log file normally contains only one record per block, and each log record contains the image of the updated records both before and after the updating. A log record also contains the address of the record that has been updated.)

2.21 In which overflow methods will it be practical to use two-pass load for re-organizing a file with random organization?

2.22 (a) A file is organized with dynamic hashing as its primary form of organization. A randomly organized index is used, whose index elements can be transformed to the root in a binary tree. How much space does the index occupy when the hashing function can address 10 000 index elements and 1000 bucket splits have occurred?

(b) How can dynamic hashing be used as a secondary form of organization?

(c) As an alternative to dynamic hashing, index organization with a B^+-tree can be used. How much space does this index occupy if the key is 10 bytes and the block length of the index file is 2004 bytes?

2.23 What are the advantages of the 'classical' types of random organization compared to dynamic hashing?

2.24 Table 2.1 shows what types of relationship can be implemented by means of the various types of file organization. Describe how the relationship types can be implemented.

2.25 Example 1.6 gave an E–R diagram covering a firm with an invoicing system, an inventory management system and a back order system. What physical files would you create to implement this database, and what primary and secondary organizations and clustering (if any) must these files have if the firm's applications have the following priority as regards fast response times?

(a) An on-line survey of contractual obligations where the search criterion is the customer's name and perhaps also his address. Output must be a screen picture showing the customers who satisfy the search criterion. If only one customer satisfies the search criterion, a screen picture is produced with the fields of the customer records as well as an outline of orders and back orders that have been placed by the customer. Note that the order lines must include both product number and product name.

(b) Real-time invoicing.

(c) Inventory management.

(d) Back order invoicing.

2.26 Two files are stored in a disk storage, both of which use a block size of 4820 bytes. In peak hours an average of three transactions per second arrive for each of the two files. One file has random organization with a search length of 1.2, while the other file has index organization with an index height of 3.

(a) Estimate the utilization of the disk storage.

(b) What is the response time for the two files, including the waiting time in a possible queue of transactions waiting to gain access to the disk storage?

(c) The firm has another disk storage with available space where the index for the indexed organized file may be stored. During peak hours this disk storage is utilized 50% of the time. It is possible to improve the response time for the two files by transferring the index to the other disk storage?

Chapter 3
Physical Database Structures – II

3.1 Introduction

In practical applications, efficiency, both in terms of cost of implementation and computer time, is a major consideration in choosing what type of organization to use when creating a database. Each type of file organization has its advantages and disadvantages in use that make it more applicable for some applications than others. Thus, optimization of the database system clearly depends on the correct choice of approach to organizing the files for the system during development.

This chapter continues the theme of Chapter 2, discussing the organization of the physical database. It begins by covering the various types of list organization and then moves on to discuss the relative merits of the different techniques applied to different situations, taking into account the number and type of transactions taking place, and considerations such as disk usage and computer facilities. Comparisons are drawn and conclusions are presented in the form of tables.

3.2 List organization

List organizations can be defined as organizations in which relationships are implemented by means of lists; that is, relationships are implemented directly by linking together those records that are related to each other (see Appendix A).

It is quite simple to implement the sequential relationship by means of a list because a list, by definition, is an ordered set of records. When it comes to the equivalence relationship we want to be able to search for all records in a group; this can be implemented by chaining them together. In the following description of special forms of list organization, the implementation of the $1{:}n$ relation is particularly important since it has been shown that the $n{:}m$ relationship, the network relationship and relationships of order n can be transformed to one or more $1{:}n$ relationships.

If the relationships are represented by means of inverted lists, the file is said to have **inverted list organization** (see Section 3.2.2).

3.2.1 Multilist organization

Multilist organization is defined as an organization in which different groups of records are chained together in such a way that the individual file contains many different lists. In this section, we shall examine those types of relationship that are well suited to implementation by a multilist organization.

The one-to-many relationship

It is easy to implement the $1{:}n$ relationship by lists since the parent record can serve as list head for its child records, which are chained together in the list itself.

EXAMPLE 3.1

In Figure 3.1 a $1{:}n$ relationship exists between the file holding details about current accounts and the file holding account statements. The relationship has been implemented by using a current account as list head for all the account statements belonging to the account in question. If the list elements are chained together in descending order by date, we get the added advantage that the first element in the list is the latest account statement. Normally, there are most queries about the latest account statement.

The many-to-many relationship

The various types of database management systems are normally classified according to the technique used to implement the $n{:}m$ relationship. In Section 4.2, which analyses the various types of database management systems, five different methods of implementing the $n{:}m$ relationship are discussed. Example 3.2 describes yet another method,

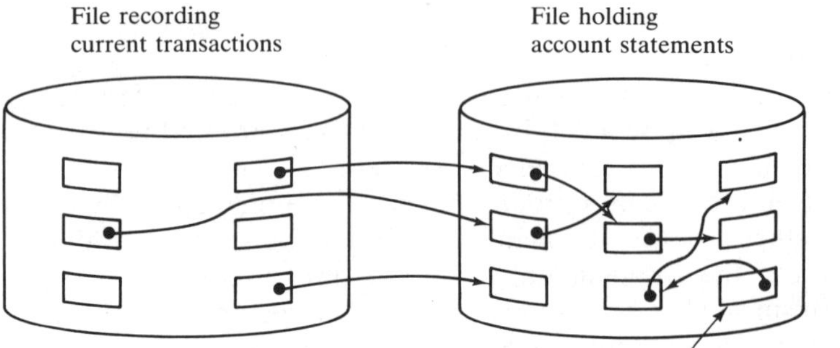

Figure 3.1 The relationship between bank accounts and statements implemented as a list with the account acting as list head for a list of statements. These will normally be chained together, ordered by date.

which is of particular interest when it is transformed to inverted list organization (see Section 3.2.2).

EXAMPLE 3.2

Figure 3.2 describes a book file and a topic file. There is an $n:m$ relationship between the book file and the topic file because a book may deal with several different topics, and a topic may be dealt with in several different books. The relationship has been implemented by chaining together all books dealing with a particular topic. The topic record serves as list head for the books dealing with the subject described in the list head. As several pointer chains may intersect in the same book record, the pointer must consist of both the pointer to the book record and the number of the field in the book record holding the next pointer in the chain.

The organization illustrated in Figure 3.2 is oriented towards the retrieval of literature. It is assumed that a student wants to find literature dealing with 'The influence of South Africa's racial policy on her exports'. The figure shows lists for the topics Africa, Apartheid policy and Foreign trade. If we want a survey of literature dealing with all three topics, we simply need to search through the three lists with the aid of a program and output all records that appear in all of them.

The list elements in the individual topic lists in the figure are sorted by the addresses where the list elements are stored. We can find the intersection of the three lists by merging them. Such merging requires almost as many searches on the disk storage as there are list elements in the three lists.

Trees

If the address of the parent is stored as a pointer in each record, as shown in Figure 3.3, these pointers can be used to search in the direction

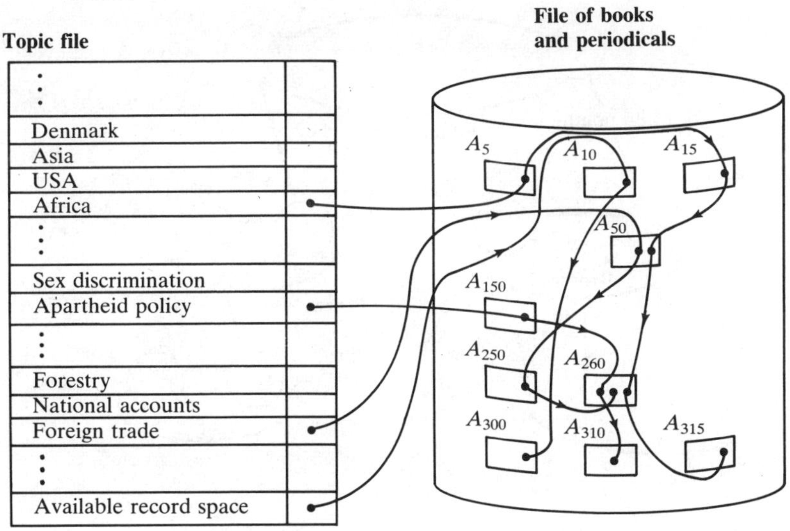

Figure 3.2 A system for retrieving books on particular topics. The entry in the topic file serves as a list head for all the book file entries (books) that deal with the topic. A book dealing with two topics will be a member of the two lists. From the figure, it can be seen that only the book whose details are stored at address 260 on the book file deals with Africa, Apartheid policy and Foreign trade.

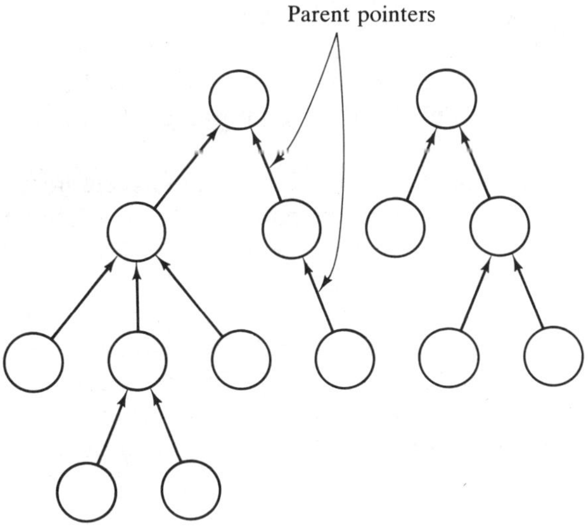

Figure 3.3 A tree structure in which the search direction from the leaves to the root is implemented.

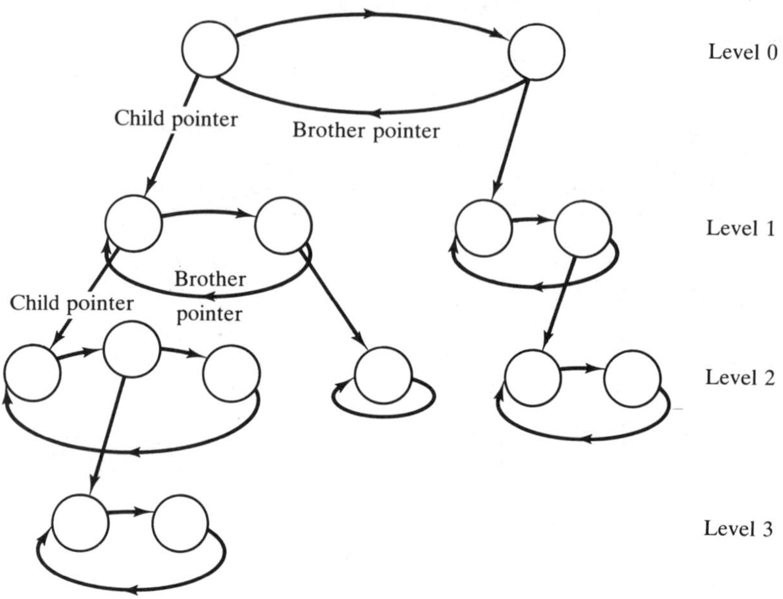

Figure 3.4 A tree structure in which the search direction from the root to the leaves is implemented.

from leaf to root. Similarly, we can store the address of the record's children in each record and use these pointers to search from lower levels towards higher levels (root to leaf). As the number of children of a record often varies a great deal, this technique requires the use of a variable record length. The problems that this raises can be avoided by using a parent record as list head for a list that chains together all the children of the parent record. This method of implementation is illustrated in Figure 3.4.

A list may be defined as an ordered set of list elements in which the list elements are either lists (represented by the list heads) or ordinary records. The relationship illustrated in Figure 3.4 can be seen as a list whose two list elements at level 0 are list heads.

In IBM's hierarchical database management system, IMS, $1:n$ relationships and tree structures can be implemented in the way just outlined. In IMS terminology, a hierarchy like the one illustrated in Figure 3.4 is called a database, and each record at level 0 is called a **database record**. Thus, in IMS terminology, the total database of a firm may comprise many different databases, corresponding to the different hierarchies implemented.

In a CODASYL system (see Chapter 11 for a detailed description), $1:n$ relationships and tree structures can also be implemented as shown here. In CODASYL terminology, a list is called a 'set'. The list head is called an 'owner' and the list elements 'members'.

The network relationship

Networks can be implemented by using each node as list head for a list that chains together the records related to the list head. As a node may be related to many other nodes, a great number of different lists will traverse each individual record. This may result in highly variable record lengths in the file and the maximum block length may be exceeded for those records that are traversed by many pointer chains. As a result, networks are often implemented by transforming the relationship into $1:n$ relationships between a 'node file' and a 'branch file' (see Section 2.4.2). Example 3.3 illustrates the implementation of an oriented network.

EXAMPLE 3.3

Figure 3.5 shows how the finished products P_1 and P_2 are produced by means of the components P_3 and P_4 as well as the raw materials P_5, P_6 and P_7.

Figure 3.6 illustrates the physical implementation of the product file, the branch file and the two $1:n$ relationships. The PRODUCT NUMBER field is shown in the product records. The branch file contains the product numbers of the two product records that it connects, as well as the number of pieces used in the production process. In the left-hand side of the record types, the pointer fields used to implement the 'consists of' relationship, are shown, and likewise in the right-hand side of the record types, the pointer fields used to implement the 'forms a part of' relationship are shown.

If, for example, we are going to search downwards through the structure from product P_4, we can use the 'consists of' relationship to search for the two branch records P_4–P_6 and P_4–P_7. The branch records contain the identifier number of the children P_6 and P_7. These pointers can be used to search for the two child records via a product number entrance to the product file. Similarly, the 'forms part of' relationship can be used to search upwards through the structure.

In network database management systems, such as CODASYL, the network structure can be implemented in the way just described, since a

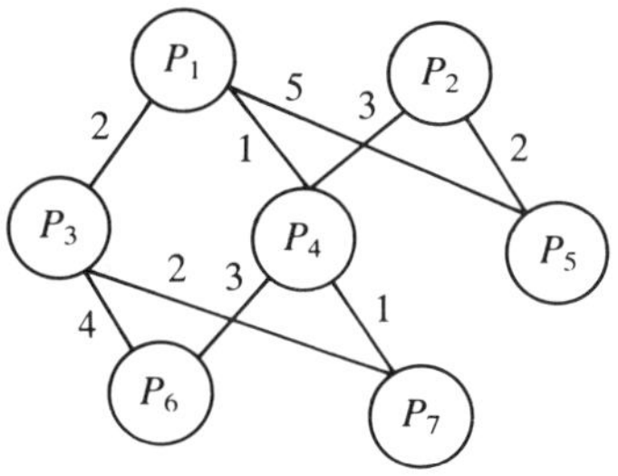

Figure 3.5 Network showing the composition of the finished products P_1 and P_2.

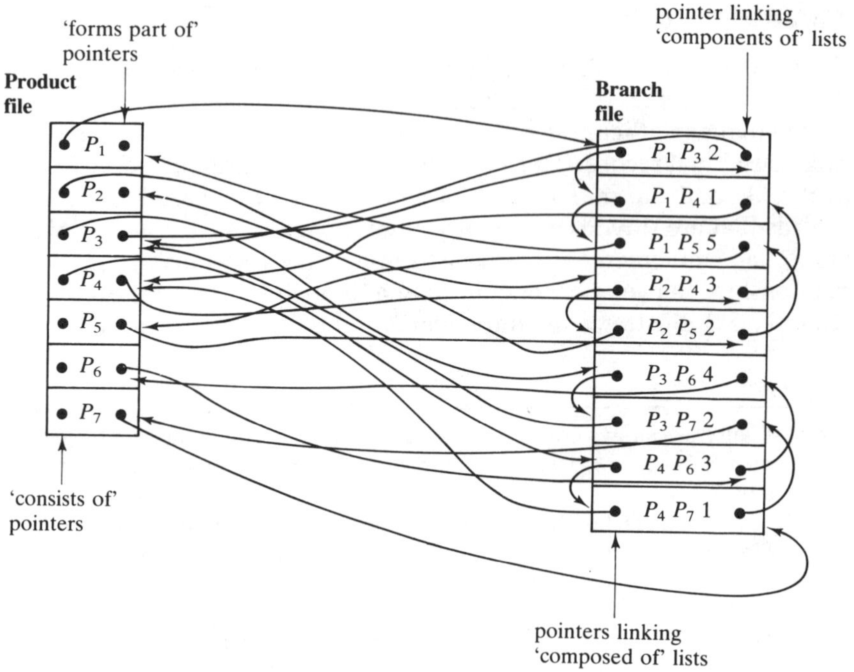

Figure 3.6 The network shown in Figure 3.5 implemented as a product file and a branch file. Each entity in the product file can act as a list head for a list of 'composed of' branches (following the pointers from the left-hand side of the record) or a list of 'component of' branches. A list is terminated by a pointer back to the list head. Note that the finished products (P_1 and P_2) have no 'forms part of' lists, and that, similarly, raw materials do not act as list heads for 'composed of' lists.

record may be a member of more than one $1:n$ relationship. In a hierarchical system, on the other hand, a member record can only be a member in one $1:n$ relationship. If we want to implement the network structure with a hierarchical system, it is therefore necessary to create redundant branch records. This technique is illustrated in Section 4.2.

In the much used system TOTAL, network structures can also be implemented in the way shown in Example 3.3. Unlike CODASYL, TOTAL is limited by the fact that a record serving as a list element (and therefore a member record in a $1:n$ relationship) cannot at the same time serve as list head in another relationship. If we are to implement tree structures with more than two levels in TOTAL, we have to implement them as if they were networks.

Relationships of order *n*

In the previous section, we illustrated a branch file that was traversed by two different lists corresponding to $1:n$ relationships. Relationships of order n can be implemented by letting n different lists traverse the records of the relationship file.

3.2.2 Inverted list organization

All the forms of organization mentioned in Section 3.2.1 on Multilist organization can also be implemented by inverted lists. This is done by removing all the pointer fields from the individual list elements and storing them in the list head instead. To gain faster access to data, the lowest level in a secondary index is frequently used as list head in inverted list organization. To provide space for all the pointers in the list head, it may become necessary to extend the list head with an overflow list.

In what follows, we shall examine how the most important relationship types can be implemented by inverted list database management systems such as ADABAS, DATACOM and SYSTEM 2000. The principal differences between these systems will be mentioned in connection with the description of the methods of implementation for the individual relationship types. The reader should note, however, that the implementation methods mentioned here cannot always be used with an inverted list system. The reason for this is that often inverted list systems are used to construct relational databases. Developments in this direction are spurred on by the fact that suppliers of database software also develop programming languages having the relational, fourth-generation languages as their ideal (see Chapters 12 and 13).

The one-to-many relationship

If we remove all pointers chaining together records with the same owner and store these pointers in the owner record, the result is an inverted list that connects an owner with its member records. The field in the owner record in which the pointers are stored is a **repeating field**. This is normally implemented with variable length because the number of pointers may vary substantially. An owner record may contain several different repeating fields as long as the maximum block length is not exceeded. The physical location of the repeating fields is normally determined by the database management system.

This implementation method can be applied to the ADABAS and DATACOM systems. In SYSTEM 2000, the inverted list head can be stored at the lowest level in an index for the file holding owner records. The advantage of this is that it becomes possible to read member records without first having to read the owner record.

We have just seen how we can get from an owner to its members. The other search direction of the relationship can be implemented by inserting a pointer to the owner in every member record.

Lowest level of the
topics file with the inverted list heads

List heads	Addresses			
⋮				
Africa	A_5	A_{15}	A_{50}	A_{260}
⋮				
Apartheid policy	A_{150}	A_{260}	A_{310}	∞
⋮				
Foreign trade	A_{50}	A_{250}	A_{260}	∞
⋮				
Available record space	A_{10}	A_{300}		

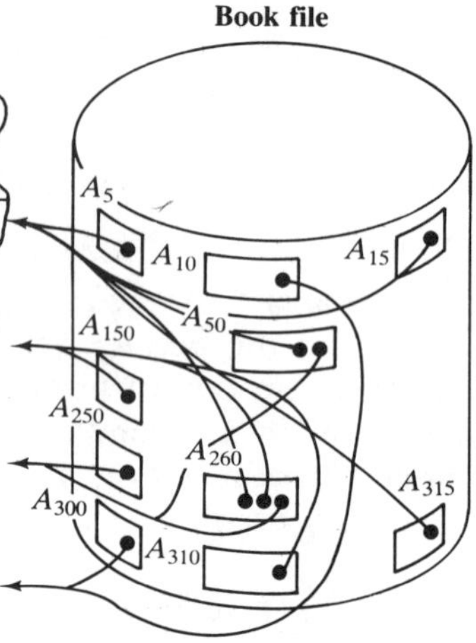

Figure 3.7 The book retrieval system shown in Figure 3.2 implemented using inverted lists.

The many-to-many relationship

In Section 4.2, we shall see two different methods of implementing $n:m$ relationships by means of inverted lists. Example 3.4 outlines yet another method, which can be used in, for example, ADABAS and DATACOM.

EXAMPLE 3.4

Figure 3.7 further illustrates the system used to search for literature, which was introduced in connection with multilist organization in Example 3.2. The $n:m$ relationship existing between topics and books is implemented by inverting the lists described in Example 3.2. In the book record the subjects treated in a book are stored in a repeating field. After that, a secondary index is built over the contents of the repeating field. The building up of such an index is equivalent to storing the inverted lists at the lowest level in the subject index.

The pointers in the individual book records are sorted in ascending order, so that the intersection of a number of lists can be found by merging the pointers in the corresponding lists. As many pointers can be stored in a block, the intersection can be found very quickly. This searching method is therefore much faster than the method described earlier, in which ordinary lists were used.

Trees

SYSTEM 2000 is a hierarchical, inverted list database management system in which all the parent, child and twin pointers can be stored at the bottom level of an index on the root segments of the file. This storage method makes for fast access to an arbitrary level in the tree structure. In ADABAS and DATACOM, the tree structures can be implemented as $1:n$ relationships, placed on top of each other; that is, a parent record contains the pointers to its own child records and its child record contains the pointers to its grandchildren, etc.

The network relationship

By using repeating fields it becomes simple to implement arbitrarily combined network relationships. If data is associated with the branches of the relationship, we have to analyse where it is most convenient to store such data as redundancy will occur if the relationship data is stored in both the nodes connected by a relationship branch.

EXAMPLE 3.5

In Example 3.3 we saw how the production structure shown in Figure 3.5 could be implemented by means of lists. In contrast, Figure 3.8 shows how the relationship can be implemented using inverted lists. Note that product records contains two different repeating fields. The 'consists of' repeating field is used to search downwards through the structure and also stores data about the quantity of the product referred to in the pointer field to be used. The 'forms part of' repeating field is used to search upwards through the production structure.

The contents of the P_4 record are read as follows: The product P_4 is produced by means of three P_6 and one P_7 and the product P_4 enters into the process of production used for the products P_1 and P_2. In Figure 3.8, the repeating fields are empty in a number of cases. ADABAS and DATACOM have solved this problem by data compression, so that empty or partly empty fields do not occupy space in disk storage.

The production structure as illustrated can also be implemented by a single repeating field and a secondary index on the repeating field. This method of implementation is dealt with further in Section 4.2.

Product number	'Consists of' pointers and number of items				'Forms part of' pointers		
P_1	P_3 2	P_4 1	P_5 5	. . .			
P_2	P_4 3	P_5 2					
P_3	P_6 4	P_7 2			P_1		
P_4	P_6 3	P_7 1			P_1	P_2	
P_5					P_1	P_2	
P_6					P_3	P_4	
P_7					P_3	P_4	

Figure 3.8 The network shown in Figure 3.5 implemented as an inverted list structure involving two repeating fields, one for each direction of branching.

Combined queries

Hierarchical secondary indexes, whose bottom level contains inverted lists with pointers to the file itself, are very well suited for the implementation of fourth-generation programming languages. The most characteristic property of this type of language is that the individual statements operate on sets of records. By using logical operators whose arguments may include field values, we can select the records that satisfy the logical selection criterion of the search statement. From these selected records we can search for related records, from amongst which we can select records whose related records we are interested in, etc.

Example 3.6 shows how this type of statement can be executed. The concept of ISN (Internal Sequence Number) is very important for the method of implementation used in this example. ISN numbers are a sequential numbering of all records in a file. Thus, each file has its own ISN numbering. The ISN numbers are used as follows: The bottom level in a secondary index contains an inverted list with ISN numbers of the records that the index points to. By means of an address conversion table, the ISN numbers can be translated into addresses of the corresponding records. The advantage of using ISN numbers and an associated conversion table is that files can be re-organized without having to re-organize their indexes. Another advantage is that it is possible to move a record (for example, due to overflow in a block) without it being necessary to update the various indexes at the same time. It is enough to change just the address of the record in the address conversion table. ISN numbers can also be used to select records satisfying a logical expression.

EXAMPLE 3.6

Figure 3.9 illustrates a physical implementation of the salesman–product database described in Chapter 1 and illustrated in Figure 1.27. It is assumed that the secondary indexes are built on all relevant fields in the various files. Thus, only part of the database is illustrated in the figure.

To search for all salesman records with TOWN = Copenhagen, we can see in the TOWN index that the two records with ISN numbers 3 and 4, respectively, satisfy the requirement. The address conversion table shows that these records are located in block addresses 1 and 2, respectively. To search for all SALESMAN records not associated with Copenhagen, we must use those ISN numbers that serve as the complement for the above-mentioned ISN numbers; that is, records with the ISN numbers 1 and 2, respectively, must be searched for. To search for all SALESMAN records with TOWN = Copenhagen or TOWN = Odense, we must use the ISN numbers found by merging the ISN lists belonging to TOWN = Copenhagen and TOWN = Odense. Note that the merging of the ISN lists is fast because all ISN lists are sorted. To search for the SALESMAN–PRODUCT records related to S_5, this is equivalent to using the SALESMAN index of the SALESMAN–PRODUCT file with SNR = S_5.

(a) **SALESMAN file with associated index**

	ISN	SNR	CODE	TOWN
Block 1	1	S_1	10	Aarhus
	3	S_2	30	Copenhagen
Block 2	2	S_4	20	Odense
	4	S_5	30	Copenhagen

Bottom level in SALESMAN index

SNR	ISN
S_1	1
S_2	3
S_4	2
S_5	4

Address conversion table

ISN	Block Address
1	1
2	2
3	1
4	2

Bottom level in TOWN index

TOWN	ISN
Copenhagen	3 4
Odense	2
Aarhus	1

(b) **SALESMAN PRODUCT file with associated index**

	ISN	SNR	PRODUCT	AMOUNT
Block 1	1	S_2	P_1	200
	2	S_2	P_3	100
Block 2	3	S_4	P_5	200
	4	S_4	P_8	100
Block 3	5	S_5	P_1	50
	6	S_5	P_3	500
Block 4	7	S_5	P_4	200
	8	S_5	P_5	500
Block 5	9	S_5	P_8	100

Bottom level in index

SNR	ISN
S_2	1 2
S_4	3 4
S_5	5 6 7 8 9

Address conversion table

ISN	Block Address
1	1
2	1
3	2
4	2
5	3
6	3
7	4
8	4
9	5

Figure 3.9 The SALESMAN–PRODUCT database introduced in Figure 1.27 showing secondary indexes built up on ISN numbers.

Table 3.1 Implementation of logical operators.

Search criterion	*Description of how the search can be implemented*
p AND q	The ISN lists for p and q are merged, so that a new ISN list is created with the ISN numbers belonging to both p and q.
NOT p	The complement for p's ISN numbers; ie., those ISN numbers in the extraction file not belonging to p.
p AND (NOT q)	p's ISN list is merged with the complement for q's ISN list, as described under AND.
$\exists s : p$	Logical expression that is true if there are records in the file s for which the expression p is true.
$\forall s : p$	Logical expression that is true if there are no ISN numbers in the complement for p's ISN numbers.
Field value constant $\geqslant$	The result is the records whose ISN numbers are retrieved by using the search argument Field value = constant, and all the ISN numbers found by sequential reading from this key value.
Field value constant $\leqslant$	As above, only this time the sequential reading is performed in descending key order.

Table 3.1 contains a survey of how the logical operators in a search strategy can be implemented. The operands p and q are search criteria that are matched by a particular ISN list. Thus, p may be an expression such as TOWN = Copenhagen.

3.2.3 Multilist organization versus inverted list organization

Inverted list organization has some important advantages over multilist organization:

- If the inverted lists are stored at the bottom level in an index, the result corresponding to a logical search expression can be calculated on the basis of the list elements.
- Inverted list organization often requires shorter search times because fewer records are to be searched for.
- If ISN numbers are used a file can be re-organized without it being necessary to re-organize the index and the lists.

However, the use of inverted list organization does have the following drawbacks:

- If the inverted lists are stored in the individual records, overflow may occur because a record may exceed the block size. Normally, the database management system cannot solve this problem. In the case of multilist organization, the various relationship types can be implemented by using files with fixed record lengths.

- If the inverted lists are stored at the bottom level in an index, overflow may occur in the index blocks. This is not a serious problem, as normally steps to deal with it will be taken automatically by the database system.

3.2.4 Clustering

Clustering means that records related to each other are stored physically beside each other. It is especially used in the various forms of list organization, because these organizations make no demands on where the individual records are located physically. Clustering can be used in the implementation of hierarchical relationships in which the individual records are physically loaded sequentially in preorder at the same time as the lists are built up. If a suitable loading factor is used and if regular reorganizations are performed, child or member records will probably be physically stored immediately after their parent or owner record.

In practice, it will often be necessary to carry out a considerable amount of analysis to find the best possible form of clustering in a database with many files and relationships. In deciding on the form of clustering to be used, the following factors have to be examined:

- If the member record has more than one different owner, care must be exercised in deciding which owner type it will be best to group the member records under.
- If the owners need to be processed sequentially, an estimate has to be made of the additional costs of doing so. These additional costs are caused by the fact that the distance between the owners is greater because member records are inserted between them.
- The amount of direct access to the root segments of the file will probably increase. If we have a case of random organization this is due to the fact that the blocking factor of the root segments is lower because space must be made available for member records in a block (see Section 2.3.3). In the case of hierarchical primary indexes the search length also increases because the number of blocks in the file increases as there has to be available space for member records (see Section 2.4.1).
- If some of the fields in a record are only occupied very rarely, it is necessary to examine whether they should be stored in a separate file. By doing so, we get the advantage that the original file can be processed faster, both sequentially and directly (see earlier).

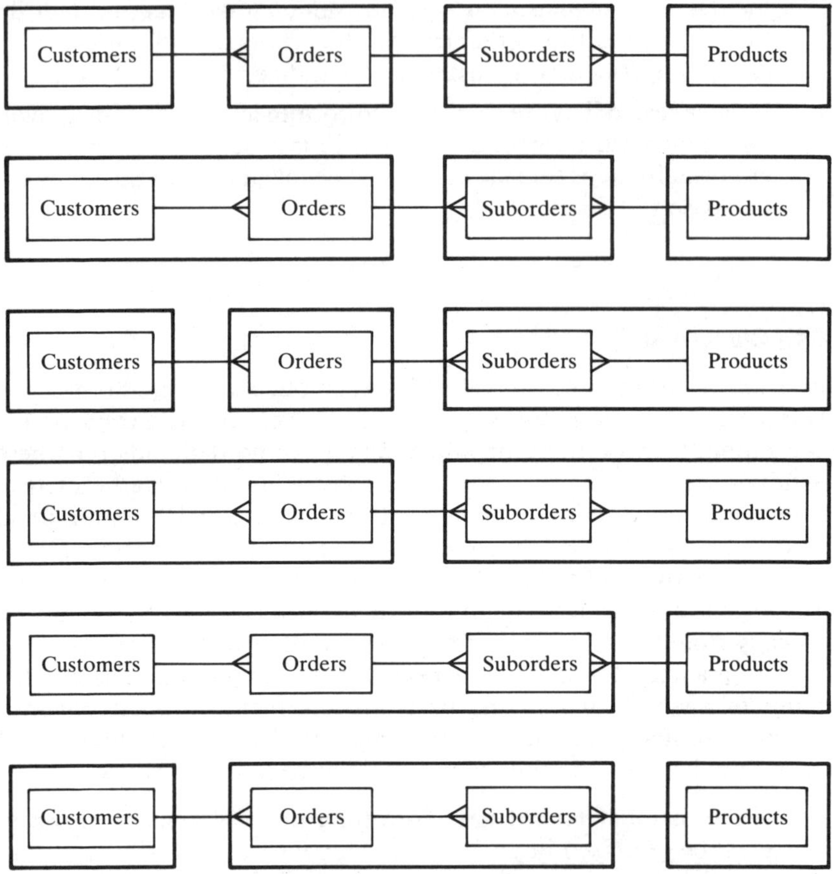

Figure 3.10 Possible ways of clustering customers, orders, suborders and products. The heavy lines enclose a clustering of files.

EXAMPLE 3.7

The connection between customers, orders, suborders and products, which has been used many times already as an example, can be clustered in many different ways. Figure 3.10 shows the various possibilities of grouping. The outer boxes represent physical files, whereas the inner boxes represent logical files, which contain one record type only.

If the aim is to construct the best possible physical database, we have, in addition to the suggestions for a solution, to examine whether it would be worthwhile to split some of the record types in order to store fields that are rarely occupied in a separate file.

Clustering is a storage technique and not an organization. It is often combined with a primary organization for the root segments while the subtrees of the root segments are stored in preorder after the root segment. In many database systems, it is only possible to read the nodes of the tree structure via the root. This may be an important argument against the use of clustering because it can be very difficult and irksome to search for the nodes of the root's subtrees if the key of the root is unknown.

EXAMPLE 3.8

It is assumed here that we have a database management system in which the nodes in a clustered hierarchy can be read by means of the root segments. If the hierarchy that exists between customers and orders is clustered, it is irksome to search for a specific order if the CUSTOMER NUMBER is unknown. One way of solving this problem is to create a redundant order file, which, for each order, contains the corresponding CUSTOMER NUMBER. By means of this CUSTOMER NUMBER, it is now possible to search for the real order record. In the situation just set out it will rarely be worthwhile to use clustering. It ought, therefore, to be possible to build up secondary indexes on the various record types making up a tree structure.

As the work of analysis required to find the best possible physical database is very comprehensive, it is often restricted in practice to examining the most promising alternatives. If we use a system with data independence – which makes the application programmes independent of the physical database – we can experiment with the physical organization of the database at a later stage and thus try to optimize it.

3.3 Sequential organization versus direct organization and list organization

We saw in Section 2.2 that the searches of practically all relationship types can be implemented by sequential organization, sorting and merging. In this section, we compare the implementation of relationships by sequential organization with similar implementations by **addressed organization**. Addressed organization is used as a collective term for the direct search possibilities provided by random, indexed and list organization. This comparison will, in most cases, only be interesting in connection with large numbers or searches, which are frequently performed in connection with batch runs.

In what follows, we will use examples to analyse, first, the use of capacity in non-multiprogrammed computers. Next, we will analyse the use of capacity in multiprogrammed computers. Finally, we will derive some general rules for choosing between sequential organization and addressed organization.

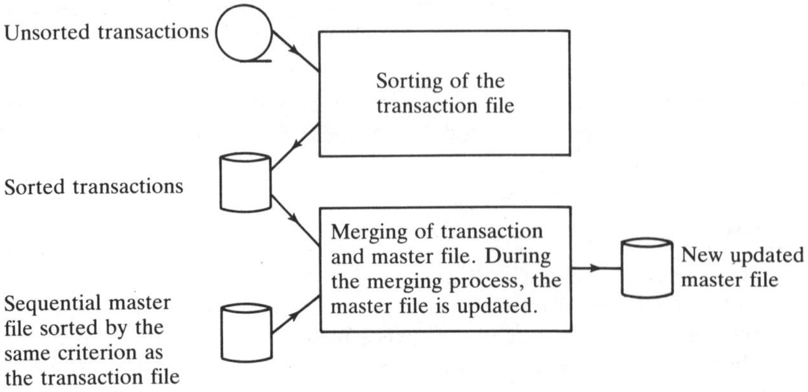

Figure 3.11 System flowchart for an update program for a sequentially organized file.

3.3.1 Use of capacity in non-multiprogrammed computers

For non-multiprogrammed computers, we can use the run time of a program as a measure of its use of capacity. Thus, in this section, we will compare the run time of update programs whose master file has sequential and direct organization, respectively.

If the master file has sequential organization, the update program can be constructed as illustrated in the system diagram shown in Figure 3.11. If the fastest sorting methods are used, the sorting time will increase progressively with the number of transactions, as illustrated in Figure 3.12 (see the sorting equations in Appendix B).

The update activity, during which the transaction file is merged with the master file, is usually characterized by simultaneity between the transaction file, the master file and the central processing unit (CPU).

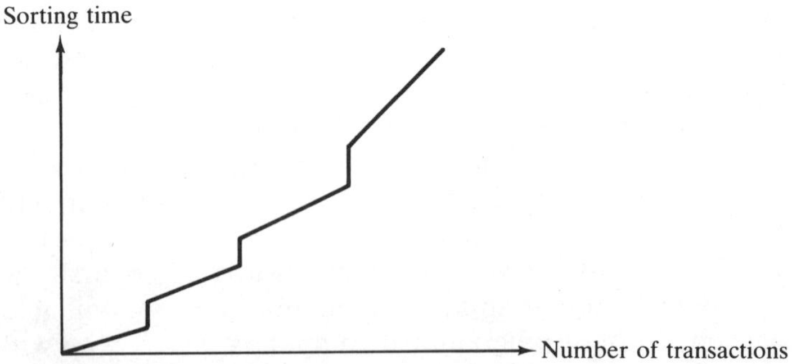

Figure 3.12 Graph of sorting time against the number of transactions in the transaction file.

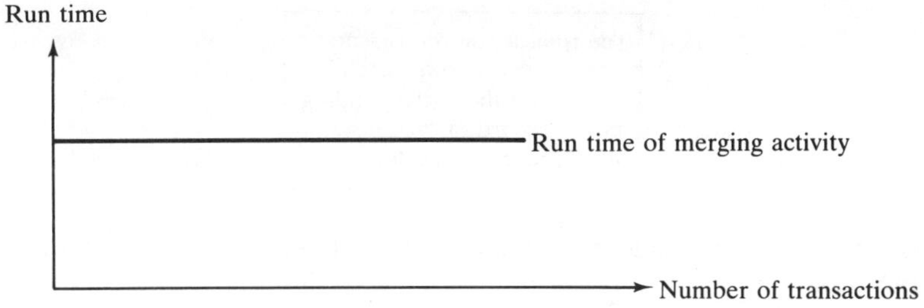

Figure 3.13 Graph of the run time of merging the transaction file with the master file against the number of transactions in the transaction file.

This means that the run time per transaction of the merging activity is independent of the number of transactions, as the master file is normally larger than the transaction file. Figure 3.13 shows the run time of the merging activity as a function of the number of transactions. The total run time of the update program as a function of the number of transactions can be calculated by combining the preceding figures, as shown in Figure 3.14.

If the master file has direct organization, the update program can be constructed as illustrated in the system diagram of Figure 3.15. It is relatively easy to prove that the run time for this update program is proportional to the number of transactions, as all the individual transactions are processed in the same way. Figure 3.16 illustrates that

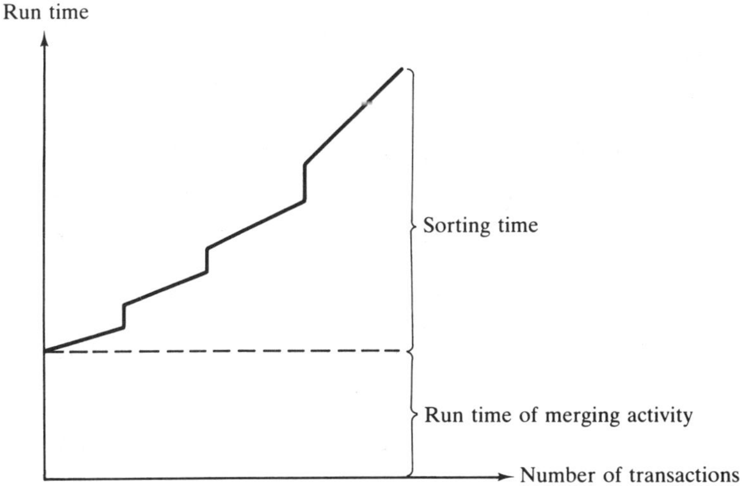

Figure 3.14 Graph of the total run time of the update process shown in Figure 3.11 against the number of transactions involved.

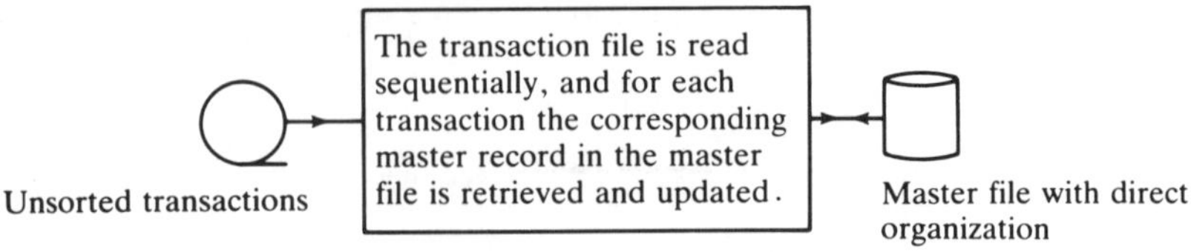

Figure 3.15 System diagram for an update program for a file with direct organization.

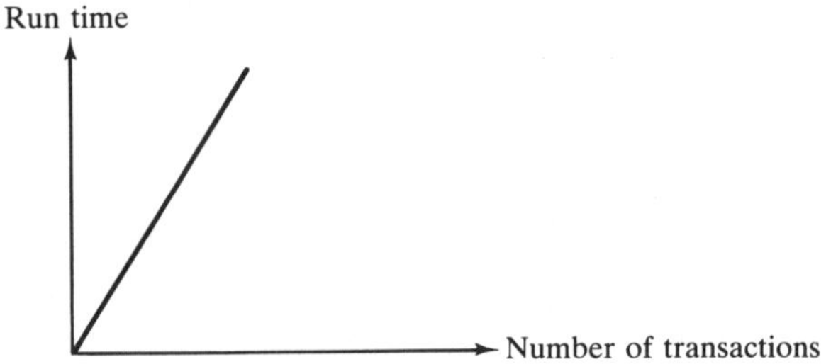

Figure 3.16 Graph of the total run time of the update process shown in Figure 3.15 against the number of transactions involved.

the run time for direct updating is proportional to the number of transactions.

Figure 3.17 illustrates the run time for the two update programs as a function of the number of transactions. It appears from this figure that the sequential updating method is fastest if there are relatively many transactions, while the direct updating method is fastest if there are relatively few transactions.

3.3.2 Use of capacity in multiprogrammed computers

Appendix B shows that it is practicable to use the work load on the individual units as a multidimensional measure of the use of capacity in running programs on a multiprogrammed computer. In view of the analysis presented there, we assume that either the CPU or disk storage is the bottleneck in a multiprogrammed computer, since although the CPU is a scarce factor, the work load on the disk storage may be more important because it normally has a greater influence on the response time. Taking these two cost factors as our starting point, we can analyse the use of capacity of the sequential and the direct update method as functions of the number of transactions:

- Assume that there is relatively small number of transactions and that disk storage is the scarce factor. In such a case, a solution

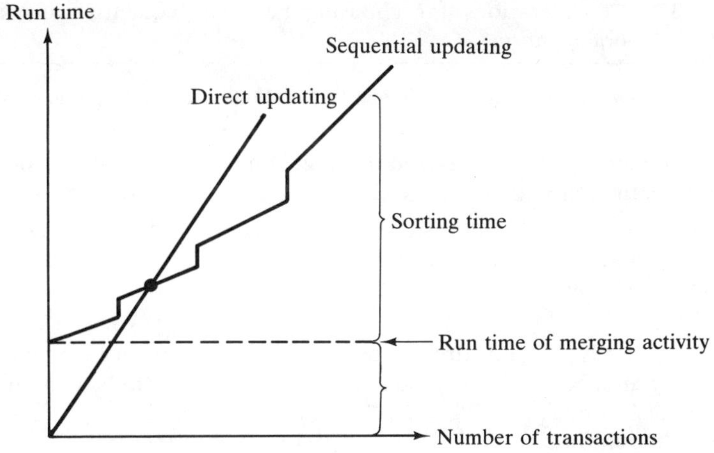

Figure 3.17 Comparison of update times in sequentially and directly organized files.

based on a file with direct organization should be chosen because the work load on the disk storage is proportional to the number of transactions, which is small.

- Assume that there is a relatively small number of transactions and that the CPU is the scarce factor of the multiprogrammed computer. In this case, too, a solution based on a file with direct organization should be chosen because the work load on the CPU caused by direct organization is proportional to the number of transactions. If sequential update is applied, the work load on the CPU during the merging stage will be proportional to the number of records in the relatively large master file.
- Assume that there is a relatively large number of transactions and that the disk storage is the scarce factor of the multiprogrammed computer. In this case, a solution based on a file with sequential organization should be chosen because the run time of the program, due to simultaneity, is equal to the work load on the disk storage, and because the run time, as shown in Section 3.3.1, is shortest if sequential organization is used.
- Assume that there is a relatively large number of transactions and that the CPU is the scarce factor. In this case, a solution based on direct organization should be chosen because:

  (1) During the sorting of a relatively large file, the CPU is relatively hard pressed so that sorting should be avoided.

  (2) In the case of direct update, the work load on the CPU is directly proportional to the number of transactions. During the

Table 3.2 Considerations for choosing between sequential and addressed organization.

Considerations	*Relatively few transactions*	*Relatively more transactions*
The computer is not multiprogrammed	Addressed organization should be chosen	Sequential organization should be chosen
The computer is multiprogrammed and the CPU is a scarce factor	Addressed organization should be chosen	Addressed organization should be chosen
The computer is multiprogrammed and the disk storage and/or the run time is a scarce factor	Addressed organization should be chosen	Sequential organization should be chosen

sequential merging of the transaction file and the master file, the work load on the CPU is almost proportional to the sum of the number of transactions and the number of master records. The work load on the CPU will therefore normally be smallest in the case of direct update, although there are relatively more transactions.

3.3.3 Which organization should be chosen?

We saw in Section 2.2 that if we use sequential organization the retrieval of information corresponding to the different relationship types could be implemented by splitting, sorting and merging of sequential files. In Sections 2.4.2 and 3.2 we saw that in the case of addressed organization the same relationships could be implemented by list organization or direct organization. On the basis of the examples given in this section, we can now assess when capacity considerations make it practical to choose sequential organization or addressed organization.

The results of these considerations are shown in Table 3.2. This table only gives rough guidance as to the choice between sequential and addressed access methods. Faced with a concrete choice, it may be necessary to use the equations given in Appendix B to decide which access method to choose. However, it should be emphasized that such an analysis is static. Some of the factors that should be considered before the choice of access method is made are as follows:

- Under normal circumstances, the expansion of the capacity of the scarce units leads to an expansion of the capacity of a multi-programmed computer. This may lead to these units no longer being scarce.
- The average number of transactions per program run may increase by having the individual programs process more transactions due, for example, to the growth of the firm.
- Disk storage that at present is not a bottleneck may later turn into one because the idea of using a database is that new programs can make use of the old files.
- CPU capacity, main storage space and disk storage space may partly replace each other and change any bottlenecks that may occur.

3.4 Random organization versus index organization

3.4.1 Comparison of primary organizations

If fast reading in key sequence is required, a primary organization with a hierarchical index, which also allows sequential processing in key sequence, should be chosen. If main storage can only hold a relatively small proportion of the index, direct searches will be fastest with random organization. Random organization used as primary organization is, however, very sensitive to pronounced growth in the number of records in the file. On the other hand, *B*-trees will be rather insensitive to such growth in the number of records.

3.4.2 Comparison of secondary organizations

It is possible to read a file in key sequence by means of a secondary hierarchical index. In the case of large files, however, it is faster to sort the entire file. Hierarchical secondary indexes are particularly suited to reading relatively few records in key sequence (see Example 2.19 on the implementation of the $n:m$ relationship in Section 2.4.3).

If the index can be held in main storage, a hierarchical index and a randomly organized index involve almost identical search lengths if a direct search is used. In the case of large hierarchical indexes, particularly where no more than one level of the index can be held in main storage, the randomly organized index involves a shorter search length than the hierarchical index. Static, secondary indexes are very sensitive to a marked growth in the number of records in the file. By using *B*-trees it is possible, however, to construct both dynamic randomly organized secondary indexes and dynamic hierarchical secondary indexes that are not sensitive to the growth of the number of records in this way.

3.5 Direct organization versus list organization

Section 2.4.2 and Section 4.2 show how all the relationship types introduced in Chapter 1 could be implemented with both direct and list organizations. Table 3.3 presents a crude comparison between list organizations and the corresponding direct organizations. The comparison applies to all the relationship types. In the case of the network relationship and the $n : m$ relationship, it is assumed that the relationship is implemented by $1 : n$ relationships, whereas the two relationships can be implemented directly in the case of list organization. This method of implementation is normally faster than transforming the relationship into $1 : n$ relationships. A more detailed comparison, if required, can be performed by calculating the search lengths in actual files.

If list organization is used, neither an index nor a low loading factor is needed to be able to implement relationships. The use of list organization, therefore, requires very little space for the implementation of relationships. If list organization with physical pointers is used, however, it is necessary, in practice, to reserve extra storage space for a redundant implementation of the relationship by means of logical pointers. Such a redundant implementation is practical for re-organizing the file and for recovery after certain types of error. In practice, therefore,

Table 3.3 Comparison between direct and list organizations.

Direct organization / ***List organization***	*Direct organization with secondary key, corresponding to clustering*	*Direct organization with primary key, corresponding to clustering*
List organization with physical pointers and without clustering	List organization is fastest	Direct organization is fastest
List organization with physical pointers and clustering	List organization is fastest	List organization is fastest
List organization with logical pointers and without clustering – the use of logical pointers assumes that the file also has direct organization	Direct organization is fastest	Direct organization is fastest

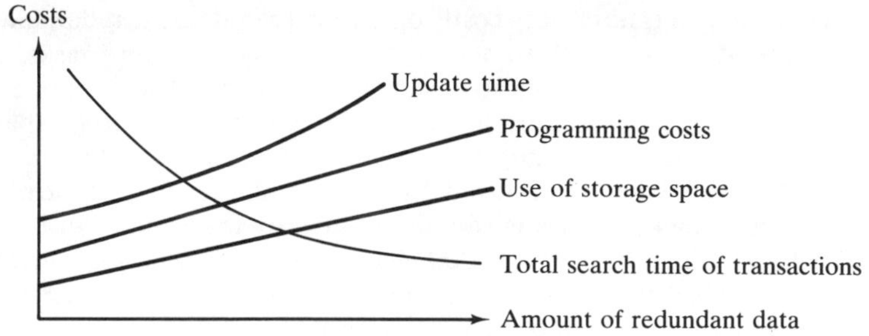

Figure 3.18 Relationship between costs and redundancy in the data. All costs except search time increase with added redundancy.

we in fact have to calculate the actual storage space required to decide which organization is the best.

3.6 Optimization by redundancy

Database techniques make it possible to construct a database without redundant data. However, there are both advantages and disadvantages associated with redundancy. This is illustrated in Figure 3.18, which demonstrates the fundamental connection between certain types of data processing costs and the amount of redundant data.

Obviously, the use of storage space and the update time increase with the amount of redundant data. There is also a tendency for the programming costs to increase, as the redundant data must be maintained and the database may be rendered less flexible for future tasks. There is, on the other hand, a tendency for the total search time of the transactions to decrease if redundancy is used. One reason for this is that the redundant data can be stored where the transactions need it. Example 3.9 examines those situations where it pays to maintain redundancy, while Example 3.10 demonstrates the opposite situation.

EXAMPLE 3.9

A bank has a customer file and an account file. If a customer dies or goes bankrupt, this fact is normally recorded, so that the customer's accounts are blocked. Data about the death or bankruptcy of the customer naturally belongs in the customer record. However, this data is useful primarily in the account file to stop payments being made from the customer's account quickly. If the data is not stored redundantly in the account file, it will be necessary, before payments are made, to look up the customer file to check whether the customer is alive, solvent, etc. As there are relatively few instances of death or bankruptcy among the customers, it is not a very costly operation to update the redundant data in the account file. With a view to flexibility for future tasks, it will probably be a good idea also to store the redundant data in the customer record where it naturally belongs. The extra use of storage space for redundant data is negligible. Assume, for example, that there are 100 000 customer records and 200 000 account records. If the code for deaths or bankruptcies is stored redundantly in the account record, it will cost an additional 200 000 characters, and it will not increase the run time substantially. If the code for deaths or bankruptcies is not stored redundantly in the account record, and if there are an average of five debit transactions per account per month, it will require 1 million additional look-ups per month to check whether an account can be debited.

EXAMPLE 3.10

Should the name and address of a supplier be stored as a field in all product records or is it necessary to create an independent supplier file, so that the name and address of each supplier are only stored once? As will be seen from the following, the size of the product file will often be of great importance in making such a decision.

If the record must provide space for the largest possible name and address of a supplier, these fields together will occupy quite a large share of the file's total storage space. If we have a product file of 10 000 records and if 'name and address' occupy 120 characters, these fields will occupy a total of 1 200 000 characters. If the firm has, say, 100 suppliers, the 'supplier's name and address' can be replaced by a double-digit number in the product record, and by a supplier file, in which each record contains the supplier number as well as the supplier's name and address. The supplier file will only occupy $100 \times (120 + 2) = 12\,200$ characters, or approximately 1/100 of the 1 200 000 characters.

Compared with the number of times the contents of the product record is needed, the supplier's name and address are needed relatively few times. Thus, the additional run time caused by searching a supplier file is not a decisive factor. Moreover, if the supplier's name and address are stored in the product record, this may cause the invoicing program to run more slowly because superfluous data about the supplier's name and address is 'carried along'.

EXERCISES

3.1 Assume that a file has random organization and that the overflow problem has been solved by means of lists. There is only room for the list heads in the main storage of the computer. The file contains 10 000 records and about 3000 list heads are used. For the sake of clarity, these figures have been reduced by a factor of 1000 in Figure 3.19. In addition,

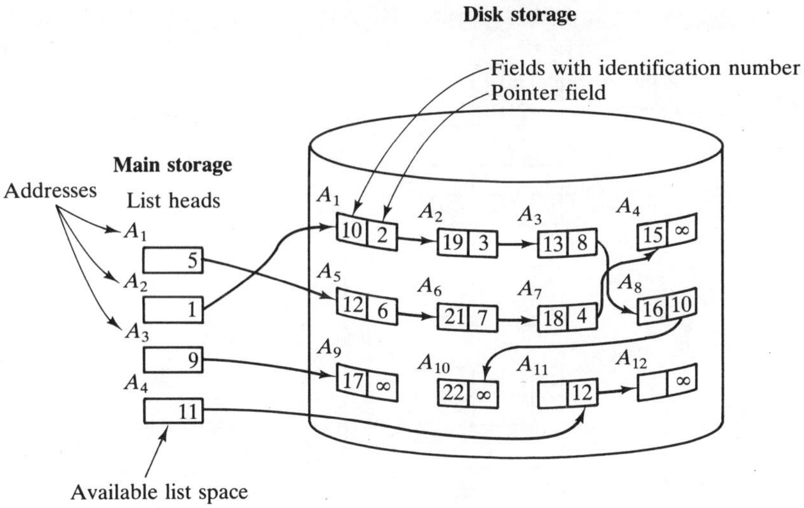

Figure 3.19 File with random organization using lists for overflow.

only the identification number and the pointer field are shown in the figure. A record's identification number is transformed to an address on a list head as follows:

$$\text{Address} = (\text{identification number modulo } 3) + 1$$

Carry out the changes that an updating program has to execute for the following transactions:

(a) Delete RECORD 16

(b) Create RECORD 25

(c) Create RECORD 24

(d) Delete RECORD 17

3.2 In Figure 3.20, the file introduced in Exercise 3.1 is organized in such a way that the overflow problem is solved by means of inverted lists. To avoid variable record lengths for the list heads, each list head is built up as a list that chains list head records together. In the figure, a list head record can contain four double fields. Each double field contains a disk storage address and the identification of the corresponding record. Additionally, there is a field that is used to point to the next list head record. Carry out the changes that an updating program has to execute for the following transactions:

(a) Delete RECORD 16

(b) Create RECORD 3

(c) Create RECORD 6

(d) Delete RECORD 17

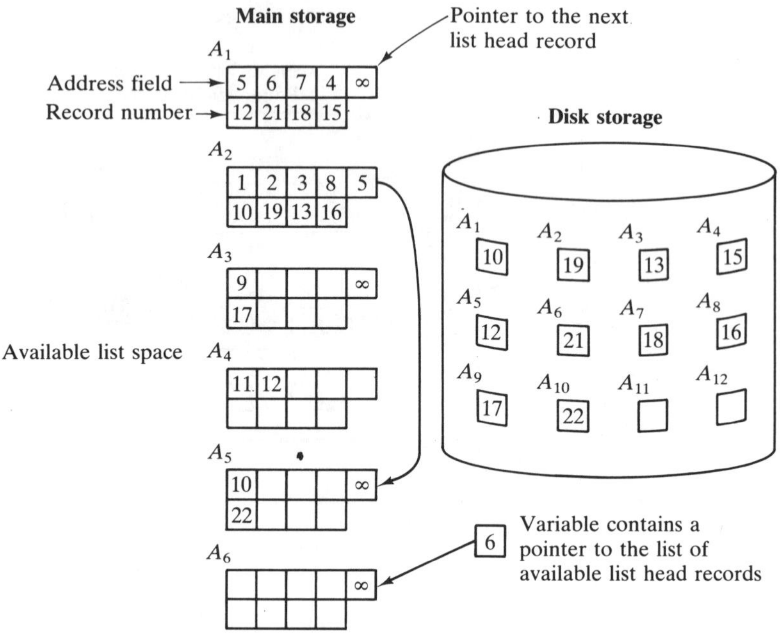

Figure 3.20 File with randomly organized index.

3.3 A file that takes up one entire IBM 3380 disk contains records with a length of 428 bytes. For the production of security copies, magnetic tapes have the technical specifications outlined in Appendix G.

(a) How many magnetic tapes does the security copy take up if the same block size is used on magnetic tapes as on disk storage?

(b) How many magnetic tapes does the security copy take up if, at the magnetic tape unit, the most space-saving block size is used?

(c) What is the work time of the disk storage and the magnetic tape unit, respectively, for copying the disk storage?

(d) How long will the security copying take if it is executed at night, after the daily production is finished?

(e) How long will the security copying take if it is executed during the daytime while on-line queries on the file are being made?

(f) What is the minimum time taken to load the security copy during a recovery operation when other systems, not affected by the recovery, are active?

3.4 A library runs its programs on a computer with the following external units:

- ten disk units
- six magnetic tape units

Field Name	Field Description	Number of Characters
BOOK NUMBER	Number identifying the book	8
TITLE	Title of the book	40
BORROWER NUMBER	Number of the borrower who has the book at present: this field has the value 0 if the book is not lent out	6
DATE	Date and time of last loan	10
AUTHOR1	Name of the author: if the book has more than one author, the following fields are used, as there is a variable record length for book records	30
AUTHOR2 ⋮	If there is more than one author, this field is used for the name of the second author	30
	On average, there is 1.2 author per book; consequently, the average record length will be:	100 characters

Figure 3.21 Library database: fields in a book record.

- one line printer, which can print 1600 lines per minute

The computer is multiprogrammed and 50 K bytes of main storage can be used for sorting buffers. The library has a file of all its books. There are 200 000 records in the file. Each book record comprises the fields shown in Figure 3.21. The book file is stored on magnetic tapes. Once a year the book file is used to print index card files, which can be used by borrowers searching for books manually. An index card can hold eight lines. The system flowchart shown in Figure 3.22 illustrates how the library has a manual file printed, in which the index cards are sorted by book titles. Note that it is necessary to start the flowchart by sorting by TITLE because book files are normally sorted by BOOK NUMBER.

(a) Outline by means of a system flowchart how a manual book file may be printed in which the index cards are primarily sorted by author and secondarily by title, so that if an author has written more than one book, then the index cards are sorted by TITLE. In addition, if a book has been written by more than one author, there must be index cards for each of the authors. Estimate the run time assuming that the program is run with first priority.

The library has a file of borrowers. There are 50 000 borrowers and each borrower record contains the fields shown in Figure 3.23. When a borrower wants to take out or return a book, the data on each book, shown

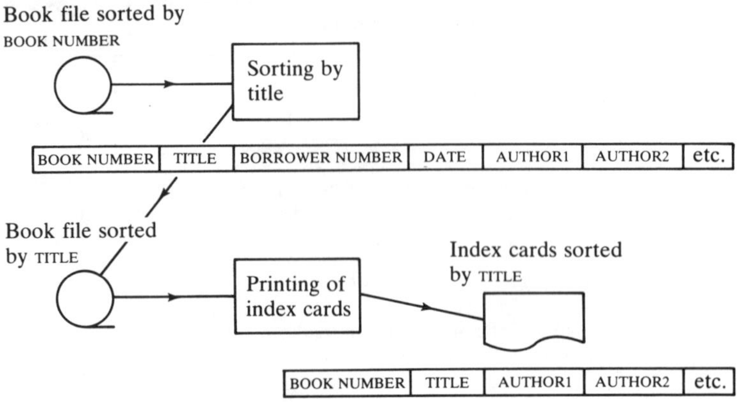

Figure 3.22 Library database: system design for the production of a manual book index printed on index cards.

in Figure 3.24, will be recorded. The system flowchart shown in Figure 3.25 illustrates how, once a week, the library runs a program to update the fields BORROWER NUMBER and DATE in the book file, and which prints overdue notices to borrowers who have not returned a book at the appointed time. Every week there are an average of 5000 transactions concerning books lent out and books returned, and about 100 overdue notices of eight lines each are printed. An average of 10 000 books are lent out. As shown in the system flowchart, both the book file and the borrower file are stored on magnetic tapes. The management of the library is considering building up a modern library system, which makes on-line searching for literature possible. In the following questions it is assumed that a normalized database without redundancy is used. That is, the database must include amongst others the following files:

- a file of the physical books;
- a file of book types (on average the library has two physical copies of each book type);

Field Name	Field Description	Number of Characters
BORROWER NUMBER	Number identifying the borrower	6
ADDRESS	Name and address of the borrower	94
	The record length will be:	100 characters

Figure 3.23 Library database: fields in a borrower record.

Field Name	Field description	Number of Characters
BORROWER NUMBER	Number of the borrower	6
BOOK NUMBER	Number of the borrowed book	8
DATE	Date and time of lending out and return, respectively	10
CODE	Contents of this field indicate whether a book is lent out or returned	1
	The record length for transaction records will be:	25 characters

Figure 3.24 Library database: data recorded when a borrower takes out or returns a book.

- a borrower file;
- an author file;
- a subject file.

When choosing an organization for the files, the on-line queries are to be given a higher priority than the requirements of the batch programs. To answer the following questions, assume that (i) a hierarchical, (ii) a network, and (iii) an inverted list database management system is used. It is particularly important to make use of these systems' individual file structures as described in Section 4.2. In the case of inverted list systems, you may only use repeating fields if you are sure that the maximum block size or record length will not be exceeded.

(b) Outline by means of a system flowchart how the recording of books returned and lent out can be performed. Estimate the run time.

(c) Outline by means of a system flowchart how overdue notices can be produced. Estimate the run time.

(d) What is the average work time required for disk storage when searching for books with a given title if there is an average of 1.2 books with the same title?

(e) What is the average work time required for disk storage when searching for books written by a given author or co-author? Authors have written an average of three books.

(f) What is the average work time required for disk storage when searching for books dealing with two different subjects? On average, such a search will result in 20 different book types.

(g) Assume that a book can be found uniquely by means of an author name and two different subjects. What is the work time required for disk storage for such a book type?

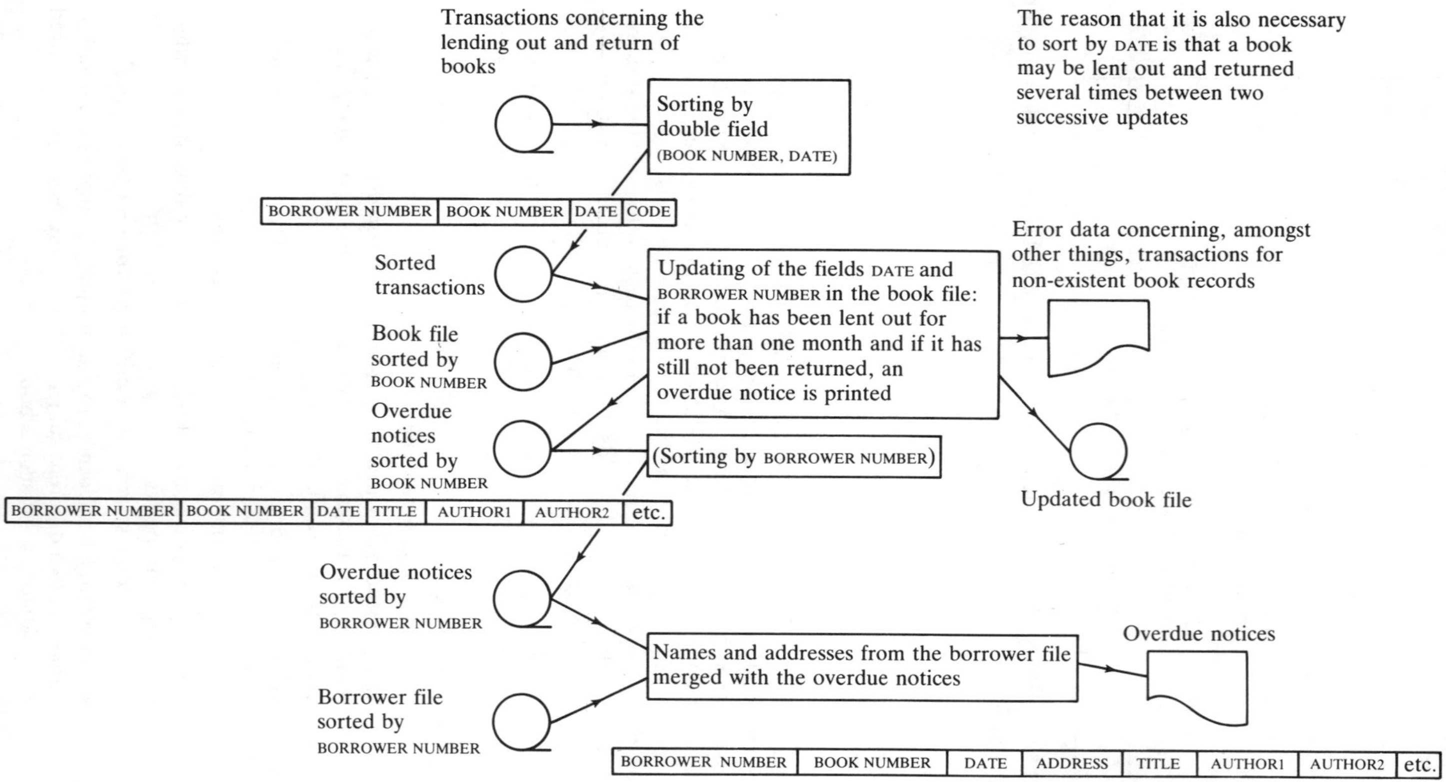

Figure 3.25 Library database: system flowchart of a weekly update that inserts BORROWER NUMBER and DATE in the book file, checks for overdue books and prints overdue notices.

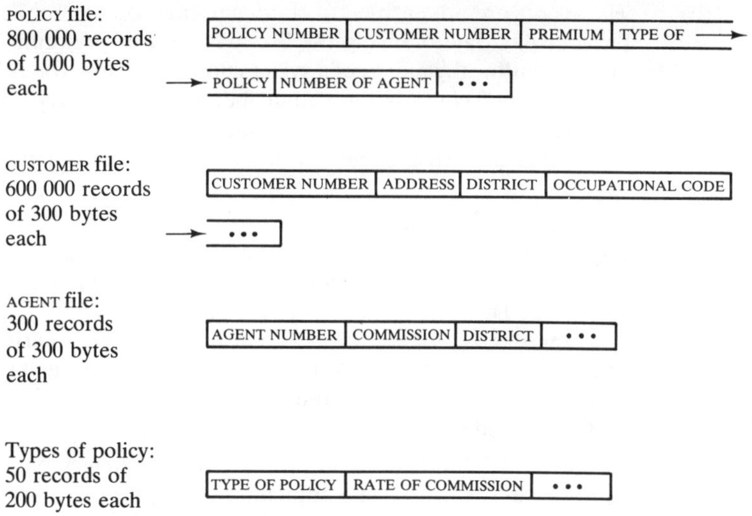

Figure 3.26 Relational model of an insurance database.

3.5 An insurance company has a multiprogrammed computer with disk storages connected to it. Figure 3.26 is a relational model of a section of the insurance company's database. The files in the figure satisfy all normal forms. For all files, the first field contains a unique identification key for the records of the file. A policy can only be written by one agent. For each new policy, the agent receives commission, which is dependent upon the size of the premium and the rate of commission stored in the types of policy file. The commission accruing to the agents is added to the COMMISSION field, which is set at zero when the commission has been paid to the agents after the monthly wages have been run. When choosing an organization for the files, the on-line queries are to be given higher priority than the requirements for file organization of the batch programs. However, this does not apply to the large quarterly runs mentioned in part (a) – it has to be possible to perform these runs during the night. To answer the following questions, assume that you use (i) a hierarchical, (ii) a network and (iii) an inverted list database management system. It is particularly important that you make use of these systems' individual file structures, as described in Section 4.2. In the case of inverted list systems, you may only use repeating fields if you are sure that the maximum block size or record length will not be exceeded.

(a) Collections of policy payments are printed every day. These batch runs normally contain a maximum of 10 000 collections. Once every quarter, policy collections are printed, comprising about 600 000 policy collections. Outline, by means of a system flowchart, how you propose to build up a system that processes ingoing payments and the printing of collections. Estimate the run time.

(b) The agents are not entitled to claim commission on a policy until the first pay day following the first payment of premium on the policy. Outline, by means of a system flowchart, how you think the calculation of commission should be effected. Estimate the additional work required for disk storage caused by the calculation of commission. An average of 1000 new policies are written every day.

(c) The customers are divided into 100 districts and 200 different occupational codes or company codes. Assume that in a given district there are 200 customers with a given occupational code. Of these, 20 have not taken out a particular type of policy. Outline how these customers can be found by on-line queries, and calculate the work time required for disk storage for such queries. Your solution must show the most practical way of indexing customers and policies.

(d) At the end of the accounting year, the management of the company needs to know the total amount of premium income per district. Outline how this calculation can be performed and calculate the additional work time required for disk storage.

3.6 A bank wants to build up a real-time system of 1 000 000 accounts of an average 3000 bytes. One account number occupies 10 bytes. This large record length is due to the large number of fields designed to collect statistical data: it has to be possible to regulate the computation of interest since cheques cannot be cleared on the same day as they have been drawn. During peak hours the system must be able to process 50 updating transactions per second. An average of 200 000 transactions are processed every day, but on busy days there may be up to about 600 000 real-time updates. To be able to process this large number of transactions, it has been decided to organize the file randomly and to solve the overflow problem by means of linear open overflow.

(a) Assume that IBM 3380 disks are used for storage and that a maximum 60 K bytes can be allocated for buffers in main storage. What block size would you choose?

(b) How many disk units does the file occupy if a block size of 15 479 bytes is used (see the storage table in Appendix G) and the loading factor is 0.7?

(c) Assume that the physical record length can be reduced by 40% by means of data compression. How much space does this save in main storage and disk storage if the block size remains the same and the blocking factor, the loading factor and the number of buffers cannot be changed, so that the updating time is increased or the capacity of the system is reduced?

(d) Assume that the individual disk storage units work simultaneously. On how many disk storage units will it be necessary to distribute the file, if the system must be able to cope with the peak load of 600 000 real-time updates?

POLICY file:
800 000 records of 1000 bytes each

POLICY NUMBER	CUSTOMER NUMBER	PREMIUM	TYPE OF POLICY	NUMBER OF AGENT	• • •

CUSTOMER file:
600 000 records of 300 bytes each

CUSTOMER NUMBER	ADDRESS	DISTRICT	OCCUPATIONAL CODE	• • •

AGENT file:
300 records of 300 bytes each

AGENT NUMBER	COMMISSION	DISTRICT	• • •

Types of policy:
50 records of 200 bytes each

TYPE OF POLICY	RATE OF COMMISSION	• • •

Figure 3.26 Relational model of an insurance database.

3.5 An insurance company has a multiprogrammed computer with disk storages connected to it. Figure 3.26 is a relational model of a section of the insurance company's database. The files in the figure satisfy all normal forms. For all files, the first field contains a unique identification key for the records of the file. A policy can only be written by one agent. For each new policy, the agent receives commission, which is dependent upon the size of the premium and the rate of commission stored in the types of policy file. The commission accruing to the agents is added to the COMMISSION field, which is set at zero when the commission has been paid to the agents after the monthly wages have been run. When choosing an organization for the files, the on-line queries are to be given higher priority than the requirements for file organization of the batch programs. However, this does not apply to the large quarterly runs mentioned in part (a) – it has to be possible to perform these runs during the night. To answer the following questions, assume that you use (i) a hierarchical, (ii) a network and (iii) an inverted list database management system. It is particularly important that you make use of these systems' individual file structures, as described in Section 4.2. In the case of inverted list systems, you may only use repeating fields if you are sure that the maximum block size or record length will not be exceeded.

(a) Collections of policy payments are printed every day. These batch runs normally contain a maximum of 10 000 collections. Once every quarter, policy collections are printed, comprising about 600 000 policy collections. Outline, by means of a system flowchart, how you propose to build up a system that processes ingoing payments and the printing of collections. Estimate the run time.

(b) The agents are not entitled to claim commission on a policy until the first pay day following the first payment of premium on the policy. Outline, by means of a system flowchart, how you think the calculation of commission should be effected. Estimate the additional work required for disk storage caused by the calculation of commission. An average of 1000 new policies are written every day.

(c) The customers are divided into 100 districts and 200 different occupational codes or company codes. Assume that in a given district there are 200 customers with a given occupational code. Of these, 20 have not taken out a particular type of policy. Outline how these customers can be found by on-line queries, and calculate the work time required for disk storage for such queries. Your solution must show the most practical way of indexing customers and policies.

(d) At the end of the accounting year, the management of the company needs to know the total amount of premium income per district. Outline how this calculation can be performed and calculate the additional work time required for disk storage.

3.6 A bank wants to build up a real-time system of 1 000 000 accounts of an average 3000 bytes. One account number occupies 10 bytes. This large record length is due to the large number of fields designed to collect statistical data: it has to be possible to regulate the computation of interest since cheques cannot be cleared on the same day as they have been drawn. During peak hours the system must be able to process 50 updating transactions per second. An average of 200 000 transactions are processed every day, but on busy days there may be up to about 600 000 real-time updates. To be able to process this large number of transactions, it has been decided to organize the file randomly and to solve the overflow problem by means of linear open overflow.

(a) Assume that IBM 3380 disks are used for storage and that a maximum 60 K bytes can be allocated for buffers in main storage. What block size would you choose?

(b) How many disk units does the file occupy if a block size of 15 479 bytes is used (see the storage table in Appendix G) and the loading factor is 0.7?

(c) Assume that the physical record length can be reduced by 40% by means of data compression. How much space does this save in main storage and disk storage if the block size remains the same and the blocking factor, the loading factor and the number of buffers cannot be changed, so that the updating time is increased or the capacity of the system is reduced?

(d) Assume that the individual disk storage units work simultaneously. On how many disk storage units will it be necessary to distribute the file, if the system must be able to cope with the peak load of 600 000 real-time updates?

(e) Assume that the randomizing function used spreads the individual records evenly throughout the entire file. How many records will be stored in overflow blocks?

(f) Assume that 90% of the update transactions only require access to the same 200 bytes of the account record. It appears from part (g) that the access time can be reduced if the account file is divided into two files, so that the 200 bytes become a separate file. What block sizes would you choose for the two files if the total use of disk storage space is not allowed to increase? Naturally, the total capacity and the work required of the disk storage cannot be increased.

(g) How big a reduction in the work time required of the disk storage can be achieved if the two files are distributed on the original disk storages? (Use the block sizes given in part (f).) It is further assumed that the average time required for moving the read/write head is reduced by 50% when searching the small file with the 200 bytes record length.

(h) The field containing the interest added to the account is stored in the 200 bytes record, but the data for updating this field is distributed on both of the two record types. Outline alternative proposals for building up a batch program that can regularly add interest to all accounts. Estimate the run time for all suggested solutions and, if some of the solutions require changes in the file organization or the use of storage space, describe the effect this has on the real-time system.

(i) It is necessary to store the individual entries so that statements of account can be produced later. An entry occupies 30 bytes. A statement of account can contain a maximum of 30 entries. Outline alternative solutions for collecting entries in the real-time system. Design the solutions to give on-line access to the contents of old account statements. It must also be possible to have statements of the latest printed out entries. Estimate the average increase in response time caused by the requirement that entries are stored. Also estimate the additional use of storage space required to obtain on-line access to all statements of account less than six months old.

(j) Assume that the bank employs account managers who, on average, are responsible for 2000 customers with a total of about 3000 accounts. From time to time the account managers need to build up an analysis file with data from the 3000 accounts and 2000 customer records. The analysis file contains an average of 3000 records of 500 bytes each. Data for the analysis file has to be extracted via secondary indexes over the customer file and the two account files. What block size is required in these indexes if a maximum of three index levels in the secondary accesses are allowed?

(k) The extraction program for the account managers is run with a

Field Name	Field Description	Number of Characters
PNR	Number of the product produced by the work group on that particular day: note that several working groups may produce the same product on the same day	8
QTY	Quantity of product PNR produced by the working group on that particular day: the piece rate for the product is stored in the product record for the product in question	5
T1	Number of hours during which the working group has been doing piece work	2
T2	Number of hours during which the production has been discontinued, when workers are paid by a uniform hourly rate	2
WNR	Number of the workers who make up the working group on the day the work ticket is filled in: worker number occupies five characters and on average a working group consists of six workers	30
	Average record length	47 characters

Figure 3.27 Manufacturing database: fields of a work ticket.

lower priority than the real-time updatings. What is the longest time required to extract account data for an account manager if up to five different account managers want to extract data at the same time?

(l) The extracted data is stored in a PC floppy disk. How many floppy disks will the analysis file occupy on average? How long will the maximum and minimum response times be for customer analyses where the PC reads the entire analysis file? Assume that the analysis file satisfies first normal form and that there are secondary indexes available for the customer's occupational code and account type.

(m) Decide what indexes will be practical for searching for all wage earner customers who have no wages account. It is assumed here that an average of 10% of the bank's customers are wage earners who have no wages account. Estimate the work time required from the floppy disks.

3.7 A manufacturing company employs 2000 workers in the production of 5000 different products. The company wants to calculate the marginal return required of the individual production series, and also wants to distribute its wage costs on separate production series. The workers are divided into groups, each group looking after a machine or production line. Each group is headed by a group foreman who fills in work tickets for

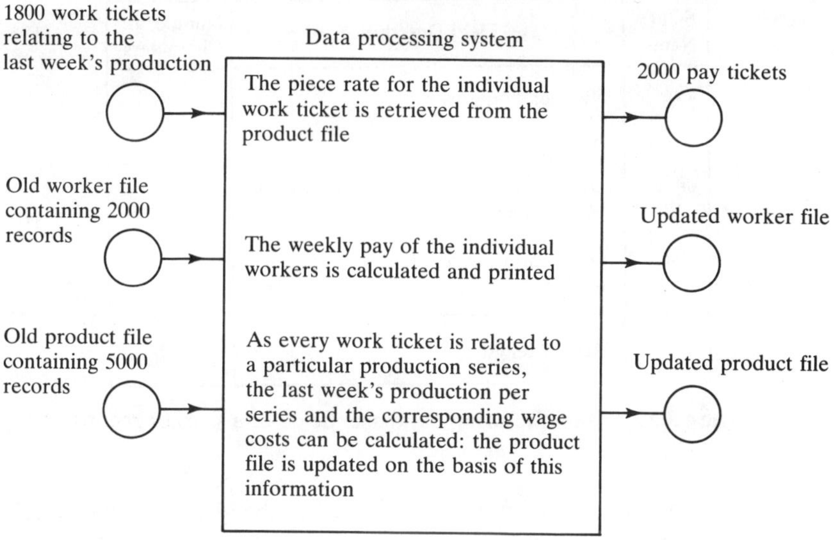

Figure 3.28 Manufacturing database: system flowchart for wage calculation and cost distribution systems.

the group's production every day. Figure 3.27 describes the fields of a work ticket. The workers are paid at a group piece rate for production time and at a fixed hourly rate for time wasted due to production stoppages. The production is regularly discontinued for a few hours due to unforeseen contingencies. The management of the company wants a system which, in addition to calculating the workers' pay, can also distribute wage costs on the separate production series. The system flowchart shown in Figure 3.28 illustrates input and output for the required wage calculation and cost distribution system. Figure 3.29 and 3.30 show worker and product records. As a work ticket can only contain one PNR, the group foreman has to fill in two work tickets if a working group switches from one product to another. An average of 1800 work tickets are filled in per week. The company is producing for stock, so that an average of only 100 different products of a total range of 5000 product numbers are being produced each week. Each week, 2000 pay tickets divided among eight lines are to be printed out. The company runs its programs on a computer with the following external units:

- three disk units
- two magnetic tape units
- one line printer capable of printing 1000 lines per minute
- various screen terminals used for data entry and query.

The computer has simultaneous units and it is multi-programmed. For sorting the file, a sorting area of 10 000 bytes is used in the computer's main storage.

Field Name	Field Description	Number of Characters
WNR	Number of the worker	5
WADDR	Address of the worker	30
GPAY	Gross pay earned by the worker in the year in question	8
OTHER	Other information relating to the worker	37
	Record length	80 characters

Figure 3.29 Manufacturing database: fields of a worker record.

(a) Which normal forms are satisfied by the files of the database?

To answer the following questions, assume that you are using (i) a hierarchical, (ii) a network and (iii) an inverted list database management system. It is particularly important that you make use of the systems' individual file structures, as described in Section 4.2. In the case of inverted list systems, you may only use repeating fields if you are sure that the maximum block size or record length will not be exceeded.

Field Name	Field Description	Number of Characters
PNR	Number of the product	8
RATE	Piece rate	5
QTY	Quantity of the product produced since the production of the series was started: when the series in progress has been finished, this field is adjusted to zero by a 'statistical' program, which makes reports for the management	10
COSTS	This field contains total wage costs for the working groups that have participated in producing the current series of the product: this field is also adjusted to zero by the statistical program	9
OTHERP	Other information relating to the product	68
	Record length	100 characters

Figure 3.30 Manufacturing database: fields of a product record.

(b) Use a system flowchart to outline the design of the wage calculation and cost distributing system. Estimate the work times for external units of the computer on the assumption that the program system is run with a first priority.

(c) How much storage space will the files of the database occupy?

3.8 A manufacturing company mass produces 5000 different finished products and components. For this, the company uses raw materials supplied by other companies and components that it produces itself. The company's workers are divided into working groups, each group looking after a machine or production line. At present there are 400 working groups, but as there are 420 different machines, some of the company's machines are not working to capacity. Each working group is headed by a group foreman who fills in work tickets for the group's production every day. Figure 3.31 illustrates the individual fields of a work ticket. The work tickets are to be used as input for a system that helps solve a number of the company's problems. The most important of these problems are as follows:

- With a view to fixing the prices of the company's products, the company wants to distribute the direct production costs on the individual production series. In this connection, the company wants to calculate the use of components and raw materials per series, as well as the number of hours during which a series has been occupying the various machines.
- Most of the company's machines can produce several different products. To find out whether any of the machines bottleneck the production process, the company, for each machine, requires data on the number of hours the machine has been producing, the number of hours the machine has been idle due to defects in the machine, and the number of hours production has been discontinued due to causes not directly attributable to the machine. The company wants to record such data continuously, so that it is possible to have reports on the utilization of the individual machines at any time. As it happens, the company (despite very sophisticated production planning) is having serious problems in connection with the coordination of the production of components that are to be used in the production of other components and finished products elsewhere in the company. The reason for this problem is that the company cannot afford to have large buffer stocks of raw materials and components for long periods, and that the production of components is connected with a number of uncertainties, which are mainly caused by machine defects (or a shortage of components, which in turn is caused by machine defects at an earlier stage in the production process). To be able to counter production stoppages due to acute shortages of components or raw materials, the management wants a daily report covering components and raw materials used in current production whose stocks have sunk below a certain critical lower

Field Name	Field Description	Number of Characters
PNR	Number of the product produced by the group on that particular day: note that several different working groups may produce the same product on the same day, as some of the company's machines can produce the same product	8
QTY	Quantity of product PNR produced by the working group on that particular day	5
MNR	Number of the machine operated by the working group	6
T1	Number of hours during which the working group's machine has been producing	2
T2	Number of hours production has been discontinued due to defects in the working group's machine	2
T3	Number of hours production has been discontinued due to 'contingencies' not directly attributable to the working group's machine: this includes, for example, stoppages due to a lack of raw materials and components used in the group's production	3
PNR QTY	Product number and quantity of raw materials and components used in the production on the day in question; the field name PNR represents a product number and field name QTY represents the quantity of product PNR used in the production; a PNR field occupies eight characters and a QTY field occupies five characters: as an average of six different raw materials and components are used in the production processes, these fields will, on average, occupy 78 characters	78
	Total	103 characters

Figure 3.31 Manufacturing database: fields of a work ticket.

limit. For each product, the report must contain the following data:

– product number
– stocks in hand
– numbers of machines that use the product in current production

To solve its problems, the company has built up a database which comprises a raw material file, a file of produced products and a file of

Field name	Field Description	Number of Characters
PNR	Number of product	8
TYPE	Code indicating that it is a raw material	1
STOCK	Quantity of the product presently in stock: this field is increased when new supplies arrive and is reduced when the products are used	8
MINSTOCK	If the product is used in the production in progress and the stock falls below the limit indicated by this field, a report has to be printed for the management, so that action can be taken	6
SUPPL	Name and address of the supplier	77
	Total	100 characters

Figure 3.32 Manufacturing database: fields of a raw materials record.

machine records. These are illustrated in Figures 3.32 to 3.34. The company runs its programs on a computer with the following external units:

- five disk units
- two magnetic tape units
- one line printer capable of printing 1000 lines per minute

The computer has simultaneous units and it is multiprogrammed. For sorting, a sort area of 10 000 bytes in the computer's main storage is used.

(a) Assume that the company has an inverted list database management system. Design a system flowchart that illustrates how, on the basis of the work tickets, it is possible to:

- have the fields H1TOTAL, H2TOTAL and H3TOTAL updated in the machine file
- have the fields STOCK, QTYPROD and H1SUM updated in the product file
- have the daily report printed of those components and raw materials, respectively, used in the production in progress, whose stocks have sunk below the limit indicated in the MINSTOCK field in the product record. Note that the STOCK field in a product record must be updated by the last 24 hours' production before it can be decided whether a product is to be included in the report.

Field Name	Field Description	Number of Characters
PNR	Number of product	8
TYPE	Code indicating whether it is a component or a finished product	1
STOCK	Quantity of the product presently in stock: this field is increased when the product is being produced and is reduced when the product is being used	8
MINSTOCK	If the product is a component, this field has a meaning similar to that in connection with raw material records	6
IPROD	Code indicating whether a series of the product is being produced	6
QTYPROD	If the product is being produced, this field contains the quantity of the product produced since the series was started	8
N1	Number of different raw materials and components, respectively, which go into the production of the product: on average, six different products participate in a production process	2
PNR, QSUM	Product numbers and quantities of those products that have so far been used in any series production of the product in progress: as the QSUM field occupies seven characters, these fields will, on average, occupy $(8 + 7) \times 6$ characters	90
N2	Number of different machines currently producing the product: on average, a product is produced by four different machines when a series is in progress	2
MNR, H1SUM	Machine numbers and the corresponding use of time in a series production of the product if any such is in progress: as the H1SUM field occupies five characters. these fields will on average occupy $(6 + 5) \times 4$ characters	44
	Average record length	175 characters

Figure 3.33 Manufacturing database: fields of a component or finished goods record (fields of a record in the products file).

Field Name	Field Description	Number of characters
MNR	Number of machine	6
H1TOTAL	Number of hours the machine has been producing in the current quarter	4
H2TOTAL	Number of hours the machine has been idle in the current quarter due to defects in the machine	4
H3TOTAL	Number of hours the machine has been idle in the current quarter due to causes not directly attributable to the machine	4
	Total	18 characters

Figure 3.34 Manufacturing database: fields of a machine record.

Estimate the system's run time on the assumption that it is being run with first priority.

(b) Assume that an average of 30 production processes go into manufacturing a finished product. What is the total work required from disk storage if we want to get an on-line overview of those raw materials that form part of a given finished product?

(c) What is the total work time required from the disk storage if we want an on-line overview of the finished products that might be affected by a shortage of a given raw material?

(d) What use of storage space by the database is implied by your answers to the previous questions?

(e) Normalize the database so that it at least satisfies third normal form and repeat the answers to the previous questions on the assumption that (i) a hierarchical, (ii) a network and (iii) a relational database management system is used. It is particularly important that you utilize the systems' individual facilities, as described in Section 4.2.

3.9 In Example 3.6, complex queries were executed by means of secondary indexes whose lowest level consisted of a list with ISN numbers.

(a) How can the set operators used in fourth-generation programming languages be implemented?

(b) Can the use of ISN numbers be combined with the use of primary hierarchical indexes?

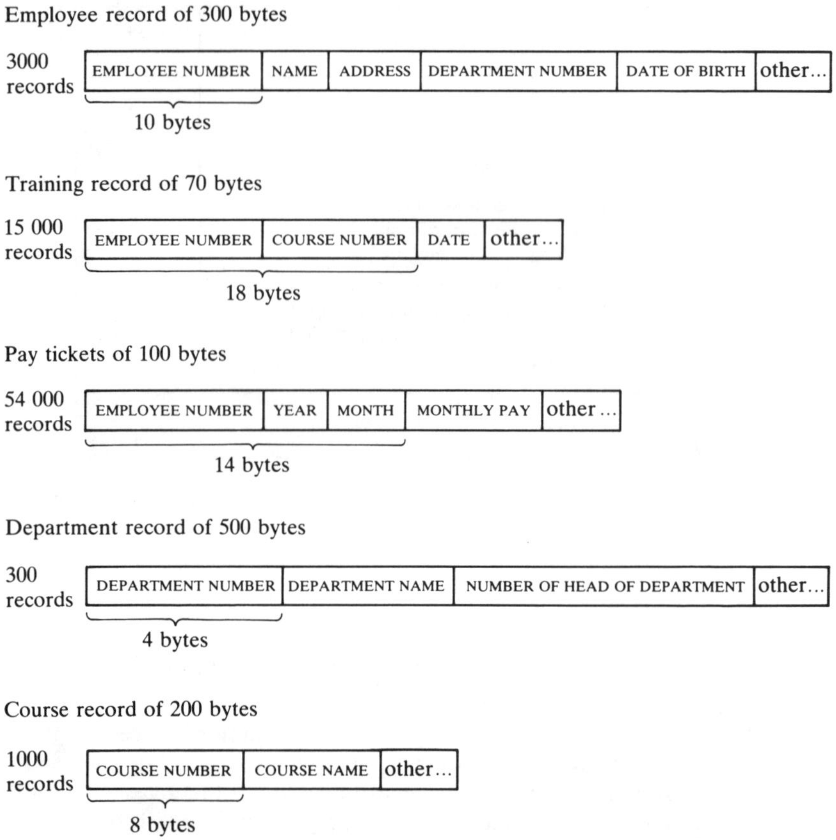

Figure 3.35 Tables in a relational employee database.

3.10 Figure 3.35 illustrates a relational model of an employee database. The number of records of various types and the length of the identification key of the various records are given in the figure. If you do not have enough information for a full answer to the following questions, make a 'reasonable guess' at any extra data you need. Select a concrete database management system and describe how you propose to construct the physical database if the most important application areas are covered by the following questions.

(a) Estimate the disk storage work required for the monthly wages run. For the printing of wage sheets, data from the employee file and the department file will be required.

(b) There are 2000 on-line queries per day of which 90% involve the retrieving of an employee record on the basis of the person's name. For 5% of these queries, it is also necessary to have the name of the department in which the person works. What is the average disk work time for on-line retrieval of an employee record?

(c) General on-line queries are rare and need not be optimized if the normal disk work time is under 5 seconds. As an example of a query of this type, the retrieval of employees who have taken part in two particular courses and who are under 40 years of age may be cited. Estimate the average disk work time.

Part Two
DATABASE MANAGEMENT

Chapter 4
Types of Database Manager

4.1 Introduction

A **database management system (DBMS)** is software used to read, maintain and provide security for a database. A great number of these systems are now on the market, either for sale or rent. Unfortunately, it is very difficult to assess and compare the various systems because the suppliers of database software use different concepts and terminologies for describing their products.

Chapters 4 to 8 deal with the most important facilities that such systems should provide. The facilities described are the following:

- The standard method used by the DBMS to implement relationships.
- Data dictionary documentation, etc.
- Data independence – that is, the possibility of changing the physical database without having to make alterations to old programs that operate on the database.
- Database languages.
- Recovery facilities.
- File protection.

These database facilities provide the most important criteria for choosing between alternative DBMSs. In some situations database facilities may be absolutely indispensable for a firm. The DBMSs on the market today, however, often have serious shortcomings, and in addition are expensive and difficult to use. In Chapter 8, therefore, we mention whether the facilities described can be bought in isolation, or whether it is difficult or easy to acquire the facilities by developing software oneself.

The names and addresses of the various database suppliers are listed in several publications of which the DATAPRO Reports (see Bibliography) are probably the most useful. The Reports also contain current information on the status of individual software products.

4.2 Standard methods for the implementation of relationships

Normally, database products are classified according to the method the software supplier recommends for implementing network and $n:m$ relationships. For our purposes, however, we distinguish between the following types of database products:

- hierarchical DBMSs
- network DBMSs
- inverted list DBMSs
- relational DBMSs

In what follows, examples are used to demonstrate how the different DBMSs can implement the $n:m$ relationship. These examples are based on a bank database with customer records and account records. The two record types are related by an $n:m$ relationship, since a customer may have several accounts and an account may be connected to several customers. Examples of relationships are account holders, guarantors, recipients of statements of account, etc.

4.2.1 Hierarchical DBMSs

Hierarchical DBMSs are oriented towards the implementation of tree structures and $1:n$ relationships. To implement the $n:m$ relationship of the bank database, therefore, we have to construct it out of two $1:n$ relationships as illustrated in Figure 4.1.

For every account connected to a customer there is a relationship record in a list with the customer record as list head. In the relationshp record we can store the account number of the record the customer is connected to. Likewise, for every account related to a customer, we create a relationship record with the account as list-head in which the customer number is stored in the relationship record. Thus, for every relationship that holds between a customer record and an account record we create two relationship records corresponding to the two search directions of

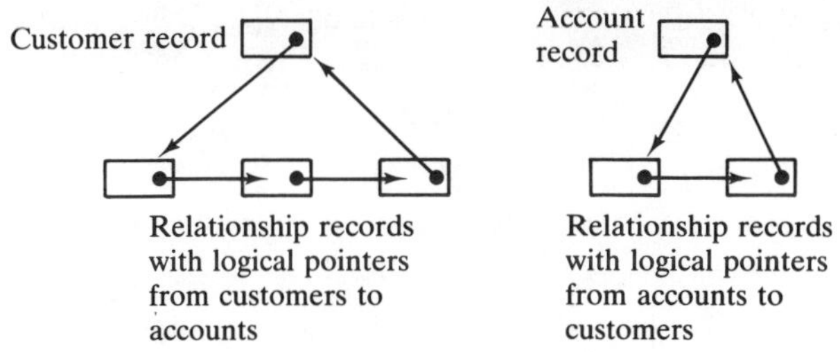

Figure 4.1 The $n:m$ relationship between bank accounts and customers realized with a hierarchical DBMS as two sets of relationship lists. The first has a customer record as list head with logical pointers to the customer's account records; the second has an account record as list head and pointers to customer records.

the relationship. In Figure 4.1, the hierarchical database has two levels. However, hierarchical DBMSs can be implemented with an arbitrary number of levels.

The DBMS, IMS, is one of the most frequently used hierarchical DBMSs. IMS terminology operates with parent records and child records, records being called **segments**. In an IMS database a parent record may be connected to child records of various types. In the bank database, for example, child segments of various types, corresponding to account relationships, deposit account relationships, etc., may be connected to the customer segment. To record that a customer has more than one telephone number, these numbers can be stored in a separate segment type, thereby making it possible to register an arbitrary number of different telephone numbers belonging to a particular custòmer. In IMS, a hierarchy of segments is called a **physical database**. As a hierarchical database often consists of many hierarchies, an IMS database will normally consist of many such physical databases. If an IMS hierarchy/physical database has been re-organized, child segments can be stored physically right after the parent segment belonging to them, so that it becomes very fast to search downwards through the hierarchy (see Section 3.2.4 on Clustering).

4.2.2 Network DBMSs

Examples of network DBMSs are IDMS and TOTAL. IDMS broadly conforms to the norms laid down by CODASYL for network DBMSs (see Chapter 11).

If we use network DBMSs we do not need to construct the bank database as two separate $1:n$ relationships, as in Section 4.2.1. Instead, we can implement the $n:m$ relationship directly. A relationship record, describing a customer's relationship to an account, may therefore be

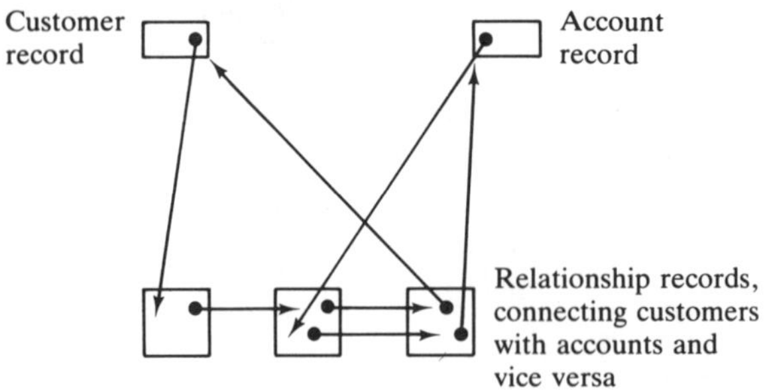

Figure 4.2 The $n:m$ relationship between bank accounts and customers with a network DBMS.

entered both into the list over the customer's accounts and into the list over the relationships of the account to the customer. Figure 4.2 illustrates how the bank database can be implemented with a network database.

In a CODASYL database, the conceptual database consists of a description of record types – the fields of the record – called **data items** and $1:n$ relationships, which are somewhat misleadingly called **sets**. The parent record in a $1:n$ relationship is known as the owner and child records as members, as shown in Figure 4.3. By means of sets ($1:n$ relationships) we can construct hierarchies, since a record that is a member of one set may be an owner in another. In a CODASYL database, a record type cannot be both owner and member for the same set. To create tree and network relationships, we therefore have to insert a branch record type, as described in connection with networks in Section 3.2 on List organization.

4.2.3 Inverted list DBMSs

ADABAS and DATACOM are examples of inverted list DBMSs. If we invert the hierarchical bank database and store the logical pointers in the customer record and the account record, respectively, the bank database can be implemented as illustrated in Figure 4.4. However, a disadvantage of this solution is that the record length may be very large if a record has many relationships to other records. A big firm, for example, often has several hundred relationships to accounts. It may also be difficult to

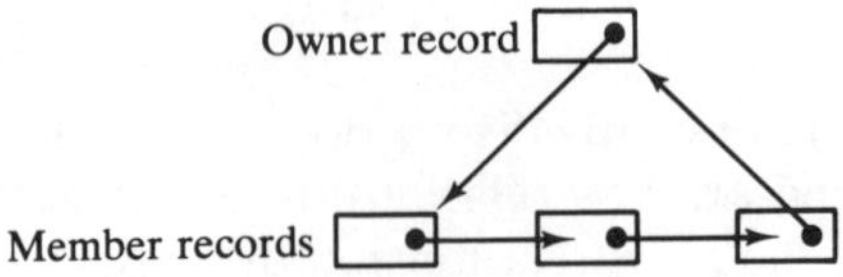

Figure 4.3 A CODASYL set.

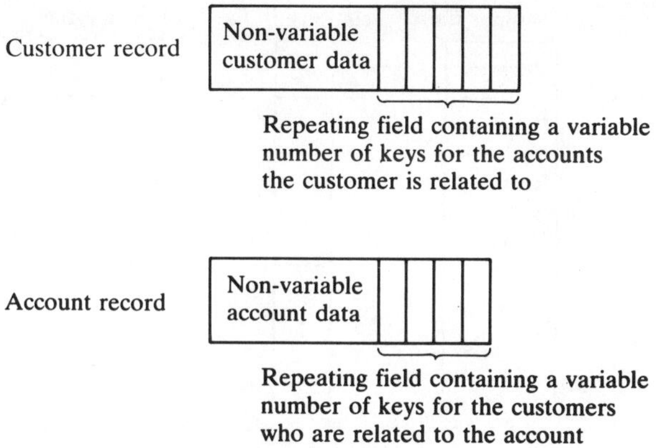

Figure 4.4 The $n:m$ relationship between bank accounts and customers realized by means of inverted lists.

determine a maximum record size, as the number of relationships may increase faster than anticipated.

In inverted list DBMSs, the bank database can also be implemented as illustrated in Figure 4.5. If this solution is used we can, for a given account number, locate the customers related to it by means of logical pointers in the variable section of the account record. Conversely, for a given customer number, we can locate the accounts related to the customer by means of the secondary index belonging to the repeating field in the account record. Thus, in an inverted list DBMS, we can build up a secondary index over the variable contents of a repeating field.

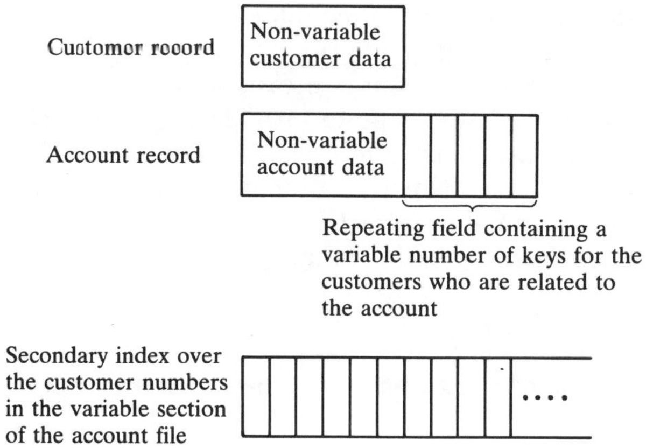

Figure 4.5 The system shown in Figure 4.4 improved by the addition of a secondary index of customer numbers in the variable section of the account file. Such a secondary index improves access.

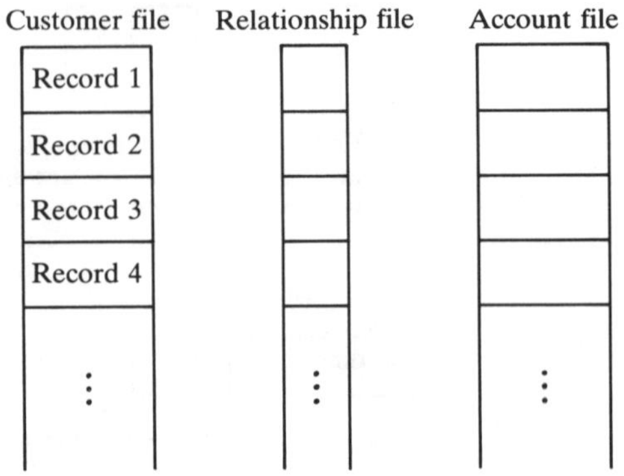

Figure 4.6 The $n:m$ relationship between bank accounts and customers in a relational DBMS. The relationship file contains customer number–account number pairs.

4.2.4 Relational DBMSs

In Chapter 1, it was explained that one of the main ideas behind the relational database theory is that the files of the database have a fixed record build-up, and that the database must be constructed in such a way that it becomes a model of reality with each file corresponding to a concept/type of object in the real world. Figure 4.6 shows how the bank database can be constructed in accordance with this principle. In the figure, the records of the relationship file contain both a customer number and an account number. Thus, a relationship record connects customers to accounts and vice versa.

The relational approach to databases is only concerned with the logical database; consequently, it gives no directions about how we can go from customer records to account records and vice versa. A natural solution to this problem would be to provide the relationship file with both a customer number index and an account number index.

The data structures in a relational database are very easy to implement. The relational DBMSs therefore allow more resources to be allocated to the data manipulation languages, which are often at a higher level than is the case with the other DBMS types. Examples of these high-level languages are given in Chapters 12 and 13.

4.2.5 Comparison of the standard methods for the implementation of relationships

The aim of this section is to compare the four standard methods for implementing relationships. The four methods are compared on the basis of occupation of disk accesses, CPU usage and programming difficulties.

The inverted list technique by which all relationships are collected and stored in the customer record and account record, respectively, naturally gives the fastest possibility of getting from a customer record to the account records related to it. It is assumed here that all the customer's relationships can be stored in the customer record itself, so that both the customer data and all the relationships of the customer can be obtained by one access to storage. In practice, it is possible to design the database in such a way that all a customer's relationships are stored together with the other customer data. However, a few records will have so many relationships that some of these have to be stored in an overflow record. As the insertion of an overflow record is a violation of the DBMS's standard method for implementing relationships, it is therefore necessary to develop special programs for the creation, deletion and reading of overflow relationships. If the database comprises many record types that cannot hold all the relationships, the database will soon become very complicated and unwieldy. Furthermore, a violation of the DBMS's standard method for implementing relationships makes it difficult for the DBMS language to follow them (see Section 5.3.2).

In hierarchical DBMSs, the reading of a customer's relationships can be performed almost as quickly as in inverted list DBMSs. A hierarchical database can be re-organized so that the relationships of the customer record are stored physically beside the customer record itself on disk storage. Thus, when the DBMS reads the customer record it will be very likely that the customer's relationships are stored in the same physical block, thereby avoiding an extra physical access to the disk storage.

Some network databases may be re-organized in such a way that a customer's relationships are stored physically next to the customer record itself (see Appendix C where the internal schema of CODASYL databases is described). However, it is not possible at the same time to physically store the relationships belonging to an account next to the account record. Consequently, a decision has to be made as to whether to optimize the search time from a customer towards an account, or conversely, from an account towards a customer.

In relational databases, the relationship file may also be re-organized in such a way that a customer's relationships are physically stored beside each other. As relational database theory is only concerned with logical databases, the customer file and the relationship file could be physically integrated with the result that the customer record is physically stored beside the customer relationships. However, as in the case of the network DBMSs, a choice has to be made as to whether to optimize the search time from customers towards accounts, or conversely, from accounts towards customers.

It appears from the foregoing discussion that the search from customers towards accounts, and, conversely, from accounts towards

Table 4.1 Criteria for assessing the merits of various DBMS types.

Assessement criterion / *Ranking*	*Disk storage accesses when searching for related records*	*CPU usage when searching for related records*	*Development and maintenance costs*
Best	Inverted list database	Inverted list database	Relational database
Second best	Hierarchical database	Relational database	Hierarchical database
Third best	—	Hierarchical database	Network database
Poorest	Network or relational database	Network database	Inverted list database

customers, can be optimized at the same time in hierarchical and inverted list DBMSs. This is not possible in the case of network DBMSs and relational DBMSs, however. The reason why the search for data in both directions of the relationship can be optimized for some implementation methods is that these methods store the relationship redundantly, precisely where it is needed.

Interested readers should consult Date (1986) for a comparison of the relational solution, the hierarchical solution and the network solution. In the example analysed there, the DBMSs are assessed on the following criteria:

- lowest number of statements for defining the database,
- lowest number of statements to develop application programs.

This analysis shows that the relational solution is the best, the hierarchical solution is the second best and the network database is the poorest.

On the basis of Date's analysis and the bank database example used here, it is concluded that it is impossible to say that a particular standard implementation method is the best, because this depends primarily on the application. It will be clear from the example used here that there is a tendency for the solutions to be ranked as illustrated in Table 4.1.

The dissimilarity between the rate of increase of hardware costs and wage costs has led to a tendency for development and maintenance costs to be considered more important than CPU usage. As this tendency will continue in the years to come, the relational DBMSs will gain a much wider popularity than today.

4.2.6 Comparison of terminology

It should be apparent from the previous sections that the various database systems have no commonly agreed terminology for the common database concepts. Table 4.2 outlines the names given to a number of central concepts in the different types of DBMSs. Blank spaces in the

Table 4.2 Comparision of the terminology for key concepts in various DBMS types.

DBMS / *Concept*	*IMS* *(hierarchical)*	*CODASYL* *(network)*	*ADABAS* *(inverted list)*	*DB2* *(relational)*
External schema	PSB = Program specification blocks	Subschema	User view	User view
Conceptual schema	DBD = Database descriptions	Schema	Conceptual database	Conceptual view
Internal schema		Storage schema		Internal view
File	Physical database	Singular set	File	Relation or table
Record	Segment	Record	Record	Tuple or row
Field	Field	Data item	Field	Attribute or column
Repeating group		Vector or repeating group	Periodic group	
Parent or owner record	Parent	Owner		
Child or member record	Child	Member		
1 : n relationship		Set		
Field's value area				Domain

table represent those instances where a particular concept is not used by a given kind of DBMS. The concepts are not fully comparable and this provides part of the explanation for the high degree of terminological confusion that characterizes database technology.

4.3 Data dictionary

A **data dictionary** may be defined as a database that contains data about the database. In other words, the dictionary describes the database and how to use it. A data dictionary has two main purposes:

(1) It must provide unique, updated documentation so that the dictionary can be used for looking up information on what types of data a firm has recorded and how the data is to be used. This avoids the problem of redundant data descriptions that are not maintained.

(2) It contains data necessary for implementing the database facilities.

The E–R diagram given in Figure 4.7 shows what types of data can be stored in a data dictionary. It contains a file for each type of data that is to be described. In the file FIELDS, there is a record for each field type in the database. A field type may occur in several different record types. The relationship r_1 connects a field with the record type in which the field occurs. By means of the relationship r_2, any possible verification rules can be found for the individual fields. These rules can be applied automatically to check the creation of new records, as well as field changes in existing ones. The verification rules can also be used by the software supplier's programs for automatic generation of files with test data. The conceptual schema consists of the files FIELDS, RECORD TYPES and RELATIONSHIPS, as well as the relationships r_1 and r_4. In the case of a relational database, the file RELATIONSHIPS can be dispensed with; in the case of a CODASYL database, RELATIONSHIPS contains the set relationships.

An external schema consists of elements from SUBRECORDS and RELATIONSHIPS. Relationships r_{15} and r_{16} are used to select the elements to be applied in a particular external schema. If the programs make use of external schemas, this gives the advantage that the external and internal schema, respectively, can be altered without affecting the old programs (see Section 5.2 on Data independence).

A distinction is drawn between an **active** and a **passive dictionary**. A dictionary is active if alterations can be made in the conceptual database without having to re-translate the programs and/or external schemas that use the altered section of the database. However, if the meaning of a field in a passive dictionary is modified, it is often

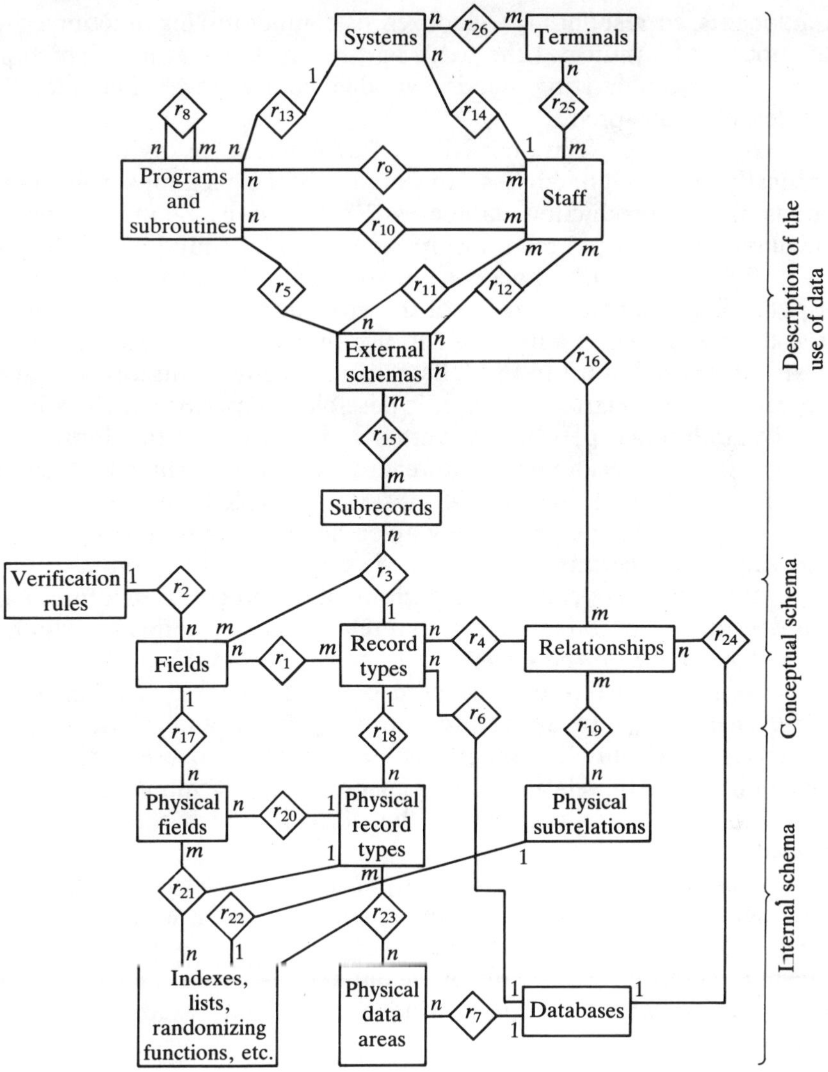

Figure 4.7 E–R diagram of the kinds of data that can be held in a data dictionary.

necessary to make alterations in the programs using that field. Programs affected by such an alteration can be found by means of the relationships r_3, r_{15} and r_5. Relationship r_{17} shows whether a logical field is composed of several different physical fields. Likewise, r_{18} indicates whether a logical record is composed of several different physical records. By means of relationship r_{19}, a logical relation is decomposed into its physical components, corresponding to indexes, lists, randomizing functions, etc. Relationship r_{21} indicates the fields and record types against which an index, list or randomizing function are defined. r_{23} shows where records, indexes, etc. are stored.

By means of relation r_7, the set of files can be divided up into physically separated databases. An example of the need for this is in test databases and production databases. Relationships r_6 and r_{24} decide which record types and relationships enter into the individual database.

Relationship r_9 connects a program with the personnel who are responsible for the maintenance of the program. Relationship r_{10} can be used to record who is authorized to use the various programs, and by means of this relationship the DBMS can stop any unauthorized use of programs. Using relationship r_{11} it is possible to describe which external schemas individual persons are authorized to use, and relationship r_{12} can be used to indicate which subrecords and relationships a person is authorized to update. In some DBMSs, it is possible to increase security so that a particular person is only given access to those records whose field values fulfil certain criteria. This is called **security by value**.

Relationship r_{13} gives a description of the programs that form part of a large data processing system, and relationship r_{14} indicates who has the responsibility for the system.

Terminals are often only used by certain people in a particular office. This fact can be utilized to improve privacy, and relationship r_{25} can ensure that only certain persons are allowed to use a particular terminal. Similarly, relationship r_{26} ensures that a terminal can only be used for the systems relevant to the office in which the terminal is located.

Normally, user input and output are not described in the data dictionary because the users' input and output are not normally integrated in the DBMS. However, there are major advantages of this type of integration, since many of the database facilities can also be used in connection with users' input and output. Some examples of such facilities are:

- data independence for transactions and reports;
- a shared description of the users' input and output;
- the possibility of re-running real-time updates by means of a logged terminal dialogue;
- the possibility of recovering output for a printer;
- extension of the different types of data manipulation languages, so that they can also operate on the users' input and output.

EXERCISES

4.1 Figure 4.7 shows an E–R diagram for a data dictionary. A data dictionary is defined as a database and therefore is a model of the entities and relationships forming part of the database. Check whether the entities and relationships shown in Figure 4.7 are in accordance with your understanding of a database.

4.2 Use an E–R diagram to illustrate how a data dictionary for a relational database can be built up.

Chapter 5
Data Independence

5.1 Introduction

This chapter covers the subject of data independence, before going on to describe the basic ideas behind database languages.

Data independence is a feature important in the upkeep of a database system. If the system programs and organization are dependent on the type of data being input, any changes that subsequently have to be made to the system (such as the introduction of an extra field to a record) would affect the programs using that record. Alterations to programs in order to take account of changes to the data are obviously undesirable as they would be costly and time-consuming, so the implementation of data independence is therefore important to the system designer.

The types of database languages are described briefly in the latter half of the chapter, with short descriptions of the ideas behind procedural and non-procedural languages.

5.2 Data independence

Data independence means that changes can be made in the physical database without having to make changes in the old programs using it. A database management system may provide different types of data independence. The most important forms of data independence are as follows:

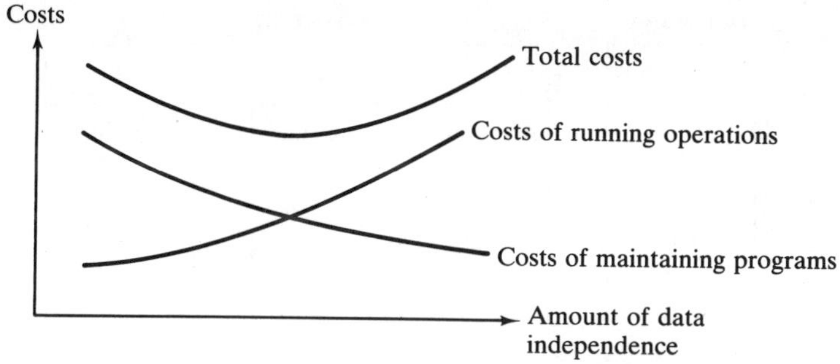

Figure 5.1 The relationship between costs and data independence.

- **Data independence at record level**: This facility makes it possible to insert new fields at the end of a record without affecting the old programs.
- **Data independence at field level**: This facility makes it possible to insert new fields in an arbitrary place in the record without affecting the old programs using the file. This facility can also be used to delete record fields without affecting the programs not using the deleted fields in their user view.
- **Independence of the file organization**: This facility enables file organizations to be changed without having to make changes in the old programs using the file. For example, it is very simple to implement the change from random organization to indexed sequential organization. In contrast, it is more problematic to implement the change from indexed sequential organization to random organization, since there may be programs that utilize the facility of reading the indexed sequential file in a fixed sorting order.
- **Independence of the physical implementation of relationships**: The relational method for describing the logical database is likely to become more common in future. It is more doubtful whether the normalization rules are also going to be observed in the physical database. However, it is possible to produce database software in which the logical database is described by means of relational terminology, whereas the physical implementation may be hierarchical, network, inverted list or relational. A software product is likely to be developed which will make it easier for the users of old DBMSs to convert to relational ones.

It is clear from the foregoing that a program may be more or less data independent. In principle, data independence is paid for by the increased costs of running independent programs, as shown in Figure 5.1.

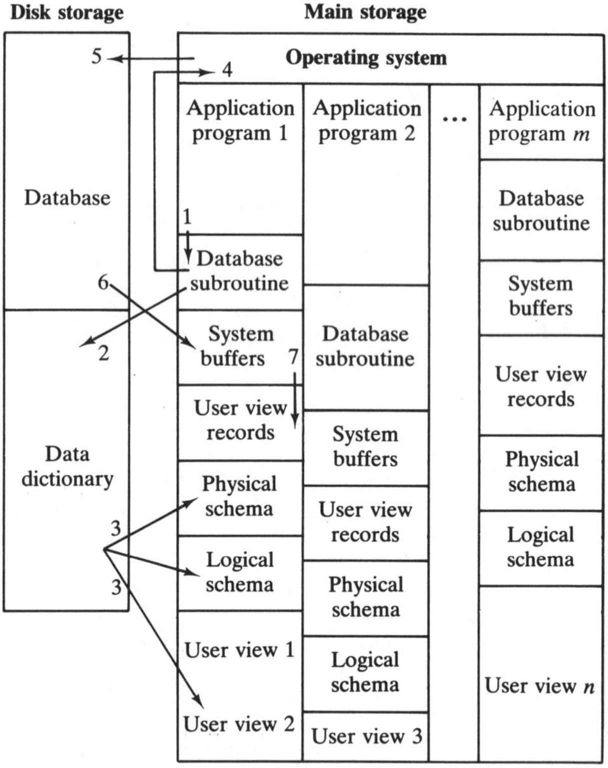

Figure 5.2 A method of implementing data independence. The following numbered activities are shown. 1: A program that has to read a record in the database is calling a database subroutine. 2 and 3: The parameters passed by the application program are analysed, and the logical and physical database descriptions as well as the user view are input to the working areas of the program. 4: The database subroutine performs further analysis of the database statements and passes any parameters necessary to the operating system. 5 and 6: Records to be operated on are transferred to the system buffers to be used by the program. 7: Using the data in the systems buffer, data can now be processed according to the user view required by the program.

On the other hand, the maintenance costs go down more the more data independent the programs are. In practice, it is a question of finding the 'amount of data independence' that results in the lowest total costs, and which at the same time yields data independence at an acceptable level.

Figure 5.2 illustrates how, in practice, data independence can be implemented. The right-hand side of the figure describes the computer's main storage, which is filled with programs and their working areas. At the top, the operating system of the computer is depicted. The computer is assumed to be multiprogrammed because under the operating system m programs have been set aside to be executed simultaneously under its control. The numbered arrows in the figure indicate the activities to be executed if an application program is to read a record from the database. The data independence at field level is achieved by keeping the user view of the application program separated from the logical database description. The independence of file organization and the physical method of implementation is achieved by separating the logical and the physical database descriptions.

In Figure 5.2, each program has a working area in which, amongst other things, the system buffers for the files the program is working with are stored. If these system buffers are stored in the program's own working area, the program can process data relatively quickly. However, the run shown has no concurrency control because the programs do not use the same system buffers. For this reason the run illustrated would only be used in connection with large batch runs where the run sequence of the programs is determined beforehand, so that the various programs do not operate on the same files at the same time.

Figure 5.3 illustrates how programs can be run in a real-time setup in which many different programs update or read the same files at the same time. As described previously, data independence is achieved by separating the physical database description, the logical database description and the external schema. The concurrency control is managed by the first program, which is the DBMS itself.

5.3 Database languages

The languages used in connection with databases fall into two main groups:

(1) database description languages
(2) data manipulation languages

5.3.1 Database description languages

There are three types of data description languages corresponding to the three types of database description:

(1) languages to define the conceptual schema;
(2) languages to define the internal schema;
(3) languages to define the external schema.

Chapter 11 describes concrete examples of these three types of language.

5.3.2 Data manipulation languages

Data manipulation languages can be divided into two main groups:

(1) procedure-oriented languages
(2) non-procedure oriented languages

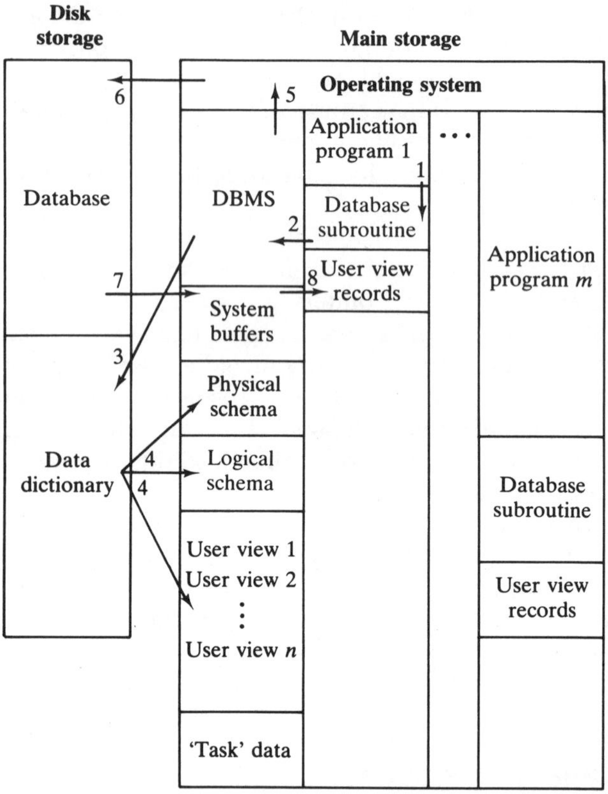

Figure 5.3 Data independence in a real-time setting. The following numbered activities are shown. 1: When a program has to read a record in the database, a database subroutine is called. 2 and 3: The database subroutine analyses the parameters it receives, and if the logical database description and the physical database description and user view are not already stored in main storage, a reading of the data dictionary is started so that the descriptions are input in the working area of the program. 4: The database subroutine analyses the database statement further and informs the operating system of any values returned from the database. 5, 6 and 7: If the required records are not already in main storage, they will be input in the system buffers of the DBMS. 8: By means of the data stored in the system buffer we can now build up records in accordance with the user views of the program.

The main difference between these two language groups is that in procedure-oriented languages the database statements treat records individually, while in non-procedure oriented languages the statements operate on sets of records. Consequently, procedure-oriented languages describe *how* output has to be produced, while non-procedure oriented languages describe *what* the output has to be.

Procedure-oriented languages

In a procedure-oriented language the database statements are normally in the form of a parameter language. This means that communication with the database is by calling subroutines, and parameters are used to indicate what operations are to be executed. Normally, there are statements that can be used to search directly for records satisfying certain search criteria. There are also statements that can be used to follow the logical relationships and search for related records. It is a characteristic of a procedure-oriented language that the programmer processes one record at a time. Thus, when the programmer processes a sequence of records he has to test with a return code to ensure that all records satisfying a given criterion have been processed. We will take a closer look at the characteristics of the procedure-oriented programming languages using the CODASYL data manipulation language as an example in Chapter 11.

Non-procedure oriented languages

Non-procedure oriented languages are normally self-contained programming languages in which the programmer does not work with the individual records, but on sets of records instead. Non-procedure oriented languages are also called **fourth-generation languages**. (Languages like COBOL, ALGOL and PL/1, in which only one record is processed at a time, are called procedure oriented languages or **third-generation languages**, while **first-** and **second-generation languages** are machine code languages and assembler languages, respectively.) The relational non-procedure oriented languages comprise statements that correspond more or less to those from the theory of sets. By using these statements, records of interest can be isolated and it is not normally necessary to be concerned with exception or error situations, which require a lot of programming work. When the records of interest have been isolated, they can be displayed on a screen or printed out on paper.

With such languages it is not necessary to design or program a screen or print layout for output because the language can fetch the data for output layout from the field descriptions of the data dictionary. Field headlines that describe the contents of output for the users are also stored here. By using parameters it is also possible to state whether statistical data is required on the selected set of records.

Some of the languages are so far developed that they can even be used to update the contents of the database. By means of the information in the data dictionary a record layout can be generated on a screen and then data input for new records or the contents of existing ones changed.

Non-procedure oriented languages are often so user friendly and easy to program that the end-users themselves can design and program small data processing systems. Some examples of relational non-procedure oriented database languages will be given in Chapters 12 and 13.

Chapter 6
Concurrency and Recovery

6.1 Introduction

Inevitably during the running of a real database, errors will occur due to program errors, or incorrect data being input into the system, and with programs running concurrently, each taking data that has been updated by other programs or by outside means, the possibility of erroneous data corrupting several different tasks that rely on it or data derived from it remains a problem.

This chapter deals with methods for detecting, correcting and preventing the occurrence of errors in a database.

6.2 Recovery

Before the use of database software gained ground, the recovery procedure usually involved making copies of the firm's files at regular intervals and keeping all the transaction files containing update information. If a file was destroyed or damaged, it could then be recovered by means of the copy and update transactions. This recovery method suffered from the following advantages and disadvantages:

- Certain types of real-time updates could not be re-run directly because re-running required a dialogue with a terminal user.

- Recovery by means of re-run operations was very time consuming if the on-line terminal users could not use the computer while the re-runs were executed.
- Before the days of integrated databases, it was easier to recover by means of re-runs, since the individual files contained no pointers to one another. Often it was sufficient to re-run those programs that updated one single file. In integrated databases, however, it is often necessary to re-run all the programs updated since the error occurred (see Section 6.5 on Recovery lines).

A **log file** is a file that records all database changes. Most database systems contain a facility that will automatically generate a log file of this kind. When a record is changed, the log file normally records the contents of the record both before and after the record change. The record contents before the change is called a **before image**, while the record contents after the change is called an **after image**.

Log records must also contain an identifier for the program run that caused the record change as well as the address of the changed record. To ensure that recovery can be accomplished by means of the log file, the database system often automatically maintains a security copy of the log file.

A transaction is said to be **atomic** or **indivisible** either if all the updates of the transaction have to be executed or if all the updates of the unfinished transaction have to be removed. The updates of a transaction can be removed by **back out** (i.e., the log file is read backwards), while the before images of the individual log records are written back onto the disk storage.

A **database checkpoint** records the state of the database at a particular point in time on the log file. This means that if it is necessary to re-run a program the database can be restored to the status it had when the checkpoint was taken. Thus, a checkpoint is connected with a program run that has been running an atomic transaction. However, a computer often runs many programs simultaneously. A **global checkpoint** is a set of checkpoints belonging to all those programs active at a given moment.

EXAMPLE 6.1

Figure 6.1 illustrates the connection between checkpoints and global checkpoints in a computer with two threads, which means that it can run two programs simultaneously. If run 4 terminates abnormally at time *M*, the checkpoint for run 4 can be used to recover run 4. If the entire transaction management system terminates abnormally at time *M*, the checkpoints for run 4 and 5 can be used as a global checkpoint.

Time	Thread 1	Thread 2	Registrations in the log file
A	Program run 1 begins		Run 1 checkpoint
B		Program run 2 begins	Run 2 checkpoint
C		Record A updated	A logged
D	Record B updated		B logged
E	End of run 1		End of run 1
F	Run 3 begins		Run 3 checkpoint
G		Record B updated	B logged
H		End of run 2	End of run 2
I		Run 4 begins	Run 4 checkpoint
J	Record A updated		A logged
K	End of run 3		End of run 3
L	Run 5 begins		Run 5 checkpoint
M		Record C updated	C logged
⋮			

Figure 6.1 The diagram shows a computer operating two program runs.

The following sections examine a number of examples of errors in which it will be an advantage to use the log file for recovery.

6.2.1 Roll forward recovery

Assume that one of the files of the database has been damaged so that parts of the file cannot be read. The damaged file can be recovered in this case by transferring an old copy of the file to disk storage. When this has been done all log files produced since the database copy has been produced are read, and each time a record belonging to the destroyed file is read, the copy can be updated. Normally, the database management system contains utility programs that use the log file to effect recovery.

6.2.2 Roll back recovery

Assume that an application program aborts because of power failure, operator error or the like. In such a situation, recovery can often be achieved by backing out the updates of the application program. This back out is performed by reading the log file backwards until the point is reached where the application program started. While reading the log file the updates made by the application program can be restored to their original contents, and then the application program started up again. If this recovery method is used, it is assumed that no other programs are simultaneously modifying the files that are being recovered.

6.3 Concurrency control

Concurrency control is the controlling of transactions that operate on the same database simultaneously. The purpose of concurrency control is to give shorter response times by running several transactions in parallel. This parallel execution of transactions does, however, cause problems. A **transaction** is usually defined as a sequence of operations (input and output instructions) that transforms the database from one consistent state to another consistent state, but this does not prevent the database being inconsistent (e.g., having an index pointing to non-existent records) while a transaction is being executed. Example 6.2 illustrates this problem.

EXAMPLE 6.2

Figure 6.2 gives some snapshots of the database while a transaction opening a new account in a hierarchical database in a bank is being run. The opening of an account is a transaction which transforms the database from one consistent state to a new consistent state. However, the database is not consistent while the transaction is being executed.

(**a**) It is assumed that the customer already has two accounts and now wishes to open a third.

(**b**) When the new account has been stored, the database is inconsistent, because the pointer to the customer's accounts has not yet been updated.

(**c**) When the new account has been stored, the pointer to the first account can be updated so that the database becomes consistent again.

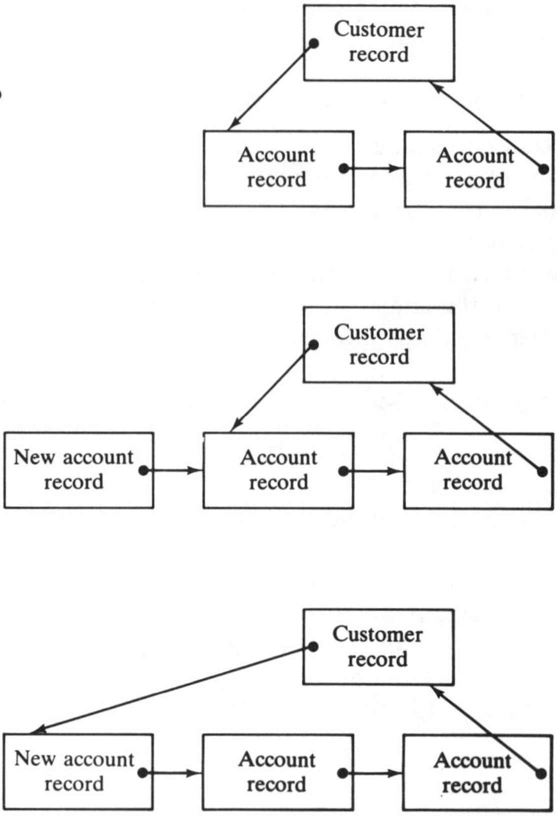

Figure 6.2 Adding a new account. In (a) the customer record with pointers to two accounts is shown. In (b) a new account record has been created but has not yet been linked to the customer owning it. The database is now inconsistent as there is an account that is not linked to any customer. In (c) a pointer to the customer has been added, restoring consistency.

Normally, transactions must operate on a consistent database. Therefore, the parallel control of the transactions must perform the following tasks:

- A transaction must be protected against inconsistencies caused by other transactions.
- If a transaction terminates abnormally or runs into unforeseen problems, the updating of the transaction must be cancelled, so that the database is left in a consistent state.

Examples 3.3 and 3.4 show errors that may arise if the database system does not protect a transaction against other concurrent transactions.

Instruction being executed	T_1's balance field	T_2's balance field	Database balance field
Status before the updating			500
T_1 reads the account record	500		500
T_2 reads the account record	500	500	500
T_1 adds $50	550	500	500
T_2 adds $100	550	600	500
T_1 updates the account record	550	600	550
T_2 updates the account record	550	600	600

Figure 6.3 Updating with two transactions run in parallel. The transactions are not coordinated, so errors occur.

EXAMPLE 6.3

Assume that the transactions T_1 and T_2 shown in Figure 6.3 are run in parallel. T_1 increases the balance in an account by $50 and T_2 increases the balance of the same account by $100. The initial balance in the account is $500. If these two transactions are run correctly, the balance will be increased to $650. The figure illustrates a parallel execution of T_1 and T_2, in which the balance has only been increased to $600; that is, the updating of T_1 has been lost.

EXAMPLE 6.4

Assume that a real-time transaction is transferring an amount from a person's wage account to the same person's savings account. Assume also that another transaction is calculating the person's total credit balance with the bank at the same time. This balance will be incorrectly calculated if the calculation takes place while the wage account has been debited but before the savings account has been credited.

The problems involved in the foregoing examples can be avoided if the parallel execution of the transactions is controlled in such a way that it proceeds as if it were a serial execution of the transactions in which a new transaction is not started until the previous one has been finished. If this requirement is fulfilled, the execution is said to be **serializable**.

There are many different methods to ensure a serializable execution of transactions. The methods applied in practice fall in two main groups:

(1) control by means of two-phase locking

(2) control by means of time-stamp order

In practice, the time-stamp order is only used in distributed database systems.

Two-phase locking makes it possible to **lock** records. There is a distinction between **read lock** and **write lock**. A read lock prevents a record from being updated until the locked record is released. However, it does allow other transactions to read the contents of the record. A write lock prevents other transactions from both reading and updating the locked record. In many database systems only a write lock is implemented so it may be necessary to use the write lock even if one is only interested in reading records. This is only necessary, however, if the transaction is required to read more than one record.

The main principles of two-phase locking are as follows:

- In the first phase, all the records needed by a particular transaction are locked. After this the transaction can perform calculations and update records, if necessary, without any other transaction being able to access them.
- The second phase begins when the transaction releases the first of the records that it has locked. At this moment all the database accesses made by the transaction must be finished: any unforeseen problems arising at this stage would cause the cancellation of the updates that the transaction has made. When a record has been released in the second phase, a new transaction can lock the record, and when this has been done there is no possibility of undoing the first transaction.

If a transaction terminates abnormally while in the first phase of two-phase locking, all the updates that the transaction has performed must be deleted. If the transaction aborts in the second stage, the updates do not need to be backed out. In the second phase, it is possible to recover the transaction simply by releasing the rest of the locked records of the transaction. Since updatings of a transaction must not be cancelled during the second phase, the transaction should be designed so that the releases of the locked records are the last instructions in the transaction.

When a transaction terminates abnormally during the first phase, the updatings of the transaction are normally cancelled automatically by the log file of the database system, in which the contents of a record, prior to its updating, has been registered.

If two-phase locking is used, it is also necessary to choose a solution to the problem of **deadly embrace** (or **deadlock**). This problem is illustrated in Example 6.5.

EXAMPLE 6.5

Assume that two transactions are to update both record *A* and record *B*. Assume also that the first transaction locks record *A*, while the second transaction locks record *B*. The first transaction now tries to lock record *B*, which is already locked by the second transaction, and goes into a wait state waiting for it to be released. Similarly, the second transaction is forced into a wait state by locking of record *A*. The two transactions now both wait for each other, so that it will never be possible to terminate them in a normal way.

Some of the most common solutions to the deadly embrace problem are as follows:

- Assume that a transaction tries to lock a record, but that it is rejected. Algorithms are available that can be used to analyse the situation and determine whether it is a case of deadlock. If it is a deadlock situation, the database system will have to back out one of the transactions.
- The deadly embrace problem can be avoided if all records are locked in accordance with a previously determined order. If this technique is used it will never become necessary to back out a transaction because of deadlock.
- For all types of transactions it is possible to set an upper limit to the run time. If this time limit is exceeded, it becomes necessary to back out the updates of the transaction. If a deadlock situation arises, one of the transactions will sooner or later be backed out. This method is often used in commercial database software products. It has to be emphasized therefore that it is important to choose a time limit for a transaction such that the transaction can only exceed it in case of deadlock. If the time limit is too small, the transaction may risk being backed out during the second phase of two-phase locking, and this may cause problems as the back out cannot be carried through if one of the records has been locked by another transaction.

When two-phase locking is employed, the updating programs are often designed not to lock while a terminal operator is examining the contents of the record(s) to be updated. Since the operator might leave his terminal, such locking would delay other transactions until the program run, and thus also the lock, is cancelled by the operating system. (It is often possible to specify to the operating system the maximum time an application programme may remain active.) This situation is illustrated in Figure 6.4.

Updating systems can be designed to read all relevant data and send it to the terminal operator, after read locks, if any, have been released. On the basis of this information the operator can submit an

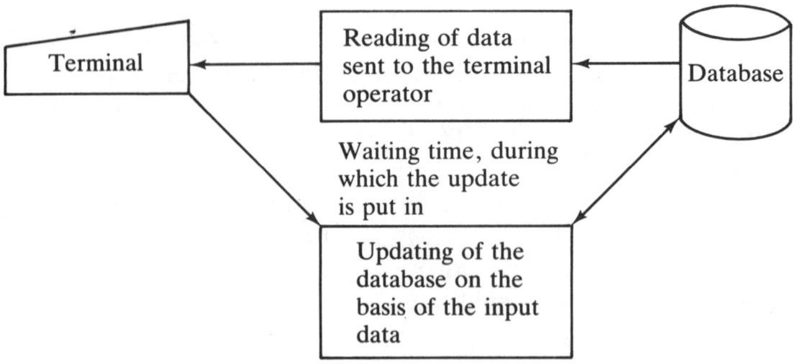

Figure 6.4 Updating via a terminal. The system is only locked after data is transferred from the terminal to the computer.

updating transaction. When this reaches the computer, the relevant record(s) can be re-read. During the second reading a write lock must be used so that the updating can be executed.

If the update is executed without checking whether other updating programs have disturbed the data to be updated, it is called **buried update**. Some suggestions for avoiding the problems that arise from buried updates are as follows:

- The data used by the terminal operator can be returned to the computer together with the updating transaction. When the record(s) to be updated is re-read, it is possible to check whether their values have been changed.
- The application program that sent the data to the terminal operator is retained in an active state, and the data sent to the operator can be stored in the variables of the program. When the updating data returns to this program, the variables of the program can be used to examine whether the conditions have been changed.
- A time value for the latest update can be stored as a field in the record itself. By storing the time it becomes possible to check whether other programs have been updating while the terminal operator keyed in the changes.

6.4 Problems relating to concurrency control and recovery of batch-oriented programs

Concurrency control and recovery of atomic transactions is oriented towards real-time systems, not towards batch-oriented systems. Even if a firm builds up real-time systems, many jobs are batch-oriented by nature;

for example, interest addition, printing of periodic statements of accounts, mortgage payment collection, overdraft lists, etc. Batch-oriented programs are often run at night, while real-time systems are run during the day. However, it is not always possible to observe this division in practice because some real-time systems run around the clock, while others use variable run hours to fit in with the busy hours during the day. Problems and errors can also arise during the running of batch programs so that they fail to terminate before the real-time systems start.

When batch-oriented systems are integrated with real-time systems problems arise, of which the most important are the following:

- If the batch programs lock entire files, the response times of the real-time systems become unacceptably long.
- If the batch programs only lock the records belonging to a particular 'batch transaction', the batch programs cannot be re-run because released records may have been updated by other programs. This can prove problematic because database systems have no facilities for recovery and restart of batch-oriented updating programs that also update sequential files, such as spool files.
- Most batch-oriented programs have to be run while the database has a particular status. Batch programs might therefore, modify records that had been updated after the status of the system had been changed.

6.4.1 Methods of concurrency control and recovery for batch-oriented programs

There is no general method for solving problems related to concurrency control and recovery in batch oriented programs. A number of suggested solutions, each with different properties, are described here so that a suitable solution can be chosen when a concrete situation arises. The various solutions are illustrated by an example in which a large database updating program has to produce output for a printer. The situation is illustrated in the system diagram in Figure 6.5. The methods described can recover both the database and the output to a spool file for printing later.

Recovery by checkpoints produced by the operating system

A checkpoint produced by the operating system consists of a copy of that part of the main storage used by an application program. If the application program terminates abnormally, it is possible to recover the contents of the main storage by means of the checkpoint and then re-start from this point.

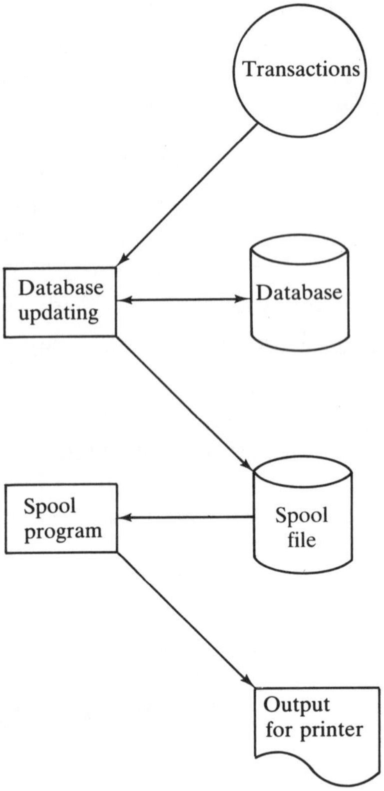

Figure 6.5 System diagram of an update program with printer output.

Checkpoints are particularly useful in connection with very large batch programs in which it would be too expensive to re-run the entire program if it aborts. The checkpoints are normally written to the same disk area, as it is always the latest checkpoint that is being used for a restart. The checkpoint must also contain buffer areas belonging to sequential files, such as input transactions and spool files. When the application program is started, reading/writing on sequential files will automatically be positioned in accordance with the contents of the buffers.

Restart by an operating system checkpoint cannot be executed if the application program is updating direct access files because the checkpoint cannot back out updates from them. In large batch programs it is necessary, therefore, to synchronize the checkpoints of the operating system and of the database. This synchronization should be run in such a way that it allows the checkpoint of the operating system to be written immediately before the database checkpoint, as the probability of the application program terminating abnormally between these two check-

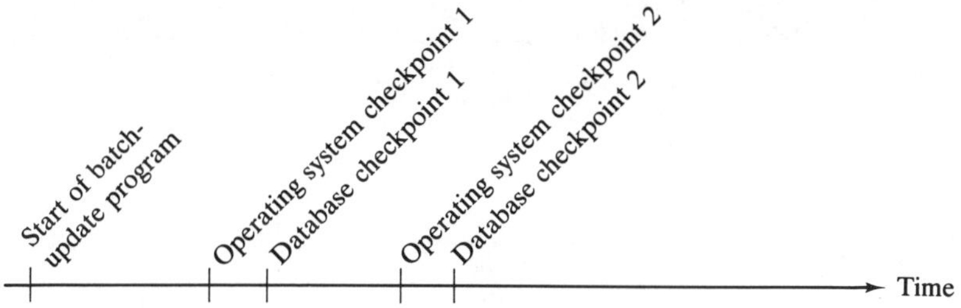

Figure 6.6 Synchronization of operating system and database checkpoints.

points is very small. If the checkpoints are written in reverse order, there will be a much stronger probability of the application program terminating abnormally between the two checkpoints, since it takes much longer to write a checkpoint of an operating system compared to that of a database.

Figure 6.6 shows two sets of synchronized checkpoints. If the application program terminates abnormally after the second checkpoint of the operating system but before the second database checkpoint has been written, the database will normally be backed out to the first database checkpoint, whereas the application program will be re-started from the second checkpoint of the operating system. In this situation, all database updates between the first and second database checkpoint will be lost. It is, however, highly unlikely that the application program would terminate at this point, since there are only a few instructions between the two synchronized checkpoints.

The method described here for synchronizing the two types of checkpoints has the disadvantage that the distance between the checkpoints of the operating system should preferably be relatively long, because it takes a relatively long time to copy that part of the main storage used by the application program, whereas the distance between the database checkpoints should preferably be short, so that the list of locked records does not become too long. This problem can be overcome by having more than one database checkpoint between two successive checkpoints of the operating system. However, this solution has the drawback that database updates cannot automatically be backed out to the correct database checkpoint. Another drawback is that other programs cannot update the files the batch program is updating, because there is the risk that the updates of the batch program may have to be backed out to the checkpoint of the operating system.

Recovery by means of user data on the log file

The following recovery methods require special facilities within the database so that it is possible to write messages to the log file of the data-

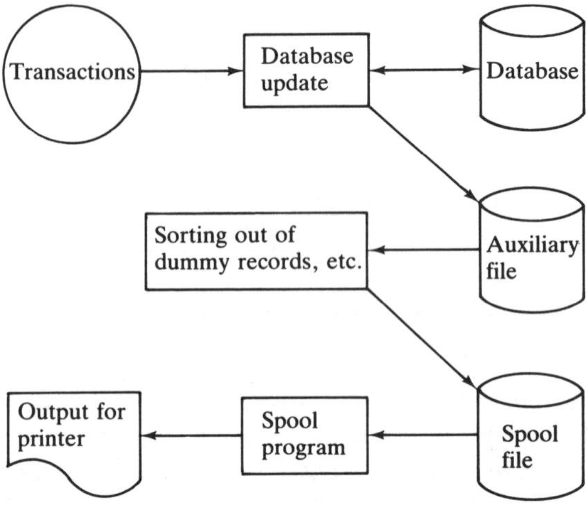

Figure 6.7 Updating with a batch system.. An auxiliary file is created by the update, which may contain dummy or duplicate records.

base at the same time as a database checkpoint is written. (If the database lacks this utility, the application programmer will have to write a similar one himself.) Together with the database checkpoint, it is possible to store information about how far the batch program has progressed in the processing of a sequential file. Program variables containing summarized data as well as statistical information about the run also have to be written to the log file together with the database checkpoint.

As output to sequential files is not recoverable, the contents of all output buffers must be physically recorded immediately before the database checkpoint is written. This can be done, for example, by writing dummy records on the sequential output file immediately before the database checkpoint is written. If it is assumed that n buffers are used by the sequential output file, the number of dummy records must be so great that at least $n + 1$ output buffers are filled between two successive database checkpoints.

After a recovery has taken place, there is a risk that output records for sequential files may be written twice. It is therefore expedient to use a serial number for all output records, so that it is possible later to sort out all those that have been double-written. Figure 6.7 illustrates how the batch system may be built up.

If the batch program terminates abnormally, the database will automatically be backed out to the nearest database checkpoint. The batch program must therefore be designed to start by examining whether user data has been stored in the last database checkpoint. If there is user data in the checkpoint, the program will have to start by reading all

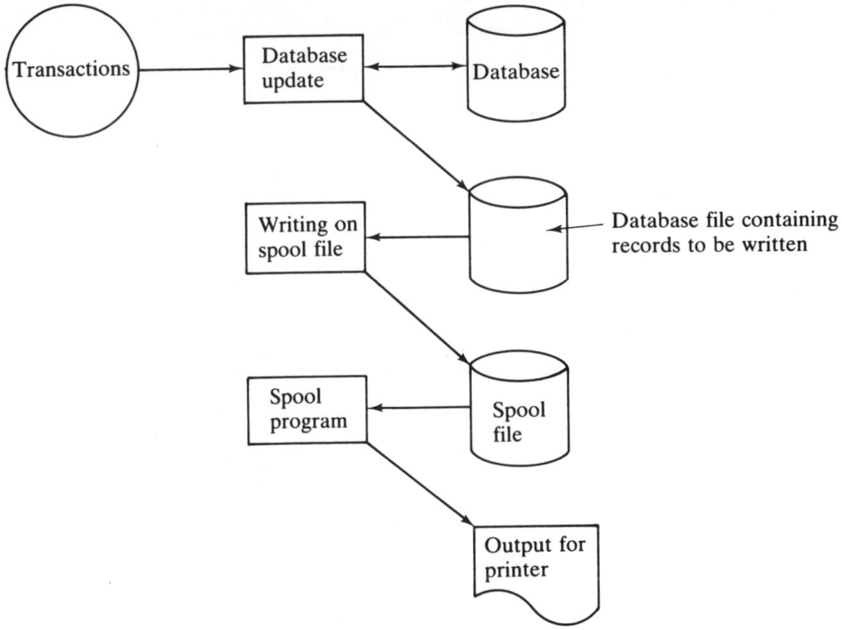

Figure 6.8 Updating by means of a database file containing the records to be printed out.

sequential input files until the program has reached the stage indicated in the user data of the checkpoint. Then the output files can be opened so that the start is made at the end of the file, and the batch run can be resumed.

Recovery by using database files only

The system diagram shown in Figure 6.8 illustrates how the updating run and production of output for the printer may take place if the spool file is replaced by a database file in which a new record is stored each time output is produced for the printer. When the database update has finished, output for the printer can be produced by means of the contents of the new database file.

Problems of recovery and concurrency control do not arise when using this method because the updating program operates through the database alone. The most serious drawback of the method is that normally it takes a lot of resources to produce a large amount of output in this way, since it takes a lot of time and capacity to store new database records. This method can, therefore, only be recommended in cases where there is only a limited amount of output for the printer.

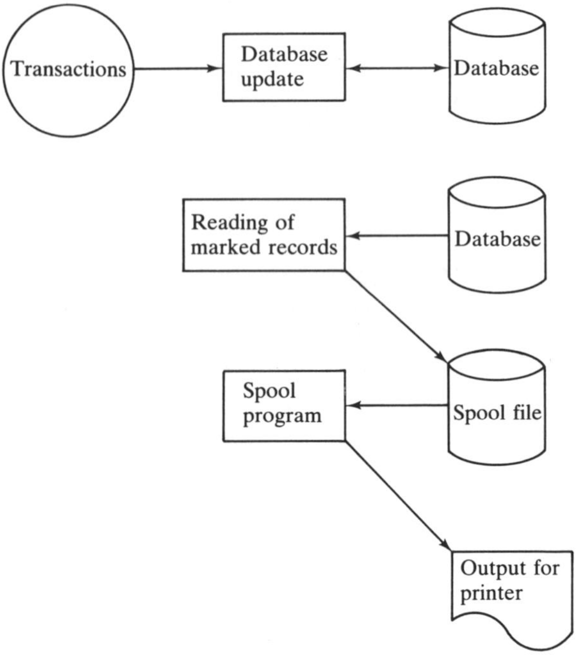

Figure 6.9 Updating by means of 'flagging' database records modified. A second search writes the flagged records to a spool file.

Recovery by dividing the application program into a database updating program and a print program

When output is produced for a printer in a program that also updates the database, it is normally because this output is connected with the updating. Instead of writing output on a spool file, however, one can mark the database record with a flag showing that output of the record is to be produced. Then, at a later stage, it is possible to search for the flagged database records and produce the necessary output. This method is illustrated in Figure 6.9.

This method presents no problems as regards recovery and concurrency control because the updating program operates through the database alone. The problem with this method is how to search for the flagged records without using too many resources. If nearly all the records of the file are marked, it will be worthwhile to read through the file sequentially and examine each record to find out whether it is marked. If there are relatively few marked records, a secondary index to the mark field can be built, or the method described in the previous section used.

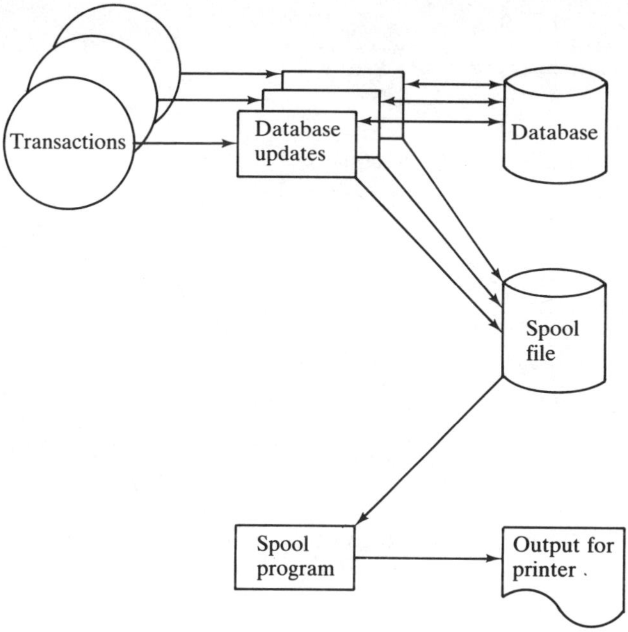

Figure 6.10 Updating by means of small application programs. Each application program updates part of the database and passes output to the spool file.

Reducing the recovery problem by dividing the application program into a number of smaller application programs

In the case of very large updating runs and print runs the application program is often divided into smaller runs, each updating its part of the database. This technique can be used to reduce the recovery time if one of the runs terminates abnormally. However, the method does not make it possible for other programs to read/update that part of the database used by the batch-oriented program. This method also requires that the batch-updating runs do not update indexes or the like, so that the individual parts of the batch updating can be re-run independently. This method is illustrated in the system diagram shown in Figure 6.10.

6.4.2 Methods of running batch programs requiring a particular database status

This section deals with a number of methods that can be used to run programs requiring a particular database status even though they are run in a real-time environment.

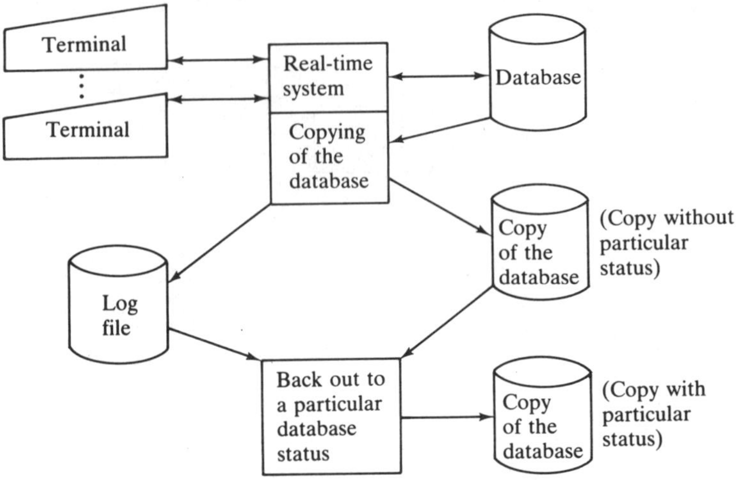

Figure 6.11 Batch updating a copy of the database to allow real-time access.

Batch run with a copy of the database

The most obvious method of ensuring that a batch program is run with a particular database status is to stop real-time updating while the batch program is run. This solution cannot be used, however, if real-time updating has to be possible around the clock. In such a situation a copy of the database may be produced and the batch program run on this. This copy cannot have a particular status because the file was being updated in real time at the same time as the batch job was producing the copy. Inconsistencies can be adjusted by means of the log file so that the result is a database copy with a particular status. The method is illustrated in Figure 6.11.

Pseudo real-time updating

Pseudo real-time updating means updating a copy of the database and meanwhile accumulating transactions so that the actual updating can be executed by a batch program. Previously, pseudo real-time updating was often used because the security of real-time systems was inadequate. Nowadays, however, pseudo real-time updating is sometimes used as it makes it possible to combine the advantages of a real-time system with the advantages of a batch setup, in which the database has a particular status when the batch program is started. The system diagram shown in Figure 6.12 illustrates this method.

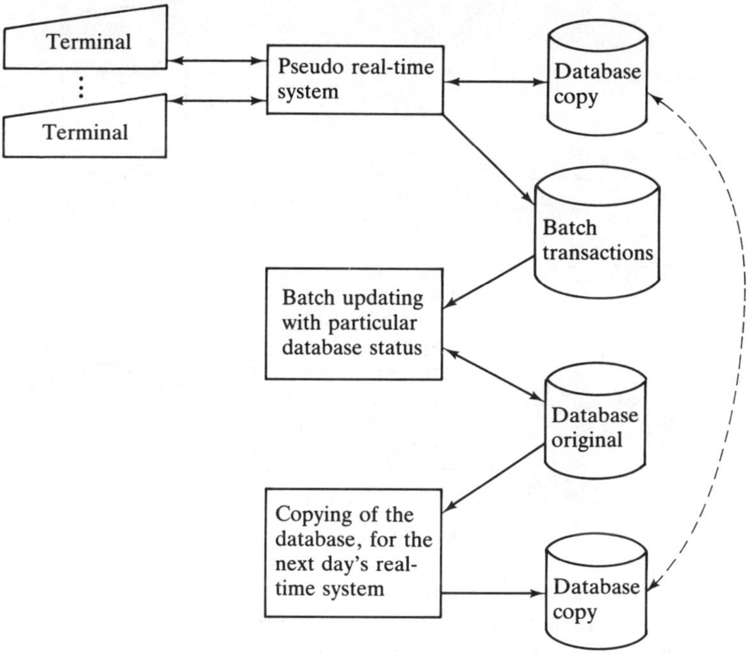

Figure 6.12 Pseudo real-time updating.

Differential files

A **differential file** is a file that contains the latest version of those database records that have been updated since a particular time. The use of differential files is illustrated in Figure 6.13.

Previously, differential files were primarily used because the security in real-time systems was inadequate. Nowadays, the method can be used if it is necessary to have a real-time updated database and at the same time need an access to the database with a given status. A major drawback of the method is that the search time for on-line inquiries is prolonged, because the differential file must first be examined to see whether it contains an updated version of the record in which the inquirer is interested.

Files with historical/budgeted data

In this section an example is used to demonstrate how a database can be built up so that it is possible to work with records that have the exact status the application requires. The example concerns a file of a bank's accounts in foreign banks. It has to be possible to:

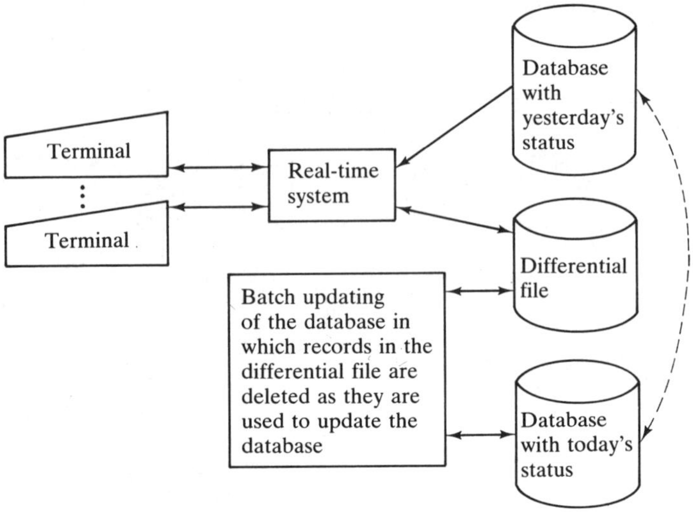

Figure 6.13 Use of a differential file.

(1) update the accounts file around the clock in real time, as the various foreign exchange markets are spread all over the world;

(2) run the day-to-day status program at the same time as the database is updated with transactions relating to the next day;

(3) calculate the future overall balance, so that the bank can cover itself against overdrafts due to movements in accounts that are not valid until later.

A database that can satisfy these requirements can be built up by supplementing the accounts file with a file containing the day-to-day turnover for each account, as illustrated in Figure 6.14. To find the balance for a particular date, it is first necessary to read the account record. When this has been done, the balance field must be adjusted by the turnover between today's date and the required balance date. In Chapter 8 we shall see how this solution can be generalized so that it can be administered automatically by a database management system.

6.5 Recovery lines

By a **recovery line** we mean a division of the database into a subdatabase that must be independently recoverable. Before the use of database technology became widespread, a firm normally had a number of data processing systems, each of which operated on its own files, and which could be run independently. If one of these systems had to be recovered, the system could merely be re-run. This is the philosophy behind the

Accounts file

Account number	Date	Balance	Other fields
1154	13.4.84	1000	
1158	13.4.84	2000	
⋮			

File recording day-to-day turnover

Account number	Date	Turnover
1154	8.4.84	+100
1154	9.4.84	−200
1154	12.4.84	−100
1154	13.4.84	+300
1158	11.4.84	−200
1158	13.4.84	−100
1158	14.4.84	−200
⋮		

Figure 6.14 The account file holding data on account balances is supplemented by a file recording day-to-day turnovers.

concept of recovery lines, as the purpose of the division into subdatabases is to limit the damage in the event of error or breakdown. However, in modern databases it may be difficult to introduce recovery lines, since the relationships can link up the systems in such a way that re-run operations can only be executed if all programs run since the error occurred are re-run.

In the following sections we analyse the most common database systems on the assumption that we want to introduce 'recovery lines'. For our analysis, we use the bank database introduced in Section 4.2. The analysis shows that it is possible to introduce 'recovery lines' into inverted list and relational database systems. In the penultimate part of this section we show how we can introduce 'recovery lines' by means of self-designed software. This is of special importance in hierarchical and network databases, where it is not possible to introduce recovery lines directly.

6.5.1 Recovery lines in inverted list databases

Figure 6.15 shows how the bank database can be implemented by means of an inverted list database. The program that updates the relationships between customers and accounts has to update both the customer file and the account file, because pointers are stored in both files. To back out the relationship updates, we also have to back out programs updating the non-variable customer data as well as programs updating the non-variable account data, because the log file will automatically delete all updates executed after the relationships were updated.

However, the customer record also contains logical pointers to the other products used by the customer, such as deposits, guarantees, bills of exchange, foreign exchange loans, etc. If just one program relating to the

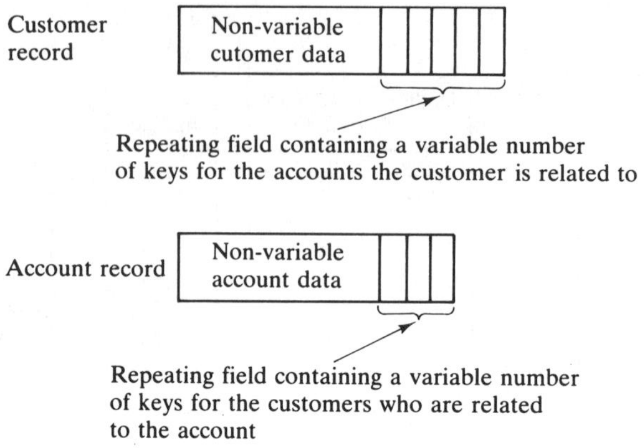

Figure 6.15 Record structure in an inverted list bank database.

updating of the customer record is to be backed out, there will be a chain reaction since it is also necessary to back out updating programs relating to accounts, deposits, guarantees, bills of exchange, foreign exchange loans, etc. Thus, practically all the bank's systems are affected by an error in only one system. This problem is called the **domino effect**.

We can see that it is impossible to introduce recovery lines in a bank database built in the way illustrated. The main reason why it is not possible to back out one single program in isolation is that normally the log file contains the entire record as it was before the update took place. When an update is backed out, all other updates that have been run after the erroneous update are backed out also. In a later part of this Section we analyse the possibility of introducing recovery lines if the log system is able to recover data at the field level.

In inverted list databases, the bank database can also be implemented as illustrated in Figure 6.16. The programs that update the account file can be built so that they only update the account data and the inverted lists belonging to the account file. If a program that is updating the account file is to be backed out, it is sufficient to back out all programs updating the account file. Similarly, the other product systems can be isolated so that in terms of updating they become mutually independent of each other, while, at the same time, the systems are totally integrated via the relationships in the inverted lists and repeating groups.

6.5.2 Recovery lines in hierarchical databases

Figure 6.17 illustrates how the bank database can be built with a hierarchical database. The program that updates the relationships between customers and accounts has to update relationship records

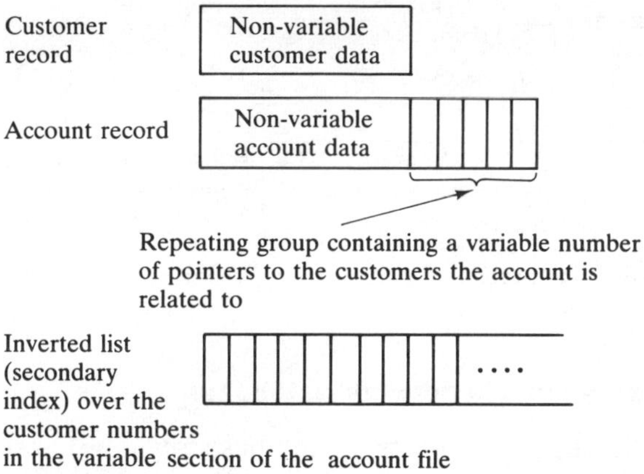

Figure 6.16 Inverted list bank database using a secondary index of customer numbers over the variable sections of the account file.

under both the customer record and the account record; hence, the physical pointers in the customer record or the account record may be changed. So, backing out the relationship program also means backing out all programs that change the customer record and the account record. As the customer record also contains pointers to deposit records, guarantee records, etc., the end result will be to back out all the update runs of the database that have been run after the relationship program.

In the foregoing discussion, the starting point was that an error had occurred in the relationship program, which therefore had to be backed out. If it is assumed instead that a program updates either the customer record or the account record, the result will be the same, because a backing out of, for example, account changes will also mean backing out pointers to relationship records. Therefore, relationship changes also have to be backed out, which brings us back to the original position, which showed that all update programs run after the relationship program had to be backed out.

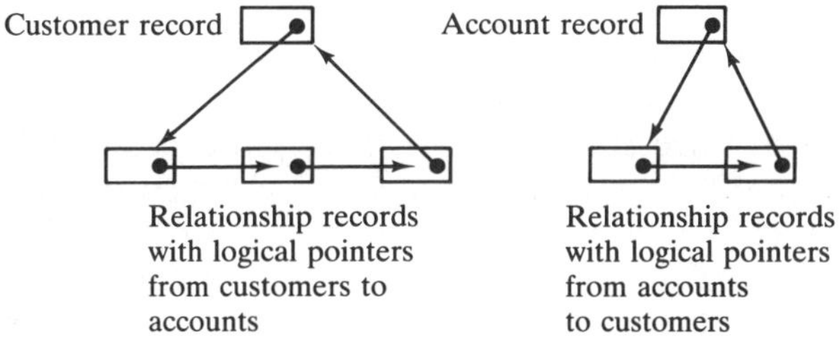

Figure 6.17 Customer and account records in a hierarchical bank database.

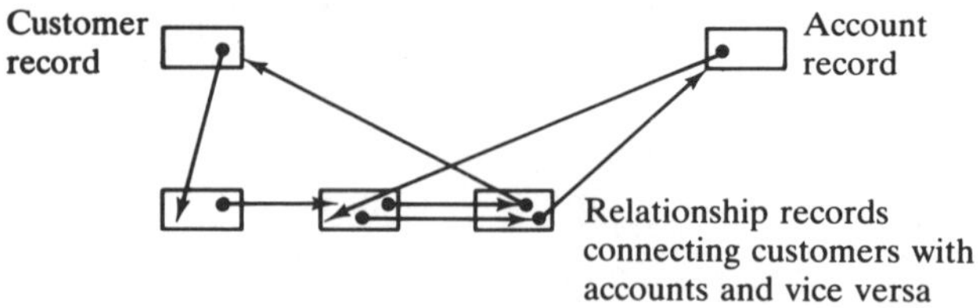

Figure 6.18 Customer and account records in a network bank database.

6.5.3 Recovery lines in network databases

Figure 6.18 illustrates how the bank database might be constructed with a network database. The program that updates the relationships holding between customers and accounts also has to update customer records and account records because of the physical pointers to the relationships. When backing out the relationship program, it is therefore necessary to back out all programs that make changes in customer records and account records. As in the case of the hierarchical databases, this results in the deposits system, the guarantee system, etc. also having to be backed out. Therefore, recovery lines cannot be introduced directly.

6.5.4 Recovery lines in relational databases

Figure 6.19 shows how the bank database can be implemented in a relational database. The account file in the figure contains no pointers to other files. Therefore, it is possible to construct the updating programs of the account system in such a way that they are not updating other files. If the other product systems are constructed similarly, recovery lines can be built up around the account system, the deposits system, the customer system, etc.

6.5.5 Recovery lines with log systems recovering at field level

The databases available on the market today normally recover at record level; that is, the entire record is logged during the updating process and written back during the recovery process. However, it is also possible to construct databases that recover at field level, so that in the recovery process it is only necessary to write back those fields that have been changed. If the database uses pointers, the changed pointer fields also have to be logged by insertion/deletion of a record in a pointer chain. During a subsequent backing out, it is then possible to insert the original pointer values without changing the contents in the record with the updated pointer values.

On the face of it, one would think that it is simple to introduce re-

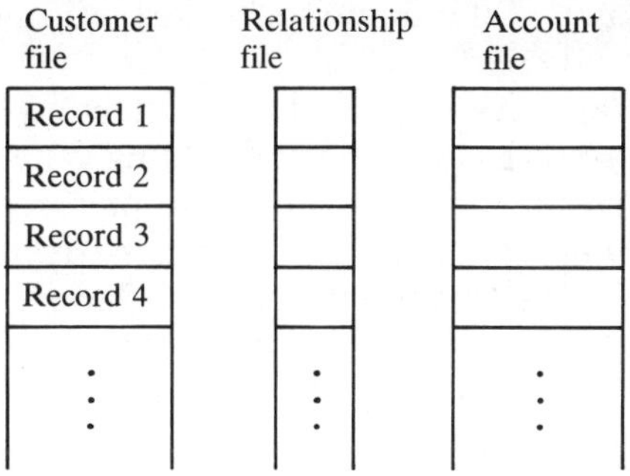

Figure 6.19 Customer and account records in a relational bank database. They are linked by means of the relationship table.

covery lines in a database whose log system recovers at field level, as the updating programs that have been operating on the error-affected fields can just be backed out. However, it is not as simple as this because, in principle, the creation and deletion of records affects all fields, which means that these will usually also have to be backed out. But if record creations and deletions are backed out, so must all programs that have been updating the record, and in such a case it is not possible to take advantage of the fact that the log system recovers at field level. Therefore, it is worthwhile checking what conditions have to be fulfilled to avoid having to back out record creations and deletions if we only want to back out a program that has made changes in a few record fields.

- A condition that has to be fulfilled to avoid having to back out record creations is that a record identification is not re-used after a record has been deleted. Record identification here means the key value that the back-out system uses when a given record is to be backed out. If this record identification is only used for one particular record, there can be no back outs relating to this particular record until the record has been created, and therefore it is not necessary to back out the record creations as long as only a few error-affected fields need to be backed out.
- The situation is completely different in the case of record deletions, since the records that are to be changed by being backed out are not re-created until the record deletions are backed out. This makes it absolutely necessary that the record deletions are backed out. This problem can be overcome by not physically deleting the records but only doing so logically by marking a field.

However, errors may also occur in the program that creates the records, so that this program has to be backed out. In such a case, it is necessary to also back out all programs that update the file, as some of these record updates will otherwise be lost during a subsequent re-running of the record creations.

If these results are applied to the inverted list bank database recovery lines can be introduced if the updating systems are designed not to create both account records and customer records in the same program. If the account system is subsequently backed out there is a risk that a few relationship fields in the customer file will have to be backed out, although it is not necessary to back out the entire customer system. If, on the other hand, the customer system is to be backed out, we risk at most having to back out a few relationship fields in the account file.

In the hierarchical databases, further demands are made on the introduction of recovery lines, since a record cannot exist if there are no records at a higher level. Thus, in backing out a record type it is also necessary to back out the programs that update the underlying record types. If the results are applied to the hierarchical bank database, the database will be designed in such a way that a backing out of the account system only means backing out relationship records at the lowest level in the customer database. Thus, the entire customer system does not have to be backed out. Likewise, the customer system can be backed out if there are errors in it.

To introduce recovery lines into a network database, it is most practical to select a system in which child records can exist without the corresponding parent record, because otherwise the backing out of a parent record may require the backing out of the child records as well. If the foregoing results are applied to the network bank database, system independence can be achieved if the updating programs are designed not to allow the creation of both account records and customer records in the same program. If the account system is then backed out, it may be necessary to back out both account records and relationship records to the customers, but the customer file itself need not be backed out.

In the case of the relational database there were no problems involved in introducing recovery lines, but the independence of the system would be improved if the log system could recover at field level, because it will then be sufficient to back out the programs that have updated the fields that may have errors in them. If the log system recovers at record level, all programs that have updated a record have to be backed out, no matter what fields the programs have been operating on.

It is particularly important to recover at field level if the database is updated by real-time transactions. In the bank database we may assume, for example, that the updating of account creations/deletions and balance adjustments is executed in real time, while the computation of interest is executed in periodic batch runs. If there are errors in the computation of interest, then the real-time updates and the erroneous interest update can be backed out so that the interest update can be re-run. Having done that it is possible to write back the correct real-time updates. If the logging of the real-time updates is not executed at field level, the erroneous interest updates can be written back with the real-time updates.

Thus, it appears that, no matter what database we are working with, the system independence can be improved if the producers of tomorrow's databases build the log system to recover at field level. In other words, the user view of the application program should be built into the recovery process.

6.5.6 Recovery lines by self-designed software

As we have seen, it is very difficult to introduce recovery lines for certain types of database software. In practice, therefore, it is often necessary to correct errors by designing special correction programs, which correct any errors introduced by a preceding program. This is often a good solution, but it may be very hazardous and time consuming in the case of complicated errors.

In the following, we shall see how it is possible to re-run one updating program without all the other updating programs having to be re-run. All suggested solutions assume the design of special programs that make correct re-runs possible. The special programs mentioned here have the advantage over the correction programs that they can be developed before errors occur so that special programming and recovery need not be subject to time pressure. However, the method requires the mutual independence of the updates of the individual updating programs.

Description of error situation

The various re-run methods are illustrated by means of a bank example. Figure 6.20 illustrates the error situation when the recovery is to be executed. The batch program containing a programming error may, for example, be a complicated addition of interest in all accounts, while the real-time system may be the creation of new records, a change of basic data, and the creation of relationships between customers and accounts and between accounts and deposit facilities, guarantees, foreign loans, etc. It is assumed in the following that the account record may contain pointers to customer records, deposits, guarantees, etc., so that the database becomes inconsistent if we only back out the updates of the account file or load a copy of the master account.

Solution 1 The solution described here assumes that it is possible to divide the fields of a record into real-time updated fields and fields that are batch-updated. If there is a field that is both real-time and batch-updated, we can try to solve the problem by creating two fields. The individual recovery activities are described in Figure 6.21.

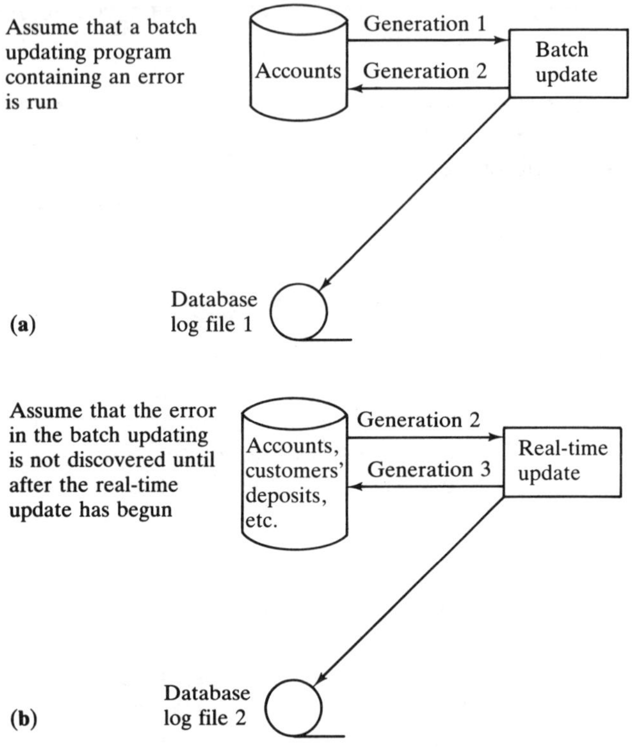

Figure 6.20 Undetected errors in a batch update. (a) may be compounded by subsequent real-time updates. (b) In this and the next two figures, Generation 1 is the consistent database before batch or real-time updates; Generation 2 is the version of the database produced by the batch update; and Generation 3 is that produced by the real-time updates.

Solution 2 In Solution 1 we extracted the non-error batch-updated fields and then placed them in the real-time updated database. In the suggested solution in Figure 6.22, the real-time fields are extracted and later returned to the database.

If the relationships between account records and other record types have been implemented by means of physical pointers, it is very cumbersome to construct the program that extracts and inserts the real-time updated pointers. In such a situation Solution 1 is to be preferred. Solution 2, however, has the advantage over Solution 1 that it runs relatively faster, since normally only few records are real-time updated, while a batch updating often changes many records. Furthermore, in Solution 1 we have to make a copy of generation 3 of the account file before the recovery process is launched. This copy has to be loaded again before activity is started. As the loading of a database file may be very

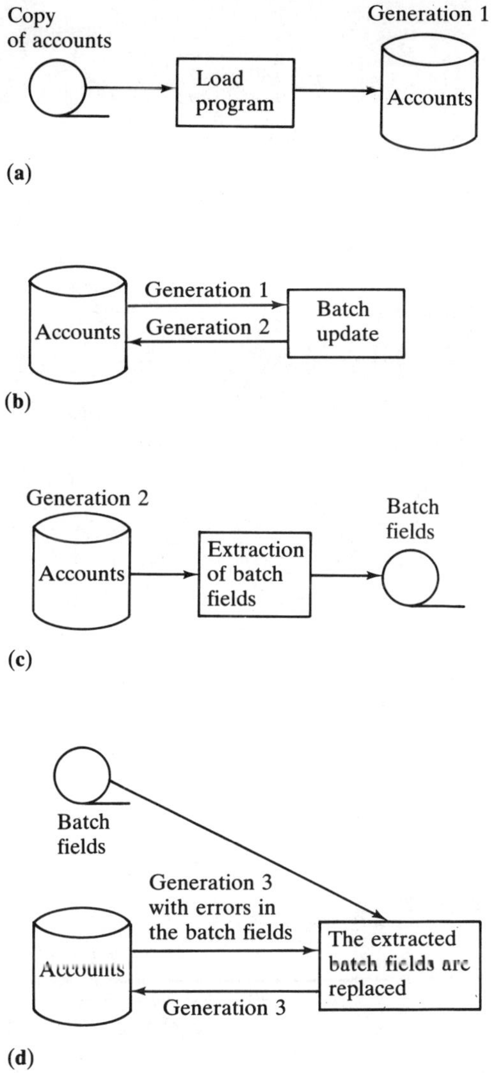

Figure 6.21 Dealing with errors in the batch update (it is assumed that no field is both batch and real-time updated). Method 1: copying the corrected batch transactions back into the live database. (a) A copy of Generation 1, the unupdated version of the database, is loaded and, (b), updated correctly. In (c) the fields that have been updated by the batch program and which are now correct are extracted from the new Generation 2 file. In (d) these values are written into the live database (Generation 3) replacing the fields that might have held errors.

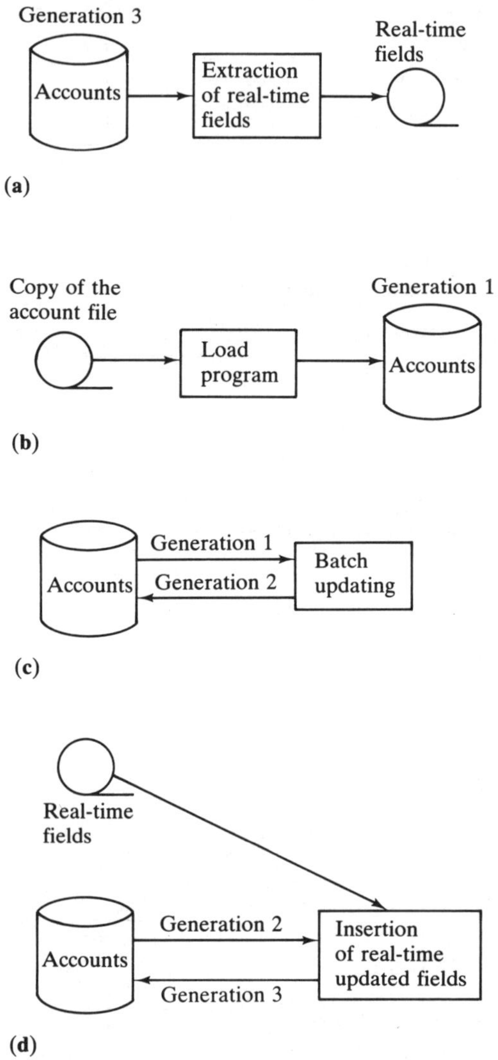

Figure 6.22 Dealing with errors in the batch update. Method 2: copying the real-time modifications back into the corrected database. In (a) the real-time fields from Generation 3 (the version in which real-time updates have been added to the erroneous batch updates) are copied. The batch update is then rerun, (b), starting from a clean copy of Generation 1. This provides a correct Generation 2, into which the real-time updated fields can be re-inserted (d).

time consuming, Solution 1 normally requires longer run times than Solution 2.

Solution 3 The solution shown in Figure 6.23 rests on the fact that relationships are normally implemented as 'two-way pointers'. If one of the pointers 'breaks', we can recover it by means of data in the other pointer.

The disadvantage of this solution is that we cannot automatically recover all real-time updates because only the relationship can be recovered. Furthermore, the running operation that extracts pointers may have to be very comprehensive if the entire database has to be searched to find pointers pointing to a single account.

Conclusions In all the solutions, we can re-run the batch program without having to re-run the real-time transactions. The reason why this is possible is that the programs do not update the same fields.

In general, if we want to be able to re-run a subsystem without having to re-run other subsystems, we have to design the updating programs in such a way that the programs are divided into groups that update in the same fields, and which therefore may be re-run without affecting the fields of other groups. If two groups of programs update the same record, we can, once and for all, construct special programs that can 'save' the fields of a program group while another group is being re-run. Once these special programs have been constructed, it becomes relatively fast to re-run a program group, no matter what the type of programming/operational error.

6.5.7 Re-running real-time transactions

It was assumed in the previous sections that the programming error did not occur in the real-time transactions. This is not an unreasonable assumption since real-time transactions are often small programs that are easy to take in. Operational errors are also rare during the running of real-time transactions because these programs are run in such a way that human errors cannot normally be a disturbing factor. However, if we still want to be able to re-run these transactions it may cause problems, as real-time transactions are normally executed as a dialogue with a terminal user. Some databases, which are integrated with the data transmission system, solve this problem by logging the terminal dialogue, so that the users' replies can be found again by re-running the real-time transactions. However, a prerequisite for using this re-running method is that the assumptions behind the users' replies in the terminal dialogue have not altered.

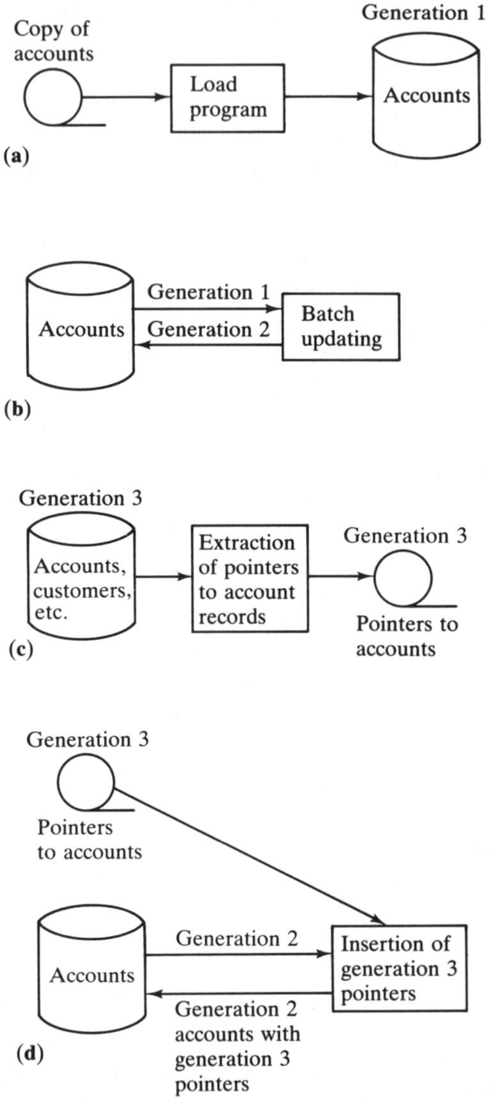

Figure 6.23 Dealing with errors in the batch update. Method 3: using two-way pointers. (a) A copy of Generation 1 of the account file is loaded. As one of the account relationships pointer directions is stored in the accounts file, the relationships are now inconsistent. (b) The database is updated correctly with the batch transactions. The entire Generation 3 database, with the exception of the accounts file (which held the original errors) is now, (c), searched for pointers to the account file, and these are copied. Finally, (d), these extracted real-time pointers are 'reversed' and inserted into the accounts file.

6.6 Consistency control

Although every effort is made to prevent them, many errors still occur in a dynamic data processing setting. Normally, these errors are found quickly and corrected. But, unfortunately, it is often necessary to have systems that can detect errors not found immediately. One of the best methods for detecting hidden errors is **consistency control**. A prerequisite for executing consistency control is that some sort of redundancy is inserted into the database. If an error occurs, it will seldom be repeated in the redundant version of the data, so that the error can be detected when the duplicate versions of the data are checked against each other. Here are some examples of consistency control.

- Two records that are related to each other are often implemented by means of a pointer from the first record to the second record and vice versa. Frequently databases are equipped with a program that can check that the 'double pointers' of the database are referring to each other. If one of these pointers is 'broken', the program 'sounds the alarm'.
- To optimize queries, it is often necessary to store certain data redundantly where it is most frequently used. It has now become possible to construct one's own programs to check that the two versions of the data tally.
- The management of a firm often need summarized data, calculated on the basis of data in the database. Such summarized data is redundant and can therefore be used for consistency control.
- When a computer reads a block of records, it usually checks that the block's contents have not been altered since it was written. This is a kind of consistency control because the outermost bytes in the block are control bytes, whose contents are calculated on the basis of the other contents of the block. The contents of the outermost control bytes are always calculated immediately before the block is written in the disk storage, and if this calculation is repeated when the block is read, it is possible to ensure that the contents of the block have undergone no unintended alterations. This control method protects the block while it is stored in disk storage. To protect the contents of the block while it is in the main storage of the computer, the individual records can be extended by control bytes, so that consistency control can also be performed on the individual records. This form of consistency control is particularly important if the operating system of the computer does not ensure that individual programs only make changes in sections of main storage where they are authorized to do so.

6.7 Validity control

Validity control comprises **semantic integrity** and **internal integrity**.

6.7.1 Semantic integrity

Controlling the semantic integrity consists of preventing users from inputting incorrect data for updating the database. Some techniques that can be used for this purpose are as follows:

- *Job design:* One of the best methods for ensuring that the database contains correct data is to design a working area so that the persons who collect and record data are also the users of that data; that is, end users are also responsible for the maintenance of data.
- *Checking the transactions:* In batch updating, the contents of a field can be summed and the result compared with a balance calculated earlier. By checking the two against each other, it is possible to check that no transactions have been forgotten or wrong data input.
- *Input control:* The input data can be input again by another person who is unlikely to repeat exactly the same errors that may have been made during the first input process.
- It is possible to describe certain constraints that the updated database must observe in the data dictionary. These constraints can be controlled directly and are described in the next section.

6.7.2 Internal integrity

Internal integrity ensures that the data stored in the database is in accordance with the data dictionary's description of it.

Internal integrity may be achieved by the following methods:

- If the data dictionary contains a description of any redundant data, consistency control may be seen as a sort of control of the internal integrity.
- The data dictionary may contain a description of each individual field's domain; i.e., a description of the authorized value area of the field. As an example, a field with an employee's date of birth must satisfy the following criteria: the day must belong to the set $\{1, 2, 3, \ldots, 31\}$, the month must belong to the set $\{1, 2, 3, \ldots, 12\}$, and the two first figures in the year must be 19.
- A particular key field can be stated to be unique or not in the data dictionary. When the key field is updated it will often be possible to ensure that a file with a unique key field contains no other records with the same key value.

- **Referential integrity** is integrity of the relationships between records. As an example of referential integrity, it is possible to store data in the data dictionary to the effect that if a customer is related to an order, the relationship must also be implemented in the opposite direction, so that the order is related to the customer. Data can also be stored to the effect that certain records may not exist in the database without being related to other records. An example of this is that an order must always be related to one or more products, while a product need not be ordered in any order.

6.8 Audit trails

An **audit trail** is a record of all the occurrences/activities in a system and the execution order of these activities. It is an important tool for the data processing auditors whose job it is to make sure that the firm's systems are secure, that they are in accordance with management's directions, and that any weak links in the system cannot be used for fraud or embezzlement. The audit trail may also be an important tool in the recovery process after an error if it is impossible to re-run the programs or recover by means of the log file. The most important demands on the system producing an audit trail are the following:

- The system must be transparent to the application systems that are to be audited; that is, no changes must be made in an application program if it is decided to produce an audit trail in connection with running it.
- The system must be able to take in all applications.
- It has to be possible to select only a few applications to be included in the audit trail.
- It has to be possible to specify the types of occurrence that can trigger off an event in the audit trail. Examples of such occurrences are start up of a transaction, start up of certain transaction types, execution of database statements and output for an external unit such as magnetic tape, screen terminal or printer.
- It has to be possible to re-construct the sequence of the occurrences.
- It must be possible to specify what is to be recorded on the audit trail for the various types of occurrence.

An audit trail usually contains data such as the following:

- the type of occurrence causing the record to be made;
- the time of the occurrence;
- the identification of the transaction that caused the occurrence;

- the name of the program that executed the transaction;
- Any user identification and identification of terminals from which the transaction was started;
- if the occurrence is transferred to/from an external unit, the name of the record type;
- if the occurrence is a database updating, both the before-image and the after-image of the updated records.

The production of an audit trail should be integrated in a DBMS, since in reading/updating a record it must be possible to record which records are read and which updates are executed. The system that writes the audit trail should also be integrated with the transaction processing (TP) management/operating system, as there may also be a need to record the data of a terminal transaction in the audit trail. This requirement can only be fulfilled if the database is integrated with the TP management/operating system. In practice, the database and the TP management system are often supplied by different software producers, so that an integrated audit trail cannot be made; consequently, the audit trails have to be merged when a total overview of the situation is needed.

This description of the demands made on an audit trail is very highly idealized and, in fact, many firms just use the log file as an audit trail. However, this is a poor replacement for a proper audit trail because the log file only contains data about database updates and gives no information about the rest of the system.

6.9 General error-preventing measures

The discussion of the previous section highlighted the fact that with modern database software we have to be prepared for new types of errors and that it may be more difficult to recover with modern day systems. It has, therefore, become more important to try to prevent errors. The most important general error-preventing methods are as follows:

- Naturally, update programs should not be tested on the production database. They have to be tested on a special database created for that purpose. It is important to know the status of the test database when the test program is run. In large data processing installations it may be necessary to create several different test databases to ensure that the different test programs do not disturb each other.
- Formally, all data processing departments require thorough testing of update programs before they go into production. In practice, this requirement may be difficult to fulfil, particularly in the case of corrections to an old program that one believes one knows. To enhance the quality of their programs some firms have started an

inspection system. Under this system a programmer who did not write the program himself has to approve it before it is allowed to go into production. The inspection of programs can be made easier if one of the many forms of structured programming is already in use.

- Hardware can be doubled and integrated with software in such a way that if a hardware unit does not work, its function will immediately be taken over by the reserve unit. It is important that such doubling is also integrated with the databases, so that the resource-demanding database updates are not executed twice. After a database update has been executed on the first disk storage, the database can transfer a copy of the update to the second disk storage, as it is much cheaper to copy it than to execute an update twice. TANDEM is an example of a system that copies updates immediately.
- Software products that can ensure that batch programs are run in the correct sequence and at the right moment are available. If such products are used, it is only necessary, once and for all, to inform the system of the dependencies that exist between the programs and how frequently the individual programs are to be run. These software products protect the database against human errors, but do not ensure a correct restart for a recovery process. Unfortunately, the greatest need to protect the run sequence often occurs after a recovery, because running a recovery phase upsets the daily routine of the operations staff.

One management method that also works after recovery, proceeds as follows: A 'date record' is created containing the date on which the firm runs its data processing production and the date of the next input into the data processing system. For each file, a copy is taken of the contents of the date record at the time when the file was last updated. When a batch update starts, the 'next run-day' in the date record of the file is checked to see if it is the same as the 'actual run-day' in the shared date record. By doing this, it is possible to ensure that an update is not forgotten or run twice. Furthermore, if the transaction files also contain a date record, a check can be made to ensure that an old transaction file is not being used. As date records are backed out in connection with recovery, the technique described here can be used to ensure correct reruns.

EXERCISES

6.1 A company has an employee file that is updated by both batch and real-time programs. The fields 'gross wages' and 'withheld tax' are updated on a batch basis once a month, and all the 2000 records of the file are updated by this wage run. The other fields in the employee file are real-time updated from a single terminal located in the staff department. An average of 100 records per month are updated by the real-time system. Assume that the company has a database that, by means of a parameter, can indicate whether record changes are to be registered in the log file. Assume that the employee file is security copied every month. The wage calculation program is run during the evening, so that real-time updatings are not run at the same time as the wage calculation program.

(a) Is it sufficiently secure not to use a log file for batch running the wage calculation run?

(b) Is it sufficiently secure not to use the log file for real-time updating of the employee file?

(c) Will it be necessary, with a view to security, for the real-time updating programs to lock records before updating if updating transactions can only be sent from one single terminal?

(d) Describe how it is possible to design a system for consistency control of the employee file. The consistency control must make it possible to detect any unauthorized changes to the fields 'gross wages' and 'withheld tax'.

(e) Can your proposed solution to part (d) also be used to detect certain types of programming errors in the wage calculation program that update the fields 'gross wages' and 'withheld tax'?

(f) Assume that a report generator can be started from a terminal that can print reports on the basis of the employee file. Could it lead to inconsistencies in a report if the report generator is started at the same time as the wage calculation program is updating the employee file? Could it lead to inconsistencies in a report if the report generator is started at the same time as the employee file is updated by the real-time system?

6.2 Assume that an employee file is updated by both real-time and batch programs. There are a large number of different terminals that can send updating transactions which can make changes in a record in the employee file. Assume that the employee file must have a particular status when the wage calculation program is being run; for example, overtime hours relating to a period must be available and the recording of overtime hours relating to the succeeding period must not have started.

(a) How is it possible to ensure that the employee file is not updated at the same time as the wage calculation program is updating the employee file?

(b) Assume that the wage calculation run has been delayed due to an error. How is it possible to prevent real-time updatings relating to the wrong period from being run?

(c) Assume that a company does not possess the control system referred to in part (b) and that the wage calculation system has been run while the employee file had a wrong status. Assume also that the employee department cannot state precisely which wage calculations are incorrect because several days elapsed before the error was discovered. How would you ensure that the incorrect wage calculations are corrected?

(d) How can the database be recovered after a power breakdown?

6.3 Assume that a real-time system has so many update transactions that writing the record changes on the log file becomes a bottleneck. Assume that in such a situation, several log records can be stored in the same block, so that the log file is no longer a bottleneck. Will this optimization reduce the possibility of recovering the database?

6.4 Assume that a company has both 'large' and 'small' real-time updating transactions. In the case of the 'small' transactions, records can be locked before the updating in the normal way. However, the 'large' transactions concern so many records that the records concerned cannot be locked in the normal way without seriously affecting the response times of the on-line/ real-time programs. (If there are many locked records, it may take a long time to find out whether a given record is locked.) How would you propose organizing the database so that both kinds of real-time update can take place?

6.5 A company has a product file in which statistical data concerning the turnover of the individual products is added up on a current basis. At the end of the accounting year, all these adding-up fields are zero-adjusted by a batch program that updates all records.

(a) How can one prevent the writing of statistical reports and the real-time updating of the statistical fields being started at the same time as the batch program is zero-adjusting the statistical fields?

(b) Assume that the product file is security copied immediately before the batch program zero-adjusts the statistical fields in the product file. Would you find it necessary or expedient for the database to write log records as the batch program zero-adjusts the product file? (It is assumed here that the system you proposed in part (a) has been implemented to prevent others from using the product file while the statistical fields are being zero-adjusted.)

6.6 Assume that a company has two types of files:

(1) files that are updated via a database

(2) 'old-fashioned' files that are not updated by a database.

(a) Describe the recovery problems that may occur if it is necessary to update both types of files in a single batch program. It is assumed here that real-time updates may not be run at the same time as the batch updates. How would you solve any problems in this connection?

(b) Describe the recovery problems that may occur if it is necessary to update both types of files in a real-time program. How would you solve any problems in this connection?

6.7 Periodically a company has some very large updating runs that simultaneously involve large amounts of output from a printer. Real-time updates may occur at the same time as the large updating run. In the large updating run, therefore, only a few records are locked at a time. If the large updating run abends, the last update may be backed out. How is it possible to synchronize this recovery of the database and the recovery of output on the printer?

6.8 A database software product backs out a transaction's real-time update if the transaction abends. How is it possible to ensure that the terminal operator is informed of the backing out if this happens?

6.9 A disk storage is destroyed physically so that part of a cylinder cannot be read. In other words, transactions that attempt to read records in the destroyed cylinders get a reply code that states that the records cannot be read.

(a) Assume that the operating system abends before the destroyed cylinders are recovered. How is it possible to recover in such a situation?

(b) How can the database be recovered if the recovery program abends due to physical defects in the log file?

6.10 Should the auxiliary programs supplied by the software producer that update, re-organize and recover the database log the executed database changes?

6.11 A file is only updated during the night so that it is possible to roll forward recover by the night log files in an old copy of the file.

(a) Is it possible to recover the file if some of the day log files produced by a real-time system are accidentally included?

(b) Can real-time transactions, which are not updating the file in the process of being recovered, be run at the same time as the recovery?

(c) Is it possible to recover the file if the night log files are rolled forward in a wrong sequence?

6.12 An operating system abends while real-time updatings are being executed. How can the database select which transactions to back out?

6.13 In files with index organization the overflow problem is sometimes solved by splitting a block into two different blocks, each containing half of the records stored in the original block. How can the database recover if it abends in the middle of a block split?

6.14 A database is to update a record. What should the database update first: the log file or the record itself?

Chapter 7
Security

7.1 Introduction

There are many aspects of database security. Normally, the problems relating to security are divided into problems of privacy and problems of integrity. In this context, **privacy** involves systems that can guarantee that only authorized users will be able to read or alter the contents of the data base, whilst **integrity** involves the reliability of the stored data – that is the requirement that the database must describe 'the real world' as credibly as possible. Integrity may be subdivided according to what is to be secured. This is illustrated in Figure 7.1.

External integrity is the requirement that the facts existing in the real world must correspond with the categories of recorded information in the database and the conceptual schema. External integrity may be divided into the integrity that holds between the real world and the conceptual schema on the one hand, and semantic integrity on the other.

The way to achieve agreement between the real world and the conceptual schema was the subject of Chapter 1. **Semantic integrity** concerns that part of integrity affected by the users' maintenance of the database. If, for example, a user accidentally inputs incorrect data about a customer, the contents of the database will not correspond with the real world for that customer, and the semantic integrity of the database is broken. This subject was discussed in Section 6.7.1.

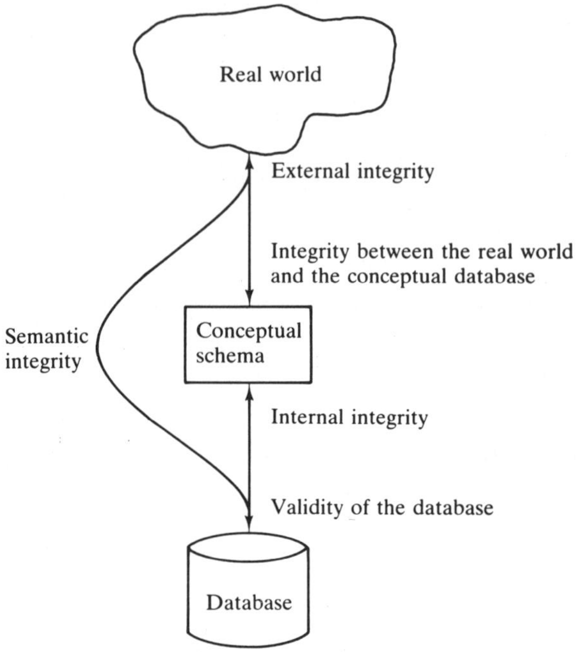

Figure 7.1 External and internal integrity.

Internal integrity is the requirement that the contents of the database must be in accordance with the conceptual schema; that is the contents of the individual fields must be in accordance with their domain, and any constraints on relationships must be observed. For example, that all employee records must contain a department number, and that there must be a department record that has the department number in question as identification key (see Section 6.7). Sometimes a field is defined by the contents of other fields. For example, the contents of a field which contains a total must be equal to the sum of the field contents of the fields that are added to get the total. The database is **consistent** if the contents of the database cross-check with each other in this way. If the contents of fields are dependent on each other, it is possible to record this connection in the conceptual schema. Thus the consistency of the database may be seen as a subset of its internal integrity (see Section 6.6 on Consistency control).

As shown in Figure 7.1 the **validity** of the database involves its internal as well as its semantic integrity (see Section 6.7).

In this chapter, we shall deal with some concrete methods that may be used to resolve the security problems related to databases. Table 7.1 classifies these methods according to whether they can be used to detect errors, prevent errors or instigate recovery after an error situation. Some of these methods have several possible applications.

Table 7.1 Methods of database security.

Error-detecting methods	***Error-preventing methods***	***Recovery methods***
Consistency control	Consistency control	Log recovery
Validity control	Validity control Concurrency control	Recovery lines Adjustment programming
Audit trails	Encryption, program inspection, hardware doubling, test databases, authorization system	Error-adjusting consistency control

7.2 Privacy

The purpose of an **authorization system** is to protect data against unauthorized use. The following is a list of examples of such protection which can be achieved by means of an authorization system:

- Updating an employee file can only be performed from specific terminals located in the staff department, and these terminals may only be used within normal office hours.
- Executive employees are authorized to see all data held on employees in their departments.
- Non-executive employees are authorized to read only those fields containing names and addresses in the employee file, while executive employees in the staff department are also authorized to read wage data, etc.
- The fields containing data on PAYE tax deductions, pension fund contributions and paid-out wages may only be updated by a batch program calculating wages, which is run once a month.
- Users in the accounts department are not authorized to read wage data in the individual employee records, but they are authorized to perform statistical operations on those fields.
- Assume that a firm has several files with employee data: an example of this would be the wage file and a curriculum vitae file containing data on the individual employee's education, training and participation in courses. A linking up of the wage file and the curriculum vitae file, for example, might only be performed by employees in the staff department.

An authorization system satisfying the foregoing requirements must be integrated with the firm's database so that it can protect files, record fields and relationships holding between files.

In practice, another type of authorization is integrated with the computer's operating system, as the operating system can often protect files, disk storages, terminals and programs against unauthorized use. It is possible to merge these two types of security systems into one authorization system, but in practice this is rarely done. The reasons for this are as follows:

- The two types of authorization systems can be built up by the same principles, but they protect different parts of a data processing installation.
- If the operating system is to protect features of the logical database, such as record fields and relationships between records, it will make the building up of the operating system more complicated since it must then have knowledge of and access to the data dictionary of the database.
- Operating systems and databases are often developed by different software suppliers. If this is so, the operating system may not be in a position to protect the record fields of the database, and the operating system will run with an extra security overhead, which cannot be exploited.

Instead of integrating the two types of security systems, it is common for the operating system to include read/write facilities that can be used by the database management system, so that the users have no access to the database round this system.

We shall now see how a user can identify himself to the authorization system by a logon procedure. In the description of how the authorization systems work, we assume that the logon procedure is executed correctly, so that the system has a unique identification for the user.

Authorization systems can be built up by many different principles. However, most systems can be classified according to whether they use an access matrix, hierarchical security levels or a combination of the two methods. In general, methods using access matrices give a greater possibility of defining the individual users' access rights. But these systems also require more administration than the systems using hierarchical security levels. A more detailed description of these methods is presented in Fernandez *et al.*(1981).

The treatment of authorization systems is followed by a description of encryption which, amongst other things, includes methods that can protect data despite failure or circumvention of the database's authorization system.

7.3 Identification and verification

An authorization system must be able to identify a user to check whether the user is authorized to gain access to protected resources. A person who tries to access resources for which he has no authorization is called an **intruder** in what follows.

Normally, the user identifies himself by typing in his **user number** or by letting the system read a plastic card, which may include a magnetic strip on which the user number is encoded. Then, the authorization system has to **authenticate** that the user is the person he claims to be: the authorization system must, for example, check that the plastic card has not been stolen and that the user is not using another person's user number. This control is normally performed by the user typing in a secret **password**: a codeword the user can choose himself. The codeword must be kept secret and should only be known by the user with the particular user number. Users can alter their passwords, if need be, and indeed should do so regularly. Authorization systems that can check the user's identity by means of fingerprints and voiceprints have also been developed.

The user's password is usually checked against data that is stored together with the user number in the password table of the authorization system. For the password to be checked, it must be transmitted from the terminal to the computer.

While the secret password is being transmitted to the computer, the transmission line could be tapped, so that an intruder could discover the password. To avoid this danger, the password can be transmitted in an encrypted form (see Section 7.5). Furthermore, to avoid the risk involved in transmitting the password down a transmission line the password can be authenticated by using a microcomputer built into the terminal, which will authenticate the password locally. The problem of securing passwords sent via a transmission line can also be solved by using **nonce passwords**. A nonce password usually consists of a permanent element and a variable element. The permanent element corresponds to a normal password, while the variable element may be a number that is a function of date and time when the logon is attempted. As the variable element of the password varies from time to time, an intruder cannot discover a password by tapping the transmission line.

The process of stating a user number and the corresponding password is called the **sign on** or **logon** procedure. When the user has finished using the terminal, the authorization system must be informed about it. This is called the **sign off** or **logoff** procedure. If a user forgets to sign off, it is possible for an intruder to use the terminal and gain access to all the resources that the user's authorization covers.

Batch programs, which are not controlled by a terminal user, must in principle also go through an identification and verification process to gain access to protected resources. If a batch program has to give a password, this will normally be stored as a part of the compiled program. Thus it is important that the authorization system also protects the compiled programs stored in program libraries.

In the following sections, describing the functions of the authorization systems, it is assumed that the sign on procedure has been executed correctly, so that the system has a unique identification of the user.

7.4 Authorization

7.4.1 By access matrices

Figure 7.2 illustrates an **access matrix** in which the rows describe the individual users' access rights and the columns describe who has access to the protected objects. The user may be either a person or a program and an object may be either a file or a field in a file. The matrix element $A\ (i, j)$ describes the rights that user 'i' has over object 'j'. Examples of rights are reading and updating. If the contents of $A\ (i, j)$ is blank, the user has no right to read or update the object.

The person '*a*' in the figure is authorized to read all fields in the first file and to read and update fields 1 and 2 in the second file. Likewise,

	Objects / Users	File 1	Field 1	Field 2	. . .	File 2	Field 1	Field 2	. . .
Persons	*a*	read					read update	read update	
	b					read			
	c	read							
	⋮								
Programs	*x*	read							
	y					update			
	⋮								

Figure 7.2 Access matrix. The columns represent files or fields in files, the rows users, which may be individuals or programs.

program x is authorized to read file 1, and program y is authorized to create new records in file 2.

Access matrices can also be used to store pointers to logical expressions that must be executed before a user gains access to the object. If, for example, a user is only authorized to read wage data on employees in the user's own department, a pointer to a logical expression in matrix field A (user identity, staff file identification) can be stored, which tests whether the user's department number corresponds to the input employee record's department number. This test is executed whenever the user wants to read an employee record. The test, which is executed before the DBMS transfers a record to an application program, may be quite complicated. For example, a test can be made to see whether the fields of the record contain certain field values, and/or the time at which the request to read the file is made is within normal office hours. This is called **content-dependent access control** or **security by value**. If the user uses a fourth-generation programming language (see Section 5.3.2) the logical expression can also test whether the user reads individual records or whether he simply sums up the contents of certain record fields. This allows a user to be authorized to perform statistical inquiries into the contents of certain record fields without having read access to the contents of the individual records that are part of his inquiries. Using a fourth-generation programming language, it will also be possible to record that a user may not use those statements that can be used to link up a file with other files. Thus, a user can be prevented from linking up the wage file with the training and education file mentioned earlier in this chapter.

7.4.2 By hierarchical security levels

Level-oriented security systems are based on the concepts of **access level** and **category**. All objects entering into the security system are given an access level number so that objects with a high access level are protected more than those with low access levels. Objects with the lowest level number, zero, thus enjoy no protection against intruders. Similarly, the users are given an access level number, which is greater than or equal to the level numbers, for those objects the user is going to have access to. Normally, users and objects have two different level numbers corresponding to the access level for reading and updating data, respectively. Examples of access levels are security classifications used for example by the military. These are shown in Figure 7.3.

Categories involve a division of objects into subsystems, which may overlap. Categories are, for example, data used in staff systems, customer information systems, invoicing systems and back-order systems. The security system uses the categories to give each object a set of

Level number	Designation of level
3	Top secret
2	Secret
1	Confidential
0	Unclassified

Figure 7.3 Military security classifications represented as access level numbers.

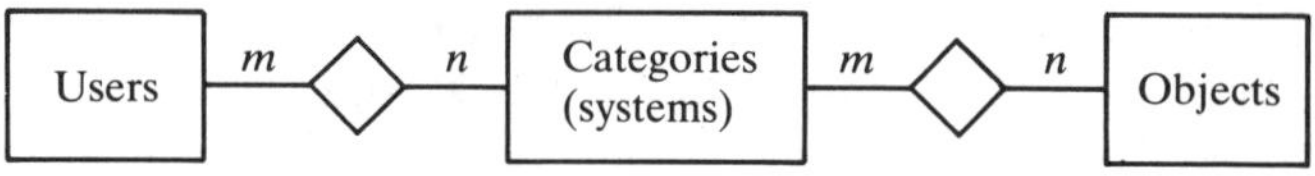

Figure 7.4 Relationship between users, categories and objects in a hierarchical security system.

categories that the object enters into. Similarly, all users are given a set of categories corresponding to the systems the user has access to. The E–R diagram in Figure 7.4 illustrates the relationships between the entities users, categories and objects.

The security system uses the access levels and categories to give the user access to an object if his level number is greater than or equal to the level number of the object, and if the object's set of categories contains a category that is also present in the user's set of categories. These access conditions can be supplemented with logical expressions that must be satisfied before the user gains access.

If the file names are used as categories, a special case of the above is obtained. In this case, an object may only have a category number attached to it which corresponds to the name of the file making up the object, or which contains the field that makes up the object. Thus, a user must have category names corresponding to all the files to which he has access.

7.4.3 By a combination of access matrices and hierarchical security levels

Authorization systems that include elements from both of the previously described methods are common in practice, and this section deals with an example of such a system. Here, files are protected by access matrices and file fields are protected by access levels. Figure 7.5 illustrates the access matrix shown in Figure 7.2, but rather than writing in the matrix whether a user is authorized to read or update an object, the user's access level number for reading and updating is placed in the cells of the matrix.

	Users \ Objects	File 1	File 2	...
National Register number	*a*	1 0	1 2	
	b		1 0	
	c	1 0		
	⋮			
Program number	*x*	1 0		
	y		0 3	
	⋮			

Figure 7.5 Access matrix containing access level numbers for particular users. The upper access level number in each cell is for reading, the lower one for updating.

In Figure 7.6, the first column contains the numbers or names of the files to be used. The second column contains the lowest access level required to read or update a field in the file. In the following columns, the element *A* (*i*, *j*) contains two numbers, corresponding to the access level for reading and updating field *j* in file *i*. If one of these table elements is not occupied, the access level of the whole file, which is stored in the second column, has to be used.

Figure 7.5 shows that person *a* has access level 1 to read file 1 and access level 0 to update it. From Figure 7.6, it can be seen that access level 1 is required to read file 1 and access level 2 to update it. Thus, person *a* can read file 1 but is prevented from updating it. Also, person *a* has access levels 1 and 2 for file 2 and so can both read and update its first two fields. He cannot, however, update field 3 since its access level is 3. Similarly, person *b* has no access to file 1, but he may read file 2; *b* is not authorized to update this file. Person *c* may read but not update file 1. Program *x* may read but not update file 1. Program *y* may update but not read file 2 – i.e., program *y* can only create new records in file 2. These authorizations correspond to the contents of the access matrix in Figure 7.2.

By means of access matrices it is possible, however, to create a

File number	Lowest access number	Field 1	Field 2	Field 3	...
1	1 2			1 3	
2	1 2	1 2	1 2	1 3	
3	0 1				
⋮					

Figure 7.6 Access matrix showing the security levels attached to files and fields of files.

more individual authorization than by the method described here. An example of this is to use access matrices to authorize a user to some fields in a record while another user can be authorized to other fields in the same record. This is not possible with the method that has been described here since the access level is set once and for all for any user.

7.5 Encryption

Encryption is defined as the transformation of data so that the meaning of it cannot be understood directly. By **decrypting** the data, its original meaning is obtained. If we can conceal how the data can be decrypted, we can protect the data against intruders. Encryption is used both in connection with data communications and for storing data in files. For data communication, the aim is to achieve protection against the data being tapped or altered while it is being transmitted via a communication line. Encryption of data in a database protects against intruders who are trying to gain access to files without using a database language and who are thereby circumventing the controls built into the authorization system of the database. Encrypted data is called **cipher text** while the original data is called **plain text**.

For encryption, a function f has to be found where f(*plain text*) = *cipher text* and where there is an inverse function f^{-1} so that f^{-1} (*cipher text*) = *plain text*. The function f must have the following characteristics:

- Finding f^{-1} must be very expensive and time consuming even if the fastest computers are used to analyse the encrypted data.
- It has to be easy to replace f and f^{-1} by other functions.

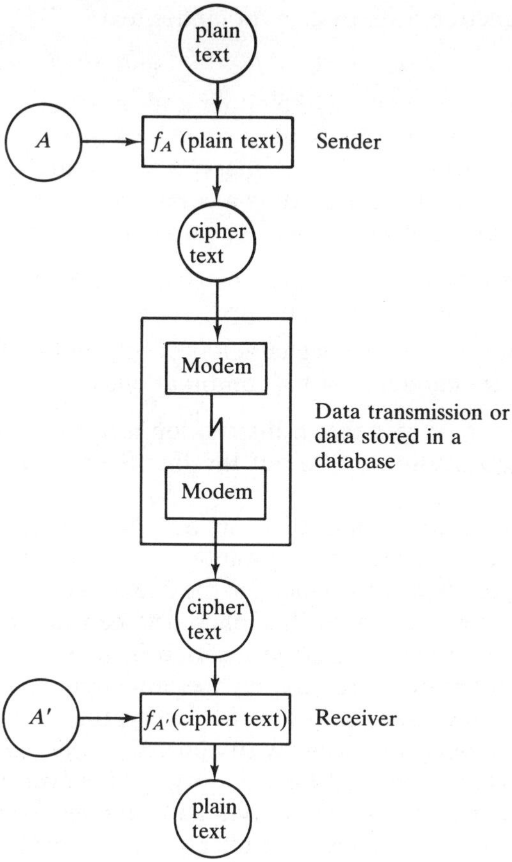

Figure 7.7 The encryption–decryption process.

- It has to be inexpensive and fast to execute the operations f and f^{-1}: it should be possible to implement these functions in the hardware of the computer.
- It has to be impossible to 'steal' the function f^{-1}.

In practice, functions satisfying these requirements are constructed as programs or hardware that use an input parameter called an **encryption key**.

In principle, the encryption *program* may be made public, since it is only necessary to keep the encryption *key* secret: to change the encryption function only involves changing the encryption key. Figure 7.7 illustrates the encryption technique involved in data communication. In this figure, A is the encryption key and A' is the corresponding key used to decrypt. The function $f_{A'}$ is the encryption function, while $f_{A'}$ is the inverse function used to decrypt cipher text:

$$f_{A'}\,(f_A\,(plain\ text)) = plain\ text$$

The sender and receiver may be either a terminal or a computer.

Encryption is normally performed by a division of plain text into fixed length blocks, which are encrypted separately. The encryption algorithm is normally produced by a combination of the following basic operations, which are well suited for implementation in a chip:

- **Transposition**: replacing a bit string from plain text by a bit string from another part of plain text.
- **Substitution**: replacing characters or bit combinations in plain text by other characters or bit combinations.

In general, it can be said that transposition mixes the characters in plain text, while substitution evens out the frequency of characters in plain text.

It is very important to even out the frequency of characters because individual characters normally occur with a fixed frequency in a given language. Thus, if the language the data is written in is known, then the frequency of characters in cipher text can be calculated and the symbols of the original language inserted in those places where cipher text has characters of approximately the same frequency. This procedure represents an important step towards decrypting cipher text. If all the characters in cipher text occur with approximately the same frequency, this method cannot be used for decryption. However, by substitution it is possible to ensure that the individual characters occur with approximately the same frequency in cipher text, as a character that occurs frequently can be converted into several different bit combinations, which all symbolize the original character.

EXERCISES

7.1 Big business customers of a bank have on-line access to their accounts and entries.

(a) How can a company be prevented from accessing another company's records?

(b) How is it possible to ensure that a parent company can access all data relating to its subsidiaries while blocking its access to data relating to other companies?

7.2 In the section on privacy, three different types of security were mentioned.

(a) Which of these security systems can secure the fields of a file so that person A may read field 1 but not field 2, while person B may read field 2 but not field 1?

(b) Which of the security systems can secure the field of a file so that all heads of departments have access to field 1, about 50% have access to field 2 and certain specialists have access to field 2 but not to field 1?

7.3 (a) Can buried update be allowed to occur in connection with the changing of a customer's address field?

(b) Can buried update be allowed to occur if airplane tickets are booked via a real-time system?

(c) Can buried update be allowed to occur if an amount of money is transferred from one account to another?

(d) Can buried update be allowed to occur if a hospital doctor updates the diagnosis on a patient?

Chapter 8
Alternatives to Database Management Systems

8.1 Introduction

In earlier chapters, we have seen how, by means of a database management system (DBMS), we can increase a firm's flexibility in the introduction of new data processing systems, increase the productivity of programmers, reduce maintenance costs and yield a high degree of service to the users. In practice, however, the introduction of a DBMS is often not an unqualified success for many reasons. Factors that play a role are as follows:

- With the DBMSs presently available the programmers often have to work at too low a programming level, since they often have to navigate their way through chains of pointers or indexes.
- The database is not flexible to unforeseen tasks because old programs are often dependent upon the physical structure of the database.
- Only in recent years have the high-level database languages become good enough to replace low-level database languages.
- The data model used by the DBMSs is often very complex. It introduces many irrelevant concepts and each DBMS often has its own terminology.
- Documentation is often poor.

- There are often errors both in the software and in manuals.
- Although the price of CPU capacity is falling rapidly, the use of capacity by the DBMS itself is still an important factor in large administrative data processing systems.
- In systems with many transactions, it may be very expensive to use all the facilities provided by a DBMS.

As firms do not often require all the facilities provided by the DBMSs, we will now go through some simple methods that can partly satisfy the demands that might be made on a DBMS.

8.2 Demands on database facilities

8.2.1 Implementation of relationships

The relational database model is so simple to work with that it is quite unnecessary to use a DBMS merely for the implementation of relationships.

According to the analysis in Section 4.2, the use of resources of the relational data model is low compared with that of other methods of implementation. Thus, a DBMS should normally not be bought only with the purpose of implementing relationships.

8.2.2. Data dictionary

If a firm is interested in data dictionary documentation, there are a wide range of different dictionary products to choose from. Sometimes these products are so good that the database software supplier recommends them as a supplement to the product. A data dictionary that is not integrated with a DBMS is not particularly well suited for the achievement of data independence, but it is possible, however, to build up the application programs in such a way that they fetch the record descriptions from the data dictionary when they are translated. This method ensures that the latest version of the record description is inserted in the application program.

8.2.3 Recovery

In real-time systems, it is relatively easy to introduce log recovery without using a DBMS, since the transaction management system may itself contain a log recovery facility. An example of this is the very commonly used transaction management system CICS.

Batch-updating programs can be recovered by using one of the following methods:

- The batch-updating programs can be run under the control of the transaction management system and can be recovered in the same way as the real-time transactions.
- The files can be copied before the batch updatings are run.
- A subroutine can be constructed through which all the file accesses have to pass. Log records with all the file changes can be written on the basis of this subroutine.

8.2.4 File protection

It is possible to buy software products that give protection against unauthorized use of data. These software products can protect resources such as screen terminals, programs, disk storages and files. As these software products are not integrated with database software they cannot individually protect the separate fields in a record.

8.2.5 Data independence

There are no special software products that provide data independence alone. However, it is easy to achieve data independence at record level. To achieve this, it is only necessary to produce a subroutine that has as its input a database statement code, a record buffer and the number of characters from the record the program requires. As output, the subroutine reads or updates the required part of the record. If such a subroutine is used, data independence has been achieved at record level, as it is possible to add new fields at the end of the record without damaging the old application programs.

By means of this subroutine, partial independence of the files' organization is also achieved as, for example, it is possible to go from random organization to index sequential organization merely by making alterations in the subroutine. The subroutine can also provide partial independence in relation to a DBMS, as a DBMS can either be introduced or replaced with a new one by merely changing the subroutine's contents.

8.2.6 Database languages

It is possible to buy special software products that contain a high-level data manipulation language. These software products are often integrated with a data dictionary so that the high-level language can utilize its field descriptions in automatic editing of screen and print layouts.

However, high-level languages that are not integrated with a DBMS suffer from a serious shortcoming as there is no simple way to follow the relationships of the database. The application opportunities of these languages are therefore limited to the generation of reports, data entry systems and extraction of data from files. These systems are therefore poor substitutes for genuine fourth-generation languages such as those described in Chapters 12 and 13.

8.3 Additional facilities

The database facilities described are all available and implemented in existing software. However, there are many other facilities that it is worthwhile integrating with a DBMS. The purpose of this section is to outline how future DBMSs can be extended so that they can administer historical and budgeted data in a flexible and user-friendly way.

The main principle in the following proposal is that the DBMS places the corresponding time on all database changes that it makes so that it is possible to extend the traditional query statements with a time dimension indicating the database status to be used in replying to the query.

An example of a situation in which historical data is called for is the calculation of interest on bank accounts. In calculating interest, it is important to know the past balances of the individual accounts as well as the history of interest rates. The reason why it is necessary to know the historical data is that the interest calculation cannot be concluded daily since amongst other things cheque entries may not be recorded at the bank until long after the cheque was issued.

Accounting systems can be mentioned as another area where the use of historical data is necessary. In budgeting systems and liquidity management systems there is a similar need for budgeted data.

8.3.1 Data dictionary records relating to historical or budgeted data

As it is very expensive to administer historical data, it is convenient to record what record types the DBMS must be able to administer in a historical/future perspective in the data dictionary. To reduce the use of space further it is expedient to record what fields in a record are interesting in terms of time. For these fields the answers to the following further questions can be stored:

- Is the field value constant? Either the contents of the field are non-existent or unknown, or the field contains a specific value that is retained throughout the life of the record. An example of this field type is a field with a person's date of birth.

P	NOT *P*
TRUE	FALSE
UNKNOWN	UNKNOWN
FALSE	TRUE

Figure 8.1 Three-value truth table for the operator NOT.

- Does the field value vary non-continuously with time? An example of this field type is a field with a person's address.
- Is the field value a continuous function of time? An example of this field type is a field that identifies the physical position of a means of transport. For fields of this type, functions are determined that can be used for interpolation or extrapolation, so that the value of the field can be calculated for an arbitrary point in time.
- Is the value of the field a function of other fields? The balance field in an account record is an example of this, as the balance can be calculated at an arbitrary point in time, if all other relevant entries have been stored.

8.3.2 Data manipulation statements for searching historical or budgeted data

As previously described, the traditional database query statements have to be extended with a parameter that indicates the database status to be used for replying to queries. However, it is convenient to extend the data manipulation language further, because a database with historical/budgeted data will often lack field values belonging to certain periods. This problem can be neatly dealt with by using ternary logic in which a logical expression may assume the value TRUE, FALSE or UNKNOWN. Likewise, rules can be formulated for dealing with unknown field values when they are part of arithmetic expressions. By way of example, Figure 8.1 shows a truth table for the logical operator NOT within ternary logic. For further information on ternary logic the reader is referred to Reschner (1969).

Chapter 9
Database Machines

9.1 Introduction

The primary purpose of using a **database machine** is to take some of the pressure off the computer on which the application programs run so that the total capacity of the machine configuration is increased. The database machine may consist of a special purpose mini-computer, which, if its capacity is taken into account, is much cheaper than the large application computer.

9.2 Architecture of database machines

In Chapter 5 on Data independence, we saw how the necessary software functions cooperate when a DBMS is run on the same computer as the application programs. Figure 9.1 shows how the corresponding software functions cooperate when a database machine is used. It can be seen from the figure that if the software functions are distributed between the two machines, then software in the form of communication links is needed to connect the two computers. The numbered arrows in the figure illustrate the activities to be executed for an application program to read a record in the database.

Figure 9.1 shows the simplest possible connection between an

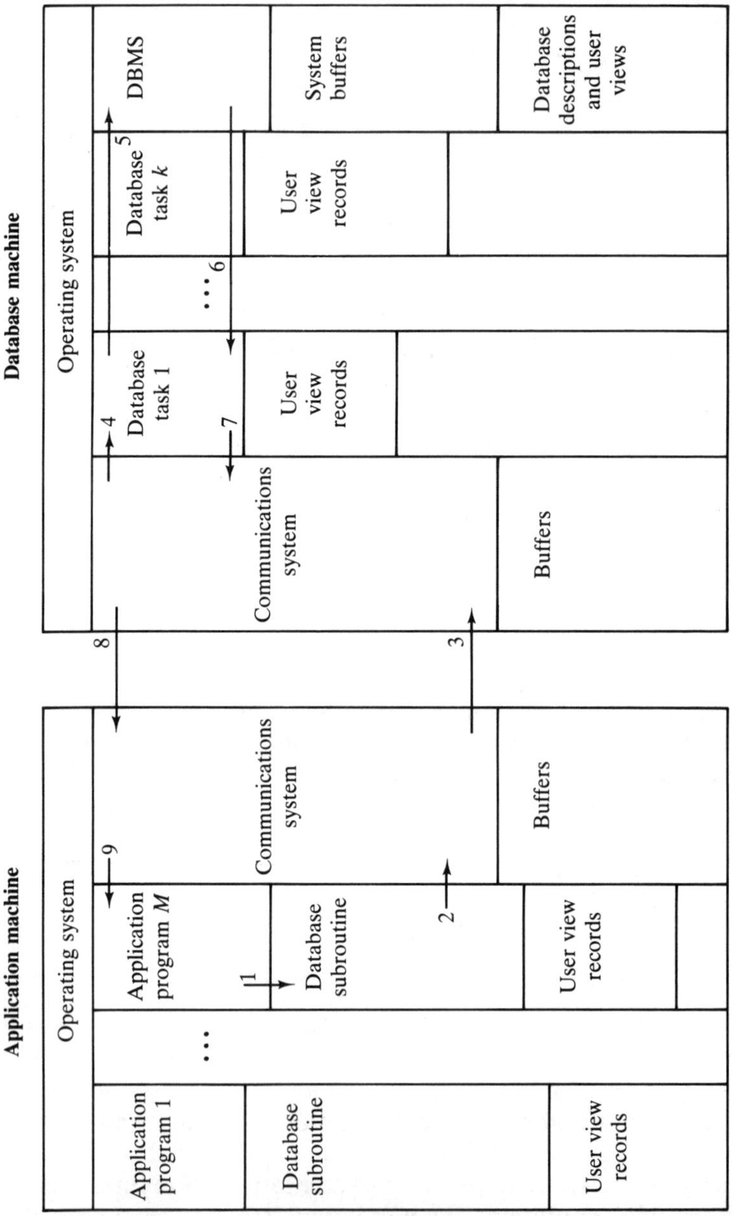
Application machine
Operating system
Application program 1
Database subroutine
User view records
Application program M
Database subroutine
User view records
Communications system
Buffers
1
2
3
4
5
6
7
8
9
Database machine
Operating system
Communications system
Buffers
Database task 1
User view records
Database task k
User view records
DBMS
System buffers
Database descriptions and user views

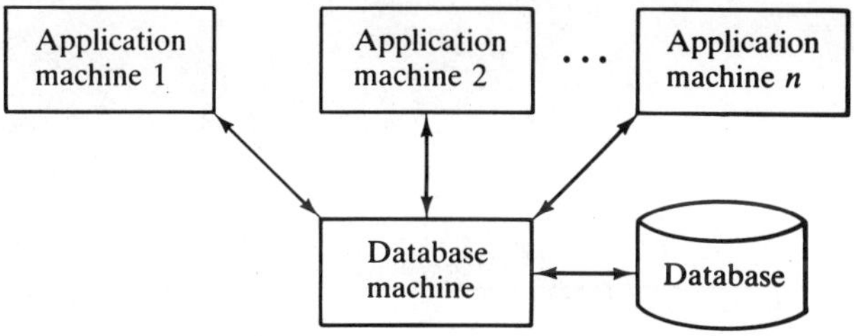

Figure 9.2 Several application machines configured with a single database machine.

application machine and a database machine. An important advantage of the database machine is that additional central or local application machines can be plugged in directly. This is illustrated in Figure 9.2. However, it is also possible to build up the database machine out of a number of different database machines. This is illustrated in Figure 9.3.

Many different types of database machines that all work according to this principle can be constructed as the distribution of work on the individual database machines may be made according to different

---

Figure 9.1 Distribution of software functions between a database machine and an application machine. The following numbered activities are shown. 1: If the program needs to read a record in the database, a database subroutine is called. 2: The application program itself must be independent of whether a database machine or database software is used on the application machine. Therefore, the database subroutine must know whether a database machine is used or not. If a database machine is used, the database statement is passed on to the communication system. 3: The communication system contains the basic components of a general transaction management system, since its task is to manage the physical connection between the two computers. Thus, the communication system must comprise a communication protocol, and a system for the detection and correction of errors, management of buffers, etc. By means of this software, the database statement of the application program can be transferred to the database machine. 4: When the database machine has received the database statement a 'task' for the statement is created; i.e., a program that analyses the contents of the database statement is started. 5 and 6: Normally, the result of the analysis above is that the DBMS is called on one or several times, corresponding to the records the database statement requires to be read. (In Section 5.2, there is a more detailed description of how the DBMS operates.) 7: After the data belonging to the database statement is located, it is passed on to the communication system of the database machine. 8: User view records are transferred from the database machine to the communication system of the application machine. 9: User view records are transferred to the working area of the original application program, after which control is passed on to the application program.

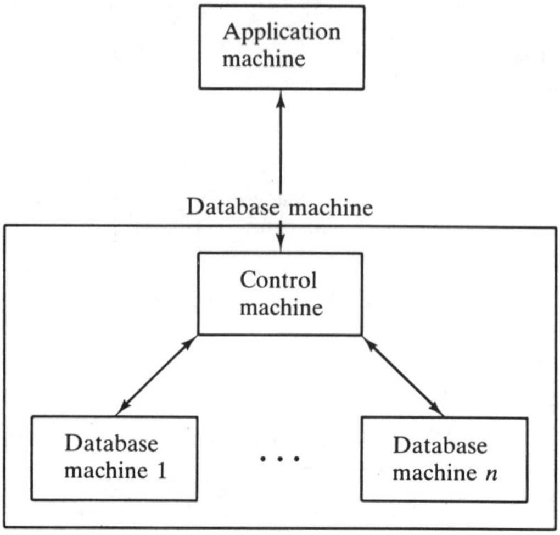

Figure 9.3 A database machine consisting of several submachines together with a control machine.

criteria. Some examples of work distribution are as follows:

- *Distribution by data:* Each individual database machine has to control a specific section of the database.
- *Distribution by function:* Each individual database machine is specialized to perform a particular task. Examples of such tasks are reading, writing and updating.

Database machines that work according to the principle illustrated in Figure 9.3 are, however, not available yet.

9.3 Advantages and disadvantages of database machines

The main advantages and disadvantages of database machines can be described as follows:

- *Capacity:* A larger total CPU capacity can be achieved by using a database machine. It is assumed here that the time for data communication is less than the time gained by the fact that the database machine can run simultaneously with the application machine.
- *Response times:* If the accesses to the database constitute a bottleneck, the average response time will decrease with a database

machine. If the accesses to the database do not constitute a bottleneck, there will be no time saved by using a database machine. In fact, in such a case the database machine might instead increase the response time because of the extra time needed for communications.

- *Costs:* Use of a database machine means that capacity on the relatively expensive application machine can be partly replaced with capacity on the relatively cheap database machine. Whether this shift from the application machine to the database machine will pay depends primarily on whether the costs of data communication are lower than the gain achieved by using the relatively cheap database machine.
- *Hardware specialization:* New hardware techniques, which are oriented towards databases, can be used more efficiently in a database machine than in a general-purpose computer. One example of such hardware is **content addressing**. When physically searching a disk, the search argument normally has to be a physical address. In the case of content addressing, the search argument is a field value, so that it is possible to search for all records with a field satisfying certain conditions. Physically content addressing can be implemented by attaching microcomputers to the read heads of the disk storage unit. These microcomputers can analyse the contents of a cylinder while the disk turns round once.
- *Operational reliability:* A database machine contains more software and hardware components than a traditional DBMS. Therefore, the probability of an operational failure is greater with a database machine.
- *Privacy:* Files connected in a database machine are easier to protect than files directly connected to an application machine. The increased privacy can be achieved by limiting the direct access to data without going through the privacy system of the database software. On the other hand, a new vulnerable link arises which has to be protected; that is, the communication system and the channel connecting the computers.
- *Modularity:* If a system is divided into subsystems, it may become easier to build the total system. The distributed DBMSs are so complicated that it is a great advantage to use the database machine concept. In a distributed DBMS, it is not necessary to physically use a database machine; it is enough to use the database machine concept as a 'logical element' for the construction of the distributed DBMS. We shall discuss this subject further in the next chapter.

Chapter 10
Distributed Databases

10.1 Introduction

A **distributed database** is a network of computers interconnected by a data communication network so that the physical database is distributed on at least two of the system's computers. A distributed database is **homogeneous** if the application programs are independent of how the database is distributed; that is, if the distribution of the physical data can be altered without having to make alterations in the application programs. In a **heterogeneously distributed database**, the application programs are dependent upon the physical location of the store data; that is, alterations have to be made to the application programs if data is moved from one locality to another.

A **DDBMS (Distributed Database Management System)** will normally have been developed by a single software supplier who will have designed the system in such a way that it has data independence, concurrency control, recovery facilities, a coordinated data dictionary, an authorization system and a shared data manipulation language. In a heterogeneously distributed database, the data is distributed physically and there will be very few database facilities since the DBMSs that run on the distributed computers are not coordinated with each other and will often have been developed by different producers. In a **distributed data processing system**, the application programs are run on distributed computers, which are linked up with each other by means of a data transmission network.

A distributed data processing system can use a distributed database, but, in practice, a central database is often used because DDBMS technology is still very new. By using a distributed database, the central computer can be supplemented with local computers, which are normally cheaper than the large central computers. A **local transaction** is a transaction that can be processed locally. A **global transaction** uses data stored in databases linked to more than one computer in the distributed database.

Table 10.1 gives a survey of the advantages and disadvantages of various configurations as functions of the degree of distribution.

10.2 Principles of data distribution

One of the greatest advantages of distributed databases is that data can be stored, thereby minimizing its transmission, which normally minimizes response times as well. The distribution of data can be based on entire files or on subdivisions of files. In the subdivision of files, we distinguish between horizontal and vertical subdivision or a combination of the two. In **horizontal subdivision**, the records of a file are divided into groups that are distributed on different local databases, as shown in Figure 10.1. In **vertical subdivision**, a logical record type is divided into two or more physical record types, which are distributed on different local databases as shown in Figure 10.2. In Figure 10.3, a file is divided both horizontally and vertically; that is, the records of the file are grouped and divided into different subrecord types.

A special form of distribution involves storing data redundantly in different **replicated databases**. By doing this, shorter response times for queries are obtained at the expense of longer processing times for updates.

10.3 Architecture of distributed database management systems

Figure 10.4 illustrates the main components normally found in a distributed DBMS. Each individual computer in the distributed system may contain a **transaction manager** (TM) and a **data manager** (DM). A TM is responsible for the transactions received by the computer, while the DM manages the database accesses on the local computer. When a transaction arrives at a TM, the TM divides the transaction into subtransactions, which are transmitted to those DM's containing data needed by the transaction. Later, the responsible TM receives responses from the subtransactions and processes the collected data into the final result. Thus, any TM can communicate with all DMs and vice versa.

Table 10.1 Survey of distributed databases.

Degree of distribution / ***Evaluation criterion***	*Central data processing with central database*	*Decentral data processing with central database*	*Distributed data processing with homogeneously distributed database*	*Distributed data processing with heterogeneously distributed database*
Complexity of the DDBMS	Known and thoroughly tested technology is used		DDBMS involves very complex software	Very complex as all problems are left to the application programmers and users
Response time for local transactions	Long transmission time to the central computer		Short	Short
Response time for global transactions	Not defined	Not defined	Very long	Very long
Reliability	Very vulnerable towards all error types	Very vulnerable towards individual errors in the the central computer	Good reliability as no individual error can paralyse the whole system	
Total capacity of the data processing system	Relatively small as many firms cannot buy single machines that are large enough	Large, but the central database is a potential bottleneck	Very large	Very large
Hardware costs	Large machines are relatively expensive	Small computers are relatively cheap and their prices fall faster than the prices of the large ones		
Development costs	Small	Small	Small	Large
Fast recovery possibility	Good	Good	Good	Poor
Flexibility	Good	Good	Good	Poor

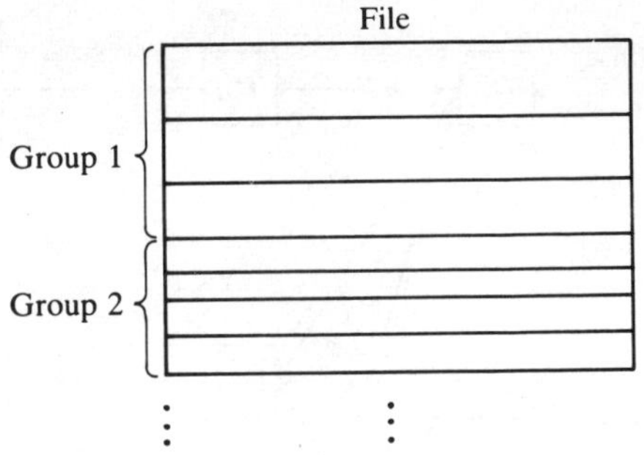

Figure 10.1 Horizontal subdivision of a file.

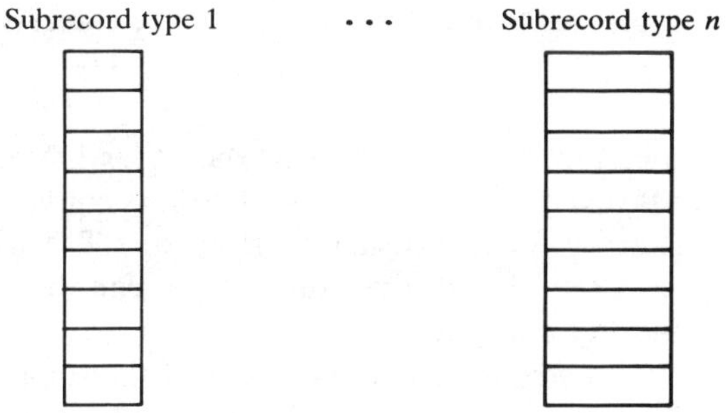

Figure 10.2 Vertical subdivision of the records of a file.

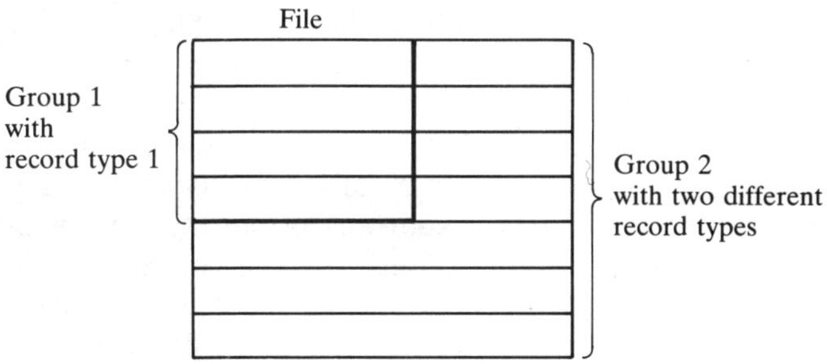

Figure 10.3 Horizontal and vertical subdivision of a file.

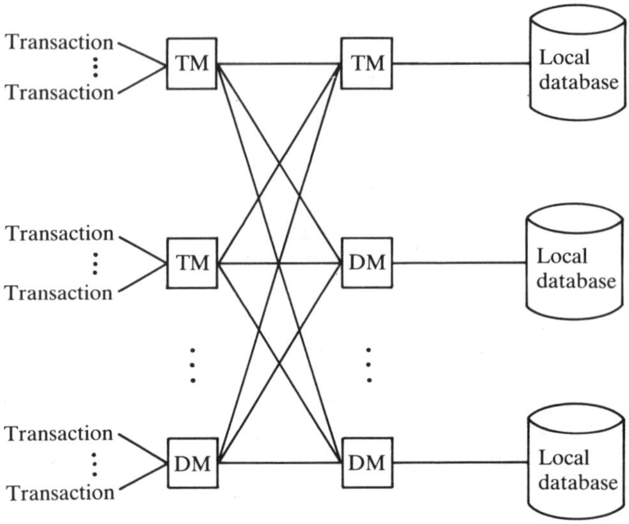

Figure 10.4 Components of a distributed database management system.

The DMs cannot transmit data to the other DMs, and the same applies to the TMs, except in those cases when it is convenient to transfer the total responsibility for a transaction from one TM to another. This may happen, for example, if the transaction can be run as a local transaction on another computer.

Figure 10.5 illustrates the cooperation of the separate subsystems in a DDBMS. The numbered arrows illustrate data streams while these are being run by a global query transaction. The data dictionary in the figure is divided into two different main types, corresponding to the data descriptions used by a TM and a DM, respectively.

The distributed external schema contains external schemas for the programs that can be run from the local TM. The distributed conceptual schema contains that section of the total conceptual schema which is relevant for the transactions that can be run on the local TM. The distribution description describes how the logical files are divided into horizontal and/or vertical subdivisions and where these subdivisions are stored. If the database contains redundant subdivisions this is also described here, so that it is possible to optimize query transactions and to get redundant data updated automatically. The local external schema contains external schemas for the subtransactions that can be processed in the local DM. The local conceptual schema contains a conceptual schema for the local database. The total conceptual database can be defined as the union of all the local conceptual databases. The local internal schema contains an internal schema for the local database.

In addition, Figure 10.5 illustrates three different types of multi-threaded management systems:

- The operating system, which can run several different programs at the same time.
- The TM-DDBMS, which can run several different database statements at the same time. The DDBMS divides the individual statement into subtransactions and transmits these to the DMs that can process them.
- The DM-DDBMS, which can run several different subtransactions transmitted from the different TMs at the same time.

10.4 Distributed concurrency control

As outlined in Chapter 6, the methods of concurrency control can be divided into two main groups:

(1) control by means of two-phase locking.

(2) control by means of time-stamp order.

Within these two main groups, there are many variations for controlling the transactions' parallel use of the database. In the following sections, a method is described from each of the two main groups. It is not possible to point to one particular method as the best, because the various methods of control have very different characteristics as regards updating times, reading times and occupation of the communication network.

10.4.1 Control by means of two-phase locking

Centralized two phase locking can be generalized to cover distributed DBMSs in the following manner. When a transaction arrives at a TM, a working area is created for the transaction. All records the transaction has to read are copied into this working area; when the transaction is to update a record the updating process takes place only in this working area. The locking of the record is executed in the local DM, while the record is read into the working area. When all updates in the working area have been finished, the contents of the updated records are transferred to the TM's log file in case a recovery becomes necessary. When the updated records are secured in the TM's log file, the first phase of two-phase locking is finished. During the second phase of two-phase locking, the locked records are released. A write lock is established by the responsible TM to transmit the updated value of the record from the transaction's working area to the local DM, where the record is updated in the database. Now the write lock can be released. If a read lock has also

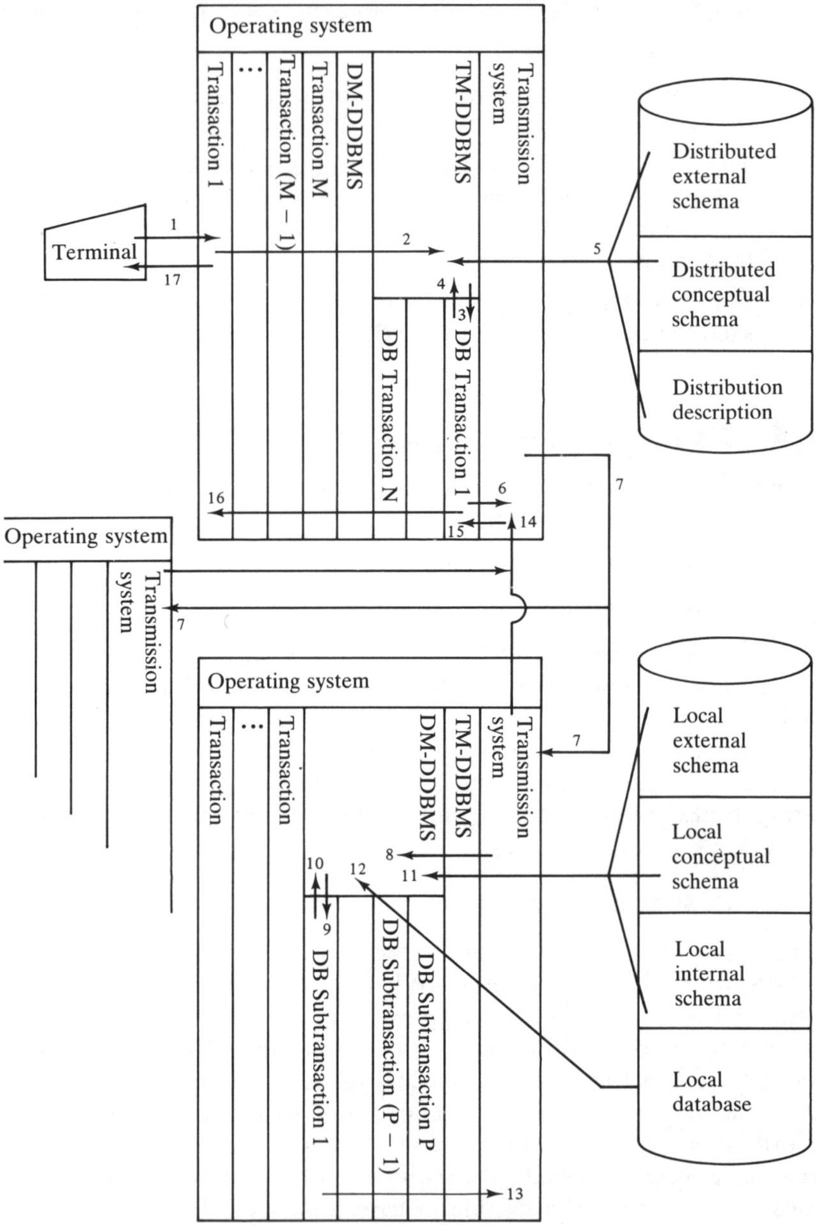

Figure 10.5 The subsystems of a DDBMS. The numbered arrows designate the following activities. 1: A transaction arrives at a local computer and an application program is started with the data of the transaction as input. 2: If the application program has to execute a database statement, this is transmitted to the TM-DDBMS management system, which can run database statements from all the application programs at the same time. 3 and 4: Working areas are created

to be released, it will be necessary to send a special message to the DM, where the record is stored, to effect this.

To recover a transaction during the first phase of two-phase locking, the responsible TM has to send a message to the DMs to the effect that all locks used by the transaction have to be released. During this phase it is not necessary to remove record updates because these are only executed in the working area of the transaction. To recover while the transaction is in the second phase of two-phase locking, the updates done by the transaction cannot be backed out as some of the locks may already have been released and the records re-locked by other transactions. Instead, the record updates must be sent to those DMs where the updating failed the first time. When the record updates are to be transmitted the second time, it may be necessary to use the log file of the responsible TM in which the updated record is stored with a view to any re-transmission that may be necessary.

If the communication line is broken so that re-transmission cannot be executed, the transmission system should be able to log the subtransaction, so that it can be transmitted as soon as the line can be used again. Such a broken line situation may be very inconvenient if some of the transactions are in the second phase of two-phase locking. The problem is that the transaction cannot be removed because some of the locked records may be released. On the other hand, the updating cannot be forced because of the broken communication line. If it takes a long time to recover the communication line, it may be necessary to update the isolated DMs manually, so that the locked records can be released.

In distributed two-phase locking, the deadly embrace problem can be solved in the same ways as outlined in connection with centralized two-phase locking (see Section 6.3).

---

in which to run the database statement received. 5: The different TM dictionary descriptions are read into the main storage of the computer. 6: The database statement is divided into subtransactions corresponding to the DM-machines controlling the data involved. 7: The subtransactions are transmitted to the relevant distributed computers. 8: DM-DDBMS receives a subtransaction from a TM. 9 and 10: Working areas are created in which to run the subtransaction received. 11: The local schemas are read. 12: Data from the physical database is input into the buffer in DM-DDBMS. 13: An external view from a local database is transferred to the transmission system. 14: The external view from a local database arrives at the TM that managed the original database query. 15: The responses of the original subtransactions from the local DMs are collected for a total response. 16: The result of the database statement is transmitted to the application program that originally sent the query.

10.4.2 Control by means of time-stamp order

The basic method of control by means of time-stamp order works as follows: When a transaction arrives at a TM, it is given a unique time stamp. When the responsible TM transmits subtransactions to the DMs, the time stamp of the transaction is transmitted to the DMs as well. Then the individual DMs process the subtransactions in such a way that database accesses relating to the same record are executed in time-stamp sequence; that is subtransactions with a low time stamp have to be processed before subtransactions with a higher time stamp. If a subtransaction arrives at a DM so late that it cannot be processed in time-stamp order, the transaction has to be rejected to avoid inconsistency. If a DM rejects a subtransaction, the responsible TM can give the transaction a new time stamp, after which the transaction can be re-started. If two different transactions are given the same time stamp by different TMs, the DMs cannot always process subtransactions in time-stamp order. This problem can be solved by adding the TMs' identification number to the time stamp of the transactions.

One of the primary advantages of using the time-stamp order method is that it avoids the deadly embrace situation which may arise when using two-phase locking. A problem that cannot be avoided, however, is that it has to be possible to remove the updates of a transaction if anything has gone wrong. This subject is discussed further later in the chapter.

10.5 Distributed atomic transactions

We have already seen that an atomic transaction is indivisible; that is, either all updates of a transaction have to be executed or all updates of the unfinished transaction have to be removed. If two-phase locking is used, as previously described, it is easy to implement automatic recovery of atomic transactions. If time-stamp order is used, atomic transactions can be recovered by means of a **two-phase commit** procedure. First, the TM transmits 'ready to commit' messages to the DMs involved in the transaction. When the TM has received an 'acceptance to commit' from the DMs involved, the TM transmits the 'commit statement'. If the TM does not receive the 'acceptance to commit' message from every DM involved the transaction has failed and must be recovered by backing out. If recovery is to occur after the commit statement has been transmitted the updating has to be forced through, possibly by means of the TM's log file.

10.6 Heterogeneously distributed databases

As mentioned earlier, a database is heterogeneous if the application programs are dependent upon how the database is distributed. Heterogeneously distributed databases are often managed by DBMSs supplied by different producers; therefore, it is very difficult to coordinate the database facilities in the different DBMSs.

It is still not possible to buy software that can solve this problem, but a great deal of research has been carried out on this subject in universities (see Schneider, 1982). One example of the results of this research is that it is possible that in the future we have to expect that practically all large data processing systems will be interconnected via a public data transmission network. This means that if we have access to a distributed data manipulation language that can operate on all database types, we will be able, by using a few statements, to extract data from any computer connected to the public data network. It must be emphasized that in a system of this type it will also be necessary to have a distributed authorization system to give protection against unauthorized use of data.

Figure 10.6 illustrates the build up of a DDBMS that can control the access to the distributed databases, in which the individual local databases are managed by DBMSs from different producers. This figure resembles Figure 10.5 showing the architecture of a DDBMS which is run on a homogeneously distributed database. The main difference is that the individual local computers are equipped with a local DBMS, which operates like a traditional central DBMS. As a central DBMS is multi-threaded, the figure contains four different types of multi-threaded management systems:

(1) the operating system
(2) the TM-DDBMS
(3) the DM-DDBMS
(4) the 'central' DBMS, which manages the local database.

In the case of distributed update transactions, the reading of records has to be executed by the DM-DDBMS; that is, local updating transactions have to transmit lock statements to the DM-DDBMS if distributed updating transactions are to be executed.

We have just seen that it may be very cumbersome to insert database facilities into a heterogeneously distributed database. In practice, therefore, we will often just restrict ourselves to inserting coordinated recovery facilities which can recover atomic transactions as illustrated in Figure 10.7. We assume that certain transactions arriving at system *A* are to update both the local databases. We give these updating transactions a serial number and store them in a database file at the same time as the updates of system *A* are executed. If the transaction terminates abnormally, all the updates – including the transaction file – are backed out.

System *B* contains a program that transfers transactions from system *A* to system *B*. This program is run at short intervals. The program

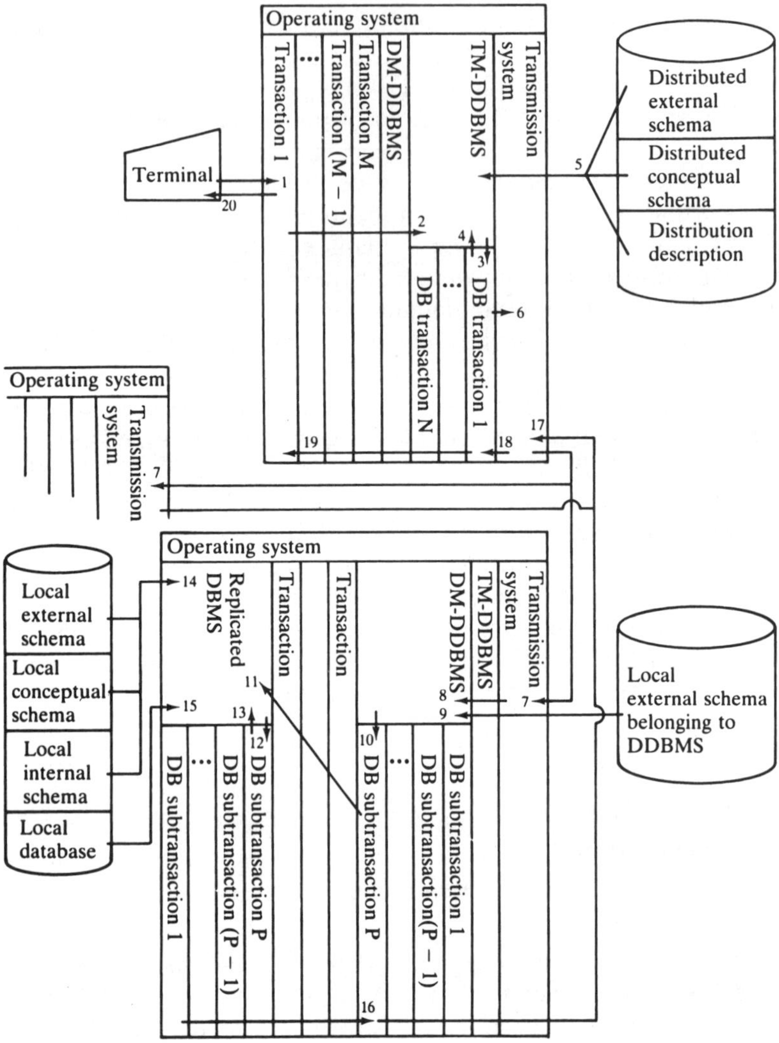

Figure 10.6 The subsystems of a heterogeneously distributed DDBMS in which each local database has its own DBMS. The numbered arrows represent the data streams of a query transaction. Numbers 1–8 are the same activities as those shown in Figure 10.5. 9: The local external schema belonging to a subtransaction is read. This external schema is only required if the DDBMS and the local DBMS are of two different types. If, for example, the DDBMS is a relational DBMS and the local DBMS is hierarchical, data will have to be read in to show how to convert data between the two forms of representation. 10: Working areas are reserved to process the subtransaction received. 11: The subtransaction is transmitted to the local 'central' DBMS. 12 and 13: Working areas are reserved to process the local subtransaction. 14 and 15: The 'central' DBMS reads the local dictionary and database. 16: The control is transferred to DM-DDBMS, which processes the subtransaction in the same way as described previously.

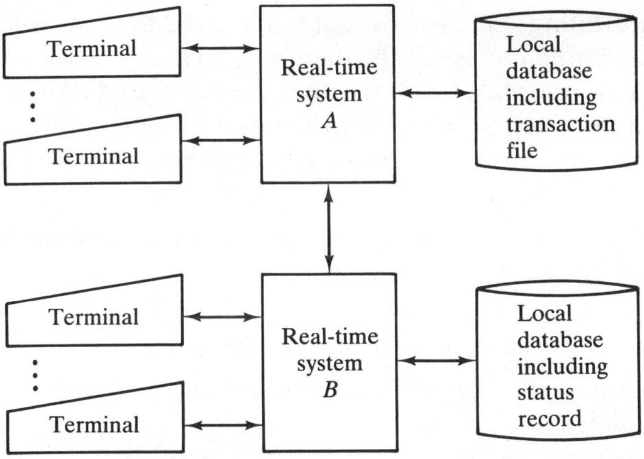

Figure 10.7 Coordinated recovery facilities for atomic transactions.

first reads a status record, which contains the serial number of the last transaction transferred. Then a query is transmitted to system *A* about transfer of the next updating transaction stored in system *A*'s database. When the transaction arrives at system *B*, system *B*'s database – including the status record – is updated. If the transaction terminates abnormally, the updatings of system B are backed out and, as the status record is therefore also backed out, the transaction will automatically be re-started the next time a transaction is transferred to system *B*.

10.7 Database administration

Most of the database facilities described in Chapters 4 to 8 require administration. Consequently, a new administrative function arises with the introduction of database software in a firm. Furthermore, the possibilities for integration presented by database technique have made it difficult to allocate the responsibility for the updating, recovery and consistency of files. Before large databases became widespread, it was usual to place the responsibility for a file with the project group that was updating it. If database techniques are used, however, there will be many different project groups that may have programs updating a particular file. It may therefore be difficult to place the responsibility for a file with one particular project group.

The following list describes the various tasks that can be placed under a database administrator. The tasks of the database administration are only described briefly, since these are implicit in the description of the database facilities the users and the database administrator use.

- Maintenance of the data dictionary (description of fields, files, relationships, etc. as well as the connections between these).

- Controlling the use of data: the DBMS can collect statistics concerning the use of the database, so that a check can be made at regular intervals to see whether the physical database is organized in an optimized way from the point of view of the current use of data. The database administrator can also have lists printed out of any attempts at unauthorized use of data.
- Preparation of recovery procedures corresponding to the various error situations that may arise.
- Preparation of programs for consistency control and periodical control of the consistency of the database.
- Planning the logical database and construction of the physical database.
- Instruction or advisory services for the end users of the database.
- Periodic checking of whether parts of the database have to be reorganized.
- Contact with the software suppliers with a view to updating database software, reporting of errors, etc.
- Collection of information and material with a view to database enhancement. It is easier for a centralized database administrator to keep up with the rapid developments that take place in connection with database techniques and theory. Such know-how may be necessary to perform the aforementioned tasks satisfactorily.

EXERCISES

10.1 Figure 10.7 shows a method of concurrency control and recovery of heterogeneously distributed databases.

(a) How can update transactions that arrive at system *B* execute consistent updates in both the local databases?

(b) Can this method be extended so that several transactions, which are updating several different local databases, can be processed in parallel?

(c) Does the status record in system *B* have to be locked while a transaction from system *A* is transferred to system *B*?

10.2 How can a heterogeneously distributed database be recovered if one of the local files is physically destroyed?

10.3 Application programs have been developed that use a heterogeneously distributed database. Do the application programs have to be changed or rewritten, either totally or partially, if new fields are inserted into a record type?

10.4 A data processing system, which uses a heterogeneously distributed database, has some query transactions that require concurrency control to ensure that the database is consistent. The update transactions do not require an equally high degree of consistency. How can both of these requirements be satisfied without having to buy a DDBMS?

10.5 (a) How is a homogeneously distributed database recovered if the operating system of one of the local computers breaks down?

(b) How is a homogeneously distributed database recovered if two or more local databases are physically destroyed?

10.6 In Section 10.7, a number of working tasks that can be solved in a centralized database administration are outlined. For each of the tasks mentioned, make an assessment of the possible advantages and disadvantages of decentralizing the work.

Part Three
DATABASE LANGUAGES

Chapter 11
CODASYL Database Languages

11.1 Introduction

CODASYL is an acronym for **Conference On Data Systems Languages**. The CODASYL organization consists of various committees with representatives from United States government departments, trade and commerce, the data processing industry, etc. The CODASYL standards for database software described in this chapter are developed and maintained by the COBOL Committee and the Data Description Language Committee following the specifications of the 1971 COBOL Data Base Task Group for a network DBMS. Appendix C contains a more detailed description of CODASYL database languages, but for the most up to date description the reader is referred to CODASYL (1978, 1981a, 1981b).

In this book, CODASYL's proposal is selected as representative of the third-generation database software products, because it is not connected with any one particular producer and because it is a network database system. (Network database systems incorporate so many of the concepts of database theory that with a little ingenuity the hierarchical and relational systems can be seen as special cases of network systems.) The following sections describe the database description language (DDL) and the database manipulation language (DML) by means of an example.

Figure 11.1 shows a Bachman diagram linking salesmen, S, and products, P. The two entity types are connected by an $n : m$ relationship,

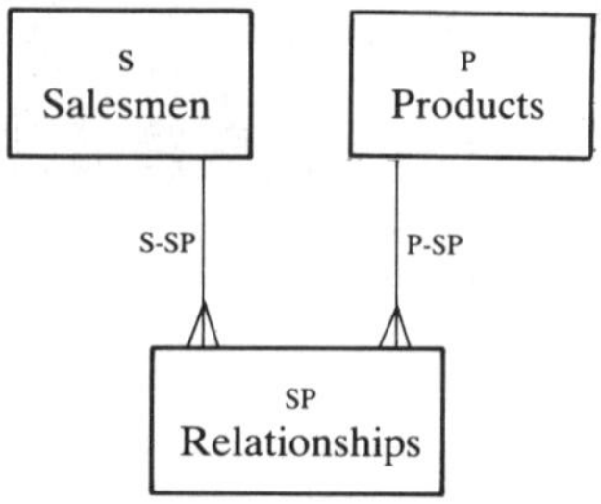

Figure 11.1 Bachman diagram of an $n:m$ relationship between sellers, S, and products, P, represented as $1:n$ relationships between sellers, products, and a relationship, SP.

as a salesman may supply several different products, and as a product may be supplied by several different salesmen. The $n:m$ relationship is implemented by means of the relationship entity SP and the two $1:n$ relationships S-SP and P-SP.

11.2 CODASYL's conceptual database description language

In Example 11.1 we see how the CODASYL DDL defines the conceptual schema for the salesman/product database. The conceptual schema in the example consists of three entries:

(1) The schema entry whose primary purpose is to name the conceptual schema.

(2) The record entry that describes the individual record types and their fields.

(3) The set entry that describes the individual set types. In CODASYL a set may be loosely defined as a relationship. If the relationship is from A to B, A is described as the owner of the set and B as a member.

EXAMPLE 11.1

Part of the conceptual schema for the database is shown in Figure 11.2. In line 1 the name of the conceptual schema is defined as SP-SCHEMA. In line 3 the name of the record type is defined as S. After that, the key of the record type is defined as the field SNR. It is decided that key values are to be assigned in ascending order and that the key field must be unique. In lines 6–9 the fields of the record type are defined in a COBOL-like notation.

```
SCHEMA NAME IS SP-SCHEMA

RECORD NAME IS S
     KEY SNR-KEY IS ASCENDING SNR
     DUPLICATES ARE NOT ALLOWED
     02 SNR          TYPE IS CHARACTER 5
     02 SNAME        TYPE IS CHARACTER 20
     02 S-CODE       TYPE IS FIXED DECIMAL 3
     02 CITY         TYPE IS CHARACTER 15

RECORD NAME IS P
     KEY PNR-KEY IS ASCENDING PNR
     DUPLICATES ARE NOT ALLOWED
     02 PNR          TYPE IS CHARACTER 6
     02 PNAME        TYPE IS CHARACTER 20

RECORD NAME IS SP
     KEY SP-KEY IS ASCENDING SNR PNR
     DUPLICATES ARE NOT ALLOWED
     02 SNR          SOURCE IS
                     SNR OF OWNER OF S-SP
     02 PNR          SOURCE IS
                     PNR OF OWNER OF P-SP
     02 QTY          TYPE IS FIXED DECIMAL 5

SET NAME IS S-SP
     OWNER IS S
     ORDER IS SORTED BY DEFINED KEYS
     MEMBER IS SP
     INSERTION IS AUTOMATIC
     RETENTION IS FIXED
     KEY IS ASCENDING PNR
     DUPLICATES ARE NOT ALLOWED
     SET SELECTION IS THRU S-SP
     OWNER IDENTIFIED BY KEY SNR

SET NAME IS P-SP
     OWNER IS P
     ORDER IS SORTED BY DEFINED KEYS
     MEMBER IS SP
     INSERTION IS AUTOMATIC
     RETENTION IS FIXED
     KEY IS ASCENDING SNR
     DUPLICATES ARE NOT ALLOWED
     SET SELECTION IS THRU P-SP
     OWNER IDENTIFIED BY KEY PNR
```

Figure 11.2 Part of the conceptual schema for a CODASYL database.

In line 20, the SP record field SNR is defined by a reference to the S record field SNR via the set (or relationship) S-SP.

In line 26, the name of a set is defined as S-SP. Line 27 defines S as owner and line 29 defines SP as member of the set S-SP. Line 28 defines the order in which member records are inserted under a given owner: member records are to be inserted in KEY order. The KEY is defined in line 32. Line 30 specifies that an SP record's insertion in the set S-SP is AUTOMATIC; i.e., the DBMS automatically inserts a member record in the set S-SP. The insertion could also be MANUAL; i.e., the programmer would be responsible for inserting member records in the set by means of special database statements.

In line 31, it is specified that a member record's attachment to the set S-SP is FIXED. This means that member records that have been inserted in the set with a particular owner S-SP cannot exist in the database unless the original owner remains in the set S-SP.

The SET SELECTION statement in line 34 tells the DBMS which owner it has to use if a new member record is to be automatically inserted in the set. In line 35 it is specified that the owner has to be selected on the basis of the value in the key field SNR.

In lines 37–46 the set P-SP is defined in roughly the same way as S-SP.

11.3 CODASYL's internal database description language

CODASYL's internal DDL consists of the following six entries:

(1) The STORAGE SCHEMA entry, which gives the internal schema a name and connects it with the name of the conceptual schema.

(2) The MAPPING entry, which describes the connection between record types in the conceptual schema and record types in the internal schema.

(3) The STORAGE AREA entry, which describes areas in the background storage where the database is stored.

(4) The STORAGE RECORD entry, which describes the record types in the internal schema.

(5) The SET entry, which describes the sets for the internal schema.

(6) The INDEX entry, which describes indexes for the various files in the database.

Example 11.2 gives an outline of these clauses. A detailed description of this syntax is to be found in Appendix C.

EXAMPLE 11.2

Part of the internal schema for the database is shown in Figure 11.3.

```
STORAGE SCHEMA NAME IS
      SP-STORAGE-SCHEMA FOR SP-SCHEMA
MAPPING FOR S
      STORAGE RECORD IS S
MAPPING FOR P
      STORAGE RECORD IS P
MAPPING FOR SP
      STORAGE RECORD IS SP
STORAGE AREA NAME IS S-AREA
      INITIAL SIZE IS 20 PAGES
      EXPANDABLE BY STEPS OF 2 PAGES TO 30 PAGES
      PAGE SIZE IS 448 WORDS
STORAGE AREA NAME IS P-AREA
      INITIAL SIZE IS 8 PAGES
      EXPANDABLE BY STEPS OF 2 PAGES TO 12 PAGES
      PAGE SIZE IS 448 WORDS
STORAGE AREA NAME IS IX-AREA
      INITIAL SIZE IS 4 PAGES
      PAGE SIZE IS 448 WORDS
STORAGE RECORD NAME IS S
      DENSITY IS 4 STORAGE RECORDS PER PAGE
      PLACEMENT IS CALC RANDOM USING SNR
      WITHIN S-AREA
      02 SNR         FORMAT IS CHARACTER
                     SIZE IS 5 CHARACTERS
      02 S NAME      FORMAT IS CHARACTER
                     SIZE IS 20 CHARACTERS
      02 S-CODE      FORMAT IS DECIMAL
                     SIZE IS 3 CHARACTERS
      02 CITY        FORMAT IS CHARACTERS
                     SIZE IS 15 CHARACTERS
      02 DATA
STORAGE RECORD NAME IS P
      DENSITY IS 20 STORAGE RECORDS PER PAGE
      PLACEMENT IS SEQUENTIAL ASCENDING PNR
      WITHIN P-AREA FROM PAGE 3 THRU 8
      02 PNR         FORMAT IS CHARACTER
                     SIZE IS 6 CHARACTERS
      02 PNAME       FORMAT IS CHARACTER
                     SIZE IS 20 CHARACTERS
      02 DATA
STORAGE RECORD NAME IS SP
      DENSITY IS 16 STORAGE RECORDS PER PAGE
```

Figure 11.3 *(Cont. overleaf.)*

```
53:         PLACEMENT IS CLUSTERED VIA S-SP NEAR OWNER
54:         WITHIN S-AREA
55:         02 SNR          FORMAT IS CHARACTER
56:                         SIZE IS 5 CHARACTERS
57:                         EVALUATION IS ON UPDATE
58:                         STORAGE IS REQUIRED
59:         02 PNR          FORMAT IS CHARACTER
60:                         SIZE IS 6 CHARACTERS
61:                         EVALUATION IS ON UPDATE
62:                         STORAGE IS REQUIRED
63:         02 QTY          FORMAT IS CHARACTER
64:                         SIZE IS 5 CHARACTERS
65:         02 DATA
66:
67:     SET S-SP
68:         OWNER RECORD S
69:         ALLOCATION IS STATIC
70:         POINTER FOR FIRST MEMBER
71:         DESTINATION OF DIRECT POINTERS
72:         MEMBER RECORD SP
73:         ALLOCATION IS STATIC
74:         POINTER FOR NEXT TENANT
75:                             INDEX SP-IX
76:         DESTINATION OF INDIRECT POINTERS
77:
78:     SET P-SP
79:         OWNER RECORD P
80:         ALLOCATION IS STATIC
81:         POINTER FOR FIRST MEMBER
82:         DESTINATION OF INDIRECT POINTERS
83:         MEMBER RECORD SP
84:         ALLOCATION IS STATIC
85:         POINTER FOR NEXT TENANT
86:         DESTINATION OF DIRECT POINTERS
87:
88:     INDEX NAME IS SP-IX
89:         PLACEMENT IS NEAR OWNER
90:         USED FOR SET S-SP
91:         KEY PNR-KEY
92:
93:     INDEX NAME IS P-IX
94:         USED FOR RECORD P KEY PNR-KEY
95:         POINTER IS DIRECT
96:
```

Figure 11.3 Part of the internal schema for a CODASYL database.

Lines 1 and 2 assign the name SP-STORAGE-SCHEMA to the storage or internal schema and link it with the conceptual schema SP-SCHEMA. Lines 5 and 6 establish that the record type S in the conceptual schema has to correspond with the record type S in the internal schema.

In line 12, an area in the background storage is named. The area is named S-AREA. The area, when created, must be of a size of 20 blocks (pages). In line 14 it is specified that S-AREA can be expanded to 30 blocks, and that the expansions have to be performed gradually, two blocks at a time. Line 15 defines a block as containing 448 words.

In line 26, record type S is named in the internal schema, and it is specified that four records have to be stored per block. Line 28 determines that S records must be randomly organized, and that we can search for S records by calling the subroutine RANDOM with the search argument SNR. Line 29 determines that S records are to be stored in the area S-AREA. The fields SNR, SNAME, S-CODE and CITY in the storage record type S are defined in lines 30–37. Lines 38, 48 and 65 define the end of the field descriptions for record types S, P and SP.

In line 42 it is specified that type P records must be organized sequentially and be stored in ascending order by the field PNR. Line 53 states that type SP records have the organization CLUSTERED; i.e., SP records with the same owner as regards S-SP have to be stored physically beside each other. NEAR OWNER means that SP records are to be stored in the same block as the owner if this is possible.

Lines 55–58 describe the field SNR. SNR is used to store characters and may contain five of them. The EVALUATION statement in line 57 means that the value of the field can be checked (the field's value is also stored in the owner record), and that the check has to be performed by updating the contents of the field. In line 58, space is reserved for the SNR field in the SP record type. This is normally not necessary because the field contains redundant data from the S record.

Lines 67–76 define the internal schema for the set S-SP. First, the fact that the owner record is S is stated. The statement ALLOCATION IS STATIC means that space is reserved for the pointer fields even though they may not be used. Line 70 specifies that the owner record S must contain a pointer to the first of its member records of type SP. Line 71 determines that direct pointers are used, pointing at records of type S. Line 72 determines that the set S-SP has member records of type SP. Line 74 specifies that member records must contain a pointer field to the next record in the list, which has the owner as list head. Line 75 determines that logical pointers to the next member record have to be used, and that the physical address of the next member record has to be found via the SP-IX index. This corresponds with the fact that in line 76 it is specified that logical pointers point at records of type SP.

Lines 88–91 define the SP-IX index for record type SP. According to line 75 the index is used to find member records belonging to a given owner. Line 89 specifies that the index is divided into a number of smaller subindexes, where the individual subindexes are stored close to the corresponding owner record.

Line 91 states that the key of the index is to be the field PNR. Lines 93–96 define a secondary index for records of type P. It appears from line 95 that the bottom level of the index contains a direct pointer to the required P record.

11.4 CODASYL's external database description language

The following types of changes are found in the external schema compared with the conceptual schema:

- Fields can be accorded another data type.
- The sequence of the record fields may be different from the sequence in the conceptual schema.
- Alias names can be defined for records, fields and sets.
- The SET SELECTION specification can be changed so that the SET SELECTION of the conceptual schema is suppressed.

The CODASYL–COBOL external schema is called a **subschema**. It consists of three main parts:

- a TITLE DIVISION, which connects the external schema and the conceptual schema.
- a MAPPING DIVISION, which makes it possible to define alias names for the record, set and field names of the conceptual schema.
- a STRUCTURE DIVISION, which defines the realms, record types and set types forming the external schema. A **realm** is a subset of the external schema that can be opened simultaneously with other realms. The external schema may contain several overlapping realms.

EXAMPLE 11.3

Figure 11.4 shows an example of a section of a CODASYL subschema.

```
TITLE DIVISION
SS PRODUCT-SALE WITHIN SP-SCHEMA
MAPPING DIVISION
ALIAS SECTION
AD RECORD PRODUCT IS P
AD RECORD SALE IS SP
STRUCTURE DIVISION
REALM SECTION
RD PRODUCT-SALE-REALM CONTAINS
  PRODUCTS, SALE RECORDS.
RECORD SECTION
01 PRODUCTS
  02 PNR PIC X (6).
  02 PNAME PIC X (24).
01 SALE
```

```
  02 SNR PIC X (6).
  02 PNR PIC X (5).
SET SECTION.
SD P-SP.
```

Figure 11.4 Part of the external schema (subschema) for a CODASYL database.

TITLE DIVISION states that the external schema is named PRODUCT-SALE and that this is a subset of the conceptual schema SP-SCHEMA. In the ALIAS SECTION, it is determined that record types P and SP are to be called PRODUCT and SALE, respectively. In the REALM SECTION, it is specified that there must only be one realm. This realm is named PRODUCT-SALE-REALM and it contains the record types PRODUCT and SALE. The RECORD SECTION defines the two record types in the normal COBOL style. Notice that the order of the fields may be changed and that some of the fields may be left out. The SET-SECTION determines that the external schema contains the set P-SP.

11.5 A data manipulation language

This section deals with CODASYL's proposal for a data manipulation language (DML). CODASYL's proposal for a low-level data manipulation language is chosen as representative because the language is so general that it may be said to incorporate other low-level data manipulation languages as subsets. In what follows, we illustrate how COBOL's DML operates. For a more detailed description, see Appendix C.

EXAMPLE 11.4

The piece of COBOL-like pseudo code shown in Figure 11.5 illustrates how we can store a new SP record in real time.

```
:
entering the SP fields
SNR, PNR, QTY from a terminal.
MOVE 'record created' to the field MESSAGE.
MOVE SNR IN SP TO SNR IN S.
MOVE PNR IN SP TO PNR IN P.
STORE SP.
COMMIT.
send the field MESSAGE to the terminal operator.
:
```

Figure 11.5 Pseudo code showing steps involved in storing a new SP record.

In line 149 text is moved to the field MESSAGE, so that in line 154 we can inform the terminal operator of how the creation worked out.

In lines 150 and 151, the input identification fields are moved to the owner record S and P's key fields, respectively. In line 152 the SP record itself is created and as SP is an AUTOMATIC member of both the S-SP and P-SP sets, SP will automatically be combined with its owners, which were identified in lines 150 and 151.

The COMMIT statement in line 153 releases all the locked records of the updating program in accordance with the rules of two-phase locking.

In line 154 a message is sent to the terminal operator about how the creation proceeded. At this point the field MESSAGE might contain an error message because the CODASYL syntax allows the treatment of errors to be initiated in an independent part of a program called DECLARATIVES which must be located at the beginning of the COBOL program.

The program code shown in Figure 11.6 illustrates how the processing of errors may be executed.

```
:
DECLARATIVES.
ERROR-MESSAGES.
   USE FOR DB-EXCEPTION ON '1501100'
ERROR-1.
   MOVE 'record updated by others'.
   TO MESSAGE
   ROLLBACK.
USE FOR DB-EXCEPTION ON '0502100'.
MESSAGE-1.
   MOVE 'no' TO MORE-SP-RECORDS.

   USE FOR DB-EXCEPTION ON OTHER.
END OF ERROR.
END DECLARATIVES.
:
```

Figure 11.6 A possible method for error processing.

The first USE statement tests whether a STORE statement has given the return code '1501100'. In this code, the first two digits are a code for the statement that caused the error code. The last five digits are the return code itself. This return code means that the STORE statement, during updating, tries to lock a record that has already been locked by another program. In this situation, deadlock may arise. However, this problem can be solved by having the ROLLBACK statement back out all updatings of the program and move an error message to the field MESSAGE.

The next USE statement tests whether a FIND statement has found the last SP record belonging to a given owner. When the last SP record has been found, the word 'no' is moved to the field MORE-SP-RECORDS. This situation is explained in further detail in the next example.

The last USE statement contains no error code but the word OTHER. All error codes not processed by the preceding USE statements will be processed here. When the USE statement belonging to an error code has been executed, the control is again transferred to the master program from which the error routine was called.

Example 11.4 showed how error processing can be removed from the master program to leave a better structured program. However, it is also possible to execute error processing in the master program itself, as a special variable DB-STATUS can always contain a return code after the execution of a database statement. DB-STATUS could be given the value '0' if the database statement is executed without any problems occurring.

To get a more thorough understanding of how the CODASYL's DML database statements function it is important to know that during each program run the DBMS maintains a table of **currency pointers**; that is, a table of variables which for each type of set contains a pointer to the set, member record and corresponding owner record that were last processed. The records the currency status table points to for a given set type are called **current owner**, **current member** and **current set**. Thus, the current record for a given record type is the record of the record type last processed; the current record is the record last processed; similarly the current set is the last set processed.

EXAMPLE 11.5

The piece of pseudo code shown in Figure 11.7 illustrates how we can produce a survey of the product numbers supplied by a given salesman on-line.

The first FIND statement uses the S record type and the salesman number as argument. This means that the S record type belonging to the input salesman number becomes current record for the S record type and the corresponding S-SP set occurrence becomes current set for S-SP. The FIND statement in line 103 causes the salesman's first SP member record to become current record for the SP record type.

We are now ready to read SP member records belonging to the first S record. The PERFORM statement executes the statements in lines 104–108 until the field MORE-SP-RECORDS gets the value 'no'. This situation occurs when there are no more member records. The result of the GET statement in line 105 is that the current SP record is read into the user work area of the program run. Once the record is in the user work area, we can refer to the contents of the record by their field names. The FIND statement in line 107 causes the next SP member record to become the current record, so that it is read in connection with the next

```
    ⋮
    The salesman's identification is input from a terminal to
    the field SNR in the salesman record
101 MOVE 'yes' TO MORE-SP-RECORDS.
102 FIND ANY S USING SNR IN S.
103 FIND FIRST SP WITHIN S-SP.
104 PERFORM UNTIL MORE-SP-RECORDS = 'no'.
105     GET SP.
106     Keep the value of the field PNR in SP-record so that
        it can later be sent to the terminal operator.
107     FIND NEXT SP WITHIN S-SP.
108 END PERFORM.
109 FREE ALL.
110 send the retained PNR numbers to the terminal.
    ⋮
```

Figure 11.7 A query: for each seller find the product numbers he supplies.

execution of the GET statement. The FREE statement in line 109 causes the current records of the program to be released, so that they can be read or updated by other programs. In line 110 the required PNR numbers are transmitted to the terminal operator.

EXAMPLE 11.6

The program outline shown in Figure 11.8 illustrates how we can search for records with a particular value in a given field. The aim is to find all salesmen with a particular name. It is assumed in the program that SNAME is defined as key field in the conceptual schema. The key field SNAME has to be a non-unique key; DUPLICATE NOT ALLOWED is not an option that we can take in the definition of the key field.

The program begins by reading the salesman's name. By means of the FIND statement the first S record with that name becomes current record for the S record type.

We are now ready to read the salesmen with the given name. The PERFORM statement in line 102 executes the statements in lines 103–106 until the field MORE-SALESMEN gets the value 'no'. It is assumed that the field gets this value from one of the first USE statements in the program. In lines 103 and 104 the current S record is read and its fields are stored for display later. The FIND statement in line 105 causes the next S record with the required name to become current record, so that it can be read when the GET statement is next executed. In line 107 the fields from the S records found are displayed.

```
⋮
read the salesman's name into the field SNAME IN S
MOVE 'yes' TO MORE-SALESMEN
FIND ANY S USING SNAME IN S
PERFORM UNTIL MORE-SALESMEN = 'no'.
    GET S.
    keep SNR and CITY to be displayed later.
    FIND DUPLICATE S USING SNAME IN S.
END PERFORM
send the retained SNRs and CITYs to the terminal operator.
⋮
```

Figure 11.8 Searching for records with a particular value in a given field.

EXERCISES

11.1 The Bachman diagram shown in Figure 11.9 illustrates the database in a production firm. Produce a diagram of the physical database. The diagram should illustrate the physical pointers in that part of the database which shows that product P_1 can be produced from one P_3 and two P_4s, and that product P_2 can be produced from four P_3s and one P_5.

11.2 Figure 11.10 illustrates a Bachman diagram for a bank database.

(a) Use the CODASYL DDL to make an outline of the bank database's conceptual schema. Include only the most necessary fields. The following examples of relationships between customers and accounts are to be included: the owner relationship, the co-owner relationship, the 'statement of account receiver' relationship and the guarantor relationship.

(b) Outline the internal schema for the bank database by means of the CODASYL DDL. The customer file is to have indexed sequential

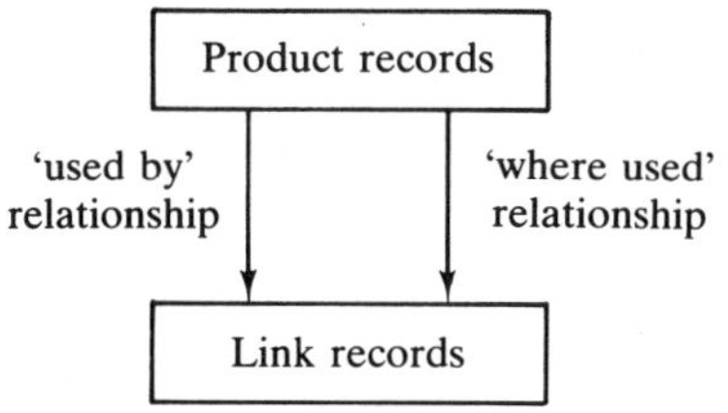

Figure 11.9 Bachman diagram of a production database.

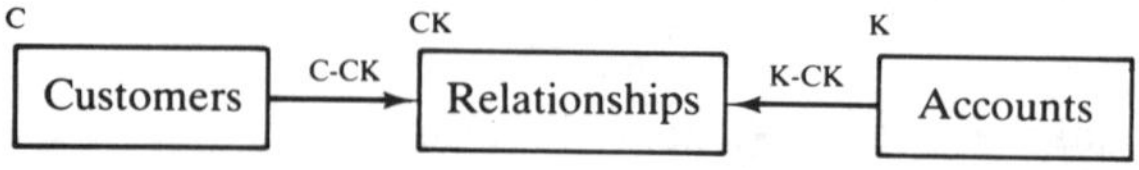

Figure 11.10 Bachman diagram for a bank database.

organization, the account file random organization and the relationship file clustered organization, so that a survey of a customer's accounts can be produced quickly. With a view to optimizing searches from accounts towards customers, the account–set relationship must be implemented by FIRST, LAST, NEXT, PRIOR and OWNER pointers.

(c) Make an outline of the external schema comprising the entire conceptual schema.

(d) Use COBOL pseudo code to make an outline of how an on-line survey of balances in a customer's accounts can be produced (both as owner and co-owner). Note that there may be real-time updates taking place at the same time.

(e) Produce a list of guarantors for an account, if there are any.

(f) Create a new account for a person who is already a customer with the bank. The pseudo code program must be terminated with a message to the terminal concerning the result of the transaction. What error situations might occur if COMMIT is the last statement in the program? (The COMMIT statement is executed after the message to the terminal operator.)

(g) Produce a batch-accounting system that can also print overdraft notices to customers. Note that while the accounting program is being run, real-time updates may arrive for the account file.

(h) How can the deadly embrace problem be solved if the DBMS includes no types of statement other than those mentioned in Appendix C? Give alternative solutions.

(i) Assume that there are decentralized mini computers in the bank's branches that can receive update transactions and send them on to the central database. Moments later the mini computers should receive a reply and edit a screen view for the terminal operator. What security problems might occur if the bank's central database recovery system is not coordinated with the decentralized mini computers' transaction recovery system?

(j) Produce those parts of the conceptual, internal and external schema that in Example 11.6 make it possible to retrieve records by the non-unique key SNAME.

11.3 Assume that a program opens a realm as follows:

'READY realm name USAGE-MOD IS EXCLUSIVE RETRIEVAL'

Will this program run faster or slower that if it was opened by the PROTECTED parameter?

11.4 (a) Use COBOL pseudo code to outline how a new S record can be

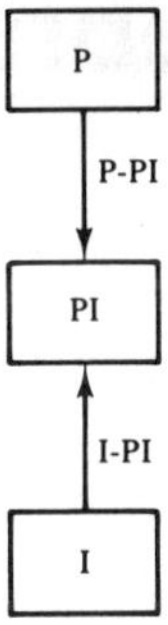

Figure 11.11 Bachman diagram for the product/inventory database described in Exercise 11.5.

created in the salesman–product database described in Section 11.2.

(b) Use COBOL pseudo code to illustrate how the QTY field in an SP record can be updated.

(c) Outline, by means of COBOL pseudo code, how the salesmen who have sold more than X units of product Z can be retrieved.

11.5 The Bachman diagram shown in Figure 11.11 illustrates the product inventory database described in Exercise 13.14. The database illustrated in the Bachman diagram is to be implemented in a CODASYL database with the names of record types and set types used in the figure. The field names used in Exercise 13.14 must be used to define the fields of the record types.

(a) Describe the conceptual schema by means of a CODASYL schema.

(b) Describe a subschema that contains the record types I and PI and the set type I-PI.

The following questions must all be solved in COBOL pseudo code. These program outlines must clearly show the treatment of:

- CODASYL DML statements
- concurrency control
- reply codes by means of DB-EXCEPTION
- currency pointers

(c) Illustrate the on-line production of a survey of a particular inventory whose INR identification is read in via a terminal. The inventory survey must contain PNR, PNAME and QTY.

(d) Outline how a new I record can be created in which the QTY field is set at zero as a real-time transaction. The field values for PNR and INR are read in via a terminal.

(e) Illustrate how the QTY field can be counted if supplies of a particular product arrive for a particular inventory as a real-time process. The field values are read in via a terminal.

Chapter 12
Relational Algebra

12.1 Introduction

Relational algebra is a technique for combining mathematical sets that have the property of being relations (see Section 1.3.1). Relations can be illustrated by means of tables such as those shown in Figure 12.1.

Relational algebra combines relations by means of **operators** to form new relations which, combined with other relations by means of a further operator, can be form further new relations. In other words, relational operators can be nested.

In this chapter, we shall examine the eight major operators of relational algebra. A database language that directly or indirectly contains these eight operators is called **relationally complete**. We will illustrate the operators using the syntax of RELAX, an experimental relational DBMS developed by Søren Holm at the University of Aarhus (Møller and Sørensen, 1982). Only a few commercial database languages directly contain the eight basic statements of relational algebra. The importance of relational algebra is in its use as a measure of the 'strength' of a relational database language.

12.2 General syntax of the RELAX data manipulation language

All operations are initiated by a statement of how the result has to be presented. There are three methods:

(a) S

SNR	SNAME	S-CODE	CITY
S_1	Petersen	10	Aarhus
S_2	Olsen	30	Copenhagen
S_4	Hansen	20	Odense
S_5	Jensen	30	Copenhagen

(b) P

PNR	PNAME	SIZE	PRICE
P_1	Shirt	6	50
P_3	Trousers	5	90
P_4	Socks	7	20
P_5	Blouse	6	50
P_8	Blouse	8	60

(c) SP

SNR	PNR	QTY
S_2	P_1	200
S_2	P_3	100
S_4	P_5	200
S_4	P_8	100
S_5	P_1	50
S_5	P_3	500
S_5	P_4	800
S_5	P_5	500
S_5	P_8	100

Figure 12.1 Tables for the relations S, P and SP. S consists of the fields SNR, SNAME, S-CODE and CITY; P of PNR, PNAME, SIZE and PRICE; and SP of SNR, PNR and QTY.

FIND *temp* = *algebraic expression;* **(12.1)**

FIND states that the result of the operation has to be presented in an auxiliary table named *temp*. The table exists until the user deletes it or the run is finished. The contents and format of *temp* are determined by the operation stated in the algebraic expression.

If the result is to appear directly on the screen we write

OUTPUT *algebraic expression;* **(12.2)**

and no auxiliary file for the table will be created.

The two forms can be combined as:

OUTPUT *temp* = *algebraic expression;* **(12.3)**

This means that the result is displayed on the screen at the same time as the result is stored in the *temp* auxiliary file. The algebraic expression may include the eight basic operations described in the rest of this chapter.

12.3 Projection

A **projection** is a vertical section of a table; the projection statement selects some columns from a table and creates a new table that only contains rows with the wanted fields.

T_1 CITY
Aarhus
Copenhagen
Odense

Figure 12.2 Projection (FIND) of CITY in S.

EXAMPLE 12.1

The following statement creates an auxiliary table T1, which contains a record for each city in which there are salesmen.

```
FIND T1 = S (CITY);
```

The algebraic expression S(CITY) means that a projection of the table S from Figure 12.1 with the field CITY has to be created. The result is illustrated in Figure 12.2.

Note that T1 contains one row less than S because there are two salesmen in Copenhagen.

12.4 Selection

A selection is a subset of the set of the rows in a table. The selection is made on the basis of the contents of one or more columns in the table.

EXAMPLE 12.2

The following statement displays a list of salesmen in Copenhagen, as shown in Figure 12.3:

```
OUTPUT S WHERE CITY = 'COPENHAGEN';
```

EXAMPLE 12.3

The query 'what quantity of product P1 has been supplied by salesman S5?' becomes the RELAX statement:

```
FIND T2 = SP WHERE SNR ='S5' AND PNR = 'P1';
```

Figure 12.4 shows this selection.

SNR	SNAME	S-CODE	CITY
S_2	Olsen	20	Copenhagen
S_5	Jensen	30	Copenhagen

Figure 12.3 Selection (WHERE) of CITY = 'Copenhagen' in S.

T_2

SNR	PNR	QTY
S_5	P_1	50

Figure 12.4 Selection over more than one column value from SP.

12.5 Union

The union of two tables is a new table containing the entries of both tables. However, the statement can only be executed if both tables use the same entry type.

EXAMPLE 12.4

The query 'which of the salesmen (SNR) are either resident in Copenhagen or have sold product P8?' becomes:

```
FIND T3 = S(SNR) WHERE CITY = 'COPENHAGEN';

FIND T4 = SP(SNR) WHERE PNR = 'P8';
```

This is illustrated in Figure 12.5.

Finally, the UNION operator combines the two resulting tables:

```
OUTPUT T3 UNION T4.
```

to give the output shown in Figure 12.6.

T_3

SNR
S_2
S_5

T_4

SNR
S_4
S_5

Figure 12.5 Projections of SNR from S WHERE CITY = 'Copenhagen' and from SP WHERE PNR = 'P8'.

SNR
S_2
S_4
S_5

Figure 12.6 Union (UNION) of the two SNR tables in Figure 12.5.

SNR
S_5

Figure 12.7 Intersection (INTERSECT) of the two SNR tables in Figure 12.5.

12.6 Intersection

The intersection of two tables is a new table containing only those entries that are members of both tables. Naturally, the statement can only be executed if both tables use the same entity type.

EXAMPLE 12.5

The query 'which salesmen (SNR) are both resident in Copenhagen and can supply product P8?' becomes:

```
OUTPUT T3 INTERSECT T4
```

The result of this operation is shown in Figure 12.7.

12.7 Difference

The difference of two tables is the set of entities that are members of the first of the tables but not the other. Of course, the statement can only be executed if the two tables use the same entity type.

EXAMPLE 12.6

The query 'output the salesman numbers for the salesmen who are resident in Copenhagen and who have not sold any of product P8' becomes

```
OUTPUT T3 − T4
```

This is shown in Figure 12.8.

SNR
S_2

Figure 12.8 Difference (−) of the two SNR tables shown in Figure 12.5.

T_5

SNR	PNR
S_1	P_1
S_1	P_3
S_1	P_4
S_1	P_5
S_1	P_8
S_2	P_1
S_2	P_3
S_2	P_4
S_2	P_5
S_2	P_8
S_4	P_1
S_4	P_3
S_4	P_4
S_4	P_5
S_4	P_8
S_5	P_1
S_5	P_3
S_5	P_4
S_5	P_5
S_5	P_8

Figure 12.9 Product (MULT). The table is produced by combining each SNR in S with every PNR in P.

12.8 Product sets

The **Cartesian product** of two tables is a new table containing entries corresponding to all combinatorial possibilities of the entities of the two tables.

EXAMPLE 12.7

The query 'produce a file containing all combinatorial possibilities of salesmen (SNR) and products (PNR)' becomes:

```
FIND T5 = MULT S (SNR) WITH P (PNR);
```

This is illustrated in Figure 12.9.

12.9 Join

The JOIN statement operates on two tables and results in the creation of a new table that is a concatenation of rows from the two tables. The JOIN statement requires the two tables to have one or more fields in common over which the join can be made. The join itself is executed as follows: For each entry in the first table we search for all the entries in the second

T_6

SNR
S_2
S_5

Figure 12.10 Salesman numbers for Copenhagen found by projection.

table having the same value in the key column as the entry from the first table file. After this, the entry from the first table is concatenated with each of the entries found in the second table.

EXAMPLE 12.8

We want to output a list of salesmen resident in Copenhagen, stating salesman numbers, product numbers and quantities sold. First, we need to find the salesman numbers for Copenhagen:

```
FIND T6 = S (SNR) WHERE CITY = 'COPENHAGEN'.
```

This is shown in Figure 12.10. We then join this to the SP table over the SNR field, which is found both in T6 and in SP:

```
OUTPUT JOIN T6 WITH SP WHERE T6 (SNR) = SP(SNR);
```

The result is illustrated in Figure 12.11.

As we can see from Example 12.8, a JOIN statement contains redundant columns, as the key column is repeated twice. To avoid this redundancy we now introduce the concept of a **natural join**, which is a JOIN operator that removes the redundant columns from the result.

SNR	SNR	PNR	QTY
S_2	S_2	P_1	200
S_2	S_2	P_3	100
S_5	S_5	P_1	50
S_5	S_5	P_3	500
S_5	S_5	P_4	800
S_5	S_5	P_5	500
S_5	S_5	P_8	100

Figure 12.11 Join (=) over SNR. Table T6 is joined over the SNR to the corresponding elements of table SP.

12.10 Division

Division comprises the concepts of dividend, divisor and quotient in the following way:

DIVIDEND ÷ DIVISOR = QUOTIENT

The division statement requires the dividend table to have $m + n$ columns and the divisor table to have n columns with the same composition as the n columns of the dividend table. The m columns in the dividend table are interpreted as a combined column X, and the n columns are interpreted as a combined column Y. The divisor file will then have type Y and the quotient file, by definition, type X. The quotient file is defined as all entries x of type X for which entry (x, y) exists in the dividend table for all values of y in the divisor table. Note that the division statement satisfies the division rule that the product set of divisor and quotient must be equal to the dividend plus any remainder.

EXAMPLE 12.9

Table SP(SNR, PNR) can be divided by table P(PNR) as column PNR is shared by both tables. This is illustrated in Figure 12.12.

This division can be used to produce an output containing the salesman numbers of the salesmen who have been selling all products:

FIND QUOTIENT = DIVD SP.(SNR, PNR) BY P (PNR)

Dividend
SP (SNR PNR)

SNR	PNR
S_2	P_1
S_2	P_3
S_4	P_5
S_4	P_8
S_5	P_1
S_5	P_3
S_5	P_4
S_5	P_5
S_5	P_8

Divisor
P (PNR)

PNR
P_1
P_3
P_4
P_5
P_8

Remainder

SNR	PNR
S_2	P_1
S_2	P_3
S_4	P_5
S_4	P_8

Quotient

SNR
S_5

Figure 12.12 Division (DIVD).

EXERCISES

12.1 Display SNAMES for salesmen with the S-CODE value 20. The database used in this and the following exercises is illustrated in Figure 12.1.

12.2 Display PNR of blouses that are available in sizes larger than 5.

12.3 Display SNR, PNR and QTY of 'blouses'.

12.4 Display SNAMES, PNAMES and QTY where QTY is greater than 300.

12.5 Display SNAME of salesmen who have sold both shirts and trousers.

12.6 Display SNAME and CITY of salesmen who have sold no products at all.

12.7 Which products are sold for more than $50 or are sold in Copenhagen?

12.8 Which products, which are sold at a price over $50, are sold in Copenhagen?

12.9 Which products, which are sold at a price under $50, are sold in Copenhagen?

12.10 Examine whether the file in first normal form in Example 1.11 can be created from the files in second normal form and vice versa.

12.11 Examine whether the file in fourth normal form in Example 1.16 can be created from the files in fifth normal form and vice versa.

12.12 Prove that the join, intersection and division operators can be dispensed with if they can be replaced by combinations of the union, difference, product, selection and projection operators.

12.13 Display all data about salesmen who have sold at least one blouse.

Chapter 13
Structured Query Language

13.1 Introduction

DB2 is a relational DBMS developed by IBM. In this chapter, we shall deal first with DB2's database description language DDL and then with the associated data manipulation language SQL (Structured Query Language). Appendix D contains descriptions of the syntax of SQL and DB2's database description language.

In the literature on databases, an early version of this software product is known as System R. The query language SQL is currently developing into a standard, as it is available for the computers of several different hardware manufacturers.

13.2 DB2 database description language

In this section, we shall see how it is possible to describe a file and the fields belonging to it. The files shown in the example will later be used to illustrate the application of SQL's data manipulation statements.

EXAMPLE 13.1

The statements illustrated in Figure 13.1 show how the salesman–product database in Chapter 12 can be defined.

```
CREATE TABLE    S
    (SNR        CHAR (2) NOT NULL,
     SNAME      CHAR (5),
     S-CODE     SMALLINT,
     CITY       CHAR (15));
CREATE TABLE    P
    (PNR        CHAR (4) NOT NULL,
     PNAME      CHAR (10),
     PSIZE      SMALLINT,
     PPRICE     INTEGER);
CREATE TABLE    SP
    (SNR        CHAR (4) NOT NULL,
     PNR        CHAR (4) NOT NULL;
     QTY        INTEGER);
```

Figure 13.1 CREATE statements defining tables (relations).

The CREATE TABLE statement creates and names a table, of which the example creates three: S, P and SP. In the first table, the SNR field is defined as a character field of four characters. The NOT NULL parameter means that records may not be stored in the table without the SNR field having a value.

The S-CODE field is defined as SMALL INT – that is, an integer that at the most may occupy one-half of a machine word. The PPRICE field is likewise defined as INTEGER – an integer that at the most may occupy one machine word.

To remove a table and the description of it from the data dictionary, the DROP TABLE statement can be used followed by the name of the table.

DB2's DDL also contains statements for the creation or removal of databases, physical disk storage space for databases, disk storage space for tables, indexes on tables and user views. Furthermore, there are statements for changing a record type, changing an index, changing of block sizes, passwords, etc.

13.3 Retrieving data using SQL

SQL is a relational data manipulation language. We can prove that SQL is a relationally complete language, as its statements, directly or indirectly, contain the eight basic operators of relational algebra.

CITY
Copenhagen
Odense
Aarhus

Figure 13.2 Projection of CITY in S in SQL.

The general syntax to be used for retrieving data by SQL is as follows :

```
SELECT fields-in-output-file
        FROM input-files
        [WHERE logical-expression
        [ORDER BY fields]];
```

A SELECT statement always results in a table. The argument for the SELECT statement must indicate what fields the output table has to contain. If the database contains no output records that satisfy the SELECT statement, the result will be an empty table with its layout as specified in the SELECT statement. The output table will normally be displayed on the user's screen terminal.

The argument of FROM contains the name of the table(s) in which the search is to be performed.

The argument of WHERE is a logical expression that determines which records the search operation is to select.

ORDER BY has one or more fields as argument. This substatement causes the output file to be sorted by the stated fields.

Example 13.2 shows how the projection operation of relational algebra can be implemented. To avoid the projection containing several identical records, the DISTINCT parameter must be used.

EXAMPLE 13.2

The query 'output a sorted list of cities where the firm is represented by salesmen' is represented by the following SQL statements:

```
SELECT DISTINCT CITY
        FROM S
        ORDER BY CITY;
```

The output is shown in Figure 13.2.

Example 13.3 illustrates how the SELECT operation of relational algebra can be executed . Note that all the fields of the file are displayed if the argument for the SELECT statement is an asterisk (*).

SNR	SNAME	S-CODE	CITY
S_2	Olsen	30	Copenhagen
S_5	Jensen	30	Copenhagen

Figure 13.3 Selection of CITY = 'Copenhagen' in SQL.

EXAMPLE 13.3

The query 'display a list of salesmen in Copenhagen' gives in SQL:

```
SELECT *
        FROM S
        WHERE CITY = 'Copenhagen'
        ORDER BY SNAME DESC;
```

The output is shown in Figure 13.3.

Note that the last line in the program causes the output table to be sorted in descending order by the field SNAME. If the DESC parameter is left out, the output file would be sorted in ascending order by SNAME.

The next example illustrates how the union operation of relational algebra can be executed.

EXAMPLE 13.4

The query 'which salesmen are either resident in Copenhagen or have been selling product P8?' requires two SQL SELECTs linked by a UNION:

```
SELECT SNR
        FROM S
        WHERE CITY = 'Copenhagen'
UNION
SELECT SNR
        FROM SP
        WHERE PNR = 'P8'
```

The output is shown in Figure 13.4.

Example 13.5 shows how SQL can be applied to implement the JOIN operation of relational algebra. If two tables are to be joined they must each contain a column with the same domain. Such columns often share the same name. To distinguish between the two columns, the table name may be added to the column name.

SNR
S_2
S_4
S_5

Figure 13.4 Result of a SQL union.

EXAMPLE 13.5

The query 'display a list of salesman names, salesman numbers, product numbers and quantities sold' can be written in SQL as :

```
SELECT SNAME, S.SNR, PNR, QTY
        FROM S, SP
        WHERE S.SNR = SP.SNR;
```

The output is shown in Figure 13.5.

The names of the tables to be joined are used as the arguments of the FROM statement, and the names of the fields over which the files are joined are used as the argument of the WHERE statement.

Example 13.6 demonstrates how the argument of a WHERE statement may be an arbitrary complex expression. In the example, a table is joined with itself. In this situation, it is necessary to give the table two different names so that the two parts of the table can be distinguished from each other when joined. The allocation of a new table is effected by writing the new table name after the name of the table in the FROM statement.

SNAME	S.SNR	PNR	QTY
Olsen	S_2	P_1	200
Olsen	S_2	P_3	100
Hansen	S_4	P_5	200
Hansen	S_4	P_8	100
Jensen	S_5	P_1	50
Jensen	S_5	P_3	500
Jensen	S_5	P_4	800
Jensen	S_5	P_5	500
Jensen	S_5	P_8	100

Figure 13.5 Join over SNR in SQL.

X.PNR
P_5

Figure 13.6 Join with a complex WHERE expression.

EXAMPLE 13.6

The query 'display a list of products that can be supplied in a size that is two sizes larger and which has the same PNAME' results in the following SQL statements:

```
SELECT X.PNR
FROM P X, P Y
WHERE (X.PNAME = Y.PNAME)
    AND (X.SIZE + 2 = Y.SIZE);
```

The output is shown in Figure 13.6.

In SQL a join does not have to take place over columns that have the same value; all that is required is that the **tuples** (columns) are linked by a logical operator such as 'greater than'.

Table 13.1 lists the most important logical operators forming part of SQL expressions. Some of the SP operators can be negated, so that a logical expression acquires the opposite logical value. This negation is achieved by putting the symbol ¬ or NOT before the operator.

EXAMPLE 13.7

The query 'display a list of all pairs of salesmen with different S-CODES' can be implemented with the SQL statement:

```
SELECT X.SNR, Y.SNR
FROM S X, S Y
WHERE (X.S-CODE < Y.S-CODE);
```

SNR is selected from S and the resulting table is joined to itself over the 'less than' operator on the S-CODE columns. Figure 13.7 shows the output table.

X.SNR	Y.SNR
S_1	S_2
S_1	S_4
S_1	S_5
S_4	S_2
S_4	S_5

Figure 13.7 Table joined to itself over 'less than'.

Table 13.1 Logical operators of SQL.

Operator	*Description*	*Negation*
=	Equal to	yes
<	Less than	yes
<=	Less than or equal to	no
>	Greater than	yes
>=	Greater than or equal to	no
OR	A logical expression is TRUE if at least one of the arguments of OR is a logical expression that is true	no
AND	The expression is TRUE if both arguments are TRUE	no
BETWEEN	The expression is TRUE if the operand lies within a specified interval, including the limits	yes
IN	The expression is TRUE if the operand is included in a stated file with one-field records; this operator corresponds to the set operator 'is a member of', which is symbolized by ∈	yes
EXIST	This operator corresponds to the mathematical existential quantifier ∃; that is, the expression is TRUE if there are records in the file serving as argument	yes
LIKE	The expression is TRUE if a character field contains certain selected combinations of characters	yes

EXAMPLE 13.8

The query 'display product numbers of blouses in the price range $30 to $60' can be formulated in SQL as:

```
SELECT PNR
   FROM P
   WHERE (PNAME = 'Blouse') AND
      (PPRICE BETWEEN 30 AND 60);
```

The output is the table shown in Figure 13.8.

PNR
P_5
P_8

Figure 13.8 The BETWEEN . . . AND . . . operator.

Example 13.8 demonstrated that if a character column is to be matched with a character string, the character string must be enclosed by quotes. If, on the other hand, a numeric field has to be matched with digits in a similar way, no quotes are needed (see Example 13.9).

EXAMPLE 13.9

The query 'display all salesman records with S-CODE 5, 8, 10 or 15, not resident in Copenhagen or Aalborg' can be formulated in SQL as:

```
SELECT*
    FROM S
    WHERE (S-CODE IN (5, 8, 10, 15))
        AND (CITY NOT IN ('Copenhagen', 'Aalborg'));
```

The output is the table shown in Figure 13.9.

In the SQL fragment, the IN operator could be replaced by a number of OR operators, and NOT IN could likewise be replaced by AND, as illustrated in the following:

```
SELECT*
    FROM S
    WHERE ((S-CODE = 5) OR (S-CODE = 8) OR
        S-CODE = 10) OR (S-CODE = 15))
    AND ((CITY NOT = 'Copenhagen') AND
        (CITY NOT = 'Aalborg'));
```

Example 13.10 shows that a logical expression with the operator EXIST has the value TRUE if the argument for EXIST is not an empty table. Note also that the argument for WHERE may be a complex expression, which may incorporate an arbitrary number of SELECT statements.

EXAMPLE 13.10

The query 'display product number and product name of products sold' gives the following SQL statement:

```
SELECT PNR, PNAME
    FROM P
    WHERE EXIST
        SELECT*
            FROM SP
            WHERE PNR = P.PNR);
```

This gives the table shown in Figure 13.10 as output.

EXAMPLE 13.11

In this example, $p(A)$ signifies a logical expression that is a function of entry A. In set theory, the existential quantifier $\exists$ and the universal

SNR	SNAME	S-CODE	CITY
S_1	Petersen	10	Aarhus

Figure 13.9 The IN operator.

quantifier ∀ are defined in such a way that:

$$\forall A : p(A) \equiv \neg(\exists A : \neg p(A))$$

'$p(A)$ must be TRUE for every entry A' is equivalent to 'it is not the case that at least one entry A exists for which it is not the case that $p(A)$ is TRUE.' As the EXIST operator corresponds to the existential quantifier ∃ we can also, by means of the above equivalent, formulate statements that use the universal quantifier ∀.

The following expression describes the set of salesmen who have been selling some of all products; $\{A \mid p(A)\}$ is the set of entries for which $p(A)$ is TRUE:

$$\{S \mid \forall P \exists SP : (SP.PNR = P.PNR) \text{ AND } (SP.SNR = S.SNR\}$$

S is the set of entries for which it is TRUE that for every entry P there is at least one entry SP such that (SP.PNR = P.PNR) AND (SP.SNR = S.SNR). In the next expression, the universal quantifier has been removed by means of the identity given above:

$$\{S \mid \neg(\exists P \neg(\exists SP : (SP.PNR = P.PNR) \text{ AND } (SP.SNR = S.SNR)))\}$$

The expression now contains only the existential quantifier ∃ and consequently it can be expressed in SQL as follows:

```
SELECT*
    FROM S
    WHERE NOT EXIST
        (SELECT*
            FROM P
            WHERE NOT EXIST
                (SELECT*
                    FROM SP
                    WHERE PNR = P.PNR
                        AND SNR = S.SNR));
```

PNR	PNAME
P_1	Shirt
P_3	Trousers
P_4	Socks
P_5	Blouse
P_8	Blouse

Figure 13.10 The EXISTS operator.

SNR	SNAME
S_5	Jensen

Figure 13.11 The LIKE operator.

Example 13.12 illustrates the use of the LIKE operator.

EXAMPLE 13.12

The query 'output SNR and SNAME for salesmen whose name starts with J and ends in SEN and where the first character in the salesman number is S' can be formated in SQL using LIKE:

```
SELECT*
        FROM S
        WHERE (SNAME LIKE 'J%SEN')
        AND (SNR LIKE 'S_');
```

The output is shown in Figure 13.11.

The LIKE statement can select columns containing one or more characters shared with the characters in the LIKE statement's other operand. The symbol % means that zero, one or more of the subsequent characters can be left out of the comparison. The symbol — means that exactly one character is left out of the comparison. The position of this character indicates the position where an arbitrary character may occur.

Note that only character fields may serve as arguments for the LIKE statement.

The ordinary rules of arithmetic applying to Boolean operators also apply to SQL, as shown in Example 13.13.

EXAMPLE 13.13

The query 'display PNR and PPRICE for products not in the price range from 50 to 80' gives the SQL statement:

```
SELECT PNR, PPRICE
        FROM P
        WHERE NOT ((PPRICE <= 80) AND (PPRICE >= 50));
```

According to Boolean algebra, NOT can be moved inside the outer parenthesis if AND is changed into OR and if the logical subexpressions are negated. The result of this is:

```
SELECT PNR, PPRICE
        FROM P
        WHERE (PPRICE >80) OR PPRICE <50);
```

The output, shown in Figure 13.12, is the same in either case.

PNR	PPRICE
P_3	90
P_4	20

Figure 13.12 Boolean arithmetic applies to SQL operators: NOT (. . . AND . . .) is equivalent to (. . . OR . . .).

A field in the output file may consists of an arithmetic expression with the operators +, −, × and / corresponding to plus, minus, multiplication and division. It is also possible to sort the output file on a calculated field. The logical expression after WHERE may contain arithmetic operators, which may only have numeric operands.

EXAMPLE 13.14

The query 'output a price list in which the products are grouped according to the price of the product including 22% VAT' would be expressed as a SQL query as:

```
SELECT PNR, PPRICE × 1.22, PNAME
    FROM P
    ORDER BY 2, PNR;
```

This gives the output shown in Figure 13.13.

Note that the output table has been sorted primarily by the second field and secondarily by PNR.

Table 13.2 gives a survey of SQL's built-in functions. These functions may form part of logical and arithmetic expressions that are arguments for the SELECT and other statements.

PNR	PRICE * 1.22	PNAME
P_4	24.4	Socks
P_1	61	Shirt
P_5	61	Blouse
P_8	73.2	Blouse
P_3	109.8	Trousers

Figure 13.13 Tuples may have arithmetic operations applied to them before a table is given as output.

Table 13.2 Built-in functions of SQL.

Function	Description
SUM (field name)	Sums up the field contents
MIN (field name)	Calculates lowest field value
AVG (field name)	Calculates average field value
MAX (field name)	Calculates greatest field value
COUNT (*)	Calculates the number of selected records
COUNT (DISTINCT field name)	Calculates the number of different field values for the selected field

EXAMPLE 13.15

The query 'display the number of salesmen who have been selling product P3' can be expressed in SQL as :

```
SELECT COUNT (*), SUM (QTY), MAX (QTY),
    MIN (QTY), AVG (QTY)
    FROM SP
    WHERE PNR='P3';
```

The output for this is shown in Figure 13.14. Note that the display must also show total sales, maximum sales, minimum sales and average sales of product P3.

The function of the SELECT statement can be altered so that it works with groups of entries. The parameter GROUP BY causes the selected entries to be grouped thereby outputting a file containing statistical information about each group. The parameter HAVING is used if the output has only to contain information about a subset of groups. Example 16 illustrates the use of GROUP BY and HAVING.

EXAMPLE 13.16

The query is 'display a list of cities with more than one salesman'. The list has to contain CITY, the number of salesmen and the average S-CODE.

COUNT (*)	SUM (QTY)	MAX (QTY)	MIN (QTY)	AVG (QTY)
2	600	500	100	300

Figure 13.14 Use of the built-in functions COUNT (*), SUM, MAX, MIN and AVG.

CITY	COUNT (*)	AVG (S-CODE)	COUNT (DISTINCT S-CODE)
Copenhagen	2	30	1

Figure 13.15 Use of GROUP BY and HAVING.

For each chosen city, we also want a list of the number of salesmen there are with different S-CODES. The list has to be ordered alphabetically by CITY. Salesmen who are not yet attached to a city are not included in the statistical material. SQL represents this enquiry in the following way:

```
SELECT CITY, COUNT (*), AVG(S-CODE),
    COUNT (DISTINCT S-CODE)
    FROM S
    WHERE NOT CITY IS NULL
    GROUP BY CITY
    HAVING COUNT (*) > 1
    ORDER BY CITY;
```

The output is shown in Figure 13.15.

Example 13.17 shows that it is also possible to combine the JOIN statement with the GROUP BY statement.

EXAMPLE 13.17

The query 'display a list of the individual salesmen's total sales' is formulated in SQL as:

```
SELECT SP.SNR, SUM (SP, QTY × P. PPRICE)
    FROM SP, P
    WHERE SP.PNR = P.PNR
    GROUP BY SP.SNR;
```

The output is shown in Figure 13.16.

SP.SNR	SUM (SP.QTY * P.PPRICE)
S_2	19 000
S_4	16 000
S_5	94 500

Figure 13.16 JOIN combined with a GROUP BY statement.

Table 13.3 Updating statements of SQL.

Statement	*Description*
INSERT	This statement can create one or more new records
DELETE	This statement can remove one or more existing records
UPDATE	This statement can alter the field contents in one or more existing records

13.4 Updating with SQL

A survey of SQL's updating statements is given in Table 13.3.

Example 13.18 illustrates how a new entry can be created.

EXAMPLE 13.18

To create a new salesman entry with the following field values:

SNR = S6
SNAME = Smith
S-CODE = 0
CITY = Berlin

the following SQL statement is used:

```
INSERT INTO S
    VALUES ('S6', 'Smith', 0, 'Berlin');
```

This adds a new entry to the S table as shown in Figure 13.17.

To record an S-CODE of NULL for the new record, we have to state that only values for SNR, SNAME and CITY are going to be provided:

```
INSERT INTO S
    (SNR, SNAME, CITY)
    VALUES ('S6', Smith, Berlin');
```

SNR	SNAME	S-CODE	CITY
S_1	Petersen	10	Aarhus
S_2	Olsen	30	Copenhagen
S_4	Hansen	20	Odense
S_5	Jensen	30	Copenhagen
S_6	Smith	0	Berlin

Figure 13.17 Creation of a new entry in the S table. S-CODE is explicitly given the value 0.

SNR	SNAME	S-CODE	CITY
S_1	Petersen	10	Aarhus
S_2	Olsen	30	Copenhagen
S_4	Hansen	20	Odense
S_5	Jensen	30	Copenhagen
S_8	Smith		Berlin

Figure 13.18 Creation of a new entry in the S table. S-CODE is not assigned a value.

This will give the S table shown in Figure 13.18. There is no value in the new entry's S-CODE field.

The next example shows how a set of new entries can be created.

EXAMPLE 13.19

In connection with the union operator in Chapter 12 we needed an auxiliary table T3, which contained the salesman number of all salesmen in Copenhagen. In SQL the corresponding exercise can be performed as follows:

```
CREATE TABLE T3
        (SNR CHAR (4));

INSERT INTO T3
        SELECT SNR
        FROM S
        WHERE CITY = 'Copenhagen',
```

Example 13.20 shows how a set of records can be deleted.

EXAMPLE 13.20

The query 'delete all salesman records with Copenhagen as CITY' in SQL is writtten:

```
DELETE
        FROM S
        WHERE CITY = 'Copenhagen'
```

And finally, Example 13.21 illustrates how the contents of a field can be updated.

EXAMPLE 13.21

To increase the S-CODE of salesman S2 by 5, the SQL instruction is:

```
UPDATE S
        SET S-CODE = S-CODE + 5:
        WHERE SNR = 'S2';
```

The following SQL statement increases the S-CODE by 5 for all salesmen in Copenhagen. At the same time, the spelling of Copenhagen is changed to 'Koebenhavn':

```
UPDATE S
        SET S-CODE = S-CODE + 5
        CITY = 'Koebenhavn'
        WHERE CITY = 'Copenhagen';
```

EXERCISES

13.1 Solve Exercises 12.1 to 12.9 by using SQL statements.

13.2 Display the product number of all products in the smallest size.

13.3 Display PNAME of products sold by seller S4.

13.4 Display PNAME of products sold in Copenhagen.

13.5 Display PNAME of products sold either in Copenhagen or in Aarhus.

13.6 How many different products are sold either in Copenhagen or in Aarhus?

13.7 Display SNR of salesmen who have sold both P1 and P3.

13.8 Display SNR of salesmen who have sold at least the same value of goods as seller S2.

13.9 Calculate the total turnover in the different cities.

13.10 Outline a syntactic change of SQL that would make it possible to have subsums of subsums displayed. An example would be turnover per city per salesman.

13.11 Increase the price by 10% for those products having more than the average turnover.

13.12 Reduce the S-CODE by 5 for those salesmen who live in cities whose turnover for blouses is lower than their turnover for trousers.

13.13 Assume that the file COSTS with the fields PNR, COSTS and PROD-COSTS

Product file

PNR	PNAME
13	Mineral water
17	Lemonade
21	Beer

Inventory file

INR	INAME
2	Copenhagen
3	Odense
8	Aalborg

Product-inventory file

PNR	INR	QTY
13	2	300
13	3	200
13	8	500
17	3	400
17	8	100
21	3	800
21	8	600

Figure 13.19 Relational inventory database for a brewery.

contain product number, fixed production costs and variable production costs of the various products. Calculate the average profits on products with the same PNAME.

13.14 The questions given in this exercise must be programmed and run on a computer with a relational non-procedure oriented programming language. Figure 13.19 illustrates a relational inventory database of a brewery whose stocks are located in different places in the country.

(a) Create files P, I and PI. Read in the data shown in the files and display a list of the contents of these files.

(b) What is the total stock of the product with PNR = 13?

(c) Display an inventory list by using the fields PNR, PNAME, INR and QTY.

(d) Display PNR, QTY and INAME for products with a remaining stock of less than 300.

(e) Which products are not in stock in Aalborg?

(f) Which products are in stock in all locations?

(g) Write a survey of total stocks of each individual product.

(h) Two hundred boxes of lemonade have been transported to the warehouse in Aalborg and 100 boxes of lemonade to Odense. Update the database with this information.

Part Four
APPENDICES

Appendix A
Lists

A **list** can be defined as an ordered set of **list elements** – in data processing the list elements are normally records. Normally, a list is implemented by chaining together the list elements in the required sequence. This can be done by storing a pointer to the next element in the list in a pointer field. The pointer is called a **physical pointer** if the pointer field contains the address of the next element in the list and a **logical pointer** if it contains the identification number of the next list element. If logical pointers are used, the file with the list elements must have either index or random organization so that the next list element can be located by means of the record's identification number. It is thus clearly faster to read a list by using physical pointers. Logical pointers, on the other hand, make the maintenance of the file more flexible, since the physical movement of records (due to reorganization or overflow in a block) can be executed without it being necessary to alter the contents of all those pointer fields pointing to the record.

EXAMPLE A1.1

The list elements *A, B, C, D* and *E* are records. Figure A1.1 illustrates how the list (*A, B, C, D, E*) can be stored on disk by having each record in the list contain a field in which the address of the next record is stored. The address of the first record in the list will usually be stored in a special record or variable called the **list head.** This list can also be implemented by using logical pointers. This is illustrated in Figure A1.2.

If the implementation of a list is the primary organization of the file, the list can be created as a **dense list,** which corresponds to physical sequential

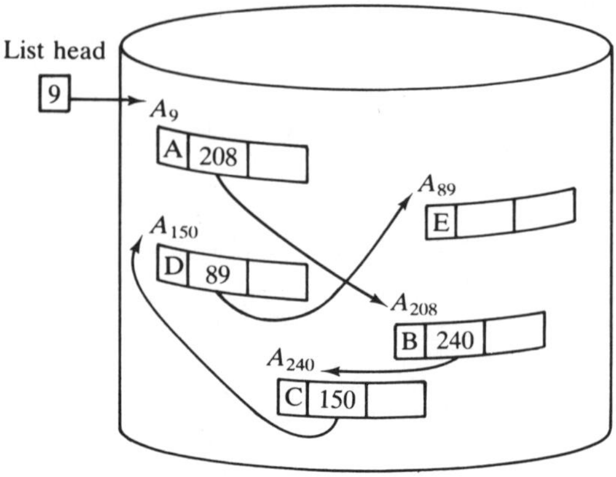

Figure A1.1 A list with physical pointers in disk storage. Each record has a field containing the address of the next element in the list (the last list element has this field blank).

organization. To avoid future maintenance problems, a dense list also has pointer fields.

It is often practical to represent the relationships between records by means of lists. Some types of relationship that can be implemented by means of lists are:

- Ordered relationships, which can be implemented by chaining together the records of the file in sorted order.
- Equivalence relationships, which can be implemented by chaining together all records from the same subset.

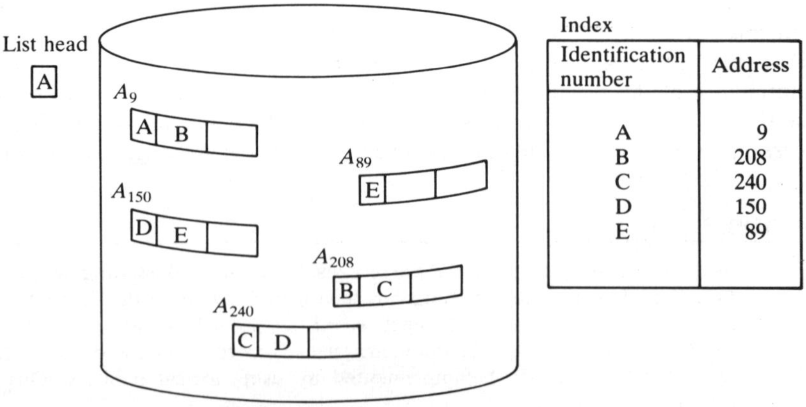

Figure A1.2 A list with logical pointers. Each element record contains a field for the next element in the list. Physical addresses of the list elements are found by means of an index of addresses.

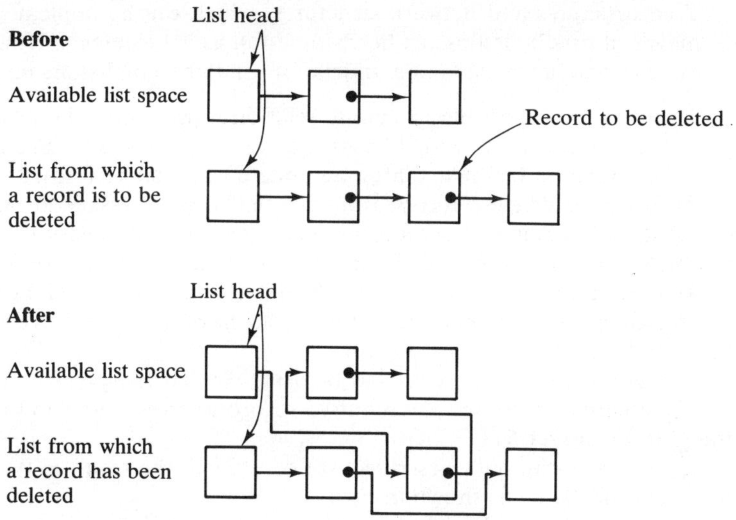

Figure A1.3 Updating a list. A deleted record is taken off the list of which it was part and the space it occupied chained back on to the available space list.

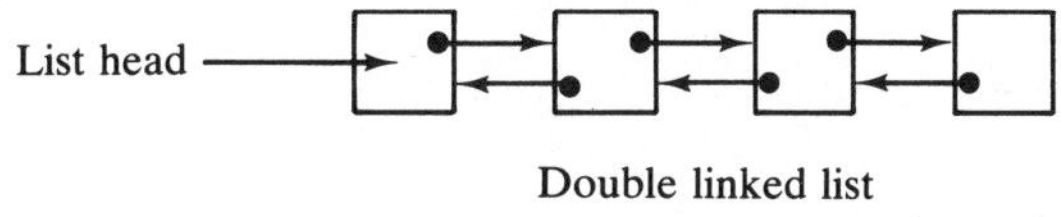

Figure A1.4 Double linked list.

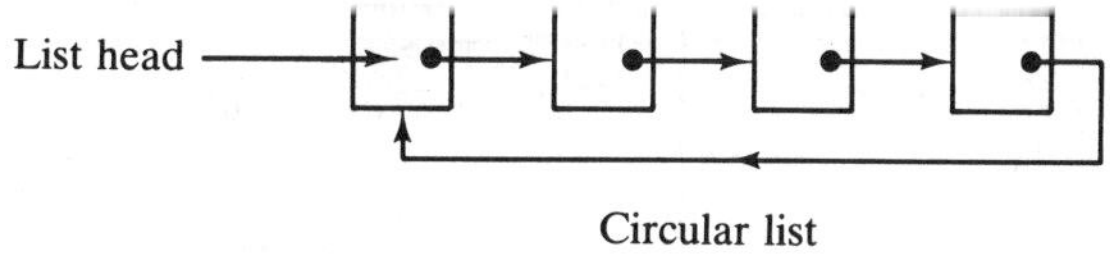

Figure A1.5 Circular list.

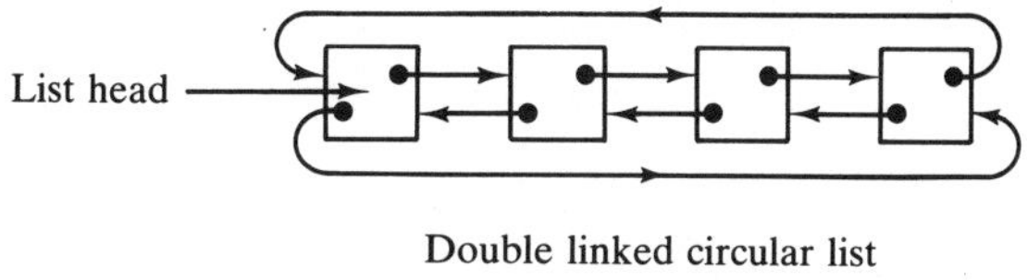

Figure A1.6 Double linked circular list.

- Tree structures and network structures, which can be implemented by means of lists by letting list heads function as list elements. How this is done in practice is explained in detail in Chapter 3 on list organizations.

As it has to be possible to update relationships, it must be possible to delete a record from a list and, likewise, to insert a new one. Figure A1.3 illustrates the situation before and after an update has been performed.

To insert or delete a record from the list, it is necessary to know the address of the preceding and succeeding record in a list. It is easy to find the address of the succeeding record if the address of the record to be deleted is known, since its address will be stored as a field in the record. To find the address of the preceding record it may be necessary to have a **double linked** list, as illustrated in Figure A1.4.

The problem can also be solved by using **circular lists,** which enables a search of the entire list to find the required record address. This kind of list is illustrated in Figure A1.5.

If the two techniques described are combined, the result is the **double linked circular list** which is shown in Figure A1.6.

An **inverted list** can be defined as a list in which all chaining pointers have been removed from the list elements and stored instead in the list head.

EXAMPLE A1.2

Figure A1.7 illustrates the list from Example A1.1 in the form of an inverted list.

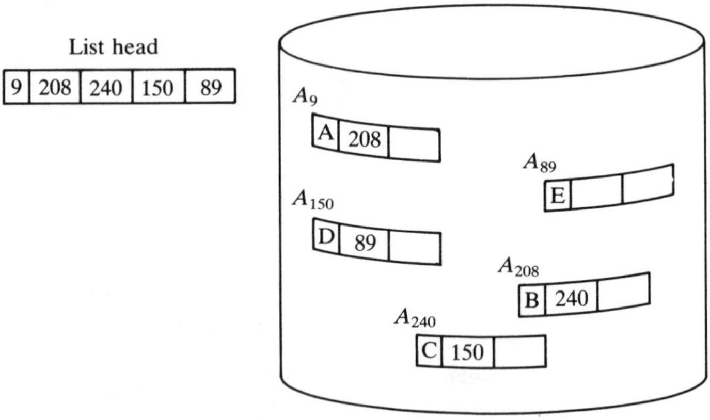

Figure A1.7 Inverted list. All the chaining pointers are now stored in the list head rather than in the list elements.

Appendix B
Estimating the use of Capacity

B1.1 Introduction

This appendix has been included in the book because although the price of CPU capacity is falling rapidly, database technology is very resource intensive. Much of the work involved in database administration, therefore, consists in optimizing the physical database. However, optimizing the database in isolation may result in poor utilization of capacity.

Normally, the capacity of a machine means the number of 'units' the machine can process in a specified period of time. Numerous attempts have been made to find such a measurable unit for the use of capacity of computer programs. These attempts fall into two main types:

(1) The multi-dimensional capacity measures, which define the capacity of a program as the capacity of the separate units making up the computer.
(2) The uni-dimensional capacity measures, which try to express the capacity in one single figure. Often, such capacity measures consist of a rather arbitrary weighting of the capacity of the separate units of the computer.

To compare the capacity of different computers multi-dimensional capacity measures are often used in which the measurements try to give an indication of the capacity of the separate untis of the computer. Table B1.1. gives an example of this.

Capacity measures of the type described in Table B1.1 are not always practical when trying to distribute the total capacity of a computer between the various programs run on it. One reason for this is that although a program may be occupying a unit, it will rarely be possible for it to utilize the unit's total capacity

Table B1.1 The capacity measures of the separate units of a computer.

Units	*Capacity*
Line printer	Number of lines that can be printed per second
Card reader	Number of cards that can be read per second
Magnetic tape unit	Number of characters that can be read per second
Disk drive†	The average number of direct searches that can be performed per second The average number of characters that can be read per second by sequential reading The number of characters that can be stored on a disk storage
CPU†	The number of 'average statements' that can be executed per second The number of characters that can be stored in main storage

† Note that for some units the capacity measure has several dimensions.

(see Examples B1.6 and B1.7). Thus, it is important to distinguish between the time during which a program is **working** on a unit (the time during which the unit is actively working at the program) and the time during which the program is **occupying** the unit (the length of time during which the program prevents other programs from using the unit).

In what follows, we will examine the most frequently used measures of use of capacity on multiprogrammed and non-multiprogrammed computers, respectively. (A multiprogrammed computer is one on which it is possible to run several programs simultaneously. The different programs each occupy a separate section of main storage, while the computer's CPU first executes a sequence of statements for the first program, then a sequence for the second program, etc. On a non-multiprogrammed computer, one program run must be completed before the next program run is started.) For each of the capacity measures discussed, we point out its serious shortcomings; that is, the properties of the capacity measure that make it difficult to make 'rational' decisions on the basis of the measures/estimates of use of capacity. However, it is difficult to find any better measures than those mentioned here. The topic is discussed in Danish at greater length in Frank (1975).

When discussing non-multiprogrammed computers, we shall use run times as a measure of a program's use of capacity. However, using run time as a capacity measure presents the following problems:

- The run time of a program is not unique, since it may vary from one computer to another.
- If the total capacity of the computer is defined as the time during which the computer can be operative, it will be possible to divide the total capacity between the program runs and a possible surplus capacity. It should be noted, however, that if this capacity measure is used there will be a hidden surplus capacity, which can be revealed by improving the **simultaneousness** of the computer. A computer with **simultaneous** units is one whose units can work simultaneously. For example, the CPU of the computer can execute calculations while, at the same time, data is

read into the computer and results are printed out. Clearly, within limits, improving **simultaneousness** can reduce the run time of a program.

In discussing multiprogrammed computers, we can use the work of the separate units as a multi-dimensional measure of the use of capacity of a program. If the storage capacity of the unit is shared with other programs, the measure of the work performed by the unit for the program should also contain information about how large a share of the unit's storage capacity the program occupies. Using the work times as capacity measures, however, presents the following problems:

- The total work times of the program runs cannot be used as an expression of the total use of capacity because the units of the computer may be occupied for longer than they are actually working. However, the time during which a program occupies the units of a computer cannot be used as measures of the use of capacity either (see Examples B1.6 and B1.7).
- If we exclude the time during which a unit is occupied but not actually working, it will be possible, in theory, to divide the total capacity of a computer between the programs run and any possible surplus capacity. However, it is impossible in practice to use all the units of the computer at the same time. This means that there will always be surplus capacity, which cannot possibly be utilized.

In this appendix, we shall first describe methods that can be used to estimate the work performed by the computer's various units. Secondly, we shall analyse the connection between the work of the units and the use of capacity, so that the use of capacity can be estimated from estimates of the work of each individual unit.

Computers can be divided into groups according to whether they are multiprogrammed or not and whether their units are simultaneous or not. If we combine these criteria we obtain four types of computer. The analysis of the connection between the use of capacity and the work performed by the external units is treated according to these different types of computer. No rigorous proof of the connection between the use of capacity and the work performed by the units is offered, rather the kinds of results we might expect to obtain are illustrated by means of examples.

B1.2 Methods to estimate the work of units

We only make use of one set of equations to estimate the work of the units, because, on the whole, the various different methods are merely variations on the same theme.

$$\text{Work time for a line printer} = \frac{\text{number of lines to be printed}}{\text{printing speed of line printer}} \qquad (1)$$

$$\text{Work time for a page printer} = \frac{\text{number of pages to be printed}}{\text{printing speed of page printer}}$$

$$\text{Work time for a card reader} = \frac{\text{number of cards to be read}}{\text{reading speed of the card reader}} \qquad (2)$$

The work time for a magnetic tape unit can be estimated by the following formula:

$$\text{number of blocks} \times \left(\frac{\text{block size}}{\text{read/write speed}} + \text{acceleration time}\right) \tag{3}$$

Note that if a small block size is used, the number of blocks in the file increases. As the size of an inter-block gap is constant, the total amount of space occupied by inter-block gaps also increases. Thus, the above equation suggests that this will result in an increase of work time because the acceleration time for moving over an inter-block gap is larger than the corresponding read/write time. Thus, it is an advantage to use a large block size. In practice, block size is limited by the space available in the computer's main storage.

In reading/writing a block in a file stored on a disk, we can use the following equation to estimate the work time of the disk storage:

$$H + \frac{R}{2} + \frac{R}{S} \tag{4}$$

where H is the average time required to move the read/write head, R is the rotational time of the disk storage and S is the number of blocks per track. We arrive at the three terms in the equation in the following way. First, the read/write head has to be moved to the right track. Then, we have to wait half a rotation, on average, before the read/write head is over the proper block. The last term in the formula is the time it takes to read or write the block when the read/write head is positioned over it.

In reading a block in a file we can, as we have just seen, use Equation (4) to calculate the work imposed on the disk storage. In practice, however, we are not always interested in finding the work time of the disk storage, but the response time of the computer after the CPU has sent the instruction to read a block. In such a case, the following formula to calculate the response time should be used:

$$H + \frac{R}{2} + \max\left\{\frac{R}{S}, \frac{B}{K}\right\} \tag{5}$$

where B is the block size and K is the transmission speed of the channel. Thus, B/K becomes the time used by the data channel to transmit a block from the CPU to the disk storage or vice versa. The two first terms in the equation describe, as before, the average time it takes to move the read/write head to the location where the required block is stored. The value of the last term in the equation depends upon whether the data channel itself, or the rotational speed of the disk storage, becomes a bottleneck when the individual bytes in a block are to be transmitted to main storage.

The total time spent on updating a block is made up of the time spent on reading a block and the time spent on writing back the changed block. In the case of multiprogrammed computers in which many different programs work on the disk storage concurrently, the actual work performed by the disk storage can be estimated by the summing Equations (4) and (5). If only a single program is operating on the disk storage, we estimate the updating time for a block as:

$$H + \frac{R}{2} + \frac{R}{S} + R \tag{6}$$

The first three terms represent the time required to read the block that is to be changed. The last term represents the writing-back time together with the waiting time before the changed block can be written back to its original place. If we check-read the updated record, the updating time will increase by R seconds. If we use a block size of one track, the updating time again increases by R seconds, as there will normally be no time for updating the block in main storage and sending the contents back to the disk storage while the read/write head is passing the inter-block gap.

If we are using a multiprogrammed computer, and if many different programs are operating on the disk storage at the same time, we can use Equation (5) to calculate the work required from the disk storage for sequential reading/writing, as we have to multiply the reading time for a block by the number of blocks in the file. If only one program is operating on the disk storage, the work time required of the disk storage can be estimated as:

$$\text{Number of cylinders in the file} \times \left(HMIN + \left(\frac{R}{S} + R\right) \times C \times S\right) \tag{7}$$

where $HMIN$ is the minimum time required to move the read/write head from one cylinder to another and C is the number of tracks per cylinder. As S contains the number of blocks per track, $C \times S$ will contain the number of blocks per cylinder. We arrive at the total work time involved in sequential reading by multiplying the number of cylinders in the file by the work time for one single cylinder. The work time required to read a cylinder includes the time for the read/write head to be moved from the neighbouring cylinder. In addition to this, we must include the reading time for a block multiplied by the number of blocks in the cylinder. The time required to read a block placed under the read/write head is fraction R/S. Then, we have to wait for one whole rotation of the disk before the next block can be read, as the transmission of the block to the CPU normally cannot be executed while the read/write head is passing the inter-block gap.

If we are to update a file stored on a disk sequentially, we will often be able to apply the following expression to calculate the work time of the disk storage:

$$\text{Number of cylinders in the file} \times \left(HMIN + \left(\frac{R}{S} + 2R\right) \times C \times S\right) \tag{8}$$

This formula is the same as that used for sequential reading apart from the fact that the work time for each block has been increased by one disk storage rotation. The reason for this increase is that the access methods are rarely devised in such a way that we can read the contents of a block immediately after writing the preceding one.

The main technique for estimating the amount of CPU work involved in executing database programs involves estimating the work times of the individual types of statement and then multiplying these by the number of times each type of statement has been used. The problem of using this method is that it is difficult to estimate the individual statements' use of CPU resources. In the following, we take a look at two different methods to estimate this work time:

- In many cases the suppliers of programs publish equations that can be used to estimate work times. However, these are often very complicated and subject to a great deal of uncertainty. This uncertainty is caused by the fact that there are numerous factors that may affect the work time of the individual statements. Examples of such factors are CPU capacity, the complexity of possible search criteria, whether the individual fields are to be changed before the record is transferred to the application program, the size of the files and the form of organization used.
- A more accurate method is to write small, simple programs that contain the individual types of statement. After doing so, we can instruct the computer to display the programs' use of CPU capacity in different situations. The use of CPU capacity in the start and finish stages of the test program can be eliminated by placing the database statement in a loop so that it is executed a great number of times while the start and finish statements are only executed once. The drawback of using this method is that many programs have to be written and test run before we know the work time of the various database statements in different situations. A further drawback is that the program runs have to be repeated whenever the firm changes the type of CPU used in its computer installation.

B1.3 Estimating the use of capacity on non-multiprogrammed computers without simultaneous units

In running a program on a computer of this type, the run time (use of capacity) is equivalent to the sum of the work required from each of the individual units of the computer. This is demonstrated in Example B1.1.

EXAMPLE B1.1

A program reads in data from cards (punched cards, optically readable paying-in forms, cards with magnetic type or the like), calculates the sum total of the input data and, finally, writes out the average. Figure B1.1 shows a Gantt diagram of the work imposed on the CPU and the card reader. The length of the lines in the figure symbolizes the time during which the corresponding unit is working. The number over the 'time lines' indicates the number of the card being processed by the unit in question. The dots indicate that the CPU is starting a data transmission.

The first dot in Figure B1.1 indicates that the CPU starts the card reader and then waits for data to be transferred from the card reader to main storage.

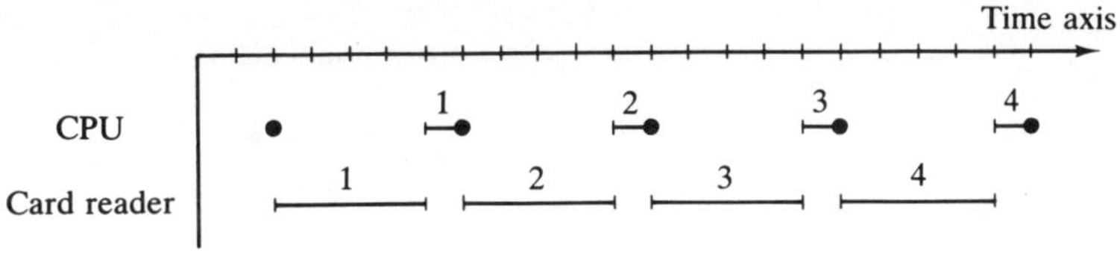

Figure B1.1 Gantt diagram of work done by a card reader and CPU without simultaneousness between the units.

The CPU now sums up the input data and then re-starts the card reader. This procedure continues until all cards have been read in. The figure shows that the run time of the program is equivalent to the sum of the work performed by the individual units.

B1.4 Estimating the use of capacity on non-multiprogrammed computers with simultaneous units

If we run on-line programs on a non-multiprogrammed computer with simultaneous units, we will, in most cases, be unable to utilize any simultaneousness, and therefore the run time of the program will be the sum of the work performed by the individual units of the computer. In the case of batch-oriented programs, we will normally be able to utilize simultaneousness so that the capacity required by a program is determined by the 'slowest' of the units used by the program.

Batch-oriented programs used in administrative data processing can be divided into activities in such a way that a new activity is started each time the processing of a file is started or terminated. Under the assumption of simultaneousness, the run time of an activity will be equivalent to the work time for the unit that acts as bottleneck in the activity; that is, the unit that is working for the longest time. The total run time of the program can now be calculated as the sum of the run times of the individual activities.

In Example B1.2 we shall try to illustrate the correctness of this method and also underline the assumptions behind it.

EXAMPLE B1.2

Figure B1.2 illustrates how the program described in the previous example can be run on a computer with synchronous units. The CPU starts the card reader and then waits for data to be transferred from the first card to main storage. When the data transmission has been terminated, the CPU re-starts the card reader and then goes on to sum up the data from the first card. When data from the second card arrives at main storage, the inputting of the third card begins while data from the second card is being processed by the CPU. This procedure continues until all the cards have been processed. The figure shows that the bottleneck is the card reader, because this is working all through the activity. Furthermore, the figure also shows that the run time of the program is equivalent to the work time for the bottleneck.

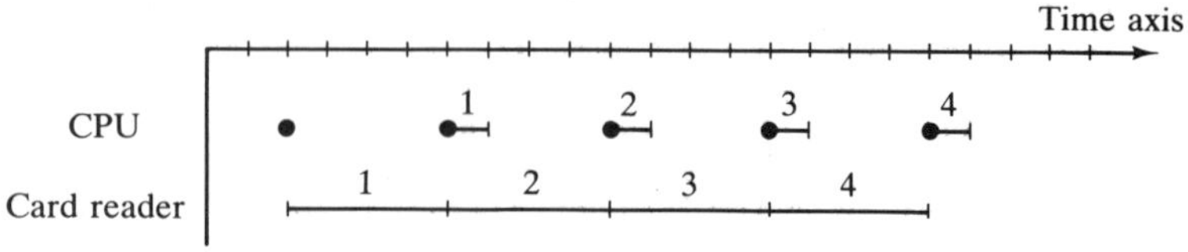

Figure B1.2 Gantt diagram of a card reader and CPU with simultaneousness between the units.

The method of reading in data just described is called the **double buffering technique,** as during the reading in of data, two buffers (areas in main storage where data to/from external units can be stored) are allocated for input. While the CPU sums data from the first buffer, data is transferred from the card reader to the second buffer. Following this, the two buffers change roles, so that data is now summed up from the second buffer while data is transferred to the first buffer. Note that it is the use of the double buffer technique that causes the run time of an activity to be equivalent to the work time of the unit acting as the bottleneck. If a program in an activity uses several different external units, it will normally be sufficient to equip the bottleneck unit with a double buffer. This situation is illustrated in Example B1.3.

EXAMPLE B1.3

Figure B1.3 illustrates a flowchart for a system designed to print a name list from a customer file while the Gantt diagram in Figure B1.4 illustrates how the individual units are working.

First, the CPU starts the magnetic tape unit. When the first customer record has been read, the CPU begins to build up a line in the first buffer of the line printer. When this line has been built up it is printed while the next customer record is being read. When this customer record has been read, the CPU can begin to build up a line in the second buffer of the line printer. The Gantt diagram shows that the line printer becomes the bottleneck, even though double buffering is not used in the magnetic tape unit. In this example, we have used a magnetic tape block size of only one record. However, this does not affect the situation if the CPU is fast compared with the magnetic tape unit.

If we are working with files with direct organization, it is not practical to use double buffers, since this facility cannot be built into standard software if the direct access to the individual records is applied. Even though a file with direct organization is the bottleneck, the run time of the activity will often be equivalent to the work required of the disk storage, as the other units can operate during the wait time that occurs while the read/write head is placed over the wanted record. This is illustrated in Example B1.4.

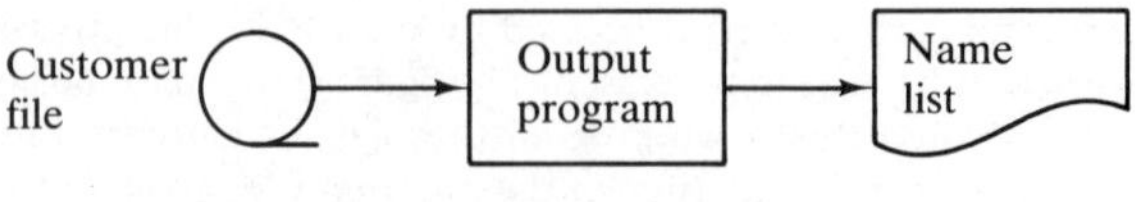

Figure B1.3 System flowchart of a program to print names from a customer file.

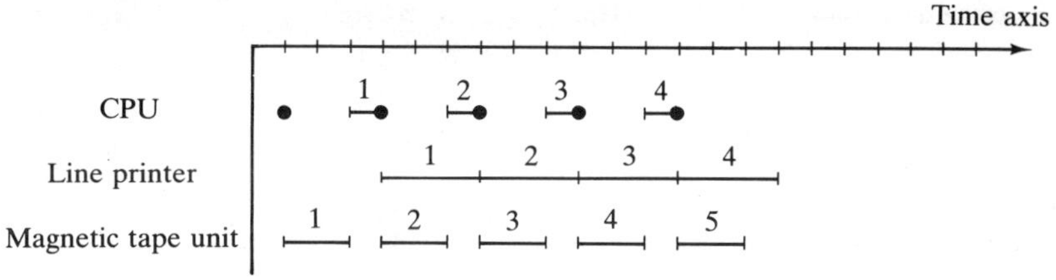

Figure B1.4 Gantt diagram of the units involved in the program shown in Figure B1.3.

EXAMPLE B1.4

The system flowchart shown in Figure B1.5 illustrates the updating of a customer file with direct organization that is stored on a disk. Figure B1.6 illustrates the work required from each individual unit. It is assumed here that the organization used makes it possible to search for a record by one single search on the disk storage.

The CPU starts the card reader and the first transaction is read. When the first transaction has been read, a search can be made for the block where the corresponding customer record is stored. Inputting the block ends $H + R/2 + R/S$ seconds later (see Equation (6) in Section B1.2). The updated customer record may be written back R seconds later, if the updating in main storage can be executed in less than $R - R/S$ seconds. We see from the diagram that the disk storage is a bottleneck even though no double buffers are used in connection with any of the external units.

If, for each transaction, several direct searches on the disk storage have to be executed, we can estimate the run time by adding the work times of each individual physical disk storage search. If, for example, the customer file has an index, we have to add the work time for searching the index and the work time for updating the customer file.

If we are going to update batch programs, the input transactions will normally be stored in a sequential file on a magnetic tape or disk, so that one entire block of transactions is read at a time. In most cases this will not change the fundamental procedure illustrated in the figure because the rotational speed of the disk is much greater than the time it takes to read in a block of transactions. However, if the transactions are stored on the same disk as the master file, the run time of the program is increased by the time it takes to read the transaction file. The reader should note that if the transactions are not updates but merely read transactions, there will be no simultaneousness between the disk storage and the CPU.

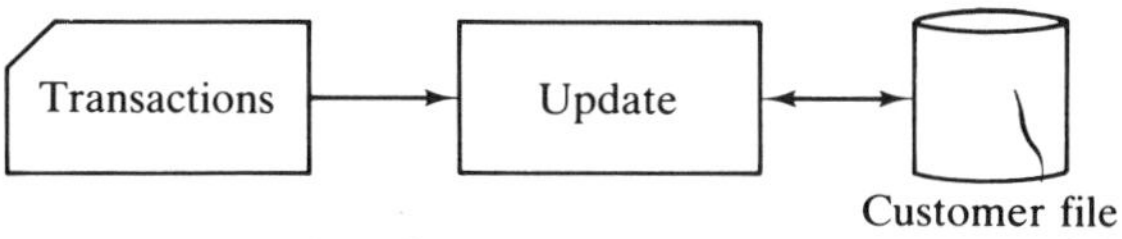

Figure B1.5 System flowchart of updates to a directly organized disk file.

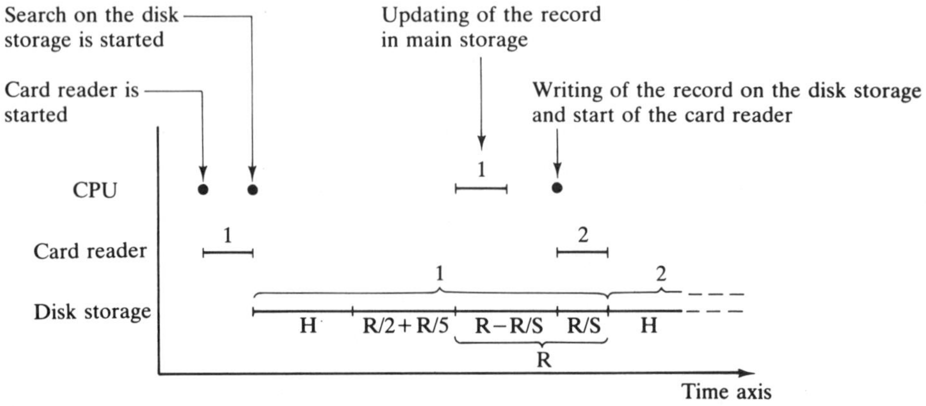

Figure B1.6 Work required from each unit to process the update shown in Figure B1.5.

At times, the bottleneck will alternate between two different external units involved in the same activity, so that the run time of the program is longer than expected. We can normally solve this problem by equipping one of the external units with so many buffers that the likelihood of them becoming bottlenecks is very limited.

EXAMPLE B1.5

The system flowchart shown in Figure B1.7 illustrates the crediting of a sequential customer file with payments received and the printing of reminders to those customers who have not settled bills due for payment. The customer file will, in most cases, be the bottleneck of the updating activity, but when it comes to printing the reminders the bottleneck is shifted from the disk unit to the line printer. If the line printer is equipped with at least as many buffers as there are lines in the reminder letter, the likelihood of the line printer becoming a bottleneck is very small.

If the connection between the work required of the units and the use of capacity is used in practice, we have to bear in mind that the programming is assumed to be optimal as regards run time; that is, the simultaneousness must be utilized. Furthermore, the reader should remember that the double buffering technique is only rarely built into, for example, FORTRAN and ALGOL, whereas it *is* used in COBOL and PL/1. The double buffering technique can also be built into the operating system.

B1.5 Estimating the use of capacity on multiprogrammed computers with simultaneous units

The run time of a program cannot be used as a measure of the use of capacity on multiprogrammed computers because the run time varies with the priority with which the program is run. This situation is illustrated in Example B1.6.

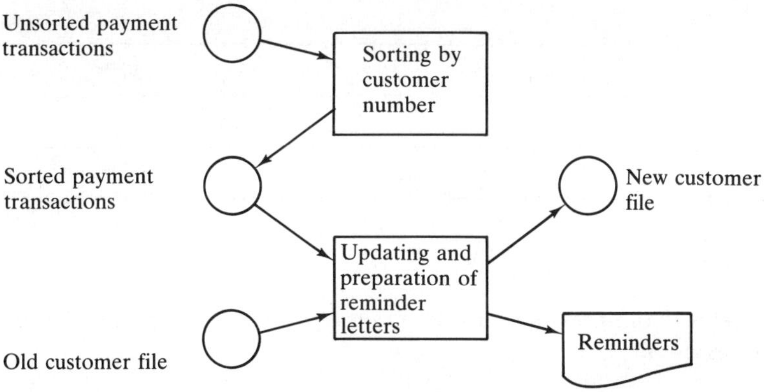

Figure B1.7 System flowchart for a billing and payment system crediting customers with payments made and sending reminders of unsettled accounts.

EXAMPLE B1.6

The diagram shown in Figure B1.8 illustrates how the individual units of a computer are working if the programs *S* and *U* are run simultaneously. Program *S* is that illustrated in Example B1.2 and program *U* is that illustrated in Example B1.3. The letters over the 'time lines' indicate which program is using the unit in question. In Figure B1.8, program *S* has priority over program *U*.

It can be seen from the figure that the card reader, which is used by the program with priority, is working at full capacity, while the line printer, which is used by the other program, is not working all the time.

Figure B1.9 shows how the two programs can be run if the output program, *U*, has priority. This time it is the line printer that is working at full capacity while the card reader is working intermittently.

When we are dealing with multiprogrammed computers, we normally use the individual units' work times to measure the use of capacity of a program. However, as we have just seen, there may be a considerable difference between the time during which a unit is working and the time during which it is occupied.

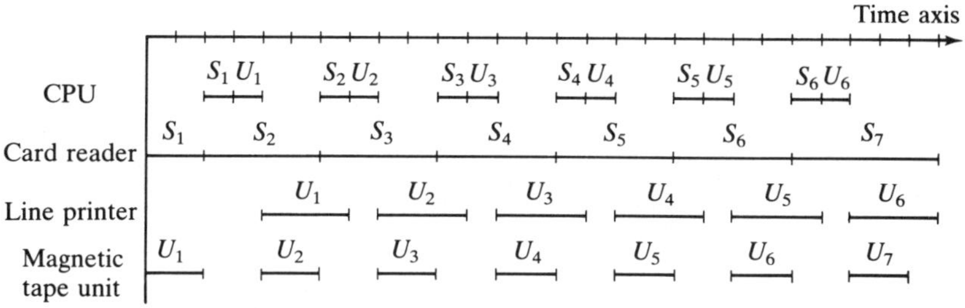

Figure B1.8 Multiprogramming. Program *S*, using the card reader, has priority over program *U*.

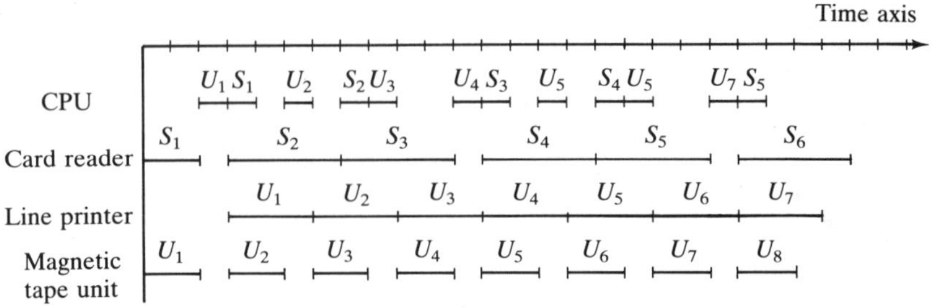

Figure B1.9 Multiprogramming. Program U, using the line printer, has priority over program S.

This applies, in particular, to slow external units – for example, the line printer. This problem is, however, of no great practical importance on multiprogrammed computers since **spooling** can be used to avoid it. This involves all input and output from slow units, which can only be used by one program, being performed by means of a standard program (the **spool program),** so that the users' programs communicate with the slow external units via a disk storage. Spooling also has the additional advantage of making better use of capacity. This is illustrated in Example B1.7.

EXAMPLE B1.7

Figure B.10 illustrates an update program run on a multiprogrammed computer. As the card reader and the line printer can only be used by one program at a time, these two units will be fully occupied while the program is running. If spooling is used, as illustrated in Figure B1.11, the card reader and the line printer will only be occupied while the spool program is running.

With multiprogrammed computers, on which interactive programs are also run, the **response times** of the programs often pose greater problems than the programs' use of resources. The response time of a program is the time that

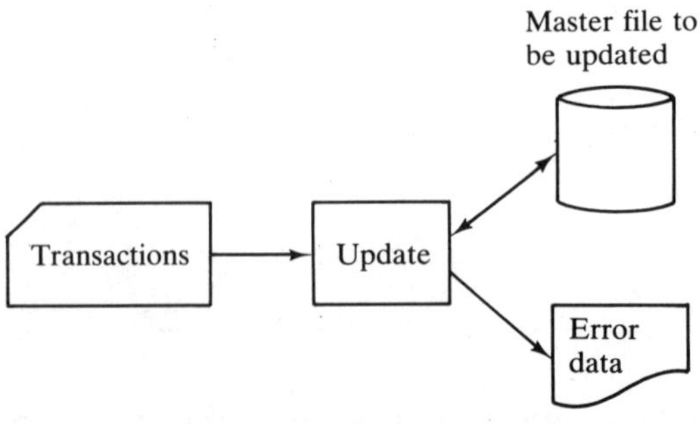

Figure B1.10 System flowchart of an update program.

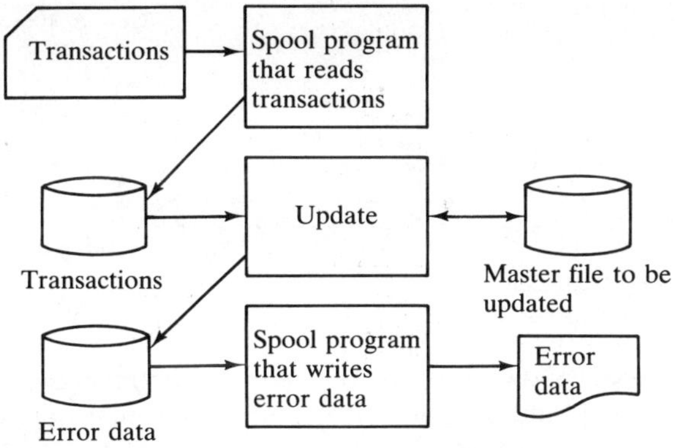

Figure B1.11 The update program shown in Figure B1.10 with spooling added, reducing the time during which the card reader and line printer are occupied.

elapses between the terminal operator hitting the 'send key' and the response being displayed on the screen. It is often difficult to estimate the response time of an interactive program because the simultaneous running of transactions causes queues to occur. Factors causing delays include queues in which transactions are waiting to use the CPU, queues for input/output service, transmission queues and waiting time for locked records – that is, records that are locked while being updated by other programs. Figure B1.12 illustrates this situation.

As transactions normally arrive in an arbitrary order, the Poisson Distribution can be used to calculate average response times and the probability of a given queue being so large that it causes response time problems (see Appendix E).

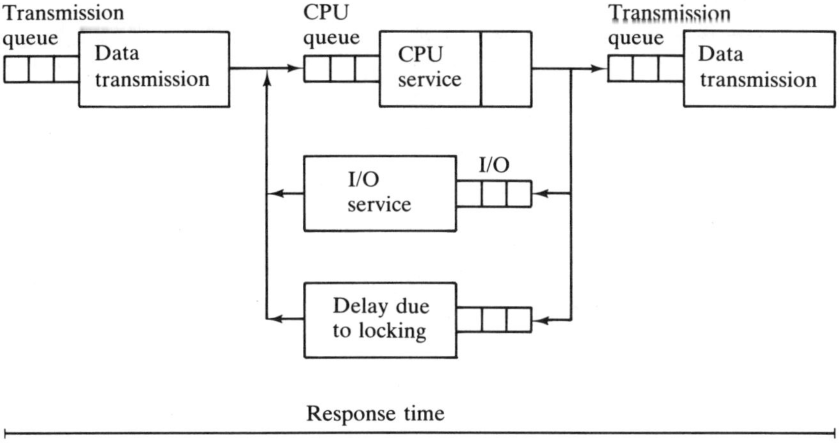

Figure B1.12 Queues affecting the response times of an interactive program.

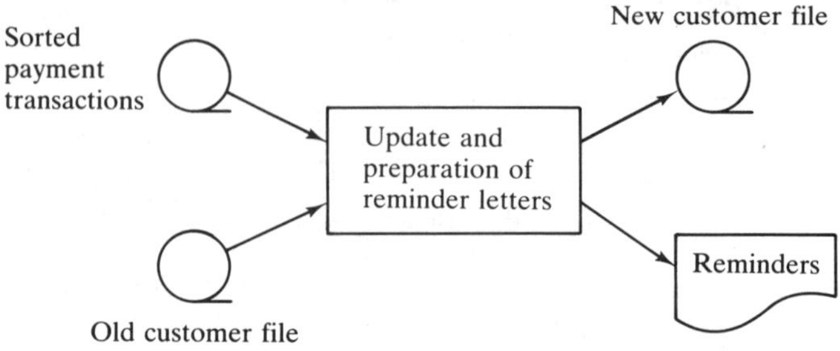

Figure B1.13 System flowchart for an accounts department that credits customers with payments made and prepares reminders where bills have not been settled.

B1.6 Estimating the use of capacity on multiprogrammed computers with partial simultaneousness

Multiprogrammed computers will always have a certain degree of simultaneousness as multiprogramming is introduced precisely to capitalize upon it. If there is only partial simultaneousness among the external units, it is frequently caused by a single data channel serving several of them. This is illustrated in Example B1.8.

EXAMPLE B1.8

The system flowchart shown in Figure B1.13 illustrates the crediting of a sequential customer file with payments received and the printing of reminders to those customers who have not paid their bills on time. If there is a large number of reminders to be printed, the line printer will probably be the unit that is occupied the longest. If the three magnetic tape units are connected to the same data channel, it is possible, however, that the total work required of the three magnetic tape units will exceed the work required of the line printer, so that the line printer is occupied for longer than it is actually working. Storage disks present similar problems, as these are often connected to the same data channel. These problems may be even greater if the files are stored on the same physical disk storage.

This example illustrates that if we are to estimate the use of capacity in a multiprogrammed computer with partial simultaneousness, it will be an advantage to see the data channels as CPUs to which external units are connected. By doing this, the estimation of the use of capacity can be performed in the same way as on fully synchronized multiprogrammed computers, as long as we bear in mind that a data channel can also be a bottleneck.

B1.7 Estimating the use of capacity in sorting

In this section, we will look at one of the best sorting methods and describe the equations for the calculation of the sorting time. The system flowchart in Figure B1.14 shows how it is possible to sort a file if we have a disk storage at our disposal.

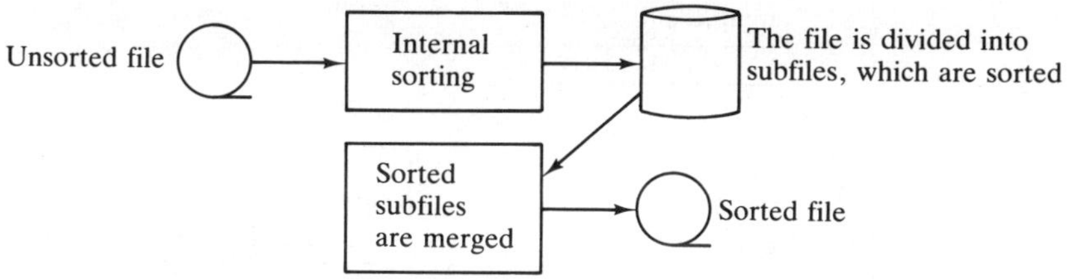

Figure B1.14 System flowchart for a method of sorting.

During the first activity, 'internal sorting', as many records as can be held are read into main storage. These records are then sorted and written to disk storage. This process is repeated until the unsorted file is divided into smaller subfiles whose records are sorted.

We start the second activity by reading the first record from each subfile. (If these cannot be held in main storage at the same time, the program must contain several different merge processes. This problem is dealt with at the end of this section.) Among the records that have been read into main storage, a search is now made for the one with the lowest value in the sort field. This record is written out and a new record is read in from the subfile holding the written out record. This process continues until all subfiles have been read. This is illustrated in Example B1.9.

EXAMPLE B1.9

In the illustration given in Figure B1.15, it is assumed that there is only room for three records in main storage. Consequently, the sorted subfiles can also only hold three records. As we are going to merge the three subfiles, we must use a blocking factor of 1. The file is sorted in descending order.

When the sorted subfiles are written out in the sort phase, we can estimate the work required of the output disk storage by means of Equation (7), if we assume that the writing out is not performed on the same disk storage that we are reading from.

When the sorted subfiles are read in the merge phase, we can calculate the work required of the disk storage by using Equation (5).

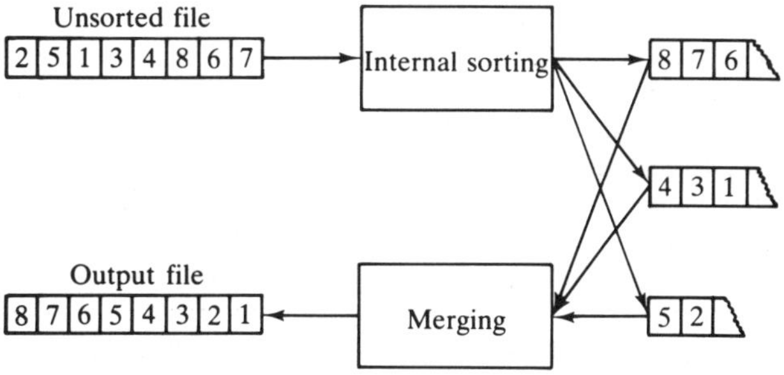

Figure B1.15 Sorting by dividing the file into sorted subfiles and merging.

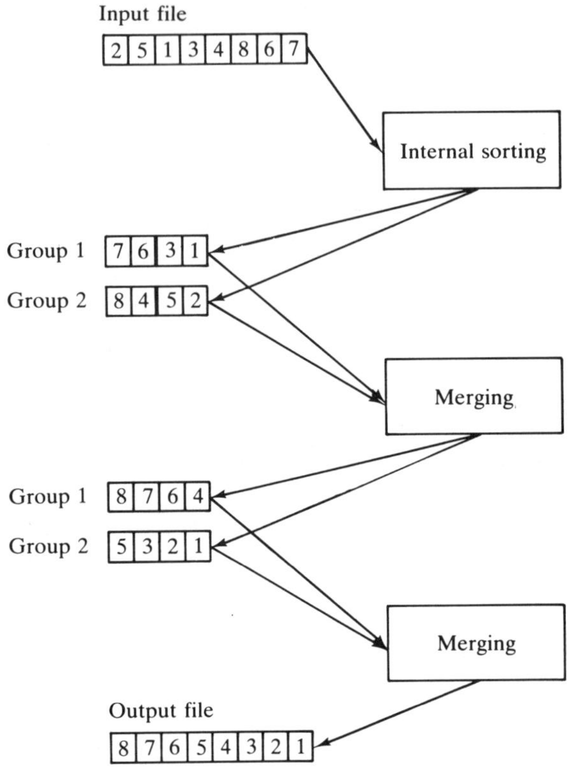

Figure B1.16 Multiway merging. In this simplified example we assume that main storage can hold only two records. The internal sort thus produces four sorted subfiles divided into two groups. Within the groups these subfiles are divided by thick vertical lines. The first merge activity merges a subfile from each group, and, since main storage is supposed to hold only two records, the resulting subfiles are again divided into two groups for further merging.

The merging activity in the preceding example assumes that main storage can hold a block from each of the sorted subfiles. In practice, however, this is not always possible, and in such a case the sorting technique known as **multiway merging,** illustrated in Figure B1.16, can be used.

When the internal sorting has finished, the sorted subfiles are divided into logical groups, corresponding to the number of buffers main storage can hold (the sorting area in main storage, which was used for the internal sorting, can now be used for buffers). The more buffers that can be put into main storage, the more subfiles can be merged at a time, and this leads to fewer merge passes.

In Figure B1.16, the sorted subfiles are divided into only two groups, which means that only two sorted subfiles can be merged at a time. In practice, this number will be much higher. When the sorted subfiles have been merged, output is again divided into two groups, corresponding to the number of buffers main storage can hold. The merging process can now be repeated as many times as is necessary. After each merge, the sorted subfiles increase in size, so that we end up with only one sorted file.

Knuth (1973) describes various methods for making subfiles bigger, so that the number of merging passes can be reduced. The most important of these methods is to read a new block from the unsorted file every time a block belonging to a sorted subfile has been written out. On the basis of the blocks that have been read, we can sort all records whose sorting key is higher than the key value of the last record written out. The writing out of a sorted subfile ends when the entire main storage is filled up with records whose sorting keys are lower than the key value in the last record written out. We can prove that if the key values are distributed evenly in the unsorted file, the sorted subfiles will, on average, contain twice as many records as main storage can hold. Furthermore, we can prove that there will be $\lceil \log_Z (a) \rceil$ merging activities after the internal sorting has been executed, where a is the number of sorted subfiles $\approx \lceil n/2L \rceil$, n is the number of blocks in the file that are sorted, L is the number of blocks that main storage can hold during the presorting and Z is the number of sorted subfiles that can be merged at a time. If the area in main storage used for the building up of the sorted subfiles is later used as input buffers in connection with the merging of the sorted subfile, then $Z = L$. Log_Z means logarithm to the base Z. This logarithm can be converted to logarithms to the base 10 by dividing by $\log_{10} Z$. That is, $\log_Z X = \log_{10} x/\log_{10} z$. Figure B1.17 contains some logarithms to the base 10. These logarithms are used in the following examples and can be used for the exercises.

If we assume that the input and output disk storages are working simultaneously, the total sorting time can be estimated by using the following equation:

$$\text{total sorting time} = \text{the number of cylinders in the file} \times \left(HMIN + \left(\frac{R}{S} + R\right) \times C \times S\right) + \left\lceil \log_Z \left\lceil \frac{n}{2L} \right\rceil \right\rceil \times \left(H + \frac{R}{2} + \max\left\{\frac{R}{S}, \frac{B}{K}\right\}\right) \quad \textbf{(9)}$$

This formula includes two terms corresponding to the internal sort and the merge, respectively. The work time for merging is calculated by multiplying the number of merges and the work time for merging the sorted subfiles. If the sorting is executed on a multiprogrammed computer, Equation (9) will give us a lower limit for the sorting time.

EXAMPLE B1.10

We want to estimate the sorting time for a file of 210 000 records of 940 bytes each. As we have a block size of 4820 bytes, 9 blocks/track (S), and 15 tracks/cylinder (C), the blocking factor will be 5 and the file will occupy 42 000 blocks, or $\frac{42\,000}{S \times C} = \frac{42\,000}{9 \times 15} = 311.1$ cylinders.

x	$\log x$
10	1.0000
11	1.0415
12	1.0792
13	1.1140
14	1.1462
15	1.1761
16	1.2042
17	1.2304
18	1.2553
19	1.2787
20	1.3010
21	1.3222
22	1.3424
23	1.3617
24	1.3802
25	1.3979
26	1.4150
27	1.4314
28	1.4472
29	1.4624

x	$\log x$
30	1.4771
31	1.4914
32	1.5052
33	1.5185
34	1.5315
35	1.5441
36	1.5563
37	1.5682
38	1.5798
39	1.5911
40	1.6021
41	1.6128
42	1.6233
43	1.6335
44	1.6434
45	1.6532
46	1.6627
47	1.6721
48	1.6812
49	1.6902

x	$\log x$
50	1.6990
51	1.7075
52	1.7160
53	1.7243
54	1.7324
55	1.7403
56	1.7482
57	1.7559
58	1.7634
59	1.7708
60	1.7782
61	1.7854
62	1.7924
63	1.7993
64	1.8062
65	1.8129
66	1.8195
67	1.8261
68	1.8325
69	1.8389

x	$\log x$
70	1.8451
71	1.8513
72	1.8573
73	1.8633
74	1.8692
75	1.8751
76	1.8808
77	1.8865
78	1.8921
79	1.8976
80	1.9031
81	1.9085
82	1.9138
83	1.9191
84	1.9243
85	1.9294
86	1.9345
87	1.9395
88	1.9445
89	1.9494
90	1.9543
91	1.9590
92	1.9638
93	1.9685
94	1.9731
95	1.9777
96	1.9823
97	1.9868
98	1.9912
99	1.9956

Figure B1.17 Logarithms to the base 10.

If the sorting is executed on a multiprogrammed computer, input and output will normally work simultaneously during the internal sorting. By using Equation (7), we get the following work time for reading in the internal sorting activity:

$$\text{Work time} = \text{number of cylinders in the file} \times \left(HMIN + \left(\frac{R}{S} + R \right) \times C \times S \right)$$

In Equation (7) we reduce this expression to:

$$\text{number of cylinders in the file} \times 2.493$$

So:

$$\text{Work time} = 311.1 \times 2.493 = 775.6 \text{ seconds}$$

We assume that 1 million bytes are used for the internal sorting in main storage, and that for the sorted subfiles we use the maximum block size of 47 476 bytes, as the merging is faster if we use a big block size:

$$\text{Number of blocks in main storage} = L = \left\lfloor \frac{1\,000\,000}{47\,476} \right\rfloor = 21$$

$$\text{Blocking factor in the sorted subfiles} = b = \left\lfloor \frac{47\,476}{940} \right\rfloor = 50$$

$$\text{Number of blocks in the presorted file} = n = \left\lceil \frac{210\,000}{50} \right\rceil = 4200$$

$$\text{Number of sorted subfiles} = \left\lceil \frac{\text{n}}{2L} \right\rceil = \left\lceil \frac{4200}{(2 \times 21)} \right\rceil = 100$$

$$\text{Number of merges} = \left\lceil \log_{21} \left\lceil \frac{n}{2L} \right\rceil \right\rceil = \left\lceil \frac{\log 100}{\log 21} \right\rceil = \left\lceil \frac{2}{1.3222} \right\rceil = 2$$

Time for the reading in of a block during the merge (from Equation (5))

$$= H + \frac{R}{2} + \max \left\{ \frac{R}{S}, \frac{\text{B}}{\text{K}} \right\}$$

$$= 0.016 + \frac{0.0166}{2} + \max \left\{ \frac{0.0166}{1}, \frac{47\,476}{1\,198\,000} \right\} = 0.0639$$

Run time of the merges = Number of merges $\times\ n \times$ 0.0639

= 2 × 4200× 0.0639 = 536.8 seconds

Therefore, the total run time will be (775.6 + 536.8) secs
= 1212.4 seconds = 20 minutes.

Appendix C
Syntax for CODASYL

C1.1 Introduction

In this appendix, we take a look at the syntax rules of the conceptual schema, internal schema, external schema and the database manipulation language contained in the CODASYL proposals. These descriptions are included in order to present a general impression of a total system, including a database language. The reader is referred to CODASYL (1978, 1981a, 1981b) for more detailed descriptions.

The following conventions will be used in describing the syntax:

- Reserved words are written in capital letters.
- Reserved words not underlined can be used optionally.
- Words in lower-case letters are replaced by suitable names or values.
- The bracketing of syntactical rules means the following:

$$\begin{bmatrix} a \\ b \\ c \end{bmatrix} \text{ one or nothing} \qquad \begin{Bmatrix} a \\ b \\ c \end{Bmatrix} \text{ exactly one} \qquad \begin{Vmatrix} a \\ b \\ c \end{Vmatrix} \text{ one and no more than one of each}$$

- ... after a bracket means that the contents of the bracket can be repeated.

C1.2 Syntax for the CODASYL conceptual schema

The conceptual schema consists of the following three entries or paragraphs:

(1) The schema entry, whose primary purpose is to name the conceptual schema.
(2) The record entry, which describes the individual record types and their fields.
(3) The set entry, in which the individual types of sets are described.

C1.2.1 Syntax of the SCHEMA entry

```
SCHEMA NAME IS schema-name-1

                            ||BEFORE          ||   ||ALTER  ||
[CALL procedure-name-1      ||ON ERROR DURING ||   ||COPY   ||  ]...
                            ||AFTER           ||   ||DISPLAY||
                                                   ||LOCKS  ||

                                    ||ALTER  ||
[ACCESS CONTROL LOCK   [FOR         ||COPY   ||  ]
                                    ||DISPLAY||
                                    ||LOCKS  ||

     { literal-1                    }
  IS { lock-name-1                  }
     { PROCEDURE procedure-name-2   }

     { literal-2                    }
 [OR { lock-name-2                  } ]...]...
     { PROCEDURE procedure-name-3   }
```

The SCHEMA statement is used to name the conceptual schema. The CALL and ACCESS CONTROL LOCK statements have a meaning similar to that of the record description.

C1.2.2 Syntax of the RECORD entry

```
RECORD NAME IS record-name-1

                      {[ASCENDING ]                  }
[KEY key-name IS      {[DESCENDING] data-identifier  } ...

                         { FIRST          }
                         { LAST           }
        DUPLICATES ARE   { NOT ALLOWED    }  ]...
                         { SYSTEM DEFAULT }
```

```
[CHECK IS condition-1] . . .

                                                          ┌ ║DELETE ║ ┐
                                                          │ ║FIND   ║ │
                            ║BEFORE              ║        │ ║GET    ║ │
[ CALL procedure-name-1     ║ON ERROR DURING     ║        │ ║INSERT ║ │ ] . . .
                            ║AFTER               ║        │ ║MODIFY ║ │
                                                          │ ║REMOVE ║ │
                                                          └ ║STORE  ║ ┘

                                      ║DELETE ║
                                      ║FIND   ║
                                      ║GET    ║
[ACCESS CONTROL LOCK  [FOR            ║INSERT ║    ]
                                      ║MODIFY ║
                                      ║REMOVE ║
                                      ║STORE  ║

     IS { literal-1
          lock-name-1
          PROCEDURE procedure-name-2 }

          [OR { literal-2
                lock-name-2
                PROCEDURE procedure-name-3 } ]... ]...
```

The RECORD NAME statement is used to name a record type; the KEY statement defines a key field and describes what to do with records that have the same identification number; the CHECK statement can be used to specify validity checks on the fields of the record; the CALL statement is used if a subroutine is to be executed while one of the listed database manipulations is being executed; the ACCESS CONTROL LOCK statement is used for file protection.

It is possible to lock record types, field types, set types, external schemas, etc. individually. The lock can be against either reading or updating. To have access to locked resources, the right 'key' must be known. This key will either be a specific code word (literal or lock name) or the name of a routine that has to be executed before access can be gained to the locked resources. The value of any such keys must be placed in the DB-ACCESS-CONTROL-KEY variable. This variable will have its values allocated by the execution of the READY statement, which, amongst other things, opens those sections of the database required by a program. The statements that have to be programmed to allocate the right key values to the DB-ACCESS-CONTROL-KEY must be placed after the USE statement. If a user cannot give a correct ACCESS-CONTROL-KEY, he will not get access to the locked resources. However, the program will be sent a return code, and by means of the USE statement outlined in Example 11.4, the programmer can decide what action to take. However, a number of details in connection with the protection of data are still left to the manufacturer of the DBMS.

C1.2.3 Syntax of the FIELD entry

The field description starts by naming the level number and data name of the field. The TYPE statement is used to give a more detailed description of the field type; thus, the field can be given a numeric, Boolean or alphanumeric bit string. The OCCURS statement is used to define a repeating group, and the CONDITIONAL statement is used, where appropriate, to state that the field only occurs in the record if certain conditions are fulfilled. The CONVERSION IS NOT ALLOWED statement can be used to make sure that no alteration of the field type takes place during the conversion from the conceptual to the external schema. The DEFAULT statement can be used to allocate a value to a field if the external schema does not contain the field. The SOURCE statement is used to state that a field must have the same value as another field. The RESULT statement is used to state that the value of a field is created by the execution of a subroutine. It can also be used to state the conditions that have to be fulfilled for the value of a field to be altered. The CHECK, CALL and ACCESS CONTROL LOCK statements have meanings similar to those outlined in connection with the record description.

```
[level-number-1] data-name-1

            { || BINARY   ||                                    }
            { || DECIMAL  ||                                    }
            { ||          ||                                    }
            { || FIXED    ||  [integer-1 [, integer-2] ]        }
            { || FLOAT    ||                                    }
            { ||          ||                                    }
[TYPE IS    { || REAL     ||                                    }
            { || COMPLEX  ||                                    }
            {                                                   }
            {  {BIT      }    [integer-3 [DEPENDING ON          }
            {  {CHARACTER}                data-identifier-1]    }
            {                                                   }
            {  BOOLEAN                                          }
            {  implementor-name                                 }

[OCCURS  {integer-4          }  TIMES]
         {data-identifier-2  }

[CONDITIONAL ON condition-1]

[CONVERSION IS NOT ALLOWED

[CHECK IS  {condition-2                    } ]
           {PROCEDURE procedure-name-1     }

[DEFAULT IS literal-1]

[SOURCE IS data-identifier-3 OF OWNER OF set-name-1]
```

```
[RESULT OF

  { condition-3
  { PROCEDURE procedure-name-2 ON CHANGE TO
  {   { {ALL DATA                  }... OF THIS RECORD
  {   { {DATA   data-identifier-4  }
  {   {
  {   { ||ALL DATA||
  {   { ||TENANCY ||  OF ALL MEMBERS OF set-name-2
  {   {
  {   { { ||ALL DATA                          } ||
  {   { { ||DATA   data-identifier-5 ...      } ||
  {   { { ||TENANCY                             ||
  {   {
  {   {   OF MEMBER record-name-1}...  OF SET set-name-3 }  }

                             ||BEFORE             ||  [ ||GET   || ]
[CALL procedure-name-3       ||ON ERROR DURING    ||  [ ||MODIFY|| ]...
                             ||AFTER              ||  [ ||STORE || ]

                                  ||GET   ||
[ACCESS CONTROL LOCK   [FOR       ||MODIFY|| ]
                                  ||STORE ||

      { literal-2                       }
   IS { lock-name-1                     } ]
      { PROCEDURE procedure-name-4      }

          { literal-3                       }
      [OR { lock-name-1                     } ]...]...
          { PROCEDURE procedure-name-5      }
```

C1.2.4 Syntax of the SET entry

The SET statement is used to name the sets. The OWNER statement is used to define the owner record type. A **singular set** is a set owned by the SYSTEM. It can be used to read a file in sorted order. The ORDER statement is used to define the insertion sequence of the member records. The CALL and ACCESS CONTROL statements have meanings similar to those outlined in connection with the record description.

```
SET NAME IS set-name-1

         { record-name-1 }
OWNER IS { SYSTEM        }
```

```
ORDER FOR INSERTION IS

{ FIRST                                                              }
{ LAST                                                               }
{ NEXT                                                               }
{ PRIOR                                                              }
{ SYSTEM DEFAULT                                                     }
{                                                                    }
{         { WITHIN RECORD TYPE                                     } }
{         { BY DEFINED KEYS                                        } }
{         { [RECORD TYPE SEQUENCE IS (record-name-1) . . . ]       } }
{ SORTED  {                                                        } }
{         {                   { FIRST          }                   } }
{         { [DUPLICATES ARE   { LAST           } ]                 } }
{         {                   { NOT ALLOWED    }                   } }
{         {                   { SYSTEM DEFAULT }                   } }

                         || BEFORE           ||  [ || FIND   || ]
[CALL procedure-name-1   || ON ERROR DURING  ||  [ || INSERT || ] ] . . .
                         || AFTER            ||  [ || REMOVE || ]

                                     || FIND   ||
[ACCESS CONTROL LOCK [FOR            || INSERT ||  ]
                                     || REMOVE ||

     { literal-1                     }
  IS { lock-name-1                   }
     { PROCEDURE procedure-name-2    }

          { literal-2                    }
      [OR { lock-name-2                  } ] . . . ] . . .
          { PROCEDURE procedure-name-3   }
```

C1.2.5 Syntax of the MEMBER description

```
MEMBER IS record-name-1

                                                  { FIXED     }
INSERTION IS { AUTOMATIC }   RETENTION IS          { MANDATORY }
             { MANUAL    }                        { OPTIONAL  }
```

```
[DUPLICATES ARE NOT ALLOWED FOR (data-identifier-1) . . . ] . . .

[   [RANGE] KEY IS {ASCENDING  } {data-identifier-2}
                   {DESCENDING } {RECORD TYPE      }

                 [ [ASCENDING ] {data-identifier-3} ] . . .
                   [DESCENDING] {RECORD TYPE      }

                         {FIRST          }
   [DUPLICATES ARE       {LAST           }  ]
                         {NOT ALLOWED    }
                         {SYSTEM DEFAULT }

   NULL IS [NOT] ALLOWED ]

[CHECK IS condition-1 ] . . .

 SET SELECTION IS

   {THRU set-name-1 OWNER IDENTIFIED BY
   {
   {  {SYSTEM
   {  {
   {  {APPLICATION
   {  {
   {  {KEY key-name-1  [data-identifier-4 EQUAL TO
   {  {
   {  {    {data-identifier-5 }  ] . . .
   {  {    {parameter-name-1  }
   {  {
   {  {SELECTION DEFINED FOR record-name-2
   {
   {  [THEN THRU set-name-2 WHERE OWNER IDENTIFIED BY ]
   {  [                                               ]
   {  [    {data-identifier-6  [EQUAL TO              ] . . .
   {  [                                               ]
   {  [        {data-identifier-7}  ]  } . . .        ]
   {  [        {parameter-name-2 }                    ]
   {
   {BY PROCEDURE procedure-name-1

                              ||BEFORE            ||   [ ||FIND  || ]
[CALL procedure-name-2        ||ON ERROR DURING   ||   [ ||INSERT|| ]   ] . . .
                              ||AFTER             ||   [ ||REMOVE|| ]
```

```
                                    ||FIND   ||
[ACCESS CONTROL LOCK  [FOR          ||INSERT || ]
                                    ||REMOVE ||

        { literal-1                      }
     IS { lock-name-1                    }
        { PROCEDURE procedure-name-3     }

           { literal-2                   }
       [OR { lock-name-2                 } ] ... ] ...
           { PROCEDURE procedure-name-4  }
```

The MEMBER statement is used to define the member record type. The INSERTION statement states whether member records are to be inserted automatically in the set, or whether an application program is to be responsible for the insertion of member records. The RETENTION statement can define three different possible statuses for member records:

(1) FIXED is used if a member record must always have the same record as owner. Thus, the member record may only be removed from the owner if it is removed from the database at the same time.

(2) MANDATORY is used if a member record must always have a specific record type as owner. In such a case, member records may not be removed from the set.

(3) OPTIONAL is used if it is permitted to remove a member record from the set.

The DUPLICATES statement is used to reject the insertion of a member record if it has the same value in a given key field as another member record. The RANGE statement can be used to state that member records having the same owner must be inserted in the set in accordance with a predetermined sorting order. The CHECK, CALL and ACCESS CONTROL LOCK statements have meanings similar to those given in connection with the record description. The SET SELECTION statement is used to give the rules that determine how a member record belonging to a given owner can be read. The SET SELECTION statement is also important if a member record is to be inserted in a set automatically.

C1.3 Syntax for the CODASYL internal schema

The internal schema consists of the following six entries:

(1) The STORAGE SCHEMA entry, which allocates a name to the internal schema and links it to the name of the conceptual schema.

(2) The MAPPING entry, which describes the connection holding between record types in the conceptual schema and record types in the internal schema.

(3) The STORAGE AREA entry, which describes areas in the background storage where the database is stored.

(4) The STORAGE RECORD entry, which describes the record type in the internal schema.

(5) The SET entry, which describes the set relationships.

(6) The INDEX entry, which describes indexes for the various files in the database.

C1.3.1 Syntax of the STORAGE SCHEMA entry

The STORAGE SCHEMA statement is used to name the internal schema. If, in connection with the STORAGE SCHEMA naming, the VERSION integer is omitted, the VERSION integer-1 will be allocated to the internal schema. Every time alterations are made to the internal schema, the VERSION integer must be increased by 1.

```
STORAGE SCHEMA NAME IS storage-schema-name-1 [VERSION integer-1]
    FOR schema-name-1 SCHEMA
```

C1.3.2 Syntax of the MAPPING entry

The MAPPING statement is used to describe the connection between record types of the conceptual and internal schema. If the MAPPING VERSION number is lower than the VERSION number for the STORAGE SCHEMA, it means that the STORAGE SCHEMA has been altered without altering the MAPPING VERSION. A similar convention applies to the following definitions of VERSION number. If there are several different physical record types corresponding to a single record type, it must be possible, by means of IF condition-1, to determine which record type is being used. This is done by introducing a field into the records carrying values for the condition-1 test.

```
MAPPING [VERSION integer-1] FOR schema-record-name-1
   [{IF condition-1 THEN}]
   [{ELSE               }]
            STORAGE [RECORD IS  ] {storage-record-name-1} ...
                    [RECORDS ARE]
```

C1.3.3 Syntax of the STORAGE AREA entry

The STORAGE AREA statement is used to name an area in background storage. Such an area can be used to store records, sets and indexes. The INITIAL SIZE statement specifies the size of the area when created. The EXPANDABLE TO ... statement specifies the upper limit of the size of the area, while the EXPANDABLE BY ... statement specifies that the expansion must take place step by step.

```
STORAGE AREA NAME IS storage-area-name-1

INITIAL SIZE IS integer-1 PAGES

[ EXPANDABLE [ || BY STEPS OF integer-2 PAGES || ] ]
             [ || TO integer-3 PAGES          || ]

PAGE SIZE IS integer-4 { CHARACTERS }
                       { WORDS      }
```

C1.3.4 Syntax of the STORAGE RECORD entry

First the STORAGE RECORD is given a name. Then, the LINK statement specifies that the record contains a pointer to another record of the storage–record–name–1 type. The RESERVE statement is used to reserve space for these pointers. The IF condition-1 statement is only used if records of the same conceptual type are stored with different DENSITY options. The DENSITY statement determines the number of records to be stored per block or PAGE. The PLACEMENT statement is used to choose the organization by which to store the records of the record type:

- CALC means random organization; and procedure-name-1 is the subprogram that is used to read or write records in the file.
- CLUSTERED means that the record type is a member record and that, as regards the schema-set-name, records with the same owner must be stored physically beside each other. NEAR OWNER means that these member records have to be stored, if possible, in the same block as the owner or integer-3 blocks from the owner.
- SEQUENTIAL means sequential organization. The sorting order may be either ascending or descending by the sorting field identifier-1.

The WITHIN statement determines where in the background storage storage-area-name-1 the records of the record type are to be stored.

```
STORAGE RECORD NAME IS storage-record-name-1 [VERSION integer-1]

   [ LINK TO storage-record-name-2 [ IS { DIRECT   } ] ] ...
                                   [    { INDIRECT } ]

      [RESERVE integer-2 POINTERS]

[ { IF condition-1 THEN } ]
[ { ELSE                } ]

   [ DENSITY IS { ONE STORAGE RECORD PER integer-1 PAGES  } ]
   [            { integer-2 STORAGE RECORDS PER PAGE      } ]
```

```
PLACEMENT IS

  ⎧ CALC [procedure-name-1] USING {identifier-1} ...                    ⎫
  ⎪ CLUSTERED VIA SET schema-set-name-1                                  ⎪
  ⎨   [NEAR OWNER [DISPLACEMENT IS integer-3 PAGES ] ]                   ⎬
  ⎪ SEQUENTIAL  ⎧ ⎧ASCENDING   {identifier-2} ... ⎫                      ⎪
  ⎩             ⎩ ⎩DESCENDING                     ⎭ ...                  ⎭

  WITHIN storage-area-name-1

    [FROM PAGE integer-4 THRU integer-5]
```

The syntactical rules for the fields of a record type are described below.

C1.3.5 Syntax of the FIELD description

The field description shown here has a lot in common with the field description of COBOL. It begins with a level number and is followed by the name of the field schema-data-name-1. If it is not necessary to refer to the contents of a field, the field name FILLER can be used. The field name DATA indicates the end of a record and can only be followed by a FILLER field. The ALIGNMENT statement can be used to shift the field integer-1 positions from the previous field in the record. The EVALUATION statement can be used if the value of a field is to be calculated or checked on the basis of the value of other fields. If the value of a field can be calculated, there is a possibility of not reserving space to hold the field (STORAGE IS NOT REQUIRED). The FORMAT statement is used to determine the representational form of the field. The NULL statement specifies a code which means that the value of the field is unknown. The SIZE statement determines how much space to reserve for the field.

```
                     ⎧ {schema-data-name-1} ... ⎫
[level-number-1]     ⎨ FILLER                   ⎬
                     ⎩ DATA ALL                 ⎭

⎡                                ⎧ BITS       ⎫ ⎤
⎢ ALIGNMENT IS integer-1         ⎨ CHARACTERS ⎬ ⎥
⎣                                ⎩ WORDS      ⎭ ⎦

⎡ EVALUATION IS ON  ⎧ ACCESS STORAGE IS [NOT] REQUIRED ⎫ ⎤
⎣                   ⎩ UPDATE                           ⎭ ⎦
```

```
[            { { UNSIGNED            }                              }  ]
[            { { EXPLICT             }                              }  ]
[            { { implementor-name-1  }                              }  ]
[            {                                                      }  ]
[            { { BINARY                                 }           }  ]
[            { { DECIMAL [implementor-name-2]           }           }  ]
[            { { PACKED DECIMAL                         }           }  ]
[            {                                                      }  ]
[ FORMAT IS  { { FIXED } integer-2 [, integer-3]                    }  ]
[            { { FLOAT }                                            }  ]
[            {                                                      }  ]
[            { { CHARACTER[implementor-name-3] }                    }  ]
[            { { BIT                           }                    }  ]
[            {                                                      }  ]
[            {    [ FRAMED integer-4 [ JUSTIFIED { LEFT  } ] ]      }  ]
[            {    [                  [           { RIGHT } ] ]      }  ]
[            {                                                      }  ]
             {      implementor-name-4                              }

[            { literal-1      } ]
[ NULL IS    { COMPACTED      } ]
[            { SYSTEM DEFAULT } ]

                          { BITS       } ]
 SIZE IS integer-5        { CHARACTERS } ]
                          { WORDS      } ]
```

C1.3.6 Syntax of the SET entry

First, the SET is given a name. Under the OWNER statement, the name of the owner record type can be specified. If space for pointer fields is not to be allocated until these fields are needed, ALLOCATION IS DYNAMIC is specified. The POINTER statement states the types of pointer used in the owner record:

- INDEX means that logical pointers are used to link owner members.
- FIRST means that the owner record contains a pointer to the first member record.
- LAST means that the owner record contains a pointer to the last member record.

The DESTINATION statement is used to indicate that other records may hold pointers to the owner. The pointer type may be DIRECT or INDIRECT; that is, physical or logical pointers can be used to retrieve the owner by means of an index. Under the MEMBER statement, the name of the member record type from the conceptual schema can be specified, as well as one or more record types from the internal schema. The ALLOCATION, POINTER and DESTINATION statements have meanings similar to those described in connection with the owner record type.

```
SET schema-set-name-1 [VERSION integer-1] [IS VALUE BASED]

[ [ OWNER
    { STORAGE RECORD {storage-record-name-1} ...
      [ [ALLOCATION IS {STATIC }]
        [              {DYNAMIC}]

        POINTER FOR  || INDEX    index-name-1 ||
                     || ||FIRST|| MEMBER      ||
                     || ||LAST ||             || ] ...

      [DESTINATION OF [DIRECT  ] POINTERS]
      [               [INDIRECT]         ]                } ... ]

  { MEMBER [RECORD schema-record-name-1]
    { STORAGE RECORD {storage-record-name-2} ...
      [ [ALLOCATION IS {STATIC }]
        [              {DYNAMIC}]

        POINTER FOR  ||   INDEX    index-name-2 ||
                     ||  ||NEXT || TENANT       ||
                     ||  ||PRIOR||              ||
                     ||   OWNER                 || ] ...

      [DESTINATION OF [DIRECT  ] POINTERS]
      [               [INDIRECT]         ]                } ... } ... ]
```

C1.3.7 Syntax of the INDEX entry

First, the INDEX is given a name. The PLACEMENT statement is used to specify the placing and organization of the index. There are three possibilities:

(1) If PLACEMENT is excluded, the manufacturer of the DBMS determines the placing of the index.

(2) By means of the CALC statement, the index can be divided into a number of smaller subindexes, in which the individual parts can be read with random organization (see Example 11.2 that deals with a special form of random organization).

(3) The NEAR OWNER statement can only be used if it is a USED FOR SET index, in which, for every owner, there is an index over the member records of the owner. By using the NEAR OWNER statement, these indexes can be placed near to the owner of the member records.

The USED statement makes it possible to specify what the index is to be used for. There are three types of index:

(1) A STORAGE KEY index is an index over those physical records whose record type is defined in storage-record-name-1.

(2) A RECORD index is normally a secondary index. It may output either a direct pointer to a record of the storage-record-name-2 type or a logical pointer, so that, via a STORAGE KEY index, a search can be made for the required record of the storage-record-name-2 type.

(3) A SET index consists of many different indexes, one for every owner record that has member records.

The WITHIN statement specifies that the index is to be stored in storage-area-name-1 in the background storage.

```
INDEX NAME IS index-name-1 [VERSION integer-1]

[                  { CALC [procedure-name-1]                                  } ]
[ PLACEMENT IS     {   USING {identifier-1} ...                               } ]
[                  {                                                          } ]
[                  { NEAR OWNER [DISPLACEMENT IS integer-2 PAGES]             } ]

             { STORAGE KEY storage-record-name-1                                      }
             {                                                                        }
             { RECORD schema-record-name-1                                            }
             {                                                                        }
             {  { KEY {identifier-2} ...                                         }    }
             {  { ORDER KEY      { {ASCENDING } }                                }    }
             {  {                { {DESCENDING} }  {identifier-3} ... } ...      }... }
             {  { SCHEMA KEY schema-key-name-1                                   }    }
USED FOR     {                                                                        }
             { POINTER IS                                                    ]        }
             { {[DIRECT  ]                                                   ]        }
             { {[INDIRECT]    [TO storage-record-name-2]... } ...            ]        }
             {                                                                        }
             { SET schema-set-name-1                                                  }
             {   [MEMBER schema-record-name-2]                                        }
             {    [KEY [identifier-4] ... ] ]...                                      }
             {      [LINK TO OWNER]                                                   }

[ WITHIN  { storage-area-name-1 [FROM PAGE integer-3 THRU integer-4] } ]
[         {              STORAGE AREA OF OWNER                        } ]
```

C1.4 Syntax for the CODASYL external schema

In this section, we will only look at some of the syntax rules for the external schema; these are the rules that can be used in a COBOL program. If the reader already knows COBOL, he will find that this section contains sufficient guidance for the solving of relatively simple exercises, and also to understand the details in Example 11.3. Readers who want a more detailed description should consult CODASYL COBOL Committee (1978). The general syntax of the external schema consists of three main parts: TITLE DIVISION, MAPPING DIVISION and STRUCTURE DIVISION (see Section 11.3). In the following sections, we shall first deal with TITLE DIVISION, and then the syntax of the individual sections. The rules relating to file protection are not discussed here, but by and large they are similar to those described for the conceptual schema.

```
TITLE DIVISION

sub-schema-description-entry

[MAPPING DIVISION

  [ALIAS SECTION
    [alias-description-entry] . . . ] ]

STRUCTURE DIVISION

  REALM SECTION
    [realm-description-entry] . . .

  RECORD SECTION
    [record-description-entry] . . .

  SET SECTION
    [set-description-entry] . . .]
```

C1.4.1 Syntax of the TITLE DIVISION

The following description links the external schema to the conceptual schema.

```
SS sub-schema-name WITHIN schema-name
```

C1.4.2 Syntax of the ALIAS SECTION

The purpose of the ALIAS SECTION is to substitute new set, record and field names for those of the conceptual schema.

```
SET set-name IS        literal-1

RECORD record-name IS  literal-2
```

```
AD
        data-name IS   literal-3   [ { IN } ]   literal-4
                                   [ { OF } ]

        CHARACTER   literal-5   IS              literal-6
```

C1.4.3 Syntax of the REALM SECTION

The letters RD have to be followed by the name of the REALM and a statement of what record types the REALM is made up of. It is possible to define several different REALMs, which means that it is possible to have several different groups of records opened at the same time.

```
                               { ALL SUB-SCHEMA         }
RD realm-name   CONTAINS       {                        }   RECORDS
                               { {record-name-1}...     }
```

C1.4.4 Syntax of the RECORD SECTION

The description of the syntax of records is omitted here because, on the whole, it corresponds to the ordinary COBOL record syntax (see Example 11.1).

C1.4.5 Syntax of the SET SECTION

The letters SD are followed by the name of the set to be included in the external schema. When this has been done, a new SET SELECTION statement can be written, if the SET SELECTION of the conceptual schema is to be suppressed.

```
SD set-name-1
[set-section-clause]...
```

C1.5 Syntax for the CODASYL COBOL data manipulation language

In what follows, we shall take a look at the most important syntax rules of the CODASYL data manipulation language used in COBOL. The statements are described in alphabetic order.

C1.5.1 Syntax of the COMMIT statement

The COMMIT statement, which has no parameters, is used to release records that have been locked by updating statements (see Section 6.3). The following statements can be used to lock records for later updating: CONNECT, DISCONNECT, ERASE, FETCH FOR UPDATE, FIND FOR UPDATE, MODIFY, RECONNECT and STORE. An updating lock can be cancelled by the following statements: COMMIT, ROLLBACK and STOP RUN, or if the program aborts.

C1.5.2 Syntax of the CONNECT statement

The CONNECT statement inserts a record as a member in one or more sets. If the ALL parameter is used, the record will be inserted into all the sets possible in the external schema. Note that the record may already have been inserted into one or more of the possible sets.

```
CONNECT [record-name] TO { {set-name-1} ... }
                         { ALL              }
```

C1.5.3 Syntax of the DISCONNECT statement

The DISCONNECT statement can logically remove a record from one or more sets if the external schema allows this. If it is, the record must appear as an OPTIONAL member of the set.

```
DISCONNECT [record-name] FROM { {set-name-1} ... }
                              { ALL              }
```

C1.5.4 Syntax of the ERASE statement

The ERASE statement logically erases a record from the database. If no record type is given as argument, the current record will be erased. If the ALL parameter is used, and if the record to be removed is an owner for other records, then the owner record and its member records, as well as any member records attached to them, etc., will be erased. If the ALL parameter is not used, and if member records, if any, are FIXED, the owner, the member records, etc. will be erased. If the member records are OPTIONAL, they are not erased. Instead, they are removed from the set of the owner. If the member records are MANDATORY, the erasing of the owner record will be rejected.

```
ERASE [ALL] [record-name]
```

C1.5.5 Syntax of the FETCH statement

The FETCH statement can be seen as a combination of a FIND statement and a GET statement. Its syntax can be best understood by referring to the FIND and GET statements.

```
FETCH [FOR UPDATE] record-selection-expression
      [USING ONLY  {identifier-1}          ...]

[              [ { REALM             } ]            ]
[ RETAINING    [ { RECORD            } ]  CURRENCY  ]
[              [ { {set-name-1}  ... } ]            ]
```

C1.5.6 Syntax of the FIND statement

The FIND statement is used to select a record to become the current record. This record can then be read into the working area of the program run by means of a GET statement. Use of the RETAINING parameter ensures that the pointers of the currency status table will not be altered for realm, record or set.

There are many different FIND statements to choose between. The choice depends upon the chosen format for record-selection-expression.

```
FIND record-selection-expression

[            [ { | REALM                  | } ]            ]
[ RETAINING  [ { | RECORD                 | } ]  CURRENCY  ]
[            [ { | {set-name-1} . . .     | } ]            ]
```

Format 1 is used for direct searching of records. The ANY parameter is used to find the first record satisfying the record-selection-expression. The USING parameter is only used to find those records that have specific values in the field identifier-1, etc. The required field value(s) must be stored in the corresponding field value(s) in the working area of the run. The USING parameter has similar consequences in subsequent formats.

Format 1

```
{ ANY       }
{           }  record-name-1  USING { identifier-1} . . .
{ DUPLICATE }
```

Format 2 is used for sequential processing of member records in a set occurrence. The records to be searched for are determined by the USING parameter.

Format 2

```
DUPLICATE WITHIN set-name-1 USING { identifier-2} . . .
```

Format 3 is used for sequential processing of member records. It can also be used for sequential processing within a realm.

Format 3

```
{ NEXT         }
{ PRIOR        }
{ FIRST        }  [record-name-2]   WITHIN   { set-name-2    }
{ LAST         }                             { realm-name-1  }
{ integer-1    }
{ identifier-3 }
```

Format 4 can be used for a direct search for records that have already been searched and whose address has been kept. As this is a case of optimization, the details will not be discussed here.

Format 4

data-base-key-identifier-1

Format 5 is used to find the owner of a given set occurrence.

Format 5

OWNER WITHIN set-name-3

Format 6 is used for sequential processing of set occurrences. If the CURRENT parameter is omitted, the member record will be selected in accordance with the SET SELECTION of the conceptual schema.

Format 6

record-name-3 WITHIN set-name-4 [CURRENT] [USING] {identifier-4} . . .]

C1.5.7 Syntax of the FINISH statement

The FINISH statement finishes the use of a realm; that is, it closes files, etc.

FINISH [realm-name-1] . . .

C1.5.8 Syntax of the FREE and KEEP statements

These statements are only mentioned briefly, as they are used for optimization purposes. By means of the KEEP statement, it is possible to retain the addresses of records that have already been read. These addresses are held in an inverted list, which elsewhere in the syntactical rules is referred to as keep-list-name. If the records are to be read again later, the search can be optimized by using the inverted list as argument of the FIND statement.

By using the FREE statement, one or more record addresses can be removed from the inverted list. Another property of the FREE statement is that it can be used to remove the current pointers of a program run from the current status table. This may be of importance as other programs are welcome to read, but not update, records that are pointed to from the current status table of the first program.

FREE { data-base-key-identifier
ALL [FROM {keep-list-name} . . .] }

C1.5.9 Syntax of the GET statement

The GET statement is used to read current records into the working area of the running program, where the fields can be referred to by means of field names.

```
GET [identifier-1]...
```

C1.5.10 Syntax of the MODIFY statement

The MODIFY statement is used to update the contents of a record having the name identifier-1 in the external schema.

```
MODIFY [identifier-1]...
```

C1.5.11 Syntax of the ORDER statement

The ORDER statement is used to re-organize the sequence of member records. The LOCALLY parameter is used if the sequence of member records in the conceptual schema is defined as non-variable. In this case, the re-organization will only affect the current program run. record-name-1, etc., determines which record types are to participate in the re-sorting. The RECORD-NAME parameter means that record types are sorted by name.

```
ORDER set-name  [LOCALLY]

{ ON { DESCENDING } KEY { | [record-name-1]... RECORD-NAME | } } ...
     { ASCENDING  }     { | {data-name-1} ...               | }
```

C1.5.12 Syntax of the READY statement

The READY statement opens one or more realms, so that the corresponding records and sets are ready to be used. If the RETRIEVAL parameter is used, the program can only read records from the opened realm(s); if the UPDATE parameter is used, the program can both read and update records. If the EXCLUSIVE parameter is used, other program runs cannot gain access to data from the realm opened by EXCLUSIVE; if the PROTECTED parameter is used, other program runs cannot open record types for updating in the realm in question. Omitting the USAGE-MODE parameter corresponds to opening by RETRIEVAL. Execution of the READY statement results in the system checking on any unauthorized use of data. Thus, any ACCESS CONTROL KEYs are checked by the corresponding ACCESS CONTROL LOCKs in the conceptual or external schema.

```
READY [[realm-name-1]...]

      [USAGE-MODE IS [EXCLUSIVE] {RETRIEVAL}]]...
                     [PROTECTED] {UPDATE   }
```

C1.5.13 Syntax of the RECONNECT statement

The RECONNECT statement can be used to move the current record in a set type. If the record to be moved is a FIXED member of the set type, it can only be moved to another location under the same owner record. The SET SELECTION statement in the conceptual or external schema determines to what location the member record is to be moved.

```
RECONNECT [record-name]  WITHIN  {set-name-1} ...
```

C1.5.14 Syntax of the ROLLBACK statement

ROLLBACK is a parameterless statement that uses the log file to remove the updates of the program run. The backing out of updates continues until a record, read on the log file, indicates that the program run has started, or that the program run has performed a COMMIT statement. If a program run aborts, the DBMS will perform a ROLLBACK statement for the program in question.

C1.5.15 Syntax of the STORE statement

The STORE statement is used for the creation of a new record and for any automatic insertion of the new record into sets. The meanings of the qualifiers in this statement have already been described in connection with the FIND statement.

```
                    [            [ { REALM                } ]          ]
STORE record-name   [ RETAINING  [ { RECORD               } ] CURRENCY ]
                    [            [ { {set-name-1} ...     } ]          ]
```

C1.5.16 Syntax of the USE statement

The main purpose of the USE statement is to render a master program easier to understand by removing tests on return codes from the master program itself. The USE statement itself cannot be executed. Instead, it is used to identify the statements to be executed for a given return code. The statements after a particular USE statement are executed if the DBMS gives a return code that corresponds to the value of literal-1 in the USE statement. literal-1 consists of seven digits. The first two digits are the code for the DML statement causing the return code. (The DML statements are numbered from 1 to 17.) The last five digits are the reply code itself, which describes how the statement was executed. All reply codes having no specific USE statement attached to them will be processed under a USE statement with the OTHER parameter.

USE statements are placed at the beginning of the program (see Example 11.4). When the statements occasioned by a USE statement have been executed, the master program again takes control. If the DBMS gives the return code 0, the relevant statement has been executed without any problems, and therefore no USE statements will be searched for.

The USE statement is also available in a special format, which is used to identify those statements that transfer key values to the DB-ACCESS-CONTROL-KEY variable, so that resources protected against unauthorized use can be accessed.

```
USE [GLOBAL] FOR DB-EXCEPTION
[ON { OTHER            } ]
[   { {literal-1} ...  } ]
```

Appendix D
Syntax for DB2

D1.1 Introduction

This appendix does not aim to give a complete syntax description of DB2; it includes only the most important statements needed to solve short exercises. Readers who want a more detailed description are referred to the IBM references in the bibliography (IBM, 1983 a–f). The following symbols are used in the syntax description:

[ ] means the contents of square brackets can be omitted.

... means the last term before the three dots can be repeated.

{ } means one of the alternatives in the curly brackets is to be chosen.

D1.2 The DB2 data definition language

The data definition language consists of the following statements:

- The CREATE statement, which is used to create databases, physical space for a database on a disk, space on disks for files, indexes to a file and user views.
- The DROP statement, which is used to delete the objects created by the CREATE statement.
- The ALTER statement, which is used to change the specifications for the objects created by CREATE.
- The COMMENT-ON statement, which is used to insert comments.

The syntax for the creation of a table, corresponding broadly to a file, is as follows:

```
CREATE TABLE file-name
  (field-definition [, field-definition] . . .);
```

in which the syntax for the field definition is

```
field-name data-type [NOT NULL]
```

NOT NULL means that the field must always have a value. The parameter data-type must have one of the following formats:

- CHAR(*n*): the field contains *n* characters.
- VARCHAR(*n*): the field has variable length and can contain *n* characters as a maximum.
- SMALLINT: the field contains an integer number and one-half of a machine word is allocated for the contents.
- INTEGER: the field contains an integer number and a whole machine word is allocated for the contents.
- DECIMAL (*p*, *s*): the field contains a signed packed decimal number which consists of *p* digits, of which the last *s* digits follow the decimal point; *s* is assumed to be 0 if omitted.
- FLOAT: the field contains a floating-point number.

Formally, a file name consists of two parts, separated by a full stop. The second part of the file name is the name used as argument to the CREATE TABLE statement. The first part of the name identifies the user who created the file. To gain access to a file created by another user, both parts of the file name must be stated.

A DB2 user view is defined as a virtual file; that is, a file that is used by a user or program, but which does not exist physically in the version the user or program requires. The syntax for the creation of a user view is as follows:

```
CREATE VIEW view-name
    (field-name [, field-name] . . .)
    AS SELECT statement;
```

The name of the user view is followed by the names of those fields that form part of the view. This is followed by a SELECT statement, which selects the records in the view. By using a JOIN statement in the SELECT statement it is possible to create a user view composed of several different files. However, it is not possible to update by using a user view composed of several different files.

The syntax for the DROP statement is as follows:

```
      ⎧ TABLE      ⎫
      ⎪ VIEW       ⎪
      ⎪ INDEX      ⎪
DROP  ⎨ STOGROUP   ⎬  name-of-object
      ⎪ DATABASE   ⎪
      ⎩ TABLESPACE ⎭
```

where name-of-object is the name of a file, an index, physical disk space for databases, a database or disk space for files.

D1.3 The SQL data manipulation language

In this section, we shall look at the syntax of the most important data manipulation statements of SQL: SELECT, INSERT, DELETE and UPDATE.

The general syntax for the SELECT statement is as follows:

$$\text{SELECT}\left[\begin{Bmatrix}\text{DISTINCT}\\ \text{ALL}\end{Bmatrix}\right]\begin{Bmatrix}\text{output-fields}\\ *\end{Bmatrix}$$

```
FROM input-file [, input-file] . . .
[WHERE search-criterion]
[GROUP BY field-name
[HAVING search-criterion] ]
[ORDER BY sorting-criterion];
```

DISTINCT is used if all records in the output-file have to be different. ALL stops duplicate records from being removed from the output-file. If a value is not specified for DISTINCT, then ALL is assumed.

* is used if the output-file has to contain the same fields as the input-file; where this is not the case, the fields for the output-file must be specified. If the output-file is a joined file, it can contain different fields with the same name. A distinction between these field names may be made by placing file names in front of them; thus:

file-name. field name

The argument of FROM contains the name of the file(s) in which the search is going to be executed. If several file names are specified, these have to be 'joined' in accordance with the subsequent search criterion. If a file is to be joined with itself, it may be necessary to give alias names to the files. An alias name is defined by writing the alias name immediately after the file name.

The argument of WHERE can be a simple logical expression used to select the records to be included in the output file. The search criterion can also be complex, in which case it incorporates arithmetic operators, set operators, quantifiers and/or new SELECT statements, which define the file or user view in which the search is to be executed.

GROUP BY causes the searched records to be grouped by the field contents in one or more fields, so that an output file can be created containing statistical data about each group. GROUP BY also has the result that the output file can contain no more than one record per group.

HAVING is used if output only has to contain data about a subset of the aforementioned groups. The argument of HAVING is a logical expression, which selects the groups to be included in the output-file.

ORDER BY has one or more fields as argument. The substatement causes the output-file to be sorted by the specified fields. Normally, the output-file is sorted in ascending order; however, by writing DESC after a sorting field, the file will be sorted on this field in descending order.

The INSERT statement is used to insert new records into a file that may already contain records. Its general syntax is as follows:

```
INSERT INTO output-file
[(field-names)]
{VALUES  (field-values)}
{SELECT statement      }
```

The argument of INTO must be the name of a file into which the new records are to be inserted. The file name can be followed by a list of the fields into which values are inserted. If there are fewer fields than in the output file, these fields are given the value NULL.

The argument of VALUES is a list of field values separated by commas. The VALUES specification can only be used to create one single record. A SELECT statement can be used instead of VALUES to extract a set of records created in the output file.

The DELETE statement is used to delete one or more records in a file. Its general syntax is as follows:

```
DELETE
FROM file-name
[WHERE search-criterion]
```

The argument of FROM is the name of the file from which records are to be deleted. The argument of WHERE is a search criterion, which selects the records to be deleted. The syntax of the search-criterion is outlined in the description of the SELECT statement.

The UPDATE statement is used to alter a field value in one or more records. Its general syntax is as follows:

```
UPDATA file-name
SET field name = expression-n
    [field-name-m = expression-m] . . .
[WHERE search-criterion]:
```

The argument of UPDATE is the name of the file to be updated. After SET, the fields whose values are to be altered are specified. The expression that specifies the new field value can be a new value, NULL or an arithmetic expression. The argument of WHERE is a search criterion that selects the records to be updated. The syntax of the search-criterion is described in further detail in the description of the SELECT statement.

Appendix E
Statistical Approximations

E1.1 The Poisson Distribution

The Poisson Distribution of the values of a variable X whose mean value is y is defined as:

$$P_y(X = j) = e^{-y} \times \frac{y^j}{j!}$$

where $P_y(X = j)$ is the probability that the variable X has the value j, j is a positive integer or zero and y a positive integer. e is the base of the natural logarithms $\simeq 2.718$.

Note in particular that 0! is defined as 1, so that

$$P_y(X = 0) = e^{-y}$$

Table E1.1 contains the values of the Poisson Distribution for a number of selected mean values. This table is used in the following examples and may be used in the exercises.

We can prove that if a randomizing function spreads the set of records arbitrarily across the buckets of the primary file, the probability that there are j records in a bucket can be approximated by the Poisson Distribution for the mean value m/n, where m is the number of records in the file, n is the number of buckets in the primary file, so that m/n is the average number of records per home bucket.

Table E1.1 Poisson Distributions.

$P_y(X=j)$ \ y	1	2	3	4	5	6	7	8	10
$P(X=0)$	0.368	0.135	0.050	0.018	0.007	0.002	0.001	0.000	0.000
$P(X=1)$	0.368	0.271	0.149	0.073	0.034	0.015	0.006	0.003	0.000
$P(X=2)$	0.184	0.271	0.224	0.147	0.084	0.045	0.023	0.011	0.002
$P(X=3)$	0.061	0.180	0.224	0.195	0.140	0.089	0.052	0.029	0.008
$P(X=4)$	0.015	0.090	0.168	0.195	0.176	0.134	0.091	0.057	0.019
$P(X=5)$	0.003	0.036	0.101	0.156	0.176	0.161	0.128	0.092	0.038
$P(X=6)$	0.000	0.012	0.050	0.104	0.146	0.161	0.149	0.122	0.063
$P(X=7)$	0	0.003	0.022	0.060	0.104	0.138	0.149	0.139	0.090
$P(X=8)$	0	0.001	0.008	0.030	0.065	0.103	0.130	0.139	0.113
$P(X=9)$	0	0.000	0.003	0.013	0.036	0.069	0.101	0.124	0.125
$P(X=10)$	0	0	0.001	0.005	0.018	0.041	0.071	0.099	0.125
$P(X=11)$	0	0	0.000	0.002	0.008	0.023	0.045	0.072	0.114
$P(X=12)$	0	0	0	0.001	0.003	0.011	0.026	0.048	0.095
$P(X=13)$	0	0	0	0.000	0.001	0.005	0.014	0.030	0.073
$P(X=14)$	0	0	0	0	0.000	0.002	0.007	0.017	0.052
$P(X=15)$	0	0	0	0	0	0.000	0.003	0.009	0.035
$P(X=16)$	0	0	0	0	0	0	0.002	0.005	0.022
$P(X=17)$	0	0	0	0	0	0	0.001	0.002	0.013
$P(X=18)$	0	0	0	0	0	0	0.000	0.001	0.007
$P(X=19)$	0	0	0	0	0	0	0	0.000	0.004
$P(X=20)$	0	0	0	0	0	0	0	0	0.001

EXAMPLE E1.1

A randomly organized file contains 70 000 records distributed over 10 000 buckets. A bucket size of 10 is used. The average number of records per bucket will then be $y = m/n = 7$. In practice, the number of records per bucket varies. By means of the Poisson Distribution, we can calculate how high a percentage of the buckets contain a particular number of synonyms. The probability that there are five synonyms, for example, can be calculated as follows:

$$P_7(X=5) = e^{-7} \times \frac{7^5}{5!} = 0.128$$

The probability of overflow occurring, i.e. that the number of records in a bucket is greater than 10, is:

$$P_7(X>10) = \sum_{j=11}^{70\,000} P_7(X=j)$$

From Table E1.1 we can see that for all $X > 17$, $P_7(X) = 0$; so:

$$\begin{aligned} P_7(X > 10) &= P_7(X = 11) + P_7(X = 12) \ldots + P_7(X = 17) \\ &= 0.045 + 0.026 + 0.014 + 0.007 + 0.003 + 0.002 \\ &\quad + 0.001 \\ &= 0.098 \end{aligned}$$

E1.2 Selection of the randomizing function

Assume that j designates the number of synonyms that can be attached to the same home bucket in a randomly organized file. P_y $(X = j)$ indicates the probability of j synonyms being attached to a home bucket. If the bucket size is b, the number of home buckets with $(j - b)$ overflow records will be $n \times P_y(X = j)$ for $j > b$. Therefore, the number of overflow records can be calculated as:

$$\sum_{j=b+1}^{m} (j - b) \times n \times P_y(X = j) \qquad (2)$$

An approximation of the number of overflow records can be used to assess whether a randomizing function is satisfactory. If more than one randomizing function is tested, the randomizing function that results in the lowest number of overflow records should be chosen. If a randomizing function in which the number of overflow records found is close to the number of overflow records predicted by approximation, we cannot expect to be able to find a better randomizing function.

E1.3 Estimation of the size of overflow storage

Equation (3) can be used to estimate the number of overflow buckets in a randomly organized file in which the bucket size of the primary file is b_1 and the bucket size of the overflow storage is b_2:

$$\text{No. of overflow buckets} = \sum_{j=b_1+1}^{m} \left\lceil \frac{j - b_1}{b_2} \right\rceil \times n \times P_y(X = j) \qquad (3)$$

EXAMPLE E1.2

Using Equation (3) we can now estimate the number of overflow blocks in the file in the previous example. A blocking factor/bucket size of 10 is assumed for both the primary file and the overflow file.

$$\begin{aligned} \text{Number of overflow buckets} &= \sum_{j=11}^{70\,000} \left\lceil \frac{j - 10}{10} \right\rceil \times 10\,000 \times P_7(X = j) \\ &= 10\,000\,(P_7(X = 11) + P_7(X = 12) \ldots + P_7(x = 17) \\ &= 980 \end{aligned}$$

Table E1.2 Overflow block calculations.

j	$n \times P_1(X=j)$ ($n = 10\,000$)	$\left\lceil \frac{j-b_1}{b_2} \right\rceil$	*Sum*
2	1840	1	1840
3	610	1	610
4	150	1	150
5	30	1	30
6	0	2	0
			Sum 2630

If we have files with a hierarchical static index and chained overflow in a separate overflow storage, Equation(3) can be used to approximate the number of overflow buckets. However, the equation can only be applied if new records, inserted after a re-organization of the file, are attached to buckets that are evenly distributed on all the n buckets of the primary file. If the equation is used, b_1 must be equivalent to the number of records that can be inserted on average after the file has been re-organized, b_2 to the bucket size of the overflow file and y to m'/n where m' is the number of records created after the file has been re-organized.

EXAMPLE E1.3

An index organized file originally contains 30 000 records distributed on 10 000 blocks in the primary file. Both the primary file and the overflow file use a bucket size of 4. Assume that 10 000 new records are created after the file has been re-organized; i.e.:

$$b_1 = 1 \qquad b_2 = 4 \qquad y = \frac{10\,000}{10\,000} = 1$$

Table E1.2 illustrates how we can calculate the number of overflow blocks. The result is 2630 overflow blocks.

EXAMPLE E1.4

Example E1.2 dealt with a randomly organized file with separate overflow storage. The number of overflow records, given by Equation (3), is:

$$\sum_{j=b+1}^{m} (j-b) \times n \times P_y(x=j)$$

with $b = 10$, $n = 10\,000$ and $m = 70\,000$. Table E1.3 illustrates how we can estimate the number of overflow records. The result will be some 2010 overflow records.

Table E1.3 More overflow block calculations.

j	$P_7(X=j)$	$n \times P(X=j)$ $(n = 10\,000)$	$j - b\ (b = 10)$	$(j - b) \times n \times P(X=j)$
11	0.045	450	1	450
12	0.026	260	2	520
13	0.014	140	3	420
14	0.007	70	4	280
15	0.003	30	5	150
16	0.002	20	6	120
17	0.001	10	7	70
18	0.000	0	8	0
				Sum 2010

E1.4 Estimates of average search length

In this section we demonstrate how we can estimate the search length in randomly organized files if the overflow problem is solved by one of the methods suggested by Knuth (1973), Severance (1976) or Teorey and Fry (1982).

In Section E1.4.1 we shall introduce a new general formula for the estimation of the search length in files that use overflow bucket chaining to store overflow records. In the subsequent sections, this formula will be used to estimate the search length in a number of different types of file organization.

E1.4.1 Search length in randomly organized files with chaining of overflow buckets in a separate overflow storage

The search length in a file in which we chain overflow buckets in a separate overflow storage can be estimated by means of the following variables and parameters.

b_1 = the bucket size in the primary file
b_2 = the bucket size in the overflow file
j = the number of records allocated to the same home address

$$j' = \text{the number of fully occupied buckets} = \begin{cases} 0 \text{ for } j < b_1 \\ 1 + \left\lfloor \dfrac{j - b_1}{b_2} \right\rfloor \text{ for } j \geq b_1 \end{cases}$$

$$j'' = \text{the number of records in a possible, partly occupied last bucket} = \begin{cases} j \text{ for } j < b_1 \\ j - b_1 - (j' - 1)\, b_2 \text{ for } j \geq b_1 \end{cases}$$

The above variables and parameters are related as shown below:

$$j = b_1 + (j' - 1)b_2 + j''$$

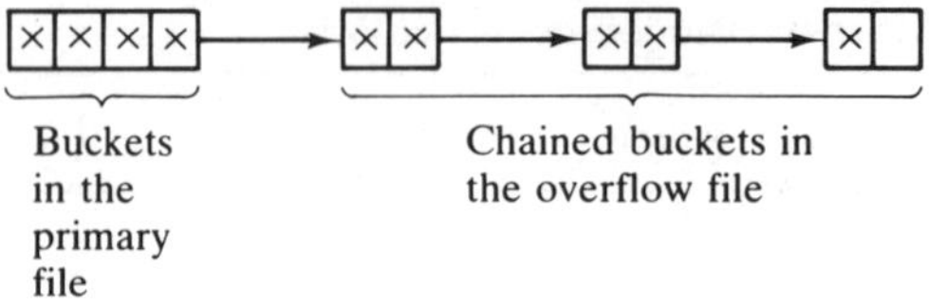

Figure E1.1 A block in a primary file with three overflow blocks chained to it. Stored records are shown by a cross.

EXAMPLE E1.5

Figure E1.1 illustrates a block in the primary file followed by three overflow blocks. The crosses illustrate stored records; that is:

$$b_1 = 4 \qquad b_2 = 2 \qquad j = 9 \qquad j' = 3 \qquad j'' = 1$$

The average search length can thus be calculated as follows. The number of home addresses with j synonyms is:

$n \times P(X = j)$ where n is the number of buckets

The number of accesses needed to read all the records in the primary file is thus:

$$\sum_{j=1}^{b_1} n \times P(X = j) \times j$$

The average search length can thus be calculated as follows. The number of home addresses with j synonyms is:

$n \times P(X = j)$ where n is the number of buckets

The number of accesses needed to read all the records in the primary file is thus:

$$\sum_{j=1}^{b_1} n \times P(X = j) \times j$$

The number of accesses required to read all the records in the j' fully occupied buckets of a chain of synonyms will be:

$$b_1 + \sum_{i=2}^{j'} i \times b_2$$

$$= b_1 + \left(\frac{b_2 \times j' \times (j' + 1)}{2} - b_2\right)$$

while the number of accesses to read the last j'' records in the final bucket will be:

$$(j' + 1) \times j''$$

Thus, the number of accesses necessary to read all the records in overflow storage will be:

$$\sum_{j=b_1+1}^{m} n \times P(X = j) \times \left(b_1 + \sum_{i=2}^{j'} i \times b_2 + (j' + 1) \times j''\right)$$

where m is the number of records

$$= \sum_{j=b_1+1}^{m} n \times P(X=j) \times \left((b_1 - b_2) + (j' + 1)\left(\frac{b_2 \times j'}{2} + j''\right)\right)$$

To obtain the average search length the total number of accesses for both primary and secondary storage are divided by the number of records, m. Thus, the average search length is:

$$\frac{1}{m} \times \sum_{j=1}^{b_1} n \times P(X = j) \times j + \frac{1}{m} \times \sum_{j=b_1+1}^{m} n \times P(X = j) \times$$

$$\left((b_1 - b_2) + (j' + 1)\left(\frac{b_2 \times j'}{2} + j''\right)\right)$$

$$= \frac{n}{m} \sum_{j=1}^{b_1} P(X = j) \times j + \frac{n}{m} \sum_{j=b_1+1}^{m} P(X = j) \times$$

$$\left((b_1 - b_2) + (j' + 1)\left(\frac{b_2 \times j'}{2} + j''\right)\right) \quad \textbf{(4)}$$

EXAMPLE E1.6

A randomly organized file with chained overflow contains 30 000 records. The primary file contains 10 000 blocks with a blocking factor of 4. The overflow blocks also have a blocking factor of 4. The overflow blocks may, for example, be stored as an extension of the primary file, so that we also have the possibility of reading the file in physical sequence. Table E1.4 illustrates how the average search length can be calculated. y for the Poisson Distribution = 30 000/ 10 000 = 3 and $b_1 = 4$, $b_2 = 4$.

The average search length will thus be $(n/m) \times 3.326 = 1/3 \times 3.326 \times 1.1087$.

EXAMPLE E1.7

Assume that the file in the previous example has chained overflow for the individual overflow records. In that case, the search length can be estimated by means of Equation (4), where $b_1 = 4$ and $b_2 = 1$. The file may be constructed so

Table E1.4 Calculation of average search length.

j	j'	j''	$P_3(X=j)$	j for $j < b_1$ or $b_1 - b_2 + (j'+1) \times \left(b_2 \times \frac{j'}{2} + j''\right)$	*Sum*
1	0	1	0.149	1	0.149
2	0	2	0.224	2	0.448
3	0	3	0.224	3	0.672
4	1	0	0.168	4	0.672
5	1	1	0.101	6	0.606
6	1	2	0.050	8	0.400
7	1	3	0.022	10	0.220
8	2	0	0.008	12	0.096
9	2	1	0.003	15	0.045
10	2	2	0.001	18	0.018
11	2	3	0.000	21	0.000
					Sum 3.326

that the blocking factor in the overflow file is still 4. However, an overflow bucket size of 1 is used because overflow records are chained together one by one, and because in the case of an arbitrary sequence of creation several overflow records belonging to the same home address are only rarely created in the same overflow block. Table E1.5 illustrates how we can calculate the search length.

The average search length will be $(n/m) \times 3.530 = 1/3 \times 3.530 = 1.177$.

The equation that uses two bucket sizes can also be used to estimate the search length in the case of linear hashing, as described in Litwin (1980). Larson (1982) establishes a formula for the estimation of the search length in the case of linear hashing which converges more slowly towards the result than the equation given here, since it includes a double summation. Furthermore, Larson's formula is not exact because, in principle, the formula requires an infinitely large file. In Knuth (1973) there is an equation that can be used if all the overflow buckets have bucket size 1. Bratbergsengen *et al.* (1983) produce an equation which applies if $b_1 = b_2$.

In Example E1.8 we need three different bucket sizes to calculate the search length. That is, first we use bucket size b_1, then bucket size b_2 and for the subsequent overflow buckets we use bucket size b_3. If we use three bucket sizes, the search length can be calculated by means of the following equation, which is derived in the same way as Equation (4).

$$\frac{n}{m}\sum_{j=1}^{b_1} P(X=j) \times j + \frac{n}{m}\sum_{j=b_1+1}^{b_1+b_2} P(X=j)(b_1 + 2j'') +$$

Table E1.5 Calculation of average search length.

j	j'	j''	$P_3(X=j)$	j for $j<b_1$ or $b_1 - b_2 + (j'+1) \times \left(b_2 \times \frac{j'}{2} + j''\right)$	Sum
1	0	1	0.149	1	0.149
2	0	2	0.224	2	0.448
3	0	3	0.224	3	0.672
4	1	0	0.168	4	0.672
5	2	0	0.105	6	0.606
6	3	0	0.050	9	0.450
7	4	0	0.022	13	0.286
8	5	0	0.008	18	0.144
9	6	0	0.003	24	0.072
10	7	0	0.001	31	0.031
11	8	0	0.000	39	0.000
					Sum 3.530

$$\frac{n}{m} \sum_{j=b_1+b_2+1}^{m} P(X=j)\left(b_1 + 2b_2 + b_3\left(j'\frac{(j'+1)}{2} - 3\right) + (j'+1)j''\right) \quad (5)$$

where:

$$j' = \begin{cases} 0 \text{ for } j < b_1 \\ 1 \text{ for } b_1 \leqslant j < b_1 + b_2 \\ 2 + \left\lfloor \frac{j - b_1 - b_2}{b_3} \right\rfloor \text{ for } j \geqslant b_1 + b_2 \end{cases}$$

and:

$$j'' = \begin{cases} j \text{ for } j < b_1 \\ j - b_1 \text{ for } b_1 \leqslant j < b_1 + b_2 \\ j - b_1 - b_2 - (j'-2)\, b_3 \text{ for } j \geqslant b_1 + b_2 \end{cases}$$

EXAMPLE E1.8

Assume that the file in Example E1.7 is loaded in sorted order, so that overflow records belonging to the same overflow chain are loaded in sequence. In that case, the first overflow block can hold an average of $b/2$ overflow records while the subsequent overflow blocks can hold b overflow records. We can calculate the search length for this situation by means of the equation for three bucket

Table E1.6 Calculation of average search length.

j	j'	j''	$P_3(X = j)$	j for $j < b_1$ or $b_1 - b_2 + (j' + 1) \times \left(b_2 \times \frac{j'}{2} + j''\right)$	*Sum*
1	0	1	0.149	1	0.149
2	0	2	0.224	2	0.448
3	0	3	0.224	3	0.672
4	1	0	0.168	4	0.672
5	1	1	0.101	6	0.606
6	2	0	0.050	8	0.400
7	2	1	0.022	11	0.242
8	2	2	0.008	14	0.112
9	2	3	0.003	17	0.051
10	3	0	0.001	20	0.020
11	3	1	0.000	24	0.000
					Sum 3.372

sizes. First, bucket size b is used and then the bucket size $b/2$, and the subsequent overflow buckets have size b. That is, $b_1 = 4$, $b_2 = b/2 = 2$ and $b_3 = 4$. The calculation of the average search length is shown in Table E1.6. The average search length will be $n/m \times 3.372 = 1/3 \times 3.372 = 1.125$.

E1.4.2 Search length in indexed organized files with overflow chaining

If we use hierarchical static indexes with overflow chaining in a separate overflow storage, the previous two bucket size equations can be used to estimate the average search length after the bottom level in the index has been read. These equations can only be used, however, if the new records inserted after a reorganization are attached to buckets that are uniformly distributed over all the n blocks of the primary file. If Equation (4) is applied, b_1 must be equivalent to the number of records which, on average, can be inserted in a bucket in the primary file after a reorganization of the file, while b_2 equals the blocking factor in the overflow file and y equals m'/n where m' is the number of records created after the file has been re-organized.

EXAMPLE E1.9

Assume that we have an indexed organized file that originally contains 30 000 records distributed on 10 000 blocks in the primary file. Both the primary file and the overflow file use the blocking factor 4. Assume also that 10 000 new records are created after the file has been re-organized; i.e.:

$$b_1 = 1 \quad b_2 = 4 \quad y = \frac{10\,000}{10\,000} = 1$$

Table E1.7 Calculation of average search length.

j	j'	j''	$P_3(X=j)$	j for $j < b_1$ or $b_1 - b_2 + (j'+1) \times \left(b_2 \times \frac{j'}{2} + j''\right)$	Sum
1	1	0	0.368	1	0.368
2	1	1	0.184	3	0.552
3	1	2	0.061	5	0.305
4	1	3	0.015	7	0.105
5	2	0	0.003	9	0.027
6	2	1	0.000	12	0.000
					Sum 1.357

Table E1.7 illustrates how we can calculate the average search length after the bottom level in the index has been read. As $m'/n = 1$, the average search length after the reading of the bottom level in the index will be 1.357.

E1.4.3 Search length in randomly organized files with coalesced chaining

If we have coalesced chaining, overflow records are not stored in a separate overflow storage but in the primary file itself. If overflow occurs in a bucket, another bucket with available space is searched for, and overflow records from the first bucket are subsequently stored in the second bucket. If overflow also occurs in this bucket, the process is repeated. Overflow records belonging to the same home address must be chained together. Assume that the file is re-organized by means of a two-pass load (i.e. first all those records that do not cause overflow are created and then overflow records are created in sequence) so that those records belonging to the same home address can be created immediately after each other.

As $P_y(X \leq b)$ is the probability that no overflow will occur in a bucket, an average of at least

$$b - \left\lceil \frac{m}{n} \times P_y(X \leq b) \right\rceil$$

overflow records can be stored in those buckets where there is available space, where $y = m/n =$ the average number of records per bucket. If we assume that two different overflow chains will not traverse the same bucket, the average search length can be approximated by means of Equation E.4 with two bucket sizes, where

$$b_1 = b \quad \text{and} \quad b_2 = b - \left\lceil \frac{m}{n} \times P_y(X \leq b) \right\rceil.$$

Knuth (1973) gives a more accurate approximation for the search length with coalesced chaining, but only in the case of $b = 1$.

E1.4.4 Search length in random organized files with open overflow

If we have open overflow the overflow records are not stored in a separate overflow file, but in available space in the primary file instead. Examples of this are linear open overflow and non-linear open overflow, such as rehashing. Knuth (1973) gives an equation for estimating the average search length with linear open overflow. In addition, Knuth (1973) and Teorey and Fry (1982) include tables giving search lengths for different values of b and f, the loading factor. The graphs giving search lengths in Section 2.4.2 are produced on the basis of these tables.

As yet, no general techniques for approximating the search length in cases of non-linear open overflow have been developed, but in McIlroy (1963) and Severance (1974) there is an equation which applies for the case of $b = 1$.

E1.5 Estimating disk storage work time for sequential updating if only some of the blocks are to be updated

If we are working with sequential updating we can adopt Equation (7) from Appendix B to give the following approximation of the work time:

$$\text{work time} = \text{number of cylinders in the file} \times \left(HMIN + \left(\frac{R}{S} + R + p \times R \right) \times C \times S \right) \qquad \textbf{(6)}$$

where p is the probability of a bucket having to be updated.

EXAMPLE E1.10

A master file of 500 000 records is to be updated sequentially on the basis of a transaction file of 100 000 records. If the master file has a blocking factor of 5 there will be an average of one record updating per block. The probability for a block *not* having to be updated can be found by means of the Poisson distribution, with y = the average number of record updatings per block. That is:

$$P_y(X = 0) = P_1(X = 0) = 0.368$$

The probability that a block has to be updated can now be calculated as:

$$1 - 0.368 = 0.632 = p$$

If we know the technical data for the disk storage, the number of cylinders and S = the number of blocks per track, we can estimate the disk storage work time by means of Equation (6).

E1.6 The effect of queue systems on the response times of transactions

The purpose of this section is to analyse the effect of the time transactions spent waiting in queues on the total response time. First we describe a model of a single-queue system. Then we shall examine some methods that can be used to estimate the response time for transactions arriving in such a queue system. And finally we shall see how the response time can be estimated with more complex systems of queueing.

E1.6.1 Single-queue system

A single-queue system is a system in which there is a single queue of transactions accumulated in front of a single processing unit that processes the transactions, which then leave the system. The processing unit may be a whole data processing system, the CPU, a transmission line or a storage disk, depending on what we want to analyse.

Figure E1.2 illustrates a queue model with a processing unit in front of which a queue of transactions accumulates. The **queue length** is the number of transactions waiting to be processed. Estimates of the queue length can be used to adjust the dimension of the buffer areas of the computer in which transactions are stored prior to processing. The **queue time** is the time a transaction in a queue waits before it can be processed. The **processing time** is the time during which the transaction occupies the processing unit. In this basic model the processing unit can only process one transaction at a time, and a transaction has to be finished before the processing of the next transaction can be commenced. The **response-time** is defined as the sum of the queue-time and the processing-time.

The **dispatching discipline** is the sequence in which the accumulated transactions are dealt with. As an example of dispatching disciplines we may mention FIFO (First-In First-Out) or FCFS (First-Come First-Served) in which the transactions are dispatched in the same order as they arrive. Data processing systems often use another important dispatching discipline as transactions are often processed in order of priority, so that important transactions can be processed before less important ones. In our account, however, we assume that the transactions are dispatched in FIFO order. It is further assumed that the time of arrival of the transactions is of no consequence. This assumption is not always justified in real situations because a peak load of user transactions can cause a subsequent peak load on the queues for CPU capacity, disk storage accesses and transmission lines. The simultaneous accumulation of transactions at the various resources of the data processing system may demand so much CPU capacity to run the operating system that the capacity of the system will be reduced, making the queues even longer. The arrival of the transactions in subsequent queues will

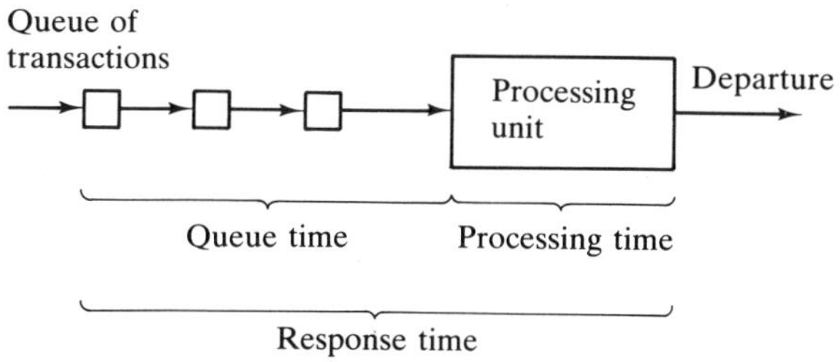

Figure E1.2 Response times in a single queue system.

thus be delayed, and therefore they will no longer arrive with the same random frequency as before. If a data processing system is in balance and not subject to extreme peak loading, however, it may be assumed that the time of arrival of the transactions is arbitrary.

E1.6.2 Exponential distribution

If an occurrence occurs arbitrarily on average a times within a given period of time, the Poisson Distribution:

$$P_a\,(X = j) = e^{-a}\frac{a_j}{j!}$$

indicates the probability of exactly j occurrences within the time period.

EXAMPLE E1.11

> Assume that on-line transactions are received in an arbitrary order by the terminal operator who is going to process them. On average, one transaction arrives each minute. By means of the Poisson Distribution with the mean value a, we can estimate the probability of j transactions arriving within one minute. The frequency of arrival of the transactions is therefore Poisson distributed.

There is a close connection between the Poisson Distribution and Exponential Distribution. Assume that an occurrence arbitrarily happens on average a times within a given period of time. The average time interval between the occurrences will then be $1/a$. We can prove that if an occurrence follows the Poisson Distribution with the mean value a the occurrence will occur ta times on average within the time interval t. By means of the Poisson Distribution with the mean value ta we can estimate the probability for the occurrence not occurring within the time interval t as:

$$P_{ta}\,(X = 0) = e^{-ta}\frac{(ta)^0}{0!} = e^{-ta}$$

This probability distribution is called the **Exponential Distribution** with the mean value $1/a$. The opposite probability – that at least one occurrence happens within the time interval – will consequently be $1 - e^{-ta}$. Thus, if an occurrence follows the Poisson Distribution with the mean value a, the time interval between the occurrences will follow an Exponential Distribution with the mean value $1/a$. The Exponential Distribution with the mean value $1/a$ is defined by the distribution function $1 - e^{-ta}$, which indicates the probability of at least one occurrence happening within the time period t.

In practice, it is often more interesting to be able to estimate the opposite probability – that an occurrence does not happen within the time interval t. This probability is defined by the function e^{-ta}. Table E1.8 gives the value of this function for different values of ta.

Table E1.8 Values of e^{-ta} for various values of *ta*.

ta	0.001	0.002	0.003	0.004	0.005	0.006	0.007	0.008	0.009	0.01
e^{-ta}	0.999	0.998	0.997	0.996	0.995	0.994	0.993	0.992	0.991	0.990
ta	0.02	0.03	0.04	0.05	0.06	0.07	0.08	0.09	0.10	0.15
e^{-ta}	0.980	0.970	0.961	0.951	0.942	0.932	0.923	0.914	0.905	0.861
ta	0.20	0.25	0.30	0.40	0.50	0.60	0.70	0.80	0.90	1.0
e^{-ta}	0.819	0.779	0.741	0.670	0.607	0.549	0.497	0.449	0.407	0.368
ta	1.1	1.2	1.3	1.4	1.5	1.6	1.7	1.8	1.9	2.0
e^{-ta}	0.333	0.301	0.273	0.247	0.223	0.202	0.183	0.165	0.150	0.135
ta	2.1	2.2	2.3	2.4	2.5	2.6	2.7	2.8	2.9	3.0
e^{-ta}	0.122	0.111	0.100	0.091	0.082	0.074	0.067	0.061	0.055	0.050
ta	3.1	3.2	3.3	3.4	3.5	3.6	3.7	3.8	3.9	4.0
e^{-ta}	0.045	0.041	0.037	0.033	0.030	0.027	0.025	0.022	0.020	0.018
ta	4.1	4.2	4.3	4.4	4.5	4.6	4.7	4.8	4.9	5.0
e^{-ta}	0.017	0.015	0.014	0.012	0.011	0.010	0.009	0.008	0.007	0.007
ta	5.1	5.2	5.3	5.4	5.5	5.6	5.7	5.8	5.9	6.0
e^{-ta}	0.006	0.006	0.005	0.005	0.004	0.004	0.003	0.003	0.003	0.002
ta	6.1	6.2	6.3	6.4	6.5	6.6	6.7	6.8	6.9	7.0
e^{-ta}	0.002	0.002	0.002	0.002	0.002	0.001	0.001	0.001	0.001	0.001
ta	7.1	7.2	7.3	7.4	7.5	8.0	8.5	9.0	9.5	10.0
e^{-ta}	0.001	0.001	0.001	0.001	0.001	0.000	0.000	0.000	0.000	0.000

EXAMPLE E1.12

Assume that on-line transactions are received in an arbitrary order by a terminal operator at an average of two transactions per minute. Thus, $a = 2$ transactions per minute. The probability that no transactions will arrive during the next three minutes will then be:

$$e^{-ta} = e^{-3\times 2} = e^{-6} = 0.002$$

E1.6.3 Estimating queue lengths and response times

The distribution function for the processing time indicates the probability of processing a transaction in less than *t* seconds. Many of the activities executed on a computer have exponentially distributed execution times. If we know the average execution time we can use the exponential distribution to estimate the probability of an activity taking less than *t* time units.

EXAMPLE E1.13

Assume that the processing time for transactions on a computer is exponentially distributed with an average processing time of 0.1 second, i.e., $a = 10$

Table E1.9 Estimates of average queue lengths and response times.

Processing time	***Constant processing time***	***Exponentially distributed processing time***
E (queue length)	$\dfrac{U^2}{2(1-U)}$	$\dfrac{U^2}{(1-U)}$
E (response time)	$\dfrac{(2-U)\,(\text{processing time})}{2\,(1-U)}$	$\dfrac{E(\text{processing time})}{(1-U)}$

transactions per second. The probability of the run time of a transaction exceeding 0.2 second will then be:

$$e^{-ta} = e^{-0.2\times 10} = e^{-2} = 0.135$$

(see Table E1.8). The probability of the run time of a transaction being less than 0.2 second will then be $1 - 0.135 = 0.865$.

There are a number of different formulae that can be used to estimate the average response time. Which of them to apply depends on the distribution function of the processing time. In what follows, we analyse only those cases in which the processing time is constant or exponentially distributed. In the case of a constant processing time, the formulae indicate the minimum average queue length and the minimum average response time that can be achieved when the transactions arrive in an arbitrary order. The processing times seen in practice will often follow a distribution somewhere between the constant processing time and the exponentially distributed processing time. The formulae applying to the exponentially distributed processing time can therefore often be used as an upper limit to the average queue length and the average response time. The variable U, standing for the **utilization** of the processing unit, is often found in equations for the average queue length and average response time. U is defined as follows:

$$U = \frac{\text{the total time during which the processing unit is occupied}}{\text{the total time during which the system is available}}$$

In the queue model, it is assumed that the system is in balance (i.e., U is constant and $U < 1$). In practice, however, U will often vary a great deal. Therefore it will be helpful to divide our analysis into peak load periods, average periods, etc.

In the following, the symbol $E(X)$ indicates the average or mean value of the variable X. E (queue length) thus indicates the average queue length and E (response time) indicates the average response time. Table E1.9 shows estimates for the average queue length and the average response time, depending on whether the processing time is constant or exponentially distributed. From the table, it can be seen that both the queue length and the response time approach infinity if the utilization factor U approaches 1. Consequently, it is impossible to work for a long time in a real-time system with a very high utilization factor.

Table E1.10 Queue lengths for different disk storage utilization.

Utilization of disk storage	*Constant block access time*	*Exponentially distributed block access time*
$U = 50\%$	0.25	0.5
$U = 90\%$	4.05	8.1

EXAMPLE E1.14

The average queue length of block readings for a particular disk storage is determined only by the utilization of the disk storage and the distribution function of the block access times. Table E1.10 gives a survey of queue lengths on the assumption of a 50% and a 90% utilization of the disk storage, and on the assumption that the block access time is constant or exponentially distributed.

Assume that the disk storage holds a file with indexed organization and an index height of three. An average of four block readings are required to read a record, and the transaction has to pass through the disk storage queue four times. The average block reading time of the disk storage is assumed to be 0.0261 second. Table E1.11 gives a survey of average response times required to read a record on the assumption of a 50% and a 90% utilization of the disk storage and where the block access time is constant or exponentially distributed.

It was assumed that the transactions arrived on the disk storage queue in an arbitrary order. This assumption is not made in the calculations of Table E1.11 because each transaction requires four disk storage accesses. In most cases, this will not have any important impact on the response time, but if the utilization factor is very high, it may lead to an increased response time because the arrival of the transactions will be more bunched.

From Table E1.11, it appears that we can reduce the response time considerably by reducing the utilization of the disk storage. This can be done, for example, by storing the master file and the index on different disks. If, after this division, we use the available disk storage space to store other files, we may lose the response time improvement as the new files may once again increase disk storage utilization.

However, by going over to random organization, it will be possible to reduce the response time considerably. Assume, for example, that the search length in a similar randomly organized file is 1.2. The disk storage utilizations of 50% and 90%, respectively, will thus be reduced by a factor 4/1.2 to 15% and 27% respectively. Table E1.12 shows the average response times for reading a record on the assumption of a disk storage utilization of 15% and 27%, respectively, and on the assumption that the block access time is constant or exponentially distributed. The table also shows how much the average response time has been improved.

Table E1.11 Response times for different disk storage utilization.

Utilization of disk storage	*Constant block access time*	*Exponentially distributed block access time*
$U = 50\%$	0.1566	0.2088
$U = 90\%$	0.5742	1.044

Table E1.12 Improved response times.

Utilization of disk storage	*Constant block access time*	*Exponentially distributed block access time*
$U = 15\%$	0.0341	0.0368
$U = 27\%$	0.0371	0.0429

From Table E1.12, it appears that by changing the file organization we have achieved a considerably improved response time, as the average response times are now 4.6, 5.7, 15.5 and 24.3 times faster, respectively, depending on the original assumptions.

E1.6.4 The spread of the response time

As previously mentioned the symbol $E(X)$ indicates the average or mean value of the variable X. Assume that X_1, X_2, ... X_n are the response times for an arbitrary selection of n transactions. The **mean value** $E(X)$ of the response time can thus be estimated from the average response time for the n transactions, i.e.:

$$E(X) = \frac{1}{n}\sum_{i=1}^{n} X_i$$

The **spread** of the response time is defined as the variation compared to the mean value. In the case of on-line systems it is not only necessary to make sure that the mean value of the response time is satisfactory. The spread of the response time must not be too large either.

The variance $VAR(X)$ and the standard deviation $STA(X)$ of the response time are often used as measures of the spread of the response time. The **variance** of the response time can be calculated as follows:

$$VAR(X) = \frac{1}{n-1}\sum_{i=1}^{n} (X_i - E(x))^2$$

The **standard deviation** of the response time is defined as the square root of the variance. For occurrences with exponential distribution it can be proved that their standard deviation is equal to their average. If we calculate the standard deviation for some measured response times, this should not normally be larger than the average response time. We can therefore check that the spread of the response times is reasonable by means of the standard deviation:

$$STA(X) = \sqrt{\sum_{i=1}^{n} \frac{(X_i - E(X))^2}{n-1}} \leqslant E(X)$$

If the response times of a transaction type do not match the figures obtained by the method outlined above, it may be due to large variations in the

Table E1.13 Response times and variance for various transactions.

Type of queue	*E (response time)*	*VAR (response time)*
CPU	0.01	0.0001
Disk storage	0.3	0.09
Transmission	0.6	0.36
Sum	0.91	0.4501

work load of the data processing system. In this case we could solve the problem by means of technical improvements to the hardware of the system.

However, the cause of the problem could also be an inappropriately designed dialogue between user and machine. If we are dealing with update transactions we may find the cause of the problem by checking the 'locking procedure' the transaction uses.

There are several measures which users can employ when they negotiate with their data processing department to ensure that the response time spread does not become too large. A well-known method is to make an agreement to the effect that 95% of the response times for a particular type of transaction must be within a certain range. The value below which 95% of the response times lie is called the **95 percentile** and it is possible to agree a value for this figure. Likewise, it is possible to define other **percentile ranges** which should be observed. Normally it is easy to check whether these ranges are being observed because most large computers can automatically output statistics which show them if so required.

E1.6.5 Complex queue systems

A transaction that is dispatched from a terminal to a computer, which later gives a response, forms part of many different queues which collectively constitute a complex queue system. Examples of these queues are the queue to get access to CPU resources, the queues to get access to data on various disks, the queue to get access to data locked by other transactions and the queues to get access to transmission lines. If the data processing system is not working to capacity, we can assume that the transactions arrive arbitrarily in the individual queues, and that the queue systems work independently. In such a situation, we can estimate the total response time of a transaction by adding up the average response times for the individual queue systems. Likewise, the variance of the total response time can be estimated by adding up the variance of the individual queue-systems.

EXAMPLE E1.15

The response times and variance in the queues for CPU, disk storage and transmission lines shown in Table E1.13 have been established for a particular type of transaction.

If the system is not working to capacity the total average response time of the transaction can be estimated as 0.91 second. The variance can be estimated as 0.4501 second, and the standard deviation as $\sqrt{0.4501} = 0.6709$.

If the computer is working to capacity the response times in the individual queues will no longer be independent of each other, and therefore the real response time may be substantially larger than the sum of the estimated response times of the individual subsystems. In such a situation, it is only possible to estimate the response time by means of simulation. In using such simulation it may be necessary to take account of the fact that it is one and the same CPU which has to administer all the lengthening queues. These have to be stored in main storage and physical main storage is likely to be so small that it will be necessary to use virtual main storage as well. Thus, some parts of the contents of main storage will have to be stored in background storage with a slower access time which will again increase the queue lengths.

Appendix F
B-trees

In a *B*-tree of order d, the nodes' maximum branching factor is $2d + 1$, which is the blocking factor of the index. Figure F1.1 illustrates two *B*-trees of order d for records with the key values $A, B, C, D, \ldots, X$. The first *B*-tree is constructed with a minimum height, whereas the second *B*-tree is constructed with a maximum height. The appearance of the index depends, in practice, on the creation sequence of the key values. In the following, we will derive formulae that can be used to estimate the maximum and minimum heights of *B*-trees or B^+-trees.

The minimum height can be calculated by means of Table F1.1, which contains a survey of the maximum number of nodes and keys that can be stored at the various levels in a *B*-tree with height h.

Table F1.1 Maximum number of nodes and keys that can be stored in *B*-trees.

Level	*Number of nodes*	*Number of keys*
0	1	$2d$
1	$2d + 1$	$2d(2d + 1)$
2	$(2d + 1)^2$	$2d(2d + 1)^2$
3	$(2d + 1)^3$	$2d(2d + 1)^3$
.	.	.
.	.	.
.	.	.
h	$(2d + 1)^h$	$2d(2d + 1)^h$

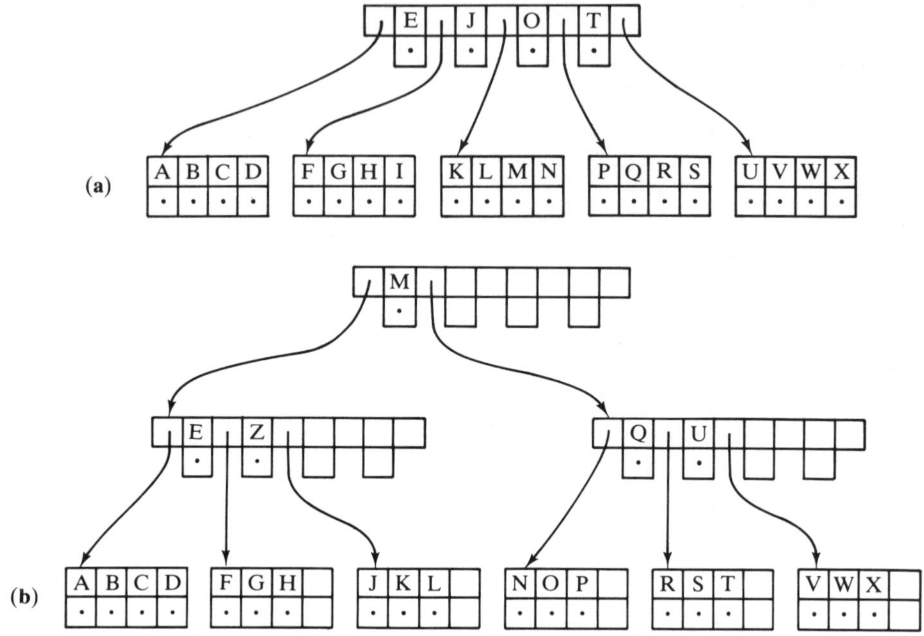

Figure F1.1 *B*-trees of (a) minimum and (b) maximum height.

Assume that the *B*-tree points to *n* blocks. A *B*-tree with height *h* can then point to a maximum of

$$n \leqslant \sum_{i=0}^{h} 2d(2d+1)^i \text{ blocks.}$$

From this inequality, the minimum height for a *B*-tree with *n* key values can be calculated as:

$$n \leqslant 2d \times \sum_{i=0}^{h} (2d+1)^i = 2d \times \frac{(2d+1)^{h+1}-1}{(2d+1)-1} = (2d+1)^{h+1}$$

Taking the logarithm with base $2d + 1$ of each side of the inequality gives the following:

$$\log_{2d+1}(n) \leqslant h + 1$$

As the height is an integer, this can be transformed to:

$$h \geqslant \left\lceil \frac{\log_n}{\log(2d+1)} \right\rceil - 1 \qquad (1)$$

Table F1.2 Minimum number of nodes and keys that can be stored in *B*-trees.

Level	*Number of nodes*	*Number of keys*
0	1	1
1	2	$2d$
2	$2(d + 1)$	$2d(d + 1)$
3	$2(d + 1)^2$	$2d(d + 1)^2$
.	.	.
.	.	.
.	.	.
h	$2(d + 1)^{h-1}$	$2d(d + 1)^{h-1}$

If the index is a B^+-tree, it has to be possible to store all keys at level h. Therefore, the following inequality will apply:

$$n \leqslant 2d\,(2d + 1)^h$$

which can be transformed to

$$\frac{n}{2d} \leqslant (2d + 1)^h$$

Taking the logarithm to base $2d + 1$ of each side of the inequality gives the following:

$$\log_{2d+1}\left(\frac{n}{2d}\right) \leqslant h$$

As the height is an integer, this can be transformed to:

$$h \geqslant \left\lceil \frac{\log\left(\dfrac{n}{2d}\right)}{\log\,(2d + 1)} \right\rceil \qquad \textbf{(2)}$$

The maximum height can be calculated by means of Table F1.2, which contains a survey of the minimum number of nodes and keys that can be stored at the various levels in a *B*-tree with height *h*.

A *B*-tree with the height *h* can point to at least

$$n \geqslant 1 + \sum_{i=0}^{h-1} 2d\,(d + 1)^i \quad \text{blocks}$$

From this inequality, the maximum height can be calculated since:

$$n \geqslant 1 + 2d \times \sum_{i=0}^{h-1} (d + 1)^i = 1 + 2d\frac{(d + 1)^h - 1}{(d + 1) - 1} = 2\,(d + 1)^h - 1$$

That is:

$$(d + 1)^h \leqslant \frac{(n + 1)}{2}$$

Taking the logarithm to base $d + 1$ of each side of the inequality gives:

$$h \leqslant \log_{d+1}\left(\frac{n + 1}{2}\right)$$

As the height is an integer, this can be transformed to:

$$h \leqslant \left\lfloor \frac{\log\left(\frac{h + 1}{2}\right)}{\log(d + 1)} \right\rfloor \tag{3}$$

If the index is a B^+-tree, it has to be possible to store all keys at level h. Therefore, the following inequality will apply:

$$n \geqslant 2d\,(d + 1)^{h-1}$$

which can be transformed to:

$$\frac{n}{2d} \geqslant (d + 1)^{h-1}$$

Taking the logarithm to base $d + 1$ of each side of the inequality gives:

$$\log_{d+1}\left(\frac{n}{2d}\right) \geqslant h - 1$$

As the height is an integer, this can be transformed to:

$$h \leqslant \left\lfloor \log_{d+1}\left(\frac{n}{2d}\right) \right\rfloor + 1 = \left\lfloor \frac{\log\left(\frac{n}{2d}\right)}{\log(d + 1)} \right\rfloor + 1 \tag{4}$$

EXAMPLE F1.1

A CUSTOMER file contains 500 000 records of 800 bytes each. In the CUSTOMER file, a block size of 4820 bytes is used, while a block size of 2004 bytes is used in the index. We want to build up a primary index over the field CUSTOMER-NUMBER of 10 bytes, and a secondary index over the field NAME of 40 bytes. If a physical address takes up four bytes, the record length in the CUSTOMER-NUMBER index will be 14 bytes and the blocking factor will be 143. If the loading factor of the CUSTOMER file is $\frac{5}{6}$, the CUSTOMER file will take up 100 000 blocks.

The CUSTOMER-NUMBER index must be a B-tree of order d, where d has to satisfy the inequality:

$$(2d + 1) \times 4 \text{ bytes} + 2d \times 10 \text{ bytes} \leqslant 2004 \text{ bytes}$$

That is, $d = 71$.

The NAME index must be a B-tree of order d, where d has to satisfy the inequality:

$$(2d + 1) \times 4 \text{ bytes} + 2d \times 40 \text{ bytes} \leqslant 2004 \text{ bytes}$$

That is, $d = 22$.

Using Equation (1), the minimum height of the CUSTOMER-NUMBER index can be estimated at:

$$h \geqslant \left\lceil \frac{\log n}{\log (2d + 1)} \right\rceil - 1 = \left\lceil \frac{\log 100\,000}{\log 143} \right\rceil - 1 = \left\lceil \frac{5}{2.1553} \right\rceil - 1 = 2$$

Using Equation (3), the maximum height of the CUSTOMER-NUMBER index can be estimated at:

$$h \leqslant \left\lfloor \frac{\log\left(\frac{(n + 1)}{2}\right)}{\log(d + 1)} \right\rfloor = \left\lfloor \frac{\log 50\,000.5}{\log 72} \right\rfloor = \left\lfloor \frac{4.6990}{1.8573} \right\rfloor = 2$$

The average height of the CUSTOMER-NUMBER index is 2.

Using Equation (1), the minimum height of the NAME index can be estimated at:

$$h \geqslant \left\lceil \frac{\log m}{\log (2d + 1)} \right\rceil - 1 = \left\lceil \frac{\log 500\,000}{\log 45} \right\rceil - 1 = \left\lceil \frac{5.6990}{1.6532} \right\rceil - 1 = 3$$

Using Equation (3), the maximum height of the NAME index can be estimated at:

$$h \leqslant \left\lfloor \frac{\log\left(\frac{(m + 1)}{2}\right)}{\log(d + 1)} \right\rfloor = \left\lfloor \frac{\log 250\,000.5}{\log 23} \right\rfloor = \left\lfloor \frac{5.3979}{1.3617} \right\rfloor = 3$$

The average height of the NAME index is 3.

If the two indexes are B^{+}-trees, using Equation (2) the minimum height of the CUSTOMER-NUMBER index can be estimated at:

$$h \geqslant \left\lceil \frac{\log\left(\frac{n}{2d}\right)}{\log(2d + 1)} \right\rceil = \left\lceil \frac{\log 704.2}{\log 143} \right\rceil = \left\lceil \frac{2.8477}{2.1553} \right\rceil = 2$$

Using Equation (4), the maximum height of the CUSTOMER-NUMBER index can be estimated at:

$$h \leqslant \left\lfloor \frac{\log\left(\frac{n}{2d}\right)}{\log(d + 1)} \right\rfloor + 1 = \left\lfloor \frac{\log 704.2}{\log 72} \right\rfloor + 1 = \left\lfloor \frac{2.8477}{2.8573} \right\rfloor + 1 = 2$$

The average height of the CUSTOMER-NUMBER index is 2.

Using Equation (2), the minimum height of the NAME index can be estimated at:

$$h \geqslant \left\lceil \frac{\log\left(\frac{m}{2d}\right)}{\log(2d+1)} \right\rceil = \left\lceil \frac{\log 11\,364}{\log 45} \right\rceil = \left\lceil \frac{4.0555}{1.6532} \right\rceil = 3$$

Using Equation (4), the maximum height of the NAME index can be estimated at:

$$h \leqslant \left\lfloor \frac{\log\left(\frac{m}{2d}\right)}{\log(d+1)} \right\rfloor + 1 = \left\lfloor \frac{\log 11\,364}{\log 23} \right\rfloor + 1 = \left\lfloor \frac{4.0555}{1.3617} \right\rfloor + 1 = 3$$

The average height of the NAME index is 3.

Appendix G
Technical Data

G1.1 Introduction

In some of the exercises, an estimate of run times and/or work times is asked for. For the purpose of these exercises, the equations given in Appendix B can be reduced to numerical values corresponding to a concrete data processing system. Use of these numerical values should make it faster to solve the exercises. Naturally, other solutions may be reached if the technical data given here is not used.

G1.1.1 Technical data for magnetic tapes and the IBM 3420 Model 8 magnetic tape unit

A magnetic tape is 2400 feet long and 6250 bytes can be stored per inch. The block gap is 0.3 inch. The maximum block size is 32 760 characters. Thus a magnetic tape can hold a maximum of 170 253 720 characters. The read/write speed of the magnetic tape unit is 200 inches per second. The time spent on accelerating the magnetic tape before reading a block is 0.001 second. The rewind speed is about 565 inches per second.

G1.1.2 Technical data for IBM 3380 disk storage

- H = the average time for moving the read/write head = 0.016 second

- $HMIN$ = the time spent on moving the head to the neighbouring cylinder = 0.003 second.
- $HMAX$ = the maximum time for moving the read/write head = 0.030 second
- R = the rotation time = 0.0166 second
- C = the number of tracks per cylinder = 15
- Number of cylinders per disk storage = 1770
- K = the transmission speed of the data channel = 1198 kilobytes

Table G1.1 shows how the track capacity varies with the number of blocks per track. This variation is caused by, amongst other things, system data, which is stored per block. In the following data for disk storage work, a block size of 4820 bytes is assumed, which corresponds to $S = 9$ blocks per track. A card reader is assumed to be able to read 300 cards per minute and the line printer is assumed to print 600 lines per minute. Now, the equations in Appendix B can be reduced as follows:

- Equation (3) If we use a block size of 4820 bytes, the work time of the magnetic tape unit for sequential reading/writing becomes:

$$\text{Number of blocks} \times \left(\frac{\text{block size}}{\text{the read/write speed}} + \text{acceleration time}\right)$$
$$= \text{number of blocks} \times 0.0039 \text{ second}$$

- Equation (4) The work time for direct reading and writing, respectively, of a block:

$$H + \frac{R}{2} + \frac{R}{S} = 0.0261 \text{ second}$$

- Equation (5) Response time for direct reading of a block:

$$H + \frac{R}{2} + \max\left\{\frac{R}{S}, \frac{B}{K}\right\} = 0.0283 \text{ second}$$

- Equation (6) Minimum work time for direct updating of a block:

$$H + \frac{R}{2} + \frac{R}{S} + R = 0.0427 \text{ second}$$

- Equation (7) Minimum work time for sequential reading/writing on a disk storage:

$$\text{Number of cylinders} \times \left(HMIN + \left(\frac{R}{S} + R\right) \times C \times S\right)$$
$$= \text{number of cylinders} \times 2.493 \text{ seconds}$$

Table G1.1 Variation of track capacity with blocks per track.

Block size	***Number of blocks per track***	***Bytes per track***
47 476	1	47 476
23 476	2	46 952
15 475	3	46 428
11 476	4	45 904
9076	5	45 380
7476	6	44 856
6356	7	44 492
5492	8	43 936
4820	9	43 380
4275	10	42 760
3860	11	42 460
3476	12	41 712
3188	13	41 444
2932	14	41 048
2576	15	40 140
2484	16	39 744
2324	17	39 508
2164	18	38 952
2004	19	38 076
1876	20	37 520
1780	21	37 380
1684	22	37 048
1588	23	36 524
1492	24	35 808
1396	25	34 900
1332	26	34 632
1268	27	34 236
1204	28	33 712
1140	29	33 060
1076	30	32 280
1044	31	32 364
980	32	31 360
948	33	31 284
916	34	31 144
852	35	29 820
820	36	29 520
788	37	29 156
756	38	28 728
724	39	28 236
692	40	27 680
660	41	27 060
628	42	26 376
596	44	26 224
564	45	25 380
532	46	24 472
500	48	24 000
468	49	22 932
436	51	22 236
404	53	21 412
372	55	20 460
340	57	19 380
308	59	18 172
276	62	17 112
244	65	15 860
212	68	14 416
180	71	12 780
148	74	10 952
116	78	9048
84	83	6972

- Equation (8) Minimum work time for sequential updating of a disk storage:

$$\text{Number of cylinders} \times \left(HMIN + \left(\frac{R}{S} + 2R\right) \times S \times C\right)$$

$$= \text{number of cylinders} \times 4.734 \text{ seconds.}$$

G1.1.3 Technical data for a floppy disk connected to an IBM Personal Computer

- H = the average time for moving the read/write head = 0.12 second
- $HMIN$ = the time for moving the head to the neighbouring cylinder = 0.006 second
- R = rotation time = 0.2 second
- Number of characters per block = 500
- S = the number of blocks per track = 9
- C = the number of tracks per cylinder = 2
- Number of cylinders per disk storage = 40

Thus a disk can hold 360 000 characters.

The equations in Appendix B can now be reduced as follows:

- Equations (4) and (5) The work time for reading/writing a block:

$$H + \frac{R}{2} + \frac{R}{S} = 0.242 \text{ second}$$

- Equation (6) Minimum work time for direct updating of a block:

$$H + \frac{R}{2} + \frac{R}{S} + R = 0.442 \text{ second}$$

- Equation (7) Minimum work time for sequential reading/writing on a disk storage:

$$\text{Number of cylinders} \times \left(HMIN + \left(\frac{R}{S} + R\right) \times C \times S\right)$$

$$= \text{number of cylinders} \times 4.006 \text{ seconds}$$

- Equation (8) Minimum work time for sequential updating of a disk storage:

$$\text{Number of cylinders} \times \left(HMIN + \left(\frac{R}{S} + 2R\right) \times C \times S\right)$$

$$= \text{number of cylinders} \times 7.606 \text{ seconds}$$

Bibliography

ANSI/X3/SPARC. (1975). Study Group on Data Base Management Systems. Interim Report. *FDT* (ACM SIGMOD bulletin) **7**(2).

Bachman, C.W. (1969). 'Data Structure Diagrams.' *Data Base,* **1**(2).

Bratbergsengen, K., Hofstad, K. and Wibe, K. (1983). *Filsystemer og Databaser.* Oslo: Tapir.

Chen, P.P.-S. (1976). 'The Entity–Relationship Model – Towards a Unified View of Data.' *ACM TODS,* **1**(1).

CODASYL COBOL Committee. (1978). *COBOL Journal of Development.*

CODASYL DDL Committee. (1981a). *Data Description Language.*

CODASYL DDL Committee. (1981b). *Draft Specification of a Data Storage Description Language.*

Codd, E.D. (1970). 'A Relational Model of Data for Large Shared Data Banks.' *CACM,* **13**(6).

Codd, E.D. (1979). 'Extending the Relational Database Model to Capture More Meaning.' *ACM TODS,* **4**(4).

DATAPRO Software Research Corporation. *Reports* (various dates). Delran, N.J.

Date, C. (1986). *An Introduction to Database Systems. Vol.1. 4th Edn.* Reading, Mass.: Addison-Wesley.

Fagin, R., Nievergelt, J., Pippenger, N. and Strong, H. (1979). 'Extendable Hashing' *ACM TODS,* **4**(3).

Fernandez, E.B., Summers, R.C. and Wood, C. (1981). *Database Security and Integrity.* Reading, Mass.: Addison-Wesley.

Frank, L. (1971). 'Datastrukturer.' *Hovedopgave ved Datalogstudiet,* 1971.

Frank, L. (1975). 'Ebd-kapacitetsforbrug og ledelsens ebd-beslutninger.' *Hovedopgave ved HD-studiet i datamatik.*

IBM. (1983a). *DB2, Relational Concepts.* Manual No.: GG24-1581-00.

IBM. (1983b). *DB2, Concepts and Facilities Guide.* Manual No.: GG24-1582.

IBM. (1983c), *DB2, SQL Usage Guide.* Manual No.: GG24-1583.

IBM. (1983d), *DB2, QMF and DXT Presentation Guide.* Manual No.: GG24-1586.

IBM. (1983e). *DB2, Interactive Demonstration Guide.* Manual No.: GG24-1587.

IBM. (1983f). *QMF Demonstration Guide.* Manual No.: GG24-1588.

Kjellberg, P. and Zahle, T. (1984). 'Cascade Hashing.' *Proc. 10th International Conference on Very Large Data Bases* (September 1984).

Knott, G.D. (1971). 'Expandable Open Addressing Hash Table Storage and Retrieval.' *Proc. 1971 ACM SIGFIDET Workshop on Data Description, Access, and Control* (November 1971).

Knuth, D.E. (1973). *The Art of Computer Programming. Vol III: Sorting and Searching.* Reading, Mass.: Addison-Wesley.

Larson, P. (1978). 'Dynamic Hashing.' *BIT,* **18**.

Larson, P. (1980). 'Linear Hashing with Partial Expansions.' *Proc. 6th International Conference on Very Large Data Bases* (October 1980).

Larson, P. (1982). 'Performance Analysis of Linear Hashing with Partial Expansions.' *ACM TODS,* **7**(4).

Larson, P. (1985). 'Linear Hashing with Overflow-Handling by Linear Probing.' *ACM TODS,* **10**(1).

Litwin, W. (1978). 'Virtual Hashing: A Dynamically Changing Hashing.' *Proc. 4th International Conference on Very Large Data Bases* (September 1978).

Litwin, W. (1980). 'Linear Hashing: A New Tool for File and Table Addressing.' *Proc. 6th International Conference on Very Large Data Bases* (October 1980).

Martin, G. (1979). *Spiral Storage: Incrementally Augmentable Hash Addressed Storage.* Theory of Computation Report No. 27. University of Warwick.

McIlroy, M.D. (1963). 'A Variant Method of File Searching.' *CACM,* **6**(1).

Møller, U. and Sørensen, R. (1982). *Noter til kursus i database systemer.* Copenhagen: Edb-skolerne.

Mullin, J.K. (1984). 'Unified Dynamic Hashing.' *Proc. 10th International Conference on Very Large Data Bases* (September 1984).

Reschner, N. (1969). *Many-Valued Logic.* New York: McGraw-Hill.

Schneider, H.-J.; Ed (1982). *Distributed Data Bases: Proc. 2nd International Symposium on Distributed Data Bases.* New York: North-Holland.

Severance, D.G. (1974). 'Identifier Search Mechanisms: A Survey and Generalized Model.' *ACM Comp. Surv.,* **6**(3).

Severance, D.G. and Duhne, R. (1976). 'A Practitioner's Guide to Addressing Algorithms.' *CACM,* **19**(6).

Sørensen, R. (1984). *Noter til modul 2.7.* Copenhagen: Edb-skolen.

Teorey, T.J. and Fry, J.P. (1982). *Design of Database Structures.* Englewood Cliffs, N.J.: Prentice-Hall.

Tsichritzis, D.C. and Klug, A.; Eds. (1978). 'The ANSI/X3/SPARC DBMS Framework: Report of the Study Group on Data Base Management Systems.' *Information Systems,* **3**.

Index